# AQA Physics

## Physics in Context

### Exclusively endorsed by AQA

Mike Bowen-Jones
Ken Price

 Nelson Thornes

Published in 2008 by:
Nelson Thornes Ltd
Delta Place
27 Bath Road
CHELTENHAM
GL53 7TH
United Kingdom

08  09  10  11 12  /  10  9  8  7  6  5  4  3  2

A catalogue record for this book is available from the British Library

ISBN 978 0 7487 8283 3

Cover photograph by Kelly Redinger/Design Pics/Corbis

Illustrations include artwork drawn by GreenGate Publishing

Page make-up by GreenGate Publishing, Kent

Printed and bound in Great Britain by Scotprint

# Contents

# AQA introduction

## Nelson Thornes and AQA

Nelson Thornes has worked in collaboration with AQA to ensure that this book offers you the best support for your AS level course and helps you to prepare for your exams. The partnership means that you can be confident that the range of learning, teaching and assessment practice materials has been checked by the senior examining team at AQA before formal approval, and is closely matched to the requirements of your specification.

## Blended learning

Printed and electronic resources are blended. This means that links between the topics and activities between the book and the electronic resources, help you to work in the way that best suits you, and enable extra support to be provided online. For example, you can test yourself online and feedback from the test will direct you back to the relevant parts of the book.

Electronic resources are available in a simple-to-use online platform called Nelson Thornes *learning space*. If your school or college has a licence to use the service, you will be given a password through which you can access the materials through any internet connection.

Icons in this book indicate where there is material online related to that topic. The following icons are used:

### Learning activity

These resources include a variety of interactive and non-interactive activities to support your learning:

- Animations
- Simulations
- Maths skills
- Key diagrams
- Glossary

### Progress tracking

These resources include a variety of tests that you can use to check your knowledge on particular topics (Test yourself) and a range of resources that enable you to analyse and understand examination questions (On your marks...). You will also find the answers to examination-style questions online.

### Research support

These resources include WebQuests, in which you are assigned a task and provided with a range of web links to use as source material for research.

These are designed as Extension resources to stretch you and broaden your learning, in order for you to attain the highest possible marks in your exams.

### Web links

Our online resources feature a list of recommended weblinks, split by chapter. This will give you a head start, helping you to navigate to the best websites that will aid your learning and understanding of the topics in your course.

### How science works

These resources are a mixtures of interactive and non-interactive activities to help you learn the skills required for success in this new area of the specification.

### Practical

This icon signals where there is a relevant practical activity to be undertaken, and support is provided online.

When you see an icon, go to Nelson Thornes *learning space* at www.nelsonthornes.com/aqagce, enter your access details and select your course. The materials are arranged in the same order as the topics in the book, so you can easily find the resources you need.

## How to use this book

This book covers the specification for your course and is arranged in a sequence approved by AQA.

The book content is divided into three units. Unit 1 is called Harmony and structure in the Universe and is divided into the two modules 'The world of music' and 'From quarks to quasars'. Unit 2, Physics keeps us going is made up of the two modules 'Moving people, people moving' and 'Energy and the environment'. These two units match the two theory units of the AQA Physics B AS specification. Unit 3 includes information and advice about practical assessment and is followed by Chapter 17 which provides advice on essential maths skills. Units are then further divided into chapters, and then topics, making the content clear and easy to use.

Unit openers for the theory units give you a summary of the content you will be covering, and a recap of ideas from GCSE that you will need.

The features in this book include:

*Learning objectives*

At the beginning of each section you will find a list of learning objectives that contain targets linked to the requirements of the specification. The relevant specification reference is also provided.

**Key terms**

Terms that you will need to be able to define and understand are highlighted in bold blue type within the text, e.g. **analogue**. You can look up these terms in the Glossary (page 237).

### ■ Hint

Hints to aid your understanding of the content.

### ■ Link

Links highlight any key areas where sections relate to one another.

### ■ How science works

'How science works' is a key part of the new A Level Physics specifications. As with the specification, 'How science works' is integrated throughout the content of the book. This feature highlights 'How science works' as it occurs within topics, so that it is always relevant to what you are studying. You will not be examined on the exact information provided in this book with relation to 'How science works''. The ideas provided in these features intends to teach you the skills you will need to tackle this part of the course, and give you experience when dealing with applying your knowledge to different contexts.

See the 'How science works' spread on page viii for more detail.

### ■ Summary questions

Short questions that test your understanding of the subject and allow you to apply the knowledge and skills you have acquired to different scenarios. Answers are supplied at the back of the book (page 241).

### AQA Examiner's tip

Hints from AQA examiners to help you with your studies and to prepare you for your exam.

## AQA Examination-style questions

Questions from past AQA papers that are in the general style that you can expect in your exam, including the new 'How science works' strand. These occur at the end of each chapter to give practice in examination-style questions for a particular topic. They also occur at the end of each unit; the questions here may cover any of the content of the unit.

When you answer the examination-style questions in this book, remember that quality of written communication (QWC) will be assessed in any question or part-question in the papers for Units 1 and 2 at AS (Units 4 and 5 at A2) where extended descriptive anwers are required. So make sure your answers to such questions are of good quality in terms of QWC as well as in terms of physics.

The answers to these questions are supplied online.

AQA examination questions are reproduced by permission of the Assessment and Qualifications Alliance.

Nelson Thornes is responsible for the solution(s) given and they may not constitute the only possible solution(s).

### Web links in the book

Because Nelson Thornes is not responsible for third party content online, there may be some changes to this material that are beyond our control. In order for us to ensure that the links referred to in the book are as up-to-date and stable as possible, the web sites provided are usually homepages with supporting instructions on how to reach the relevant pages if necessary.

Please let us know at **webadmin@nelsonthornes.com** if you find a link that doesn't work and we will do our best to correct this at reprint, or to list an alternative site.

# Studying AS Physics

## AS Physics for AQA specification B

This book is written for AS Physics students who are following AQA Physics (Specification B). It provides the entire content of all three Units in the AS course including information and advice about practical assessment. In addition, essential maths skills are provided. Guidance on how to bridge the gap between Physics at GCSE and at AS level is given below.

### About AS Physics

Welcome to Physics at AS level, the subject that helps us to understand nature from the smallest possible scale deep inside the atom to the largest conceivable distance, stretching across the entire Universe. Physics is about making predictions, testing them through observations and measurements and devising theories and laws to make more predictions. On your course, you will cover the key ideas of the subject including a study of particle physics, quantum physics and cosmology. You will study how physical principles are applied in topics such as music, communications, sport and in the production and use of electrical energy. You will learn the skills of making observations and measurements, and how to use your mathematical skills to make sense of experiments. You will also learn how to communicate your knowledge and understanding of the subject effectively. You will discover that physics is a very creative subject that calls for imagination and inventiveness. Don't be afraid to ask your teacher when something doesn't seem clear. Einstein developed a reputation for asking awkward questions and it made him into the most famous physicist ever!

You are about to set off on a course that will further develop your knowledge, understanding and skills of the subject. At this stage, your GCSE course will have provided you with solid foundations to build on as you progress through the course. To help you make a smooth transition from GCSE to AS Physics, the next part of this introduction covers the key mathematical and practical skills you need to get started on your course. Further support on practical skills, their assessment, and mathematical methods and skills is given in Chapters 15 to 17. There are also resources online that will support and develop your skills further in these areas. This book is written for the AS Physics course for AQA Specification B. It covers every topic needed for the specification, which comprises three units. The main chapters of the book, Chapters 1-14, are written in sequence to follow the content of Units 1 and 2. These are the units that are examined through written examinations offered in January or June. Practical skills are assessed internally in Unit 3 and you will be given plenty of opportunities to develop these skills as you progress through the topics in Units 1 and 2. Chapters 15–16 provide advice on the practical skills including the Investigative Skills Assignment (ISA) and the Practical Skills Assessment (PSA). At the end of the book, there is a reference section consisting of useful data, a glossary, answers to summary questions, and a comprehensive index. In addition, a full list of the data and formulae that you will be provided with in your AS examination papers is reproduced at the end of the book. Essential practical experiments are included within the relevant units. Further practical experiments and animations are available as part of the online resources .

AS course structure (% weighting of each unit shown in brackets)

**Unit 1 Harmony and structure in the Universe**
(40%)
Chapters 1–5

**Unit 2 Physics keeps us going**
(40%)
Chapters 6–14

**Unit 3 Investigative and practical skills in AS Physics**
(20%)
Chapters 15–16

This book is written to help you pass the AS examination so make sure you use it fully, particularly the final 'skills' chapters and the final reference section. It is also written to provide you with a firm foundation for your A2 course using the companion book *A2 Physics for AQA Specification B*. Working through this AS book will help you to pass your AS exam then to move on successfully to A2 Physics. More importantly, we hope it will give you a lasting interest in physics and on-going enthusiasm for this exciting subject!

# How science works

You will already have gained some skills through the 'How science works' component of your GCSE course. As you progress through your AS Physics course, you will develop your scientific skills further and learn about important new ideas and applications through the 'How science works' component of your A level course. These skills are a key part of how every scientist works. Scientists use them to probe and test new theories and applications in whatever field of work they are working in. Now you will develop them further and gain new knowledge and skills as you progress through the course.

'How science works' at A level (and at GCSE) has several different strands summarised in Table 1 and these are brought out in your course as appropriate in different topics. These strands include practical and investigative skills in science. They also consider the implications of scientific work in terms of how science is used not just by scientists and engineers but also by society at large. Science is often in the headlines, not only as a result of 'good news' such as major new discoveries but also through issues that concern us all, for example 'climate change' and 'depleting energy resources'.

Most of the strands in the table relate to practical work and the ability to communicate scientific ideas. The practical aspects are assessed in Unit 3. Other strands deal with the way scientific discoveries are made, how they change our understanding of the world we live in and the use we make of the discoveries, for example the development of diffraction techniques.

The strands relating to the implications of science are important because what scientists do affects us all, and ethical issues are often associated with their work. For example:

- Should children be banned from using mobile phones because of concerns about the effects of mobile phone radiation?
- Should scientists working on the use of radiation to treat cancer use patients to test the effectiveness of new treatments?

## How science works

### Discovering DNA

Scientists have used diffraction techniques to determine the structure of DNA. This has led to a wide range of applications from fighting disease to catching criminals.

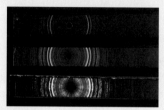

*Pattern formed from X-ray diffraction*

These strands will be tested in your AS and A level examinations; so you need to be able to discuss in depth a scientific issue by considering the benefits and the risks or the advantages and disadvantages. You will develop the necessary skills for these strands as you progress through your course and meet topics that touch on issues that show how and why science affects us all.

A major feature of this course is that you will learn the physics laws and principles through a study of their application in defined contexts that are particularly relevant in today's world. The topics also include consideration of many of the ethical issues brought about by scientific and technological developments where this is appropriate. This means that you will be learning 'How science works' throughout the course. Some particular examples are also highlighted in margin features where appropriate.

All the 'How science works' strands of AQA's Advanced level science specifications are the same. A study of the topics in this book and the 'How science works' features will help you to develop the relevant skills necessary for examination purposes. More importantly, it should give you a thorough grasp of how scientists work and what they do as well as a deeper awareness of how science is used to improve the quality life for everyone.

**Table 1** *How science works specification summary*

| Strands | Skills |
|---|---|
| **A Theories, models and ideas** are used to develop and modify scientific explanations. | Scientists make progress when validated evidence is found that supports a new theory or model. |
| **B Predictions from a hypothesis** (i.e. untested idea) or a theory need to be tested by experiment. If a reliable experiment does not support a hypothesis or theory, the hypothesis or theory must be changed. | Scientists use their knowledge and understanding in forming a hypothesis and when questioning the explanations of themselves or of other scientists. |

*continued*

**Table 1** *(continued)*

| Strands | Skills |
|---|---|
| C **Appropriate methodology**, including ICT, is used to make observations and measurements. Experiments are the key links between the 'real world' and the abstract ideas of science. | When scientists plan and carry out investigations, they need to:<br>• identify the dependent and independent variables in the investigation and the control variables,<br>• select appropriate apparatus and methods, including ICT,<br>• choose measuring instruments according to their sensitivity and precision and carry out reliable measurements. |
| D **The range of experimental skills needed** to carry out scientific investigations include manual and data skills (tabulation, graphical skills, etc.). | Scientists have to follow appropriate experimental procedures in a sensible order, use appropriate apparatus and methods to make accurate and reliable measurements, identify and minimise significant sources of experimental error and identify and take account of risks in carrying out practical work. |
| E **Data must be analysed and interpreted** to provide evidence, recognising correlations and causal relationships. When experimental data confirm predictions from a theoretical model, scientists become more confident in the theory. | Scientists look for patterns and trends in data as a first step in providing explanations of phenomena. They need to know how to:<br>• process measurement data,<br>• use equations and carry out appropriate calculations,<br>• plot and use appropriate graphs to establish or verify relationships between variables,<br>• relate the gradient and the intercepts of straight line graphs to appropriate linear equations. |
| F **The methodology used, evidence and data** must be evaluated and conflicting evidence resolved. The validity of new evidence is a stimulus for further scientific investigation, which involves refinements of experimental technique or development of new hypotheses. | Scientists need to be able to distinguish between systematic and random errors, make reasonable estimates of the errors in all measurements, use data, graphs and other evidence from experiments to draw conclusions and to use the most significant error estimates to assess the reliability of conclusions drawn. |
| G **The tentative nature of scientific knowledge** needs to be considered. Scientific knowledge changes when new experimental evidence provides a better explanation of scientific observations. | Scientists need to know that if evidence that is reliable and reproducible does not support a theory, the theory must be modified or replaced with a different theory. |
| H **Research findings** needs to be communicated to the scientific community to see if it can be replicated, thus either confirming new explanations or refuting them. | Scientists need to provide explanations using correct scientific terms, and support arguments with equations, diagrams and clear sketch graphs when appropriate. |
| I **The applications and implications of science** and their associated benefits and risks need to be considered. | Scientists apply their scientific knowledge to develop technologies that improve our lives. We all need to appreciate that the technologies themselves may pose significant risks that have to be balanced against the benefits. |
| J **The ethical issues** associated with scientific developments need to be considered. | Scientists have a duty to consider ethical issues associated with their findings. Scientists provide solutions to problems but the solutions often require society to form judgements as to whether the solution is acceptable in view of moral issues that result. Issues such as the effects on the planet, and the economic and physical well being of the living things on it should be considered. |
| K **The scientific community** itself validates new knowledge and ensures integrity. | Scientists need a common set of values and responsibilities. They should know that scientists undertake a peer-review of the work of others. They should know that scientists work with a common aim to progress scientific knowledge and understanding in a valid way and that accurate reporting of findings takes precedence over recognition of success of an individual. |
| L **Decision makers** are influenced in many ways, including their prior beliefs, their vested interests, special interest groups, public opinion and the media, as well as by expert scientific evidence. | Scientific evidence should be considered as a whole. Media and pressure groups often select parts of scientific evidence that supports a particular viewpoint and that this can influence public opinion which in turn may influences decision makers. Consequently, decision makers may make socially and politically acceptable decisions based on incomplete evidence. |

# Harmony and structure in the Universe

## Chapters in this unit

This unit consists of two topics which are in the forefront of modern research for widely different reasons: 'The world of music' and 'From quarks to quasars'.

## The world of music

What makes particular sounds so pleasing to the ear and how do we hear sounds? How has the storage of music and other data progressed from **analogue** discs and tape to **digital** media including CDs, DVDs and MP3 players? The principles involved in **sound** production, storage and reproduction are considered. The way information is communicated is continually changing and is an important aspect of life in the twenty-first century, so the benefits of digital over analogue communication and the advantages of different ways of transmitting data are compared. The study includes the use of various regions of the **electromagnetic spectrum**, **carrier waves**, **optical fibres** and **satellites**.

## From quarks to quasars

One of the awe-inspiring aspects of physics is its diversity from sub-nuclear to astronomical magnitudes. Fundamental questions such as 'how far can matter be broken down and how large is the Universe?' are considered in this unit. The development of models which help to explain our current beliefs is studied, with an emphasis that any model used must be tentative by virtue of our limited opportunity to measure quantities directly. The progression of our understanding of the atom from early ideas leading to the **kinetic theory of gases** and to the wave–particle model of light and matter is developed logically. The discovery of the wide range of **fundamental particles** and the forces of nature is studied, as are the observations of stars and galaxies which led to **Hubble's law** and the dominance of the **Big Bang** theory over other theories. Finally the unit looks at the big questions that remain unanswered and which are challenging today's leading physicists.

**What you already know:**

- Sound is a longitudinal waveform and all electromagnetic waves are transverse waveforms.

- A complete wave is from one peak to the next peak.

- Wavelength is the distance between adjacent wave peaks.

- Wave speed = wavelength × frequency.

- In order of increasing wavelength, the electromagnetic spectrum consists of gamma rays, X-rays, ultraviolet, visible, microwaves and radio waves.

- All electromagnetic waves travel through space at a speed of 300 million m s$^{-1}$.

- The use we make of radio waves depends on the frequency of the waves.

- Visible light and infrared radiation are used to carry signals in optical fibres.

- Analogue signals vary continuously in amplitude.

- Digital signals are either high ('1') or low ('0').

- Digital transmission can be free from noise and distortion. It carries more information than analogue transmission.

- Every atom has a positively charged nucleus at its centre that is surrounded by negatively charged particles called electrons.

- An atom's nucleus is composed of protons and neutrons, which have about the same mass.

- Protons and electrons have fixed equal and opposite charge; neutrons are uncharged.

- An uncharged atom has equal numbers of electrons and protons.

- Radioactive substances emit radiation because the nuclei of the atoms are unstable.

- The radiation from radioactive substances ionises substances it passes through.

- α, β and γ are the three types of radiation from radioactive substances.

- Light from a distant galaxy is red-shifted to longer wavelengths.

- The most distant galaxies are about 13 000 million light years away.

- The Universe started with the Big Bang and is expanding.

- Background microwave radiation is radiation created just after the Big Bang.

# 1.1 Music and sound

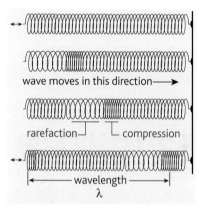

**Figure 1** *Compression pulse moving down a slinky spring*

### How science works

**Demonstration**

A tuning fork is a simple source of sound and a single musical note – its vibration can be seen by the water splashing in a beaker.

Music is a sequence of sounds that is appealing. It has all the properties of sound with some unique properties that make it music.

## What is sound?

All sounds are formed by a vibration and require a medium to travel through. Sound travels as a **longitudinal,** otherwise known as a **compression** wave, whereby it forms a series of compressions (regions of higher pressure than the surroundings) and **rarefactions** (regions of lower pressure than normal). This can be modelled by vibrating the end of a slinky spring along its length.

The distance between two successive compressions is one **wavelength** – the symbol generally given for this is a Greek 'L' called lambda ($\lambda$) see Figure 1. The frequency is the number of vibrations per second or the number of compressions passing a fixed point per second and is measured in hertz (Hz). The **frequency** and wavelength are related to the wave speed $c$ by the wave equation.

$c = f \times \lambda$. **The wave speed is the frequency multiplied by the wavelength.**

The sound from a musical instrument is caused by the instrument vibrating, the greater the number of vibrations the higher the frequency of sound that is produced.

## Detecting and measuring the frequency of sound

The typical human ear can detect a range of frequencies between 20 Hz and 20 kHz. Frequencies below this are known as **infrasound** and above this as **ultrasound**. Animals can detect frequencies well above those detected by humans, in fact some bats can hear sounds up to 110 kHz. Humpback whales produce a sequence of sounds that are called 'songs'. The frequency of these songs ranges from about 40 Hz to 5 kHz. These are believed to be territorial and mating calls.

When sounds are turned into an electrical signal with a detector, such as a microphone, the frequency can be measured with an oscilloscope. From the time-base setting the period (the time for one vibration, $T$) can be measured and hence the frequency ($f$) can be found. The time-base of an oscilloscope is a circuit which controls how long it takes for the trace to cross the screen horizontally. It is usually calibrated in $s\,cm^{-1}$ or $ms\,cm^{-1}$.

## Unique properties of sound found in music

The **pitch** of a sound from a musical instrument is produced from the fundamental frequency plus harmonics (multiples of the fundamental frequency). The brain is able to detect the same pitch when it is played by different instruments. Sound waves of certain pitches, when heard together, will produce a pleasant sensation and are said to be **consonant** or **harmonic**. These sound waves form the basis of a **musical interval**. For example, any two musical notes of frequency ratio 2 : 1 (i.e. one note is double the frequency of the other) are said to be separated by an **octave**. This is a particularly pleasing sound. Similarly two notes of frequency ratio 5 : 4 are said to be separated by an interval of a **third;** again this interval sounds pleasing.

**Quality** is sometimes called **timbre**. It is an important factor that gives a musical instrument or a voice its unique character. It is easy to observe the profile of a regular wave using an oscilloscope and microphone. The same frequency note played on two musical instruments produces very different wave forms:

The timbre of the wave is made up of three aspects – the **harmonics** present, the **attack** and **decay** of the sound and the **vibrato**.

**Harmonics** are the multiples of the fundamental wave frequency that are included. These can by analysed using **Fourier analysis**. This characterises the wave in terms of the different **amplitudes** of the frequencies that make up the harmonics of the sound wave. Harmonics can be synthesised electronically using **Fourier synthesis**. This is a process by which any regular sound can be reproduced by adding regular alternating voltages together.

The **attack** of a sound is a measure of how quickly it reaches its peak amplitude or loudness and the **decay** is a measure of how long it takes to die away.

**Vibrato** is a periodic change in the pitch of the waveform as the sound continues to be produced. It is usually accompanied with a periodic change in amplitude – which is known as **tremolo**. Musicians will often deliberately induce vibrato and/or tremolo in order to give expression or variation to music.

Imagine all these unique properties being applied to the sounds that bats make, then what may be high pitched sounds that cannot be heard by humans may be music to their ears.

### Summary questions

1. Compression waves are made on a slinky at a frequency of 2 Hz; successive compressions are separated by a distance of 0.25 m. Calculate the speed of the wave along the slinky.

2. Middle C has a frequency of 256 Hz. What are the frequencies of the Cs which are one and two octaves higher than middle C?

3. What is meant by ultrasound? The speed of sound is 340 m s$^{-1}$. Suggest a frequency of an ultrasonic wave and calculate its wavelength.

4. What is meant by the attack and decay of a musical note? Describe similarities and differences in appearance of the same note played on two different musical instruments when displayed on an oscilloscope.

### 💡 Hint

When measuring a repeating quantity such as the period on the oscilloscope – measure several periods (three here) and divide. This has the advantage of dividing the uncertainty in that measurement. This will give a more accurate value.

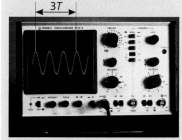

In this example the time-base is set to 2 ms cm$^{-1}$ and three periods occupy 6.0 cm. Thus the period is 4 ms. Furthermore, $f = \frac{1}{T}$ so the frequency of the sound is $\frac{1}{4} \times 10^3 = 250$ Hz.

**a** *trumpet trace*

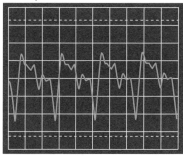

time ⟶

**b** *accordion trace*

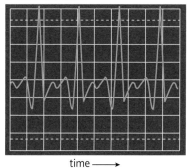

time ⟶

**Figure 2** *The upper trace (a) is produced by a trumpet while the lower trace (b) is the same note played on an accordion. Each is repetitive and has the same period and therefore frequency. When the sound is detected by the ears and processed by the brain it is possible to determine that the notes are the same pitch although they come from different instruments.*

# 1.2  Listening to sounds

*Learning objectives:*

- How are sound waves represented?

- What is the difference between light and sound?

- What are the implications of the speed of sound for music?

*Specification reference: 3.1.1A*

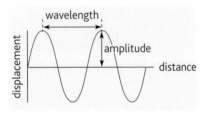

**Figure 1** *Displacement against distance graph*

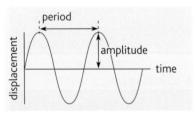

**Figure 2** *Displacement against time graph*

## Representing sound waves

Sound waves consist of a series of compressions and rarefactions that travel through a substance, usually air. It is not easy to picture both the amplitude and the frequency of a sound wave in a diagram in terms of the compressions and rarefactions. The **amplitude** is the maximum displacement from its rest position of one of the particles of the medium that carries the wave. There are two graphs that can help to visualise a sound wave more clearly: a graph showing the **displacement** of **all** the particles against distance (a sort of graphical photograph, Figure 1), and a graph showing how **one** particle moves as time changes (Figure 2). In this way sound can be treated as if it were a **transverse wave**, which is defined below.

The first of the graphs shows how the amplitude can be related to the pressure of the air molecules. The second of these graphs has the advantage that it is exactly what is seen on an **oscilloscope** and it is easy to work out the frequency of the sound from the period $T$.

## Light waves

Light stimulates the eyes whereas sound stimulates the ears, but what other differences are there between a light wave and a sound wave?

Unlike sound, which is a mechanical wave, light does not need a substance to travel through. Most substances easily absorb light. Light slows downs when travelling through transparent substances. In 1864 James Clerk Maxwell showed that light travels as an **electromagnetic wave**. This is a varying electric field and a varying magnetic field which are at right angles to each other and to the direction of travel of the wave. It is an example of a transverse wave. A transverse wave is one in which the energy travels in a direction at right angles to the direction of vibration.

The speed of light at $3.00 \times 10^8 \, \mathrm{m \, s^{-1}}$, is a factor of about a million times faster than sound.

### Polarisation

Sound and light have some properties in common. They reflect, refract, diffract and superpose. The difference between light and sound can be seen by the property of polarisation. Polarisation of a transverse wave restricts the direction of oscillation so that it only occurs in one plane perpendicular to the direction of travel. Longitudinal waves such as sound waves cannot be polarised. This is because sound waves travel in the same direction as the oscillation of the particles they travel through.

## ⚠ Measuring the speed of sound

A very simple method of measuring the speed of sound is to use two microphones connected to a fast timer. A hammer strikes a metal plate, making a pulse of sound. The nearer microphone picks this up first followed by the second microphone when the pulse of sound has travelled an extra metre. The sound pulse causes the microphones each to generate an electrical pulse; the pulses trigger the timer to start and stop. The

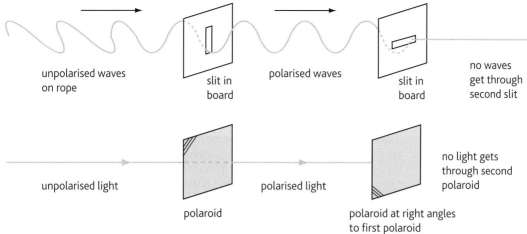

**Figure 3** *Polarising transverse waves*
*When a polariser is aligned with a wave, the polarised wave passes through. When the polariser is at right angles to the wave, it cannot pass through.*

speed of sound is simply the extra distance travelled by the sound pulse (1.0 m) divided by the time.

An alternative method is to connect a signal generator output to a loudspeaker. This sends a sound towards a microphone. The signal generator produces a pulse of voltage which in turn causes the loudspeaker to produce a sound pulse. The pulse from the signal generator also triggers the oscilloscope and the microphone picks up the pulse of sound which leads to the trace on the screen of the oscilloscope. The time taken for the sound pulse to travel from the loudspeaker to the microphone is the time from the start of the trace to the pulse shown on the oscilloscope.

So, the speed of sound $= \dfrac{\text{distance between speaker and microphone}}{\text{time read from oscilloscope trace}}$

## Music and the speed of sound

The fact that the speed of sound is relatively low has some important features when listening to music.

- The surround sound of a home theatre arrangement is initially set up assuming that the listener is equidistant from each of the speakers. If this is not the case then the sound from each speaker will have a different delay and the overall effect is spoilt. This can be corrected by balancing the system.
- Large orchestras and choirs need to watch the conductor. If they just listen, a very unpleasant sound results.
- Echoes (sound reflections) from the walls and ceilings of a building add to the overall sound. In poorly designed concert halls the echoes can add to or subtract from the initial sounds. Again this produces an unpleasant noise.

### How science works

**Accuracy**

A good thing would be to repeat this experiment for five or six distances between microphone and oscilloscope, repeating and averaging your readings. Plot a graph of distance against time. This should give a straight line origin graph of gradient equal to the speed of sound ~340 m s⁻¹.

### How science works

**Better acoustics**

Increasingly concert halls include 'hanging clouds' from the ceilings of the building to improve the acoustics and give a musical presence to the audience – so that the audience feels part of the concert. The hanging clouds reduce the time taken for a first echo to reach the audience. This apparently reduces the feeling of isolation.

### Summary questions

1. Sketch graphs to distinguish between the period and the wavelength of a sound wave.

2. State what is meant by polarisation and explain why light can be polarised whereas sound cannot.

3. Taking the speed of light to be $3.00 \times 10^8$ m s⁻¹ and the speed of sound to be 340 m s⁻¹, calculate the delay in hearing the thunder clap after seeing the lightning strike if the event occurred 5.0 km away from an observer.

4. Explain why the shape of a concert hall has a significant effect on the enjoyment of the audience.

# 1.3 Sound production

*Learning objectives:*

- How are stationary waves produced?

- How do different musical instruments produce sounds?

- What are the harmonics produced on strings and in pipes?

*Specification reference: 3.1.1A*

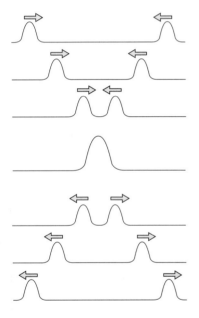

**Figure 1** *Superposition of pulses*

An important characteristic of musical instruments is that the production of their sound usually involves standing or **stationary waves**, although the eventual sound emitted is a travelling wave. Stationary waves differ from the normal travelling waves that have been considered so far. Travelling waves cause energy to move from the source of the wave to the surroundings. When a travelling wave is restricted, for example on a string with fixed ends, it reflects at each end and forms a standing wave. This can be explained in terms of the superposition of the waves.

## The principle of superposition

Unlike solid objects colliding, when two or more waves meet their total displacement is the sum of their individual displacements, taking their directions into account. Having met, the waves continue on their way as if they had never met at all. For a consistent pattern, waves need to have the same frequency and speed, and ideally the same or very similar amplitudes. Figure 1 shows two pulses approaching and passing through each other. When they meet the resultant amplitude is the sum of the two amplitudes of the individual pulses.

## Musical instruments and standing waves

The vibration of a device, such as a wire, drum, or reed, creates musical sounds. The instrument causes the surrounding air to vibrate at the same frequency as the device. Musical instruments usually fall into the categories of percussion, string or wind. In this book the focus will be on string and wind instruments.

### String instruments

Violins, pianos, 'cellos and guitars all have a stretched string that is made to vibrate either by plucking or bowing the string. This sets up a **standing wave** on the string.

The characteristic sound of, for example, an acoustic guitar is produced as a result of the shape of the body of the guitar. The strings themselves do not produce a very loud sound because of their small amplitudes and the fact that they cannot move a large volume of air. The string effectively transfers its vibration to the body of the guitar which vibrates as a whole and makes much more air move. The top plate is only a few millimetres thick and can vibrate easily. The air inside the body is important since it can vibrate just like the air in a bottle when a person blows across the top. In fact, if a speaker is placed above the sound hole and the frequency varied using a signal generator then, by listening close to the sound hole, it is possible to hear the air in the body **resonating.** This means that it vibrates at the same frequencies as the strings.

The pitch of a vibrating string depends on **three** things.

1 The **mass of the string**: more massive strings (greater mass per unit length) vibrate more slowly. On steel string guitars, the strings get thicker from high to low pitch.

2   The **tension in the string,** which is adjusted using the tuning pegs. The tighter the string, the higher the pitch.

3   The **length of the string** that is free to vibrate. When a guitar is played, the fingers press the string against the fretboard. This reduces the length of the string to the distance between the bridge and the fret. Shortening the string gives a higher pitch.

The fundamental frequency of a vibrating string is given by the equation:

$$f = \frac{1}{2l}\sqrt{\frac{T}{\mu}}$$

where $l$ is the length of the vibrating string, $T$ is the tension in the string and $\mu$ is the mass per unit length of the string material.

### Standing waves on strings

Standing waves on strings are formed from the superposition of two identical waves travelling in opposite directions. In string instruments **travelling waves** move from the point where the string is plucked or bowed. They then travel to the ends of the string where they reflect and undergo a phase change of 180° where a crest becomes a trough. Figure 3 shows two waves (blue and green) travelling towards each other. The red line shows the resultant displacement. As the green and blue waves move forwards there are points where the total displacement always remains zero. These are called nodes. At other places the displacement varies between a maximum in one direction and a maximum in the other direction. These are called antinodes.

It is usual to show the extremes of standing waves graphically as shown in Figure 4. Within each loop all parts of the string vibrate together in **phase** but loops next to each other are consistently 180° out of phase.

### Harmonics on strings

A string has a number of frequencies at which it will naturally vibrate. These natural frequencies are known as the harmonics of string. The **natural frequency** at which a string vibrates depends upon the tension of the string, the mass per unit length and the length of the string. Since both ends of a string are fixed there will be a node at either end. The fundamental frequency (or first harmonic) is the lowest frequency for which a standing wave will be set up and consists of a single loop. Doubling the frequency of vibration halves the wavelength and means that two loops are formed. This is called the second harmonic (or first overtone). Three times the fundamental frequency gives the third harmonic (see Figure 5 on the next page). In a musical instrument the rich sound comes from several harmonics occurring at the same time, and it is the balance of their amplitudes that determines the timbre.

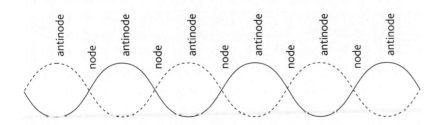

**Figure 4** *Extreme positions of standing waves*

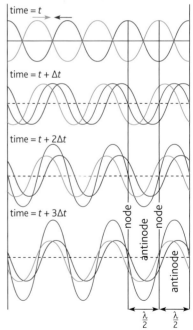

**Figure 3** *Standing waves on strings*

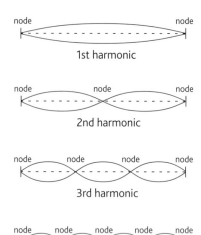

1st harmonic

2nd harmonic

3rd harmonic

4th harmonic

**Figure 5** *Harmonics on a string*

## Wind instruments

In most wind instruments air is blown into one end of a pipe and leaves at the other end. The vibration usually begins at the mouthpiece. This is the device which classifies the wind instrument. In **reed** instruments air is blown through pieces of reed plants which causes the reed to vibrate quickly. This opens and closes the pipe. The pulses of air passing through the reed cause the air in the pipe to vibrate in sympathy and sets up a standing wave. **Flutes** and recorders have a sharp 'edge mouthpiece'. The sound is produced by blowing a stream of air at this sharp edge. The stream of air vibrates above and below the edge setting up a standing wave in the pipe. In **brass** instruments, the player's lips vibrate against each other and against the rim of the mouthpiece.

### Standing waves in pipes

Standing waves in a pipe, open at one end and closed at the other end, differ from standing waves on a string. In pipes the wave medium is (usually) air and the waves themselves are longitudinal. The sound waves are reflected at both ends of the pipe. At the end of a pipe open to the air the pressure is always atmospheric and so cannot change. This is similar to the fixed end of a string and therefore at the open end of the pipe the standing sound wave must be a (pressure) node. At the closed end of the pipe the pressure varies by the greatest amount so a (pressure) antinode is formed there. However, the displacement of the air molecules in the pipe varies in exactly the opposite manner to this. There is a displacement antinode at the open end (since the molecules can be displaced by a larger amount than anywhere else in the pipe) and there will be a displacement node at the closed end. Displacement rather than pressure is used to represent the standing waves in pipes. Similar ideas to strings apply to the harmonics in pipes (see Figure 6). Strictly speaking the displacement antinode forms just beyond the open end of the pipe but you can ignore this fact for most purposes.

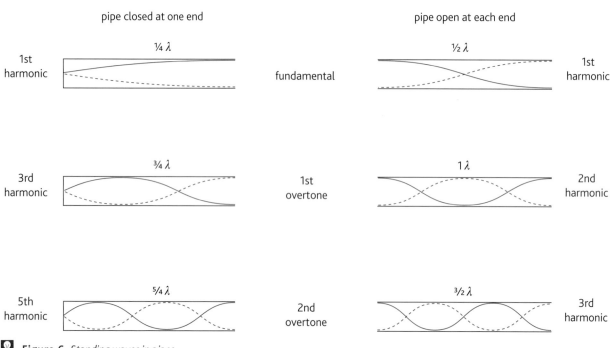

**Figure 6** *Standing waves in pipes*

## Beats

If two musical notes are sounded together, when the waves meet they will superpose and form an overall wave in a similar way to how a standing wave is set up. If the frequencies of the two waves are similar but not identical a regular rising and falling of amplitude of the resultant wave will be heard – this is known as beats (see Figure 7). When, say, two strings are in tune the beats will no longer be heard; when the strings are not in tune the beat frequency $(f_b)$ is equal to the difference between the frequencies of the individual strings.

$$f_b = f_2 - f_1$$

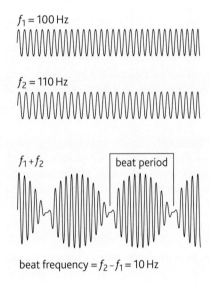

**Figure 7** *Formation of beats*

### How science works

**Tuning instruments using beats**

As two frequencies are brought closer together, the beats period will gradually increase and the beats will disappear when they become identical. Guitarists and piano tuners often use beats to hear if strings are in unison – i.e. they are in tune with each other but may be an octave or several octaves apart.

## Summary questions

1. Explain what effect increasing the tension of a drumhead has on the pitch and loudness of a kettledrum.

2. A vibrating string has length 60.0 cm and mass per unit length of $1.12 \times 10^{-3}$ kg m$^{-1}$. Calculate the frequency of the fundamental note when a tension of 12.5 N is applied to the string.

3. A tube of length 0.800 m resonates in the second harmonic mode when a tuning fork is held near it. The tube is open at both ends. Taking the speed of sound to be 340 m s$^{-1}$, calculate the most likely frequency of the tuning fork. What other frequencies could the tuning fork have?

4. Explain the difference between a travelling (sometimes called progressive) wave and a stationary wave.

5. Calculate the beat frequency and beat period produced by two notes of frequencies 320 Hz and 330 Hz.

# 1.4 Loud and soft

*Learning objectives:*

- What determines how loud a sound is?

- What is the difference between loudness and intensity?

- What is white noise and how can it pollute the environment?

*Specification reference: 3.1.1A*

### Hint

The surface area of a sphere is given by $4\pi r^2$ – this equation is given on the AS data sheet (page 235) along with some other useful mathematical equations.

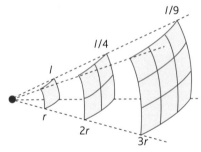

**Figure 1** *Inverse square relationship*

The loudness of a sound wave depends on the amount of energy that is transferred to the surroundings by the vibration. When a trumpeter blows harder into a trumpet, for example, then more work is being done on the air and so there will be more energy in the sound wave. The energy $E$ is found to be proportional to the square of the amplitude $A$ ($E \propto A^2$). Doubling the amplitude increases the energy by a factor of four, tripling the amplitude increases the energy by a factor of nine, etc. Loudness is the listener's perception of **intensity** of sound, but as we will see later, it is affected by the frequency.

## Intensity

If we imagine sound waves being emitted by a point source, they will spread out in all directions. This will mean that the total energy that is emitted will be spread increasingly thinly the greater the distance from the source.

In order to compare intensities easily, it is usual to use the idea of the energy transferred per second. This is the **power** ($P$) of the source. This means that the intensity ($I$) at a distance ($r$) from a point source of sound is given by the power divided by the surface area of the sphere at that radius:

$$I = \frac{P}{4\pi r^2}$$

This equation shows that intensity has an inverse square relationship with distance from the point source. This means that as the distance doubles the intensity falls to a quarter of the previous value as shown in Figure 1. The SI unit for intensity is $\mathrm{W\,m^{-2}}$.

## Loudness

Humans have very sensitive ears that can detect sound waves of extremely low intensity. The quietest sound that the typical human ear can detect has an intensity of around $1 \times 10^{-12}\,\mathrm{W\,m^{-2}}$; it does this by detecting the change in the atmospheric pressure produced by the sound. With normal atmospheric pressure being around $1 \times 10^5\,\mathrm{Pa}$, this sound would produce a pressure change of 0.00002 Pa. Remember from Key Stage 3 that $1\,\mathrm{Pa} = 1\,\mathrm{N\,m^{-2}}$. Typically, normal conversation produces a sound pressure change of 0.02 Pa. A petrol-powered lawn mower changes the pressure by about 1 Pa and sound is painfully loud at levels around 20 Pa. Thus the common sounds that are heard have sound pressure changes over a wide range (0.00002 Pa to 20 Pa).

The faintest sound that the human ear can detect is known as the **threshold of hearing**.

Since the range of intensities that the human ear can detect is so large, the scale which is frequently used by physicists to measure intensity is a scale based on multiples of 10. This is a logarithmic scale – but that is A2!

## The decibel

You will probably have seen loudness measured on the **decibel (dB)** scale. The threshold of hearing $(1 \times 10^{-12}\,\mathrm{W\,m^{-2}})$ is assigned a sound level of 0 dB. A sound which is 10 times louder $(1 \times 10^{-11}\,\mathrm{W\,m^{-2}})$ is 10 dB; a sound 100 or $10^2$ times louder is 20 dB; and a sound which is 1000 or $10^3$ times louder is 30 dB. In other words to find the number of dB, divide the intensity by $1 \times 10^{-12}\,\mathrm{W\,m^{-2}}$ and express this as a power of 10. The number of dB will be ten times this power. As a rule of thumb a 3 dB increase corresponds to a doubling of loudness and a 3 dB decrease in intensity corresponds to a halving of loudness.

 How science works

### Common sounds and their dB rating

| sound | decibel rating | noise effect |
|---|---|---|
| jet takeoff (at 25 m) | 150 | eardrum rupture |
| live rock music, thunderclap | 120 | human pain threshold |
| jet takeoff (at 300 m), petrol lawn mower | 100 | serious hearing damage after 8 hours |
| busy street traffic, vacuum cleaner | 70 | annoying |
| conversation at home | 50 | quiet |
| whispering, rustling leaves | 20 | very quiet |
| breathing | 10 | barely audible |
| mosquito hum at 3 m | 0 | threshold of hearing at 1000 Hz |

### *Frequency effects on loudness*

The intensity of a sound is an objective quantity which can be measured with sensitive instrumentation. The **loudness** of a sound depends upon the ear of the listener and is therefore subjective. Experiment has shown that a range of people do not perceive the same sound being the same loudness. Age is probably the most obvious factor which reduces the effectiveness of ears when responding to sound. The human ear does not respond equally to all frequencies: it is much more sensitive to sounds in the frequency range of about 1 to 4 kHz than to very low or high frequency sounds – the ear tends to amplify sounds in this frequency range more than those at other frequencies.

Figure 2 shows a series of curves, each of which represents how a typical listener perceives sounds of different frequencies and intensities to be of equal loudness. The dips in the curves at about 3 kHz indicate that the listener's ear is most sensitive at this frequency.

## Noise and sound

The word **noise** is used in everyday language to mean unwanted sound or noise pollution. Noise crops up in several areas of physics and we tend to use the term to mean a variation of sound or an electrical signal that obscures or reduces the clarity of a signal. This variation is often random and persistent. White noise has an equal probability of being any frequency and so has a uniform frequency spectrum (although

How science works

Exposure to loud sounds, including loud music, can affect a listener's hearing adversely. This is why employees subjected to loud noises in their work places are required to wear ear protectors.

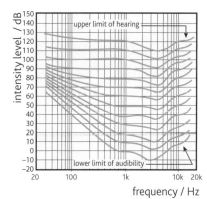

**Figure 2** *Equal loudness curves*

■ Link

Signal noise is something that affects the transmission of electrical and optical signals as we shall see in Topic 2.1.

at any one time only certain frequencies can be present). A graph of amplitude against frequency is shown in Figure 3. White noise has a typically uniform amplitude across the frequency range and produces a background hiss and hum reminiscent of the sound heard on a very old sound recording. When a television aerial is unplugged, the screen shows the effects of white electromagnetic noise. In the United Kingdom noise pollution is regulated by the Department for the Environment Food & Rural Affairs (Defra). This includes 'neighbourhood noise' and 'ambient noise' (the background noise due to traffic, machines, etc.).

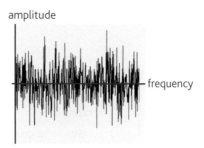

**Figure 3** *White noise energy spectrum*

Noise can be irritating to listeners. There are three things which can be done to reduce the effects of noise:

■ reducing it at the source

■ absorbing it

■ masking it

Vehicle exhaust systems use bafflers to muffle the noise produced by the engine. Defra have regulations which limit the times at which aeroplanes may fly and what constitutes unacceptably noisy neighbours.

Cubicles are often used in office buildings to section off workers from one another. These tend to be made of soft, sound absorbing 'acoustical' tiles. Carpeting on floors has a good sound-absorbing effect.

Active noise cancellation is used in headsets, headphones and earphones to reduce the effect of noise. A microphone samples the surrounding noise and elecronic circuits generate a sound of similar frequency and amplitude but antiphase with the original sound. The superposition of the two sounds cancels the original sound. Such systems tend to be more effective at lower frequencies and allow noise of chosen frequency ranges to be blocked.

## Summary questions

1. Explain the difference between loudness and intensity.

2. At a distance of 15 m from the source, the intensity of a loud sound is $2.0 \times 10^{-4}\,\mathrm{W\,m^{-2}}$. Calculate the intensity at 120 m from the source.

3. What is meant by the *threshold of human hearing*? How many decibels is a sound of intensity $1.0 \times 10^{-8}\,\mathrm{W\,m^{-2}}$?

4. Explain what is meant by noise pollution and suggest situations in which noise pollution might be a serious risk to health.

**1** (a) (i) A sound wave of frequency 250 Hz travels through air at a speed of 332 m s⁻¹. Calculate the wavelength of the sound wave.

(ii) The wavelength of a sound wave of the same frequency travelling through a block of lead is six times larger. What is the speed of sound in lead? *(3 marks)*

(b) (i) A sound wave of frequency 200 Hz is converted to an electrical signal and the signal displayed on an oscilloscope. How many cycles are observed on the screen if the time base setting is 1 ms cm⁻¹ and there are ten horizontal divisions on the screen.

(ii) What would be the new time base setting if it was required to display the same number of cycles of an electrical signal generated by a sound wave of frequency 50 Hz? *(4 marks)*

**2** (a) The speed of a wave travelling across a water surface is greater for waves of longer wavelength. If the speed of a sound wave was also dependent on wavelength, what effect would this have when listening to an orchestra? *(3 marks)*

(b) Explain why it is important that members of an orchestra watch the conductor rather than just listen to the music from the other instruments. *(2 marks)*

**3** (a) In order to measure the speed of sound, a student stands some distance from the wall of a building and uses a hammer to strike a wooden block. He listens to the echo produced by the sound wave reflecting off the wall and adjusts the rate at which he hits the block of wood so that each strike coincides with the echo from the previous one.

(i) Explain why this method of measuring the speed of sound is likely to be more accurate than simply measuring the time between striking the block of wood and hearing the first echo.

(ii) The time taken for 21 strikes of the wooden block is 10.6 s. Calculate the time taken for the sound wave to travel to the wall and back to the student.

(iii) Calculate the speed of sound if the distance from the student to the wall is 91 m. *(6 marks)*

(b) What would be the effect on the measurements if there was a breeze blowing directly towards the wall? *(2 marks)*

**4** (a) (i) A stationary wave is set up in a pipe that is closed at one end and open at the other. Explain why a pressure node is set up at the open end and a displacement node at the closed end.

(ii) Explain why the length of the pipe is slightly less than a quarter of a wavelength when the pipe is resonating in its fundamental mode. *(5 marks)*

(b) (i) A pipe open at both ends, and a pipe closed at one end have the same length. They are resonating in their fundamental mode. State and explain the relationship between the frequencies of the sound waves produced by the two pipes.

(ii) State and explain why a pipe open at each end is capable of producing more harmonics than a similar pipe closed at one end. *(5 marks)*

**5**　**Figure 1** shows the displacement of particles in an ultrasound wave at different distances from the source at a particular time. The wave travels at $3200\,\text{m}\,\text{s}^{-1}$.

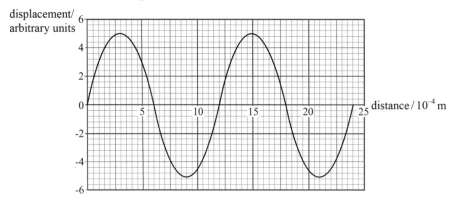

**Figure 1**

(a)　(i)　Use the graph to find the wavelength of the wave in **Figure 1**.

　　(ii)　Calculate the frequency of the ultrasound wave.　　*(3 marks)*

(b)　One industrial use for ultrasound waves is to detect flaws inside a metal block.

**Figure 2a** shows the arrangement in which the waves are fired downwards in short pulses from a transmitter. **Figure 2b** shows the amplitudes of the initial pulse and the reflected signals recorded by the receiver. You may assume that there is no reflected pulse received from the upper surface of the block.

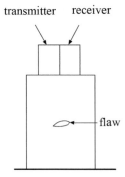

**Figure 2a**

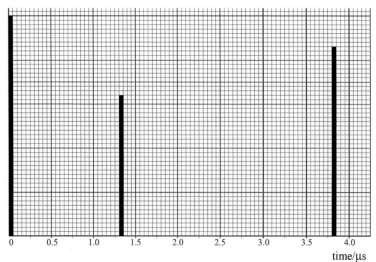

**Figure 2b**

The ultrasound wave travels at $3200\,\text{m}\,\text{s}^{-1}$. Use data from **Figure 2b** to calculate the distance of the flaw below the top of the block.　　*(3 marks)*

AQA, 2006

6    A small loudspeaker emitting sound of constant frequency is
     positioned a short distance above a long glass tube containing
     water. When water is allowed to run slowly out of the tube, the
     intensity of the sound heard increases whenever the length *l*
     (shown in **Figure 3**) takes certain values.

     (a) Explain these observations by reference to the physical
         principles involved.

         You may be awarded marks for the quality of written
         communication in your answer.                    *(4 marks)*

     (b) With the loudspeaker emitting sound of frequency 480 Hz,
         the effect described in part (a) is noticed first when
         *l* = 168 mm. It next occurs when *l* = 523 mm.

         Use both values of *l* to calculate:

         (i)  the wavelength of the sound waves in the air column,
         (ii) the speed of these sound waves.          *(4 marks)*

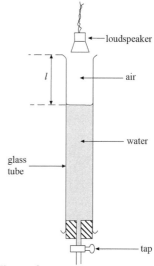

**Figure 3**

AQA, 2005

7    (a) Explain how a stationary wave is produced when a stretched string is plucked.    *(3 marks)*

     (b) (i) Copy **Figure 4** and draw on it the fundamental mode of vibration of a
             stretched string. Label any nodes with a letter **N** and any antinodes with a
             letter **A**.

     **Figure 4**

         (ii) Copy **Figure 4** again and draw on it the fourth harmonic (third overtone) for
              the stretched string. Label any nodes with a letter **N** and any anitnodes with
              a letter **A**.                                   *(4 marks)*

     (c) The fundamental frequency of vibration, *f*, of a string is given by:

$$f = \frac{1}{2l}\sqrt{\frac{T}{\mu}}$$

         where  *T* = the tension in the string
                *l* = the length of the string
                $\mu$ = the mass per unit length of the string

         A string has a tension of 180 N and a length of 0.70 m.

         (i)  What would need to be done to the length of the string in order to double
              the frequency?
         (ii) What would need to be done to the tension of the string in order to double
              the frequency?                                   *(3 marks)*

AQA, 2005

8    (a) (i)  The sound level at a distance of 10 m from a point source is 70 dB. What is
              the intensity of the sound wave at this distance from the source?
         (ii) What would be the intensity at a distance of 20 m from the same point
              source?                                           *(4 marks)*

     (b) Describe how the normal human ear has a sensitivity that varies with frequency.    *(3 marks)*

# 2.1 Recording and playback

*Learning objectives:*

- How are sounds recorded and stored?

- What is the difference between analogue and digital signals?

- How can an analogue signal be digitised?

- What are the advantages of the two types of signal?

*Specification reference: 3.1.1.B*

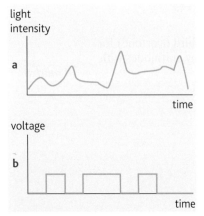

**Figure 1** *Analogue and digital signals*

### How science works

**Frequency response**

Microphones, loudspeakers and amplifiers used in recording systems may have a big impact on the final sound produced. In an ideal system each of these devices will treat each frequency present in the original sound in an identical way – however the reality is that different frequencies will be processed by different amounts and the sound output can be very different from the sound input.

## What are analogue and digital signals?

**Analogue** signals are those which vary continuously with time, for example a voltage or light intensity could vary continuously (see Figure 1a).

**Digital** signals only have two values (see Figure 1b); information is coded in binary in pulses of voltage or light.

## Stages in sound recording and playback

The first stage in analogue sound recording is when sound waves cause a membrane in a microphone to vibrate (see Figure 2). These mechanical vibrations are converted into weak electrical signals whose voltage mimics the displacement of air molecules by the sound. This signal is amplified; this means that the output of the microphone is increased using current from the amplifier's power supply. The amplified signal is then fed into the record head which is an electromagnet that produces a magnetic field. The intensity of the field varies in the same way as the current (and therefore the original sound). Recording tape consists of a thin plastic tape coated with a thin layer of ferric oxide powder which is permanently magnetised by a magnetic field. If several microphones, or a series of microphones and guitar pickups, are to be recorded together, an electronic box called a **mixer** is used to balance the relative strengths of the signals.

During playback, the reverse processes of recording occur. The tape passes the playback head where the tape's magnetic field induces currents in this head. These currents are amplified and the electrical signal is then passed to a loudspeaker where it is converted into sound by the mechanical vibrations of the loudspeaker cone or headphones.

## Converting analogue signals to digital signals

### Sampling analogue signals

Although the principles of recording and storing an analogue signal are quite straightforward there are limitations of space – a vinyl disc can store little more than 20 min worth of music per side and, although analogue tape can store quite a bit more than this, the linear nature of tape makes locating a particular part of the tape difficult and therefore slow. Storing data can be made considerably easier if the data is **digital** as is the case with compact discs (CDs) and MP3 players. At some stage, either at the microphone or other recording device, an analogue signal must be **sampled**. This is done by measuring the signal voltage at regular time intervals and then converting the measurement into a binary number. This digital number can either be stored on a CD or a computer or else transmitted to a receiver. When the sound is to be played again, the binary data must be reconverted into an analogue signal to drive a loudspeaker. Many audio systems use a digital signal processor.

During this process a microphone produces an analogue signal which an analogue-to-digital converter (ADC) digitises into binary. This signal is sent to the digital signal processor (DSP). The DSP analyses the digitised signal, and encodes it using a compression algorithm. The compressed data is then stored in memory. Upon playback, the data is retrieved from memory and is decompressed. A digital-to-analogue converter (DAC) changes the digital values back to an analogue voltage that is applied to the amplifier and speaker. The routine used in the DSP is called a *codec*, for *compression-dec*ompression. MP3 and WMA are common codecs, though there are many others.

Although we are not concerned with the details of the method, the sampling of the analogue voltage occurs at regular intervals of time. Figure 3a and b show the principle of sampling an analogue signal. Figure 3c shows how this data is then converted into a binary number.

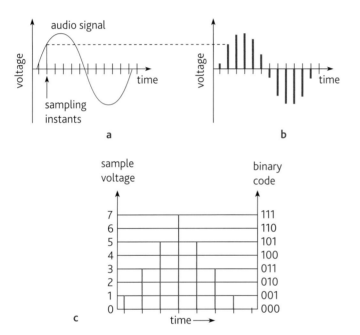

**Figure 3** *Sampling an audio signal*

### Sampling rate

The more frequently the data is sampled the closer a regenerated wave will be to the original analogue waveform.

> The rule for setting out the minimum sampling rate of a regular signal is that it must be at least twice the frequency of the signal.

If this is not the case the regenerated signal can produce false sounds in what is called aliasing. Figure 4 on the next page shows regular analogue signals being sampled at different frequencies.

The blue dots show when the signal is sampled. The graphs on the right show the digital version of the signal at the different sample rates. The black lines show the analogue signals regenerated from the digital signals. When sampling occurs at more than twice the signal frequency a reasonable signal is regenerated. When sampling occurs at the signal frequency there is no signal at all, sampling at other instants at the signal frequency would produce constant voltages. However, when the sampling

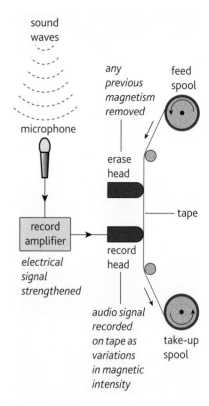

**Figure 2** *Analogue recording*

■ How science works

**Binary**

In order to store information on computers data must be converted into binary numbers, i.e. numbers which consist of just zeros and ones. Such numbers are preferable to the normal base 10 that we use because they can easily be coded as on and off using electronic switches. Each of the ones or zeros in a binary number is called a 'bit' – shortened form of **bi**nary dig**it**. The numbers 0–10 in four bit binary are 0000, 0001, 0010, 0011, 0100, 0101, 0110, 0111, 1000, 1001, 1010. A group of eight bits is called a 'byte'.

frequency is less than twice the signal frequency a very different (and useless) signal is regenerated, this signal is called an **alias**.

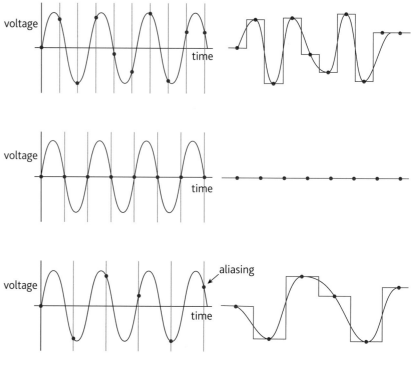

💡 **Figure 4** *Sampling rates*

### *Quantisation*

When sampled data is represented by a greater number of bits, the closer a regenerated wave will be to the original analogue waveform. Of course greater numbers of bits means more space is needed to store the data. So there has to be a compromise between faithful reproduction of the analogue signal and memory used. If a three-bit binary number is used for encoding a signal there are eight possible levels (from 000 to 111 or 0 to 7 in ordinary (base 10) numbering). This leads to a quantisation error since the signal has to be encoded so that a range of analogue values are all represented by the same digital value. If an eight-bit binary number is used to encode the same signal there are 256 $(= 2^8)$ possible values and so the quantisation error is smaller. Figure 5a shows how 2 bit encoding represents the analogue signal – the variation in voltage is poorly represented by the binary number. In Figure 5b the use of 4 bit encoding at the same sampling frequency produces a much more faithful representation of the analogue signal – but takes twice the storage space.

The sequence of binary numbers that result from the sampling process is known as the pulse code and therefore the process of assembling the sampled analogue signal into a sequence of binary numbers is called **pulse code modulation.** The pulse code is transmitted and when it is received it can either be stored or processed immediately by a pulse code demodulator. This converts each binary number into a quantised voltage pulse that can then be reformed into an analogue signal.

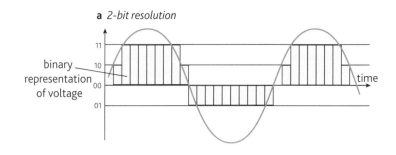

**a** *2-bit resolution*

binary representation of voltage

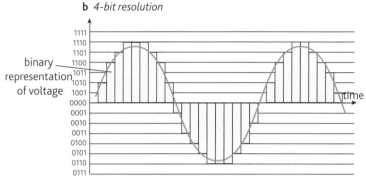

**b** *4-bit resolution*

binary representation of voltage

**Figure 5** *Quantisation using 2 bit and 4 bit coding*

## Compression

Data compression techniques have been developed in order to speed up digital data transmission and to reduce the space needed to store it. The main concept behind compression is that of elimination of redundant information. 'Lossy' compression makes use of the fact that the listener will be unable to hear small discrepancies in the signal due to the compression routine. Certain quiet frequencies received by the ear are masked by other louder frequencies so the masked frequencies become redundant and need not be recorded. As we saw in Topic 1.4 the ear is more receptive to some frequencies than others and therefore the presence of these favoured frequencies masks others occurring at the same time – again leading to the possibility of elimination. Predictive coding uses the fact that previous samples produce information which can predict the next sample – meaning that only the *difference* between the samples needs to be transmitted in order to produce the second sample. If the compression is too extreme then the effects of the compression will produce a noticeable decrease in sound quality. This technique is commonly used in the transmission of digital television where much of a picture remains unchanged from frame to frame.

## Digital filters

The function of a filter is to remove random noise from a signal or to extract useful parts of it, such as sending the high or low frequencies to different loudspeakers in a sound system. A low-pass filter removes the high frequencies and drives a subwoofer (bass speaker) whereas a high-pass filter will drive a tweeter (treble speaker). A digital filter uses a digital processor to perform numerical calculations on sampled values of the signal. The results of these calculations, which now represent sampled values of the filtered signal, are output through a digital to analogue converter (DAC) to convert the signal back to analogue form. Such techniques can be used to eliminate clicks and hiss when anlogue 'vinyl' discs are being converted to CD.

## How science works

**The future's digital**

- Semiconductor technology has a very consistent history of improvement with the processing power of microprocessors, memory, etc. traditionally doubled every 18 months. This gives designers access to tremendous capabilities at relatively low cost.

- The relative cheapness of electronic components means that the twenty-first century is truly becoming the age of communication with the UK population being said to own more than one mobile phone per head of population!

- The cloning of digital data can be a problem for people such as software developers, record companies, and film studios who want to sell digital data for profit.

## Advantages and disadvantages of digital signals

Processing techniques applied to digital signals mean that the electromagnetic interference, signal loss and noise, which restricts the quality of analogue signals, can be virtually eliminated. As long as the stream of bits is received, it can be reconstructed into a replica of the original digital source. The faithfulness of the reproduction depends on the quantisation and compression used. A digital file can be copied an infinite number of times without a loss of quality. When analogue signals attenuate and degrade the noise becomes amplified along with the signal. Digital data can also be encrypted to provide some measure of protection against unwanted viewing or listening and often it can be compressed. Digital data can be shared among many different devices – you can use your mobile phone to send e-mails or photographs, or a PC to listen to a compact disc.

One of the limitations of digital is that transducers usually generate analogue voltages which need to be sampled and then converted back to analogue at the end of the process – binary numbers can not be heard from a speaker or seen on a monitor.

### Summary questions

1 State the difference between analogue and digital signals.

2 Explain the effect that increased sampling rate and decreased quantisation levels has on the amount of storage required and the faithfulness of a digital signal.

3 Suggest why a good compression routine will mean that a compressed signal will be practically indistinguishable from an uncompressed one.

4 Outline the reasons why the music industry has mixed emotions about digital music.

# 2.2 CD and DVD

*Learning objectives:*

- What is interference and diffraction?

- What are the principal components of a CD system?

- How is music stored and played back?

*Specification reference: 3.1.1C*

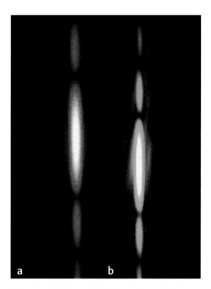

**Figure 1** *Single slit diffraction pattern*

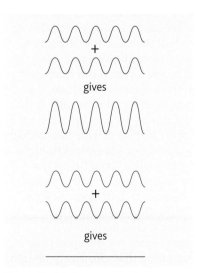

**Figure 3** *Reinforcement and cancellation*

## 🔺 💡 Diffraction and interference

When light from a laser beam passes through a narrow slit it does not produce a bright dot as an image, which is what we might expect, instead the image is that shown in Figure 1a. The wave property causing this is **diffraction** which is a property of all waves. Figure 1a and b shows the diffraction patterns produced by green and red laser beams passing through narrow slits (of the same width). The intensity of the central maximum is much greater than that of the secondary maxima and its width is about twice that of the other maxima. Red light has a longer wavelength than green and diffracts more noticeably.

### Young's double slit experiment

In this experiment a double slit is used to diffract one light beam into two which then overlap.

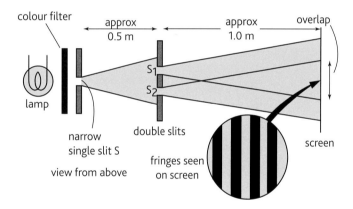

💡 **Figure 2** *Young's double slit arrangement*

The **interference** pattern that is produced is shown in Figure 2 and consists of bright and dark fringes of equal width. These fringes are formed as a result of the **superposition** of the waves coming from each of the slits. Where a bright fringe is formed the waves from each of the slits either travel the same distance (central bright fringe) or else has a **path difference** equal to a whole number of wavelengths, so that they arrive in **phase** (a crest meets a crest or a trough meets a trough) and reinforce each other giving twice the amplitude of a single wave. Where a dark fringe is formed the waves travel a path difference equal to an odd number of half-wavelengths, so they arrive 180° out of phase (a crest meets a trough, etc.) and completely cancel each other out (see Figure 3). Reinforcement is also known as **constructive interference** and cancellation as **destructive interference**. The spacing between two adjacent bright fringes $w$ is given by the equation

$$w = \frac{\lambda D}{s}$$

where $\lambda$ is the wavelength of the light, $s$ is the separation of the slits and $D$ is the distance from the double slit to the screen.

23

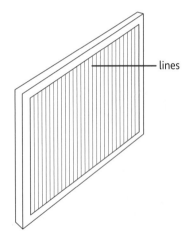

**Figure 4** *Diffraction grating*

## The diffraction grating

A transmission **diffraction grating** is constructed by drawing *lines* (usually between 100 and 600 lines per mm) on a piece of glass or transparent plastic as shown in Figure 4. The light is therefore transmitted by the transparent *slits* between the lines. The grating splits white light into different wavelengths with a high degree of precision. A reflection diffraction grating has a shiny surface between the lines so that light gets reflected off it. A compact disc acts as a reflection grating. The diffraction grating is very similar to Young's double slit but the maxima are more intense, more sharply defined and the angles the beam are diffracted through are larger so that they can be measured with greater precision. The equation for the diffraction grating is:

$$n\lambda = d\sin\theta$$

where $n$ is the order of the image (central one is 0, next on either side are 1, etc.), $\lambda$ the wavelength, $d$ the grating spacing and $\theta$ the angle the image makes with a line normal to the grating (as shown in Figure 5).

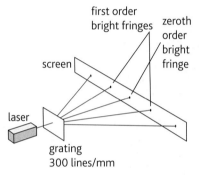

**Figure 5** *Diffraction grating images*

## The compact disc

A typical CD consists of a plastic disc that is 12 cm in diameter and 1.2 mm thick. A long single spiral track, on which microscopic bumps are recorded, runs from the centre to the outside. The track is $0.5 \times 10^{-6}$ m wide and there is a gap of $1.6 \times 10^{-6}$ m between successive loops in the spiral. The bumps are $1.25 \times 10^{-7}$ m high. If the track was stretched out it would be 5 km long (see Figure 6). Diffraction is used to help the laser reader keep on target with the very fine precision needed. A *three-beam* system is utilised; a diffraction grating produces the first order diffraction maximum to each side of the main beam. The three diffracted beams overlap the track and when the main beam is centred on the track the reflected light from the two side beams should average out to be of equal intensity. If the beams are unequal, then their difference can be used to generate an error signal which will then initiate a procedure to correct the tracking (see Figure 7). Bumps are made to be a quarter of a wavelength high. This means that light striking the flat part (called 'land') travels a quarter of a wavelength in one direction and quarter of a wavelength in the other direction (making a total distance of half a wavelength) further than light striking the top of the bump. The light reflected from the land is therefore delayed by half a wavelength and so is exactly out of phase with the light reflected from the bump. These two waves will interfere destructively meaning that effectively no light has been reflected. This means that the detecting optical sensor senses bumps as binary zeros whereas the land does not produce destructive interference and is sensed as ones. A motor rotates the disc at between 200 and 500 revolutions per minute – the reason for this variation in speed is so that the laser can pick up data at the same rate whether the beam is scanning near the centre where the disc is moving quickly or scanning at the outer parts where it is moving less quickly. The laser tracks in order to follow the spiral, detecting the bumps and land precisely. The disc is recorded and read from the inside to the outside.

**Figure 6** *The spiral track on a CD*

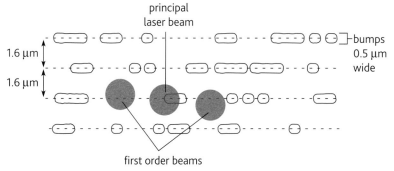

**Figure 7** *Tracking on a CD*

A computer drive or CD recorder must be able to write data on a CD-R (recordable CD). For this to work the laser creates a non-reflective area on the disc by darkening an area in the layer of dye positioned underneath the reflective aluminium surface (the laser beam shining upwards from below the disc). A less powerful laser is then used to read the pattern with the darkened area not reflecting the light (as with bumps) while the remainder of the dye remains translucent and allows the aluminium surface to reflect the light. In CD-RW (rewritable) discs the dye layer is replaced by a special compound that melts above 600 °C but crystallises (and is translucent) below 200 °C. By melting the compound, pits made during the *burning* of the CD can be filled in again.

### How science works

#### DVDs

**DVDs** use a very similar technology to CDs but single-sided DVDs have about seven times the capacity for storing music. This comes from having a tighter spiral, shorter bumps and a more efficient tracking system than a CD. DVDs often have two layers, where the laser can pass through the first one to reach the second, thereby increasing the capacity still further. DVD and HD-DVD (high definition DVD) recordable discs can be made compatible by using two layers of dye and different coloured lasers. DVD and HD-DVD are made compatible by being accessed from the top and the bottom of the same disc by the read-write lasers.

### Summary questions

1. Describe Young's double slit experiment and go on to explain how bright and dark fringes are produced by constructive and destructive interference.

2. Calculate the angle measured from the straight through position of the first order maximum, when light of wavelength 630 nm is incident on a grating of 400 lines per millimetre.

3. Explain how a compact disc stores binary information and how a laser beam is used to read the 0's and 1's on the disc.

# 2.3 Electromagnetic waves used for wireless communication

*Learning objectives:*

- What frequencies of the electromagnetic spectrum are used for communication?

- What is meant by the modulation of a carrier wave?

- How can pulse code modulation and time division multiplexing techniques be used?

*Specification reference: 3.1.1D*

## Properties of electromagnetic waves

All **electromagnetic (e-m) waves**:

- consist of a varying electric and a varying magnetic field vibrating at right angles to each other
- travel at the same speed in a vacuum ($3.00 \times 10^8\,\mathrm{m\,s^{-1}}$)
- are unaffected by electric or magnetic fields
- obey the inverse square law in the absence of absorption
- may be **polarised**
- have properties of **reflection**, **refraction**, **diffraction** and **interference**.

## Differences between e-m waves

Although there is significant overlap in terms of wavelength and frequency, e-m waves are usually distinguished from each other by how they were produced. Figure 1 includes the frequencies and wavelengths in a vacuum of e-m waves. Of these waves there are only a limited number that are used to transmit and receive information without the need for connecting wires or fibres. These tend to be in the family of waves called 'radio' but include microwaves and, to some extent, light.

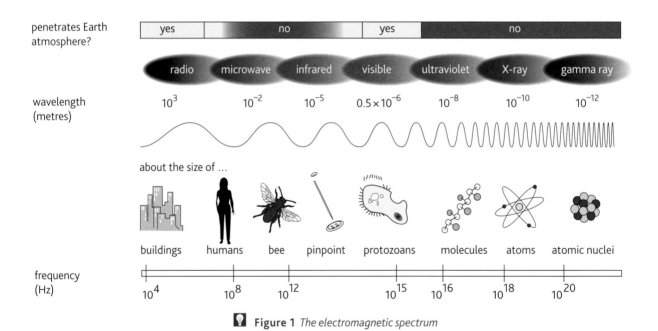

**Figure 1** *The electromagnetic spectrum*

## Uses of e-m waves

The different frequencies and energies of various regions of the electromagnetic spectrum mean that they can be used for a variety of applications. Table 1 shows a summary of the properties and uses of each region of the e-m spectrum.

**Table 1** *Uses of e-m waves*

| region of e-m spectrum | main properties and some uses | |
|---|---|---|
| radio waves | radio and TV communications | |
| microwaves | satellite communications<br>wireless computer connections including *blue-tooth*<br>radar detection of ships and aircraft | some mobile phone networks<br>heating effect used in microwave ovens |
| infrared | cooking or heating using radiant heater<br>photography in the dark | remote controllers for TV, hi fi etc.<br>thermographs |
| visible | human and animal vision | photosynthesis in plants |
| ultraviolet | produces vitamin D in the skin<br>forgery detection | can cause sun-tan, eye damage and skin cancer<br>causes fluorescence in certain mineral salts |
| X-rays | form images in medicine (radiography)<br>non-destructive testing of welds or joints etc. in metals | measurement of thickness<br>imaging internal structures of objects |
| gamma rays | sterilise food or medical equipment<br>treat cancer (radiotherapy) | kill bacteria |

## Windows for e-m waves

Not all electromagnetic waves can pass through the atmosphere. Most radiation is absorbed. The atmosphere is effectively opaque to all electromagnetic waves with the exception of:

- some radio wavebands,
- the light in the optical window – the entire visible region (of wavelength from 390 to 780 nm),
- the near ultraviolet,
- the near infrared and some far infrared.

Infrared of wavelengths between 1 and 20 mm is absorbed by water, oxygen and carbon dioxide molecules in the air. Most ultraviolet is absorbed by the ozone layer. X-rays and gamma rays are absorbed by gas molecules. Although the atmosphere is transparent to many radio wavelengths, atmospheric absorption becomes a problem for wavelengths of less than 2 cm and the ionosphere reflects radio waves of wavelength more than a few metres.

## Modulation and carrier waves

All forms of wireless communication rely on a carrier signal such as an electromagnetic wave with a particular frequency. By **modulating** the carrier, we can encode the information to be transmitted; the higher the carrier frequency, the more information a signal can hold. When the whole signal has been received, the carrier wave is filtered out leaving only the **demodulated** signal behind. Tuning a radio to a particular station means that you are selecting the frequency of the carrier wave. However, modulation can be applied to any form of electromagnetic wave.

The medium wave (MW) and long wave (LW) bands on an analogue radio use **amplitude modulation** or AM. The information is added to the carrier wave, producing a signal of greater amplitude variation when the information is a loud sound and smaller amplitude variation for quiet sounds. The modulated carrier wave is filtered by the radio leaving the information (speech or music) to be amplified and fed to the loudspeaker (see Figure 2).

audio frequency signal

unmodulated radio frequency carrier wave

carrier wave amplitude modulated by audio frequency signal

**Figure 2** *Amplitude modulation*

audio frequency signal

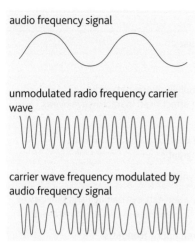

unmodulated radio frequency carrier wave

carrier wave frequency modulated by audio frequency signal

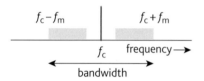

**Figure 3** *Frequency modulation*

**Figure 4** *Frequency spectrum of carrier wave and signal*

FM stands for **frequency modulation**. The information signal modifies the carrier wave by changing its frequency very slightly (see Figure 3). There are two changes possible: the overall change in frequency above and below the carrier frequency, and the number of times the frequency changes between these limits every second. The first represents the amplitude of the information signal, the second the frequency.

## Bandwidth and sidebands

When a carrier signal is modulated, frequencies other than those of the carrier and the signal are produced. These extra frequencies are equal to the sum of and the difference between the carrier and the signal. For a carrier frequency $f_c$ and a single signal frequency $f_s$ the frequencies produced will be $f_c + f_s$ and $f_c - f_s$. This means that, in order to avoid interference with signals from other sources, an amount of the spectrum equal to $2f_s$ based on $f_c$ must be allotted to the signal. This value of $2f_s$ is called the **channel bandwidth**. In a real modulating signal there will be a range of frequencies and so there will be sidebands on either side of the carrier frequency as shown in Figure 4.

## ■ Pulse code modulation

As you have seen in Topic 2.1, pulse code modulation (PCM) is a digital technique for transmitting analogue data. Using PCM, it is possible to digitise all forms of analogue data. To obtain PCM from an analogue waveform the signal is sampled at regular time intervals and then quantised. The output of a pulse code modulator is thus a series of binary numbers which are transmitted in sequence. At the receiver a pulse code demodulator converts the binary numbers back into pulses having the same quantum levels as those in the modulator. These pulses are further processed to restore the original analogue waveform.

## 💡 Time division multiplexing

This is a technique which is used to send several PCM or digital signals from a number of devices (computers, telephones, fax machines, etc.) along the same transmission path at what seems to be the same time (see Figure 5). The signal from each device is split into packets of bits which are then sent in sequence to the receiver from the transmitter. When the signals reach their destination they are reassembled in sequence by a demultiplexer. They are then passed to the appropriate device for decoding.

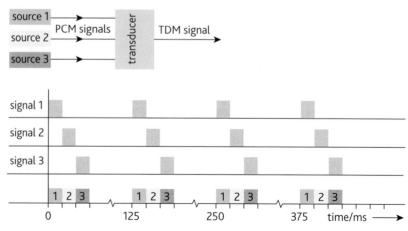

**Figure 5** *Time division multiplexing*

## Summary questions

1. List the regions of the electromagnetic spectrum which are used for wireless communication.

2. Explain what is meant by saying that the atmosphere has windows for certain electromagnetic waves.

3. A carrier frequency of 1.5 GHz is modulated by speech in the range from 300–5000 Hz. What is the bandwidth occupied by the speech channel?

# 2.4 Radio transmission

*Learning objectives:*

- Why is it not possible to receive FM signals in some places?

- How do the different frequencies travel from transmitters to receivers?

- Why do aerials need to be correctly aligned?

*Specification reference: 3.1.1D*

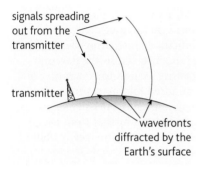

**Figure 1** *Ground waves*

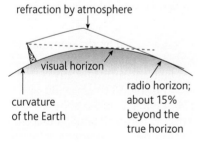

**Figure 2** *Space waves*

## Transmission paths

There are several ways in which radio can be transmitted from a transmitter to a receiver – each of these is called a transmission path. At very high frequency (VHF) and above, line-of-sight propagation is the most significant method of transmission. At high frequency (HF), the two main methods of transmission are by **ground waves** and **sky waves**. Ground waves are radio waves that travel near the surface of the Earth. Sky waves are radio waves that are refracted back to Earth from the ionosphere.

### Ground waves

These may be of two types called **surface waves** and **space waves**.

Surface waves are transmitted as waves with a long wavelength typically 1 km (such as with LW radio) and reach the receiver by diffracting around the surface of the Earth (see Figure 1). Waves can diffract around objects when the dimensions of the object do not exceed the wavelength (this includes hills and buildings for LW radio) meaning that surface waves can reach places that shorter wavelength radio cannot. The surface wave attenuates (weakens) by inducing a voltage in the Earth's surface thereby reducing wave energy. By using vertically **polarised** waves the extent to which the electric field of the wave is in contact with the Earth is reduced; this is achieved using a vertical dipole aerial. LW radio covers the whole of the country from a single transmitter and it requires no retuning when listening in a car travelling the length of the country. TV and VHF radio signals have wavelengths typically of a few metres; such waves cannot diffract around hills or over large buildings; this means FM transmitters only cover a small region and car radios need retuning during long journeys.

Space waves either travel in the line-of-sight or else refract off the Earth's surface to the receiving aerial. The different densities of the atmosphere means that waves travel at a slightly higher speed in the upper than in the lower parts of the atmosphere causing them to **refract**. This means that the space waves travel further than might be expected giving reception up to 15% beyond the **visual horizon** (see Figure 2).

### Sky waves

In this mode, the signal sent out radiates towards the ionosphere, a layer of ionised atoms between 90 and 300 km above the surface of the Earth. Depending upon the frequency of the radio waves, the power of the transmitter and the level of ionisation at the time, the signal appears to be reflected by the ionosphere leaving a region where no signal can be received (a skip zone). The waves can be reflected again back and forth between the Earth's surface and the ionosphere giving several skip zones. In fact the signal is refracted by the ionosphere. The refraction is gradual but increases deeper into the ionosphere. The wave exits from the ionosphere either at the top or goes back to the Earth (see Figure 3). Sky waves occur with short wavelength waves and so are usually HF or MW radio waves.

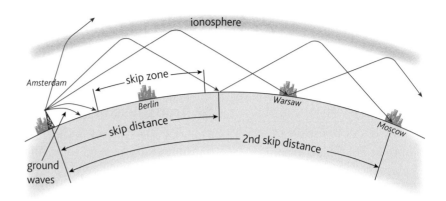

**Figure 3** *Sky waves*

## ■ AM versus FM radio

AM radio is broadcast on three frequency bands: LW (153–279 kHz), MW (520–1610 kHz) and short wave (SW) (2.3–26.1 MHz). The LW and MW are each allotted a 9 kHz channel bandwidth and SW is allocated 5 kHz. The main drawback of AM is that electromagnetic interference can modify the carrier wave – this noise is difficult to filter from the audio signal when the signal is demodulated at the receiver. In the daytime AM signals travel as ground waves, diffracting around the curvature of the Earth over a distance of up to a few hundred kilometres from their transmitter; at night changes in the ionosphere cause AM signals to travel by sky waves and they can be received much further from the transmitter. As a result of this some AM transmitters are legally obliged to reduce their power at night or else use directional aerials to avoid interference with other signals. AM radio signals can be interfered with by tall buildings and electrical noise such as the noise from vehicle ignition systems. Consequently AM radio is used for 'talk radio' where the fidelity need not be too high.

Because the amplitude of its carrier wave is not varied by the information signal, FM radio is much less susceptible to noise than AM radio and gives far better fidelity. Although FM could be transmitted on any wave band it has come to mean transmission in the VHF range (30 to 300 MHz). Due to its higher frequency VHF radio has much shorter wavelengths than AM radio and so it is affected by much smaller objects and also reflected by many objects (causing 'multipath' interference). VHF is not diffracted by the Earth's surface or reflected by the ionosphere and so is limited to line of sight transmission. The much greater bandwidth of FM means that more information can be carried allowing stereo transmissions. As electromagnetic noise affects the amplitude of a wave, FM is relatively unaffected by this. The amplitude of the wave can be filtered, removing the noise, because the signal information is encoded as the change in frequency of the carrier wave.

### Bandwidth limitations within the e-m spectrum

A large portion of the e-m spectrum is used for communication purposes. However, since AM, FM, television, etc. require a particular bandwidth for successful transmission there is clearly a limit to the number of stations that can exist at the same time. A typical FM radio signal has a bandwidth of about 200 kHz while a typical analogue television broadcast video signal has a bandwidth of 6 MHz.

## How science works

### Digital audio broadcasting

Digital broadcasting works by superimposing a digital signal on a carrier wave. A *multiplexer* then attaches any supplementary data to the signal. Since transmission is digital, text or images can be broadcast, meaning that useful information (e.g. song titles, news and weather) can be transmitted. Unlike analogue radio stations, digital audio broadcasting (DAB) stations do not use single carrier frequencies; DAB services are combined into a *multiplex*. At the receiver, multiplex is split down into channels, thereby allowing more stations to transmit on less radio space. The individual multiplexes are distributed across up to 1536 carrier frequencies. Receivers use decoders which put the digital signal in the correct sequence. Finally, the digital signal is converted back into analogue sound for the listener. The result is CD-quality sound output, and although AM/FM radio quality can suffer from interference, digital radio receivers show little interference.

The same problem exists for all forms of communication that make use of e-m radiation transmitted through the 'air'. The government strictly controls the bandwidths available in each particular band of the spectrum (AM, FM, TV, mobile phones, microwave, etc.) with FM being allotted the range of frequencies from 88–108 MHz. As channels require a bandwidth of 200 kHz, the maximum number of channels available is 100. Researchers continue to explore the range of the e-m spectrum that can be used for communication purposes with work being done on infrared carrier frequencies.

Bandwidth limitation does not apply to 'hard-wired' systems such as copper cable or optical fibre systems, since bandwidth can be expanded without limit simply by installing more cable.

## Radio aerials

Radio waves are produced by accelerating electrons in a wire which acts as a transmission aerial. An ideal length of wire needed to generate waves of a particular frequency is equal to half a wavelength at that frequency. The alternating currents in the aerial set up a standing wave in a similar way to a vibrating string. The transmitting aerial polarises the wave so that the receiving aerial must be aligned with the electric field in order to be able to receive the wave (Figure 4).

### Summary questions

1. Explain the difference between surface and space waves.

2. What are the advantages and disadvantages of using FM radio transmission compared with AM transmission?

3. Explain why medium and short-wave radio transmission requires a smaller bandwidth than FM.

## Link

See Topic 1.3 for a discussion of standing waves on strings.

horizontal position

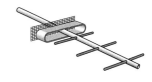

vertical position

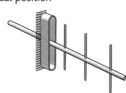

**Figure 4** *Radio waves are polarised by the transmitting aerial*
*Look at tv or radio aerials – you will see that in a particular area they point in the same direction and have the same orientation showing that the waves are polarised.*

# 2.5 Satellite communication

*Learning objectives:*

- What are the main features of a communication satellite system?

- How does radiation spread from a satellite dish?

- What is meant by a satellite's *footprint*?

*Specification reference: 3.1.1D*

**Figure 1** *A communications satellite*

## Link

The cost of launching satellites into geosynchronous orbits is very high due to the altitude of the orbit – see Chapter 2 of the A2 book for discussion of rocket launching and the mechanics of satellite orbits.

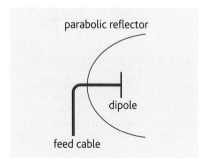

**Figure 2** *Parabolic reflector*

## Communication satellites

Communications satellites are usually put in a high altitude, geosynchronous orbit above a ground station which has a large dish for transmitting and receiving radio signals. The satellites serve as relay stations, receiving radio signals from one location and transmitting them to another. A single communications satellite can relay many thousands of signals at once. Sometimes, a group of low orbit communications satellites arranged in a network, called a constellation, work together by relaying information to each other and to users on the ground. Through international agreement, three frequency bands have been assigned for non-military satellite communication. A lower frequency band is chosen for the downlink compared with the uplink because rain and atmospheric attenuation of the radio waves are reduced at lower frequencies. The full range of frequencies used in these bands are between 4 and 20 GHz (i.e. the UHF/microwave region) (see Figure 1).

### Geosynchronous orbits

**Geosynchronous** or **geostationary** orbits are those in which the satellite is always positioned over the same point on the Earth's surface – for this they must have an orbital **period** of 24 h. Since the orbit is fixed, receiving dishes do not need to change direction (*track*) in order to receive the signal from the satellite. Most geosynchronous satellites occupy a band above the equator at an altitude of about 35 800 km. Although just three geosynchronous satellites would be needed to cover the vast majority of the Earth's surface, currently there are several hundred television, weather and communication satellites occupying this band; each satellite must be precisely positioned to prevent its signals from interfering with those from neighbouring satellites. The main disadvantage of the geostationary orbit is that there is a noticeable delay between transmission and reception of the signal – because the electromagnetic waves are travelling nearly 72 000 km.

### The satellite dish

The power of electromagnetic waves spreads out with distance from the transmitter obeying the inverse square law (see Topic 1.4). In order to avoid loss of power from a transmitting aerial it is vital therefore that the transmitted beam is very narrow. This is done by positioning the aerial at the focus of a parabolic reflecting dish (see Figure 2). Designing receiving dishes in the same way means that the receiving dish has a high gain; it has a stronger signal output than from a low gain aerial. The gain can also be improved by increasing the diameter of the dish. The amount of energy collected by a dish is proportional to the area of the circle enclosed by the edge of the dish – since the area is given by $\pi D^2/4$, doubling the diameter of the dish increases the power by a factor of four, etc. A satellite dish does not have to be solid. Provided it is composed of a mesh of spacing less than the wavelength of the waves, it will behave as if it were solid. This principle allows a large reflector to be built without too much concern about its weight; large dishes are used for radio astronomy but X-rays have too short a wavelength to contemplate using a mesh structure for the reflector so the weight of the dish becomes a very significant factor here.

## Diffraction and the satellite dish

When radiation is emitted from a transmitting dish, the waves spread out from the dish in a similar way to waves passing through a narrow slit (see Figure 3). This diffraction occurs with the diameter of the dish being treated as the width of the slit. Figure 4 shows how the intensity of the diffracted beam emitted by the satellite transmitter varies. It can be shown that the angle $\theta$ is related to the dish aperture diameter $a$ by the equation:

$$\sin\theta = \frac{\lambda}{a}$$

Increasing the wavelength increases the angle through which the waves become diffracted. Increasing the diameter of the dish narrows the beam.

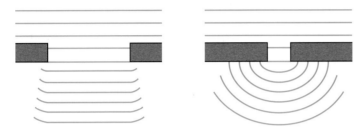

**Figure 3** *Diffraction at a single slit*

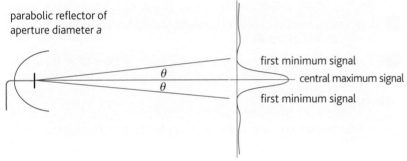

parabolic reflector of aperture diameter $a$

first minimum signal
central maximum signal
first minimum signal

 **Figure 4** *Diffraction by a parabolic reflector*

## The footprint of a satellite

In satellite communications the footprint is the portion of the Earth's surface over which the satellite dish delivers a specified amount of signal power under specified conditions. Dishes with a small diameter will give a large footprint but the intensity may be quite low since the power is distributed over a large area. Figure 5 shows a communication satellite's footprint.

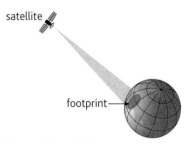

satellite

footprint

**Figure 5** *Satellite footprint*

■ How science works

### Loudspeakers

Loudspeakers diffract sound in a similar way to how satellite dishes diffract radio waves but, with a range of wavelengths making up speech or music, the minima will be in different places. The position of the listener is vital with a loudspeaker set up – the central maximum will always be in the same place but $\sin\theta$ increases with $\lambda$. For such reasons stereo systems must have loudspeakers containing cones of different diameters so that the cone aperture $a$ can be matched to $\lambda$ to give minima in the same places, for at least some frequencies.

AQA **Examiner's tip**

When performing calculations, it is essential to choose the correct equation appropriate to single slit (or speaker/satellite dish) diffraction, double slit interference and the diffraction grating.

## How science works

### Space debris

There are currently so many disused or broken up satellites and other large pieces of space debris (such as ejected rocket stages) in orbit around the Earth that NASA publishes an 'Orbital Debris Quarterly News.' More than 10 000 sizeable items had been catalogued at the start of 2007. The space debris problem is such an issue that an international Inter-Agency Space Debris Coordination Committee (IADC) exists. One of the fundamental principles of the United Nations Office for Outer Space Affairs is that 'States shall be liable for damage caused by their space objects; and States shall avoid harmful contamination of space and celestial bodies'.

## Summary questions

1 Explain whether satellite transmissions are in the microwave or UHF region of the electromagnetic spectrum.

2 Calculate the delay between transmission and reception of a signal via a geosynchronous satellite at a height of $3.6 \times 10^7$ m. The speed of e-m waves in vacuo $= 3.00 \times 10^8\,\mathrm{m\,s^{-1}}$.

3 Explain why parabolic reflectors are essential for transmitting or receiving satellite signals.

4 A satellite is in geosynchronous orbit at a height of $3.6 \times 10^7$ m above the Earth's surface. The satellite uses waves of wavelength $2.6 \times 10^{-2}$ m and has a dish of diameter 1.4 m.

   a Calculate the diffraction angle $\theta$.

   b Calculate the diameter of the satellite's footprint on the surface of the Earth.

# 2.6 Fibre optics

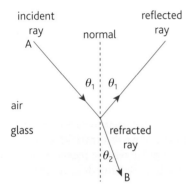

**Figure 1** *Reflection and refraction*

## ⚠ 💡 Ray optics

There are several ways to think about light. It can be useful to imagine it as travelling in very narrow beams which we call **rays**. A ray represents the direction in which a light wave travels and is therefore always at right angles to the **wavefronts** that we have previously considered.

### Laws of reflection and refraction of light

Figure 1 shows how a ray incident upon an air/water boundary behaves. Three things happen to the incident ray: it partially reflects, partially refracts and partially becomes absorbed at the surface. Since energy must be conserved, the total incident energy will be equal to that reflected, refracted and absorbed. Key concepts illustrated by this diagram are:

▪ The law of reflection: the angle of reflection ($\theta_1$ on one side of the normal) = the angle of incidence ($\theta_1$ on the other side of the normal).

▪ Snell's law: the ratio of the sine of the angle of incidence ($\theta_1$) to the sine of the angle of refraction ($\theta_2$) is a constant for two different transparent substances. This constant is the refractive index going from substance 1 to 2 ($_1n_2$). This can be written as:

$$n_1 \sin\theta_1 = n_2 \sin\theta_2$$

▪ $n_1$ and $n_2$ are the absolute refractive indices of the transparent substances 1 and 2.

### Speed and refractive index

When e-m waves enter an optically denser substance they slow down (and, since rays travel along the same path irrespective of direction, e-m waves speed up as they enter an optically less dense substance). This gives a definition of the absolute refractive index of a substance ($n_s$):

$$n_s = \frac{c}{c_s}$$

where $c$ is the speed of e-m waves in a vacuum and $c_s$ is its speed in the substance.

Using the reversibility of e-m waves we see that when a ray goes from substance 2 into substance 1 we can write:

$$_2n_1 = \frac{1}{_1n_2}$$

If medium 2 is the substance s and medium 1 is a vacuum we drop the 1 symbol (or write it as 'vac') and so:

$$_sn_{vac} = \frac{1}{n_s}$$

### Total internal reflection

When a ray travels into a less optically dense substance it refracts away from the normal. Increasing the angle of incidence, as shown in Figure 2, eventually means that the angle of refraction will become 90° and lie along the boundary between the two substances. The value of the angle of incidence when this happens is called the **critical angle** $\theta_c$.

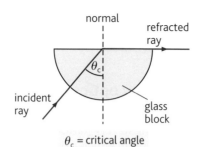

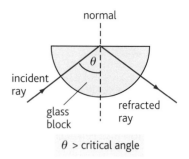

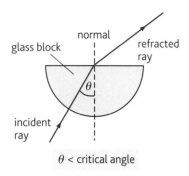

$\theta$ < critical angle

$\theta_c$ = critical angle

$\theta$ > critical angle

💡 **Figure 2** *Total internal reflection*

■ How science works

**Variation in refractive index**

The absolute refractive index of a substance ($n_s$) is the ratio of the speed of an e-m wave in a vacuum to that in the substance; $n_s$ must therefore be the ratio of the wavelength of the e-m waves in a vacuum to that in the substance (since frequency does not change on entering different substances). Light of different frequencies travels at the same speed in a vacuum but at different speeds in substances. Dispersion is detrimental to transmission of signals in optical fibres and therefore it is important to ensure that light transmitted along such fibres is as monochromatic (single wavelength) as possible.

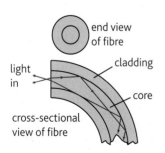

light in

end view of fibre

cladding

core

cross-sectional view of fibre

**Figure 3** *Structure of optical fibres*

When the angle of incidence becomes greater than the critical angle, the ray is **totally internally reflected** and trapped in the optically denser substance – there is now no refracted ray, although some of the energy will be absorbed within the substance.

The critical angle for two substances is given by $\sin\theta_c = \dfrac{n_2}{n_1}$ when $n_1$ is higher than $n_2$.

Air has a refractive index of almost exactly 1 so when a ray travels in substance s towards the air boundary:

$$n_s = \frac{1}{\sin\theta_c}$$

■ Optical fibres used for communication

Optical fibres are thin threads of glass or plastic designed to carry light waves (or infra-red) with the minimum of attenuation using total internal reflection (TIR). When a pulse of light is passed into an ideal fibre from a transmitter at one end, the same pulse will be picked up by the receiver at the other end. This ideal situation is difficult to achieve in practice. In practical optical fibres a transparent core is surrounded with a transparent cladding of slightly lower refractive index than the core. Any light ray in the core reaching the cladding boundary will be totally internally reflected when the angle of incidence is greater than the critical angle (see Figure 3). Around the fibre is a plastic sheath which strengthens the fibre and protects it from damaging scratches which could leak light.

Cladding is necessary to surround the core with a material of lower refractive index and also to make sure that light will not pass directly from one fibre to another if two fibres were to come into contact; this would mean cross-over of signals and a very insecure communication channel.

Increasingly cores are made ever thinner to avoid **multi-path dispersion** as shown in Figure 4. This effect would be significant in a wide core because the rays from the same part of a pulse would travel very different distances when travelling along the axis compared with making many reflections off the core/cladding boundary. The effect of this would be to spread the pulse out. This limits the number of pulses per second that could be transmitted down a fibre and still be recognisable as separate pulses at the other end (i.e. the **bit rate** or **bandwidth** would typically be 10–20 MHz over a length of 1 km). Figure 5 shows how multi-path dispersion can be reduced by using a **graded-index core**.

In the case of a graded-index fibre, the refractive index across the core is gradually reduced from the centre to the edges. Because light travels faster

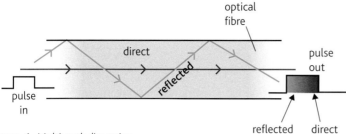

**Figure 4** *Multi-path dispersion*

in a low refractive index material than in a high-index material, the light rays near the edges of the core travel faster but over a longer distance, meaning that they curve due to refraction and travel through the core in approximately the same time as the straighter rays travelling more slowly near the centre of the core. This significantly reduces the pulse spreading and means that graded-index fibres can cope with pulses closer together without spreading into each other; graded-index fibres can support a bandwidth of over 1 GHz per km. Due to interference between the rays, only certain angles of incidence at the fibre/cladding boundary will allow rays to be transmitted. The angles that are allowed are called **modes** and they satisfy the conditions for **constructive interference** – other directions will result in cancellation by **destructive interference**.

## Attenuation of the signal

The signal travelling through an optical fibre will be attenuated as a result of absorption, scattering and bends in the fibre.

Absorption occurs when the light encounters impurities or atomic defects in the glass. Some absorption is due to the glass itself whereby infra-red and ultraviolet are naturally absorbed because their frequencies match the **natural frequencies** of the glass atoms. Scattering occurs when the light 'collides' with certain molecules in the glass and scatters the beam in all directions, limiting the energy in the forward direction.

Attenuation can be compensated for by **repeaters**. These are positioned at regular intervals and convert the signal to an electrical signal which is fed to a transmitter which sends the optical signal onwards at a higher intensity.

## ■ Comparison of optical fibre with copper cable

Optical fibres are usually chosen for systems requiring a higher bandwidth or spanning longer distances than copper cable (they are much lighter then equivalent lengths of copper cable). The main benefits of fibres over copper cables are their exceptionally low losses, allowing very long distances between repeaters and much greater bandwidth. Optical fibres exclude electromagnetic interference and cross-talk – no signal in one fibre can induce a signal in a nearby one, as can happen with copper cable; they are also very secure from being tapped into. The high electrical resistance of optical fibre means that it is safe near high voltage equipment and cannot produce sparks when circuits are made or broken. Copper cables are still used for short distances and relatively low bandwidth applications because of the lower cost of materials and transmitters and receivers. Copper cables are much easier to join together than optical fibres and they can carry electrical power as well as the signal. The main reason that copper cabling has not been superseded by optical fibres is that there is so much of it in place already.

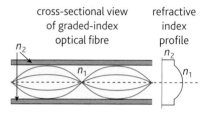

**Figure 5** *Graded-index fibre. The refractive index of the cladding is fixed at value $n_2$. The refractive index $n_1$ of the core decreases gradually from the centre of the fibre to the boundary with the cladding.*

### Summary questions

1 Explain what is meant by total internal reflection of light.

2 Water has a refractive index of 1.3 and glass of 1.5. Calculate the critical angle for light going from glass to water.

3 State what is meant by the 'pulse spreading' and explain why a thin fibre carrying monochromatic light reduces this.

4 What is meant by the attenuation of a signal and list **two** causes of attenuation in optical fibres.

# AQA Examination-style questions

1  (a) (i) A diffraction grating has $4.5 \times 10^5$ lines per metre. Calculate the separation between lines.

 (ii) The grating is illuminated with a parallel beam of light of wavelength 750 nm. Calculate the angle between the first and second order diffracted beams.

 (iii) What is the maximum order visible with this grating when it is illuminated by a parallel beam of light of wavelength 750 nm? *(8 marks)*

 (b) (i) The grating in part (a) is now illuminated with a parallel beam of light which is a mixture of light with wavelength 420 nm and 750 nm. Calculate the angle between the first orders produced by these two wavelengths.

 (ii) Show that the second order of the longer wavelength overlaps with the third order of the shorter wavelength.

 (iii) Explain why the overlap will occur whatever the line spacing of the grating happens to be. *(7 marks)*

2  A motorist is driving along a straight road listening to the radio. His radio is receiving signals from two transmitters both broadcasting the same programme at the same frequency and in phase. The motorist notices that the intensity of the signal varies regularly from a maximum to a minimum and back to a maximum again. **Figure 1** shows the arrangement seen from above.

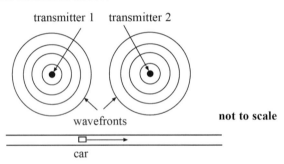

**Figure 1**

 (a) (i) Explain how a maximum of signal intensity occurs. You may wish to draw on a copy of **Figure 1** to help your explanation.

 (ii) The distance travelled by the car between successive maxima is 1.7 km and the wavelength of the signals is 0.54 km. The transmitters are both 570 km from the road.

 Calculate the distance between the transmitters. *(4 marks)*

 (b) The radio is tuned to a frequency of 560 kHz. The loudspeaker emits a maximum frequency of 8 kHz. Explain the significance of using these frequencies. *(2 marks)*

 (c) The transmitters emit an analogue signal. An alternative is to transmit the signal in a digital form.

 Explain how an analogue signal such as that shown in **Figure 2** may be converted into a digital form. *(3 marks)*

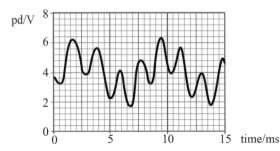

**Figure 2**

AQA, 2006

3    (a)  A 400 kHz carrier wave is modulated by a square wave of frequency 40 kHz. The carrier has an amplitude of 8.0 V and the square wave an amplitude of 1.5 V.
         Calculate:
         (i)   the frequency of the upper and lower sideband,
         (ii)  the bandwidth of the resultant waveform,
         (iii) the maximum and minimum amplitude of the resultant waveform.        *(5 marks)*
     (b)  State **three** advantages and **one** disadvantage of using FM radio transmissions instead of AM radio transmissions.        *(3 marks)*

4    A communication system is designed to sample and digitise voice frequencies in the range 100 Hz to 3.5 kHz. The sampled signal is stored as one of a possible 64 levels before transmission.
         (i)   What would be a suitable sampling frequency?
         (ii)  Express the number 63 as a binary number.
         (iii) How many bits are required to transmit each sample?
         (iv)  How many bits need to be transmitted per second to transmit the signal?
         (v)   What is the maximum duration of a bit?        *(7 marks)*

5    A satellite in geostationary orbit transmits to Earth at a frequency of 11 GHz using a transmitter of diameter 1.6 m. The height of the satellite above the Earth's surface is 36 000 km. Calculate:
     (a)  (i)   the wavelength of the transmitted signal,
          (ii)  the half-beamwidth angle of the transmitter at this frequency,
          (iii) the area of the footprint of the signal received at the equator.        *(6 marks)*
     (b)  (i)   The diameter of the dish designed to receive a signal from the satellite at the equator is about 0.5 m. State and explain why a larger diameter dish is needed to receive signals from the satellite as you move further away from the equator.
          (ii)  State an advantage of using a satellite transmission system instead of a ground based transmission system.        *(3 mark)*

6    (a)  (i)   Explain why cladding is necessary in an optic fibre used as a communications link.
          (ii)  Explain why graded index optic fibres are preferred to a fibre of a single refractive index for long distance transmissions.        *(3 marks)*
     (b)  A step-index multimode fibre has a length of 5 km and a core diameter of 100 μm. The refractive index of the core is 1.511 and the cladding 1.485.
         Calculate:
         (i)   the critical angle of the boundary between the core and cladding,
         (ii)  the time taken for light to travel along the axis of the core,
         (iii) the time taken by a light ray travelling down the fibre with the greatest number of reflections.        *(6 marks)*

# 3.1 Why believe in atoms?

*Learning objectives:*

- What evidence is there for the existence of atoms?
- How small is an atom?

*Specification reference: 3.1.2A*

### Hint

Large and small numbers are difficult to comprehend. Look at the distance between two adjacent millimetre scale marks on your ruler. There would be 10 million atoms between the two marks.

### How science works

#### Changing ideas

Dalton's law relating masses was correct given the limited accuracy of measurements that could be made. Energy cannot come from nowhere so if thermal energy is released in a chemical reaction the mass will be reduced and vice versa.

### How science works

#### Discovering DNA

Scientists have used diffraction techniques to determine the structure of DNA. This has led to a wide range of applications from fighting disease to catching criminals.

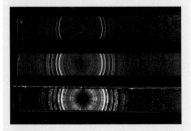

### Creating models

Scientists make up models to explain experimental observations and to explain natural phenomena. Sometimes these are visual models but they can also be in the form of mathematical equations. The models are used to predict the outcome of other experiments and this chapter explores some of the ways in which scientists had to invent new models to explain results which did not fit with the existing model of matter.

#### From Democritus to Dalton

Explaining what matter is has challenged scientists down the ages. The Greek philosopher Democritus proposed the existence of atoms (from *atomos* meaning indivisible) in about 400 BC. He suggested that matter was made of different types of tiny discrete particles and that these particles determined the properties of matter. The theory remained untested and it was many centuries before experimental science was able to provide the evidence to support the theory. The alchemists continued with their work on the basis that everything could be made from four 'elements'; *earth, air, fire* and *water.*

Isaac Newton in 1675 suggested that new particles were produced when stable particles separated and reformed. This theory was formalised in the nineteenth century by John Dalton who showed that the mass of the products was equal to the mass of the reactants in a chemical change. Experimental evidence that 'atoms' existed came from confirmation of two chemical laws.

**The law of constant composition (Proust):** The ratio of the masses of elements in a compound is the same, however much of it there is.

For example, in water, hydrogen combines with oxygen so that the ratio is

$$\frac{\text{mass of oxygen}}{\text{mass of hydrogen}} \approx \frac{16}{2}$$

**The law of multiple proportions (Dalton):** When two elements combine to produce different compounds the mass of one element that combines with a fixed mass of another element is in a simple ratio $1:1$, $1:2$, $2:3$, etc.

*Examples:*

1 When a fixed mass of carbon combines with oxygen it can produce two compounds. One contains twice the mass of oxygen as the other. This is explained by:

1 atom of carbon combining with one atom of oxygen (carbon monoxide)

1 atom of carbon combining with two atoms of oxygen (carbon dioxide)

2 Nitrogen and oxygen form a number of compounds:

$N + O$ (NO);   $2N + O$ ($N_2O$);   $N + 2O$ ($NO_2$);   $2N + 3O$ ($N_2O_3$);

$2N + 5O$ ($N_2O_5$);   $N + 3O$ ($NO_3$)

The ratio of the mass of oxygen for a given mass of nitrogen in these compounds is 1; 0.5; 2; 1.5; 2.5; 3.

## Evidence for atoms and molecules from gas behaviour

### Diffusion

The way that the smell of a gas spreads slowly across a room cannot be explained if a gas is just one homogeneous mass. Atoms of one gas, however, can move around freely amongst other gas atoms. Diffusion can be demonstrated in an experiment using bromine.

- The bromine liquid vaporises when the phial in the rubber tube is broken and can move into the other tube.
- If the space in the tube is evacuated the brown colour of bromine immediately fills the tube showing that the atoms move at a high speed.
- If the space contains air the colour spreads slowly because the bromine atoms collide with the atoms and molecules which make up air so hindering their progress. This also shows that within the gas there is space for atoms and molecules to move between each other.

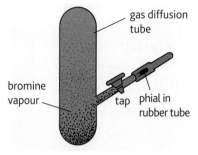

**Figure 1** *Apparatus to demonstrate diffusion of bromine*

### Brownian motion

This was first observed by the biologist Robert Brown who noticed the random movement of pollen suspended in a liquid. The same effect is observed when smoke particles suspended in air are viewed under a microscope.

The following points explain Brownian motion in terms of atoms.

- Smoke particles are bombarded by atoms and molecules in air.
- The atoms and molecules have momentum and exert a force on the smoke particle.
- The collisions are random and the smoke particles are small.
- At any time a resultant force exists as there are more collisions taking place on one side of the particle than the other.
- The direction of the resultant force continually changes direction and produces the 'jerky' random motion.

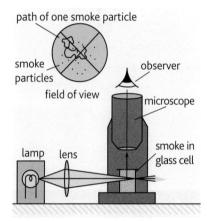

**Figure 2** *Apparatus to demonstrate Brownian motion*

## How large are atoms?

To produce the statistical imbalance of forces necessary to produce the jerky Brownian motion, the atoms have to be considerably smaller than the particles that they are colliding with. They turn out to be like spheres with radii varying from $1.2 \times 10^{-10}$ m for hydrogen to $7.4 \times 10^{-10}$ m for uranium.

In Topic 2.2 it was shown that the separation of lines in a diffraction grating can be found from the interference pattern if the wavelength of light is known. In a similar way the distance between layers of atoms can be found from an X-ray diffraction pattern. The atoms in a crystal are arranged as a regular structure and a diffraction pattern is formed by superposition of X-rays reflected by these layers. The distance between the layers and an approximate diameter for an atom can be found from measurements of the diffraction pattern. The arrangement of atoms in the structure can also be found from the pattern.

### Summary questions

1 Explain how Brownian motion provides evidence for atoms and molecules.

2 Explain how Dalton could have used the following data for two samples of different compounds of carbon to provide evidence for an atomic model.

Sample 1 contained 1.2 mg of carbon and 1.6 mg of oxygen.

Sample 2 contained 2.4 mg of carbon and 6.4 mg of oxygen.

# 3.2 Electrons and nuclei

*Learning objectives:*

■ How were electrons discovered?

■ What is the evidence for a nuclear atom?

■ How small is a nucleus?

*Specification reference: 3.1.2A*

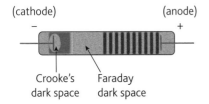

(cathode)   (anode)

Crooke's dark space    Faraday dark space

**Figure 1** *Glowing discharge tube*

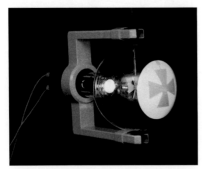

**Figure 2** *Maltese cross experiment*

## Discovering electrons

It has already been shown that atoms are visualised as small spheres, but what are they made of? The first clues came from experiments with gas-filled discharge tubes. With a high voltage between the electrodes (about 5000 V) different features appeared as the pressure was reduced (Figure 1). With an air-filled tube, as pressure was reduced, first lightning-type sparks appeared between the electrodes. Then at lower pressures observers noticed dark spaces followed by regions where the tube glowed blue or pink, sometimes with a striped effect (called striations). At these low pressures conduction is known to have occurred because of charged ions and electrons produced due to **ionisation** of the gas by the high voltage. The glow is due to **excitation** of the atoms (see Topic 5.4).

At a pressure of about 1 Pa the tube becomes completely dark and the Crooke's dark space shown in Figure 1 fills the tube. When this happened the glass envelope glowed at the end where the electrode was positive. The glow was thought to be produced by some sort of radiation coming from the cathode and so they were called cathode rays.

Some scientists thought cathode rays were something like light or some new form of radiation. William Crooke thought they were 'matter radiation' but Hertz observed that the rays could pass through thin gold sheets and it seemed unlikely that particles could pass through solid matter.

In 1897 J.J. Thomson demonstrated that the rays were negatively-charged particles of small mass. He called them corpuscles but we now call them electrons.

In TV sets, oscilloscopes and experimental tubes like the one shown in Figure 2, electrons are freed from a heated cathode. This is called thermionic emission. For the Maltese cross experiment, a metal cross was placed in between the cathode and a phosphorescent screen. The shadow showed that the cathode rays moved in straight lines and were absorbed by the metal. The shadow could be moved using a magnet, a fact later used in television receivers. The direction of the deflection was as expected for a negatively-charged particle.

The particle properties were shown by the change in speed using different accelerating voltages. Thomson demonstrated the negative charge by deflecting them towards a positively charged plate which led to the development of the cathode ray oscilloscope.

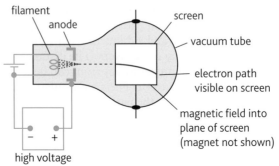

filament
anode
screen
vacuum tube
electron path visible on screen
magnetic field into plane of screen (magnet not shown)
high voltage

**Figure 3** *Deflection of electrons*

The evidence showed that the electrons came from the cathode and so must come from atoms. So atoms have a substructure, but what is it?

## ⚙ Models of the atom

Thomson suggested that an atom is like a 'plum pudding' or 'raisin cake'. In this model the tiny negatively charged electrons move around inside a cloud of massless positive charge and the mass of a hydrogen atom was due to the mass of thousands of electrons.

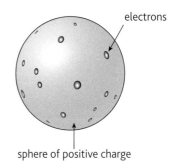

**Figure 4** *Thomson's 'plum pudding' model*

### Geiger and Marsden's alpha particle scattering experiment

This experiment gave results that showed that Thomson's model was incorrect. Alpha particles were fired at a thin gold foil and, based on the predictions of the plum pudding model, only slight deflections were expected.

It was found that:

▪ most of the alpha particles passed through with small deviations,

▪ about 1 in 8000 particles was scattered more than 90°.

The second observation surprised Rutherford and caused him to comment that 'it was as if you fired a 15-inch shell at a piece of tissue paper and it came back and hit you'. He concluded that:

▪ most of the atom is empty space,

▪ the atom must have a small nucleus containing most of the mass of the atom,

▪ the nucleus is positively charged with the electrons in the space around it.

He then suggested that the deviation was caused by the positively charged alpha particle being repelled by the positively charged nucleus. Alpha particles that went closer to the nucleus were deviated more.

Rutherford went on to predict the correct distribution for the deflected alpha particles which provided evidence for the existence of an atom with a nucleus.

Niels Bohr developed the model further and suggested that the atom contained a nucleus with the electrons in orbit around it. This model is still used to visualise atoms even though this model has been replaced by one based on quantum mechanics, see Topic 4.2.

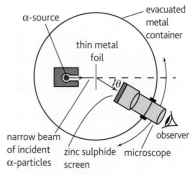

**Figure 5** *Arrangement used to investigate alpha particle scattering*

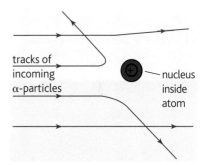

**Figure 6** *Paths of alpha particle near a nucleus*

### Size of the nucleus

When higher energy alpha particles are used in the scattering experiment, the results eventually fail to match the prediction from Rutherford's theory. This happens when the alpha particle is so close to the nucleus that the nuclear strong force dominates (see Topic 4.5). Using the rules that govern forces between charged particles (to be studied in A2), the radius of a gold nucleus can be shown to be about $7 \times 10^{-15}$ m. The smallest nucleus is hydrogen with a radius of $1.2 \times 10^{-15}$ m.

### ▪ Summary questions

**1** Calculate the approximate ratio of the radius of a hydrogen atom to the radius of its nucleus.

**2** How was it shown that electrons are negatively charged?

**3** State two ways of producing free electrons.

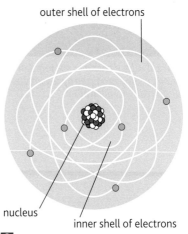

**Figure 7** *Bohr's model of the atom*

# 3.3  Inside the nucleus

*Learning objectives:*

- How were the proton and neutron discovered?

- What is the difference between the nuclei of different elements?

- What happens to a nucleus when it emits an alpha or beta particle?

*Specification reference: 3.1.2A*

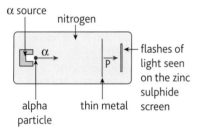

**Figure 1** *Discovery of the proton*

**Figure 2** *Cloud chamber photograph showing proton produced by α-particle collision with nitrogen atom*

## Rutherford 'splits the atom' and discovers the proton

Rutherford bombarded nitrogen with alpha particles using the apparatus shown in Figure 1. The metal film, placed in front of the zinc sulphide detector, absorbed alpha particles and he concluded that the film ejected a new more penetrating particle which was a proton. As a result of the emission of the proton, nitrogen was changed into oxygen (a process called transmutation).

The nuclear equation that describes the reaction is $^{4}_{2}\alpha + ^{14}_{7}N \longrightarrow ^{17}_{8}O + ^{1}_{1}p$

The alpha particle is now known to be a helium nucleus and the proton (named by Rutherford) is the nucleus of the simplest form of hydrogen.

The mass and charge of the proton were deduced from the tracks that they formed in a cloud chamber (see Figure 2).

- The proton charge $q_{p}$ = $+1.6 \times 10^{-19}$ C
- The proton mass $m_{p}$ = $1.673 \times 10^{-27}$ kg

So the model of the nucleus that was accepted by scientists in the first 30 years of the twentieth century made the assumption that the nucleus consisted of protons and electrons. There would need to be fewer electrons than protons to give the nucleus a positive charge. So, for example, a helium nucleus would consist of four protons and two electrons giving it a mass of four times that of hydrogen and a charge twice that of hydrogen.

It was the discovery of the neutron in 1932 that led to further revision of the model.

## Chadwick discovers the neutron

Rutherford and Chadwick believed that neutrons existed and in 1932 Chadwick performed experiments that led to their discovery. The arrangement of the apparatus is shown in Figure 3. In his experiment alpha particles bombarded beryllium and the result was radiation that had a weak ionising effect. When this radiation was incident on paraffin wax (which contains lots of protons) the radiation knocked protons out of the wax. One suggestion was that this unknown radiation was extremely energetic gamma radiation. Chadwick did not agree with this and he went on to show conclusively that the radiation was in fact a stream of neutrons.

A neutron has a similar mass to the proton ($m_{n} = 1.675 \times 10^{-27}$ kg) and the proton was knocked out of the wax, like the head-on collision between two pool balls.

The nuclear equation for the production of the neutron is:

$$^{4}_{2}\alpha + ^{9}_{4}Be \longrightarrow ^{12}_{6}C + ^{1}_{0}n$$

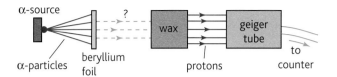

🔔 **Figure 3** *Chadwick's apparatus*

### How science works

**Chadwick keeps an open mind**

The final sentence in Chadwick's original report acknowledged that the radiation could still be gamma radiation but only if two well-established laws were flawed:

'Up to the present, all the evidence is in favour of the neutron, while the quantum hypothesis can only be upheld if the conservation of energy and momentum be relinquished at some point.'

## Nuclear structure

So by 1932 scientists had arrived at the familiar model of a nucleus consisting of protons and neutrons called **nucleons**. Each type of nucleus is referred to as a **nuclide.** The number of protons in the nucleus, the **proton number Z,** defines the element and the number of protons and neutrons, the **nucleon number A,** defines a particular **isotope** of the element. A neutral atom has the same number of electrons surrounding the nucleus as there are protons in the nucleus.

A nuclide of an element X is represented as $^A_Z$X. There are $Z$ protons and $(A - Z)$ neutrons in the nuclide.

So, for example, the nuclides $^3_2$He and $^4_2$He are isotopes of helium. These are often written as helium-3 and helium-4. A helium nucleus contains two protons. $^3_2$He contains 2 protons and 1 neutron. $^4_2$He contains 2 protons and 2 neutrons. Isotopes of hydrogen are shown in Figure 4.

## Radiation from the nucleus

Becquerel discovered radioactivity in 1896 and so it was known that alpha particles and beta particles were emitted spontaneously from some nuclei. Spontaneous means that nothing outside the nucleus caused the nucleus to emit particles. This is different from induced fission in which a particle is absorbed by the nucleus making the nucleus unstable so that it decays.

The proton and neutron model of the nucleus that followed Chadwick's discovery led to an understanding of the changes that occur during radioactive decay. In any decay or reaction involving nuclei:

▪ charge is conserved, so the sum of the $Z$ numbers on each side must be the same,

▪ nucleon number is conserved, so the sum of the $A$ numbers on each side must be the same.

The alpha particle is a helium nucleus (2 protons and 2 neutrons) and so carries a charge $+2e$ and has a mass four times that of a single nucleon. The beta particle was known to be an electron (represented by the symbol $^0_{-1}$e or $^0_{-1}$β).

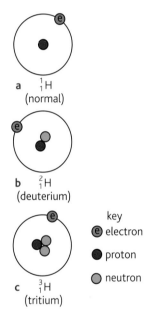

a  $^1_1$H
(normal)

b  $^2_1$H
(deuterium)

key
ⓔ electron
● proton
⚪ neutron

c  $^3_1$H
(tritium)

**Figure 4** *Isotopes of hydrogen*

### Hint

Nuclear reactions take one of the following forms:

▪ an unstable radioactive nuclide decays by emitting α, β or γ radiation

▪ two nuclei fuse together to form a new nuclide

▪ a nucleus collides with another nucleus or with a particle producing different nuclei or particles.

When an alpha particle is emitted the $Z$ number decreases by 2 and the $A$ number decreases by 4:

$$^{A}_{Z}X \longrightarrow\ ^{A-4}_{Z-2}Y +\ ^{4}_{2}\alpha$$

When a beta⁻ particle is emitted, a neutron effectively becomes a proton so the $Z$ number increases by 1 and the $A$ number remains the same. It is now known that an electron antineutrino is emitted at the same time as the beta⁻ particle in this process (see Topic 4.3):

$$^{A}_{Z}X \longrightarrow\ ^{A}_{Z+1}Y +\ ^{0}_{-1}\beta + \overline{v}_e$$

Nuclides have now been found that decay by emitting a positively charged beta particle called a positron $\left(^{0}_{+1}\beta\right)$. An electron neutrino is emitted at the same time. In this case the $Z$ number is reduced by 1 and the $A$ number remains the same.

$$^{A}_{Z}X \longrightarrow\ ^{A}_{Z-1}Y +\ ^{0}_{+1}\beta + v_e$$

*Examples:*

$$^{235}_{92}U \longrightarrow\ ^{231}_{90}Th +\ ^{4}_{2}\alpha$$

$$^{241}_{94}Pu \longrightarrow\ ^{241}_{95}Am +\ ^{0}_{-1}\beta + \overline{v}_e$$

$$^{113}_{49}In \longrightarrow\ ^{113}_{48}Cd +\ ^{0}_{+1}\beta + v_e$$

## Summary questions

1  Describe the structure of neutral atoms of $^{12}_{6}C$, $^{241}_{95}Am$, $^{16}_{8}O$

2  How many nucleons are there in $^{238}_{92}U$?

3  Insert the missing numbers in the following equations:

$$^{220}_{x}Rn \longrightarrow\ ^{y}_{84}Po +\ ^{4}_{2}\alpha \quad ; \qquad ^{x}_{91}Pa \longrightarrow\ ^{234}_{y}U +\ ^{0}_{-1}\beta + \overline{v}_e$$

4  Explain why Chadwick believed that the unknown radiation in his experiment were neutrons rather than gamma radiation.

# 3.4  Probing nucleons

## Learning objectives:

- What is deep inelastic scattering?
- What are quarks?
- What is the evidence for their existence?

*Specification reference: 3.1.2C*

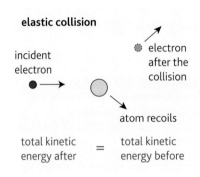

**elastic collision**

incident electron

electron after the collision

atom recoils

total kinetic energy after  =  total kinetic energy before

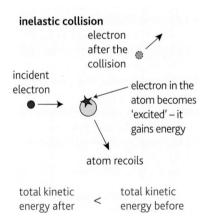

**inelastic collision**

electron after the collision

incident electron

electron in the atom becomes 'excited' – it gains energy

atom recoils

total kinetic energy after  <  total kinetic energy before

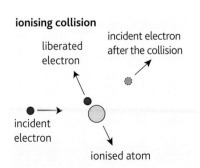

**ionising collision**

liberated electron

incident electron after the collision

incident electron

ionised atom

**Figure 1** *Electron collisions with an atom*

## Deeper and deeper

For a while the proton and neutron were thought to be **fundamental particles**, which means that they were not made from smaller particles. The situation was no different from the early view that atoms themselves were fundamental. However, particle physics experiments started to produce some unexpected results and this led to the development of the quark model (see Chapter 4). Experiments that probed deep into the nucleons were necessary to show that they existed.

The name 'quark' was given to the particles by Murray Gell-Mann probably from a novel by James Joyce. A quark was the name that Joyce gave to a rather sarcastic 'cheer' sounding like a seagull. "Three quarks for Muster Mark!"

## Deep inelastic scattering

When electrons collide with atoms a collision can:

1  be **elastic** – so that after the collision the total kinetic energy of the electron and the recoiling atom is equal to the kinetic energy of the incident electron

2  be **inelastic** – so that there is a loss of kinetic energy which is caused by electrons in the atom becoming excited

3  liberate an electron – so kinetic energy is lost in **ionising** the atom.

Elastic collisions provide no evidence of any atomic substructure but collision type 2 suggests that there is a process inside the atom that takes up some of the electron's energy. The third type of collision, in which an electron is knocked out of the atom, provides evidence for what makes up an atom.

Rutherford's experiments using alpha particles probed further into the atom. The results of Geiger and Marsden's experiment were consistent with elastic scattering of the alpha particles but higher energy alpha particles probed further into the nucleus and suggested an internal structure.

So, to investigate whether there are particles that make up a nucleon, experiments have to probe even deeper. If a particle new to science could be knocked out of the nucleon then this would suggest that the nucleon is made of smaller particles. Equally an inelastic collision of an electron with a nucleon can suggest an internal substructure for the nucleon. Scientists therefore searched for this **deep inelastic scattering.**

## Particle accelerators

The size of the experiments needed to probe deeper into matter have become bigger and bigger as the particles being looked for have become smaller and smaller. To produce higher energies the accelerators have become larger, as have the detectors. Compare Geiger and Rutherford's apparatus (Figure 2) which stood on a laboratory bench with the magnet that is only part of a particle detector at CERN (Figure 3). The man in

**Are particle accelerators worth it?**

Although built to advance human knowledge and understanding, there are many 'spin-offs'. For example, accelerators are used in the production of radioisotopes in medicine and the magnet technology developed has led to magnetic resonance imaging (MRI) scanners. There have been advances in materials science and electronics. The need to share and communicate vast amounts of information led to the creation of the internet.

the middle of the picture gives you an idea of the scale. The path of the particles in the large electron positron (LEP) collider at CERN (Figure 4) has a circumference of 27 km. Such machines cost enormous sums to build and provide vast amounts of data, so particle physics has had to develop into a multinational co-operative venture involving thousands of scientists and engineers.

**Figure 2** *Geiger and Rutherford with alpha particle scattering apparatus*

**Figure 3** *The ATLAS detector at CERN*

**Figure 4** *Circular path of the LEP collider at CERN*

## ■ Discovery of quarks

So far, free quarks have never been observed. They only exist in combinations that produce other particles. However in 1968 physicists bombarding protons with very high energy electrons at Stanford university found the first evidence of a nucleon substructure and this led to confirmation of the existence of quarks.

The electrons at Stanford had very high energies and therefore short wavelengths (see Topic 4.1) which enabled them to probe the protons. At low energies the proportion of the electrons scattered at any angle was just as predicted by assuming the proton to be a fundamental particle. However, as the energy was increased, the proportion scattered at large angles increased. Just as results like this had predicted the existence of a nucleus, this experiment showed that there are particles inside the proton. The incident electrons appeared to be undergoing collision with charged point-like particles inside the proton. These were referred to as 'partons' but experiments went on to show that they were the quarks with charge $\frac{2}{3}$ and $-\frac{1}{3}$ as predicted by Murray Gell-Mann. Further evidence for quarks is provided by the tracks, such as those in Figure 5, formed by new particles that result from high energy collisions between electrons and protons.

Although present theories suggest the quarks to be fundamental, given what has happened before there may still be more to come in the particle story.

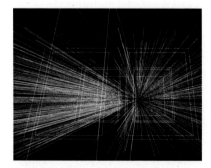

**Figure 5** *A quark 'starburst' in an experiment at CERN*

### ■ Summary questions

**1** Explain what is meant by a 'fundamental particle'.

**2** Explain why deep inelastic scattering shows that protons are not fundamental.

# AQA Examination-style questions

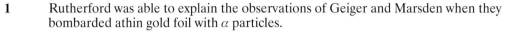

1 Rutherford was able to explain the observations of Geiger and Marsden when they bombarded athin gold foil with $\alpha$ particles.

   (a) Describe the plum pudding model suggested by Thomson. *(3 marks)*

   (b) State and explain the observations that Rutherford could have expected to make had Thomson's 'plum-pudding model' of the atom been correct. *(3 marks)*

   (c) State the main observations made by Geiger and Marsden of the scattering of $\alpha$ particles by gold nuclei. *(2 marks)*

   (d) State and explain the conclusions that Rutherford was able to make from these observations. *(3 marks)*

2 **Figure 1** shows a single atomic nucleus that is part of a thin foil. **A**, **B** and **C** are the paths of three $\alpha$ particles directed at the foil. All three paths are approaching close to the nucleus.

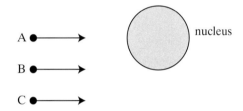

**Figure 1**

   (a) Copy and complete the diagram to carefully show the subsequent paths of the $\alpha$ particle. *(3 marks)*

   (b) Suggest **two** pieces of scientific information that can be gained by bombarding matter with particles in this way. *(2 marks)*

3 In 1932 Chadwick carried out experiments that led to the discovery of the neutron. He bombarded beryllium ($^{9}_{4}Be$ ) with a stream of particles. Carbon-12 was formed in the reaction.

   (a) Name the bombarding particles that he used . *(1 mark)*

   (b) Write down the full nuclear equation that was occurring in the beryllium. Include the nucleon and proton numbers in the equation. *(2 marks)*

   (c) Outline the observations that Chadwick made. *(2 marks)*

   (d) Explain how Chadwick was able to confirm the likely presence of the neutron. *(2 marks)*

4 For each of the following, write down the equation that represents the nuclear reaction when:

   (a) $^{238}_{92}U$ decays to thorium (Th) with the emission of an $\alpha$ particle. *(2 marks)*

   (b) The thorium formed in part (a) decays to protactinium (Pa) with the emission of a $\beta$ particle. *(2 marks)*

   (c) The protactinium formed in (b) decays to actinium-230. *(2 marks)*

5    Deep inelastic scattering is a technique used by nuclear scientists to investigate the nature of nucleons.

    (a)  Explain what is meant by *deep inelastic scattering*. Go on to explain why elastic scattering does not provide so much evidence as inelastic scattering.  *(5 marks)*

    (b)  Particle accelerators are constructed ever larger as time goes on. Suggest why the study of the nucleus needs progressively larger machines.  *(3 marks)*

6    A student carries out an experiment to estimate the size of a molecule of a liquid oil. The shape of the molecule is known to be linear and about 12 carbon atoms in length (**Figure 2**). When on the surface of water, one end of the molecule is attracted to the water and the other end is repelled so that the molecule sticks straight up out of the water.

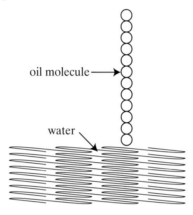

**Figure 2**

A small spherical drop of the oil with a radius of 1.2 mm is placed on the surface of a large bowl of water and the oil is allowed to spread until the layer is one molecule thick. The diameter of the resulting oil slick is 0.7 m.

    (a)  Show that the volume of the oil is about $7 \times 10^{-9} \, \text{m}^3$.  *(2 marks)*

    (b)  Estimate the radius of a carbon atom.  *(4 marks)*

7    Experiments involving deep inelastic scattering enable scientists to investigate the sub-structure of nucleons. Nucleons are believed to be constructed of either two or three quarks.

    (a)  (i)   Explain what is meant by a *nucleon*.

        (ii)  Give an example of a nucleon.  *(2 marks)*

    (b)  Gell–Mann suggested that quarks have charge. State the charges he assigned to the quarks.  *(2 marks)*

    (c)  Show how the quarks may combine to produce:

        (i)   a neutral nucleon,

        (ii)  a positively charged nucleon with a charge equal in magnitude to that of the electron.  *(4 marks)*

**8** (a) State Dalton's law of multiple proportions. *(1 mark)*

(b) Sodium hydrogen carbonate has the formula $NaHCO_3$. The table indicates the atomic and nuclear properties of the elements concerned.

|  | H | C | O | Na |
|---|---|---|---|---|
| proton number | 1 | 6 | 8 | 11 |
| nucleon number | 1 | 12 | 16 | 23 |

(i) State the type and number of nucleons in sodium (Na).

(ii) A mass of 11 g of sodium is to react with hydrogen, carbon, and oxygen to form sodium hydrogen carbonate with no sodium remaining. Calculate the mass of the other three reagents that would be required for this to occur. *(6 marks)*

**9** **Figure 3** shows the path taken by an $\alpha$ particle, **B**, as it is deflected by a gold nucleus, **G**, in Rutherford's alpha scattering experiment. Also marked on **Figure 2** are the starts of two further tracks, **A** and **C**, made by $\alpha$ particles travelling with the same initial speed as **B**.

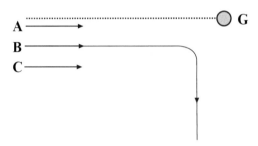

**Figure 3**

(a) Re-draw **Figure 3**, completing the tracks of the $\alpha$ particles marked **A** and **C**. *(2 marks)*

(b) State and explain what the results of the experiment indicated about the structure of the gold atom. *(4 marks)*

AQA, 2004

# 4.1 Why photons?

*Learning objectives:*

- What is the evidence for a photon model of electromagnetic radiation?

- What is the energy of a photon?

- How are the wave and photon models used to predict the behaviour of radiation?

*Specification reference: 3.1.2B*

The previous topics have concentrated on the particles that make up the atom and the particles that are emitted. But what about the nature of electromagnetic radiation that is emitted by hot bodies and the gamma radiation from the nucleus?

## The ultraviolet catastrophe

In the late nineteenth century scientists were developing theories to predict how the intensity of the electromagnetic radiation from a **black body** varied with wavelength. A black body is one that emits all possible wavelengths for its temperature (perfect emitter). The theory developed worked well for very long wavelength radiation but at short (ultraviolet) wavelengths the theory predicted that intensity would become infinite, which cannot be possible. In practice the intensity rises to a maximum and falls again at short wavelengths. The theoretical and practical curves are shown in Figure 1. The position of the peak in the practical curve depended on the temperature of the body. Scientists called the failure to predict what happened at short wavelengths the **ultraviolet catastrophe**.

Max Planck resolved the problem by suggesting that the electron oscillations in hot bodies could only take certain (discrete) values given by $nhf$, where $n$ is an integer, $h$ is the Planck constant and $f$ the frequency of the radiation. These are called 'quanta'. This enabled Planck to produce a mathematical equation for the way intensity varied with wavelength for the black body radiation, which gave a theoretical prediction that matched the practical curve. However, he did not have the evidence for his assumption and scientists did not take the quantum idea seriously until Einstein explained the photoelectric effect using the quantum idea.

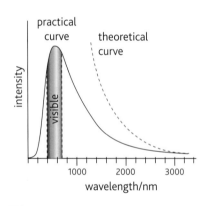

**Figure 1** *Practical curve for a black body and the prediction based on 'classical' physics*

## The photoelectric effect

The **photoelectric effect** is the emission of electrons from a metal surface when electromagnetic radiation is incident on it. A simple experimental arrangement to demonstrate the effect is shown in Figure 2.

The clean zinc plate of the gold leaf electroscope is first given a negative charge. Electrostatic repulsion of like charges causes the leaf to rise. When ultraviolet radiation is incident on the surface the leaf falls showing that the electroscope is losing its negative charge; electrons are being lost from the surface of the zinc plate.

Further important observations can be made:

- If a glass plate is inserted between the ultraviolet lamp and the zinc plate, the electron emission ceases.
- If an ordinary filament lamp (emitting no ultraviolet light) is used, the electroscope does not discharge.
- Even if a very intense visible light is used, no electrons are emitted.

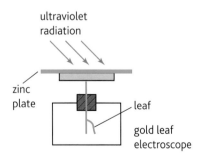

**Figure 2** *Demonstrating the photoelectric effect*

■ If the ultraviolet radiation is very weak the discharge still starts immediately.

The first and second observations show that there is a **threshold frequency** below which the photoelectric effect does not occur. The third and fourth observations can only be explained using the idea of photons.

## 💡 Einstein's explanation of the photoelectric effect

Einstein was awarded the Nobel Prize for physics in 1921 for his explanation of the photoelectric effect. He came up with the idea that the energy in electromagnetic radiation can only be transferred in well defined 'lumps'. The energy is said to be **quantised** and a quantum of electromagnetic radiation is called a **photon**.

$$\text{Photon energy } E = hf$$

where $f$ is the frequency of the radiation and $h$ is the Planck constant, which has a value of $6.63 \times 10^{-34}\,\text{J s}$.

For electromagnetic radiation $c = f\lambda$, where $c$ is the speed of electromagnetic radiation. It follows that the photon energy $E = \dfrac{hc}{\lambda}$

Einstein's explanation of the photoelectric effect works like this. Electrons are bound to a metal surface rather like gravity holds us to the Earth. To remove an electron from a metal surface a **minimum amount** of energy is needed. This is called the **work function** $\varphi$. An electron that is more tightly bound to the surface needs more energy than this. Most importantly, the energy to remove an electron has to be delivered at one instant – an electron cannot store energy up a bit at a time.

When $hf < \varphi$ the photon has insufficient energy to liberate an electron.

When $hf = \varphi$ the electron can just leave the surface and $f$ in this case is the threshold frequency $f_0$.

If the $hf > \varphi$ there is energy to spare and this becomes kinetic energy of the electron.

This led to Einstein's photoelectric equation:

$$hf = \varphi + E_{k(max)}$$

The graph in Figure 3 shows how the maximum kinetic energy of the photoelectrons varies with the frequency energy of the radiation falling on a metal surface. Rearranging Einstein's equation to $E_{k(max)} = hf - \varphi$ and comparing it with $y = mx + c$ shows that the gradient is the Planck constant. The $x$ intercept gives the threshold frequency $f_0$ and the $y$ intercept is $-\varphi$.

### Explaining the observations in the gold leaf electroscope experiment

The observations described in the photoelectric effect demonstration can now be explained.

■ The glass plate absorbs the high energy (uv) photons so that only low energy, visible photons remain.

■ Ordinary visible light photon energies are below the work function of the zinc and do not release electrons.

■ Although there are lots of low energy photons in intense light, each one alone is incapable of liberating an electron.

■ Even if there are very few photons of ultraviolet light, each one can liberate an electron.

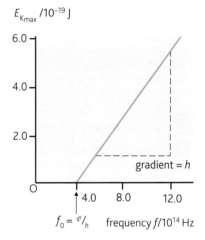

💡 **Figure 3** *Graph of maximum kinetic energy of photoelectrons against frequency*

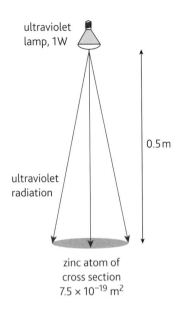

ultraviolet
lamp, 1W

0.5m

ultraviolet
radiation

zinc atom of
cross section
$7.5 \times 10^{-19} m^2$

**Figure 4** *Wave energy incident on an atom*

### Summary questions

1  Explain the significance of a *threshold frequency* in the photoelectric effect.

2  Radiation has photons of $3.32 \times 10^{-19}$ J.

   a Calculate the frequency of the radiation that has photons of this energy

   b Calculate the maximum speed of a photoelectron emitted from the surface of potassium by photons of this energy.
   Work function of potassium $= 2.90 \times 10^{-19}$ J
   Mass of an electron = $9.11 \times 10^{-31}$ kg
   Planck constant = $6.6 \times 10^{-34}$ J s

3  How would the graph in Figure 3 (previous page) change if a material with a higher work function were used?

## *Work functions*

Work functions are energies. The energies are small and for convenience they are usually given in a unit called an electron-volt (eV). This is the energy gained by an electron when it is accelerated through a potential difference of 1 V.

$1$ electron-volt $= 1.6 \times 10^{-19}$ J

Work function of zinc $= 4.3$ eV $= 6.9 \times 10^{-19}$ J

## ■ Why does the wave theory fail to explain the photoelectric effect?

According to the wave theory, energy arrives at the surface continually. Low frequency light of high intensity should liberate electrons when it delivers sufficient energy per second, but it liberates none at all. Weak radiation should lead to an electron taking a long time to gain sufficient energy to become free but, provided the frequency is high enough, the emission starts almost instantly.

The time delay expected using a wave theory is illustrated in the following calculation (see Figure 4).

The energy falling per second on each square metre of a surface that is 0.5 m from a source that emits 1 W of ultraviolet radiation

$$= \frac{1}{4 \times 3.14 \times 0.5^2} = 0.32 \text{ J}$$

The energy falling per second on a zinc atom of cross-sectional area $7.5 \times 10^{-19} m^2 = 2.4 \times 10^{-19}$ J

Time for energy equal to the work function ($6.9 \times 10^{-19}$ J) to fall on the atom $= 2.9$ s

There is no such delay before an electron is emitted.

## ■ Wave–particle duality

So is light a wave or a particle? It is neither but the way electromagnetic radiation behaves can sometimes be described by assuming wave properties and sometimes by assuming particle properties. It depends on the experiment that is being performed so it is said to show **wave–particle duality.**

To find out where the energy in a light wave goes, it is treated as a wave. To find out what happens when the light energy interacts with matter, such as in the photoelectric effect or when it is detected by a photographic plate, it is treated as a particle (photon).

In wave theory the square of the amplitude of a wave ($A^2$) is proportional to the wave energy arriving per square metre per second. This is the intensity of the wave. So when light travels through slits as in Young's experiment (Topic 2.2), the wave property of light is used to predict the amplitude of the wave at a point on the screen. This is related to the energy arriving per second, and since this can only be detected as photons, $A^2$ is proportional to the number of photons arriving at the point each second.

The tie-up between waves and particles is to realise that the square of the amplitude is related to the chance of a photon arriving at a point. The greater the amplitude, the greater the probability of detecting a photon. So if there are lots of photons, more are detected where the amplitude is greatest.

# 4.2  Matter waves

*Learning objectives:*

- What is the evidence that particles have wave properties?

- What determines the wavelength of the wave?

- How has the wave–particle model been applied in practice?

*Specification reference: 3.1.2B*

Optical microscopes are a familiar laboratory tool in school laboratories but in hospitals and university research departments, electron microscopes are used to produce startling images of tiny objects (see Figure 1). The development of these microscopes and what determines the size of the smallest object that can be seen using them followed the discovery that particles have wave properties and that the wavelength can be controlled.

Louis de Broglie thought that since a wave can behave as a stream of particles, perhaps particles can also behave like waves. He suggested that the wavelength $\lambda$ associated with a particle is given by:

$$\lambda = \frac{h}{mv}$$

where $h$ is the Planck constant and $mv$ is the momentum of the particle. The wavelength is known as the de Broglie wavelength.

So what is the evidence for a stream of particles behaving like a wave?

## ⚡ ℹ️ 🔬 Electron diffraction

Soon after de Broglie suggested the above equation two physicists, Davisson and Germer, obtained experimental proof of the hypothesis by demonstrating interference maxima when an electron stream was reflected from a nickel crystal. This led to a Nobel Prize for de Broglie in 1929.

Figure 2 shows a laboratory arrangement for demonstrating the effect. Electrons from an electron gun pass through a thin sheet of graphite or aluminium. If the electrons behaved like particles they would be only slightly deviated by collisions with the atoms and form a bright region in the centre of the screen.

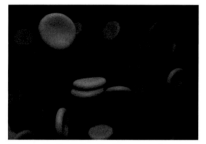

**Figure 1** *Red blood cells seen using an electron microscope*

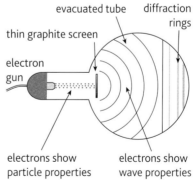

**Figure 2** *Electron diffraction experiment*

The bright rings shown in Figure 3 identify where the electrons land on the screen. The rings are the regions where the electron waves interfere constructively to produce a maximum. This shows that the electrons are more likely to arrive at certain parts of the screen than they are at others and that there are parts where no electrons arrive at all. The same pattern builds up slowly even if there are only a few electrons travelling in the tube at any one time.

---

$\boxed{\text{AQA}}$ **Examiner's tip**

Remember that the velocity used in $\lambda = \dfrac{h}{mv}$ is the velocity of the electrons and not the speed of light .

Do not confuse the equations for electromagnetic waves and those for particles.

---

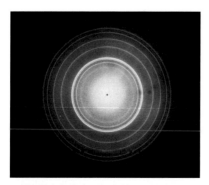

**Figure 3** *Electron interference pattern from aluminium target*

## Calculating wavelength

The energy gained by the electrons $= eV$ and this becomes kinetic energy $\frac{1}{2}mv^2$.

So when electrons are accelerated by a voltage of $2000\,\mathrm{V}$ they reach a speed of $2.7 \times 10^7\,\mathrm{m\,s^{-1}}$.

Their momentum is then $(9.11 \times 10^{-31}\,\mathrm{kg}) \times (2.7 \times 10^7\,\mathrm{m\,s^{-1}})$ which is $2.5 \times 10^{-23}\,\mathrm{kg\,m\,s^{-1}}$ (or $\mathrm{N\,s}$)

The de Broglie wavelength of these electrons is

$$\frac{6.6 \times 10^{-34}}{2.5 \times 10^{-23}} = 2.6 \times 10^{-11}\,\mathrm{m}$$

This is similar to the wavelength of the X-rays used to form diffraction patterns when they are incident on crystals (Topic 3.1). Increasing the accelerating voltage, increases the energy and momentum of the electrons. The wavelength therefore decreases. Shorter wavelength blue light falling on a diffraction grating produces fringes that are closer together. In this case increasing the accelerating voltage produces smaller rings with smaller spacing between them.

## Seeing small objects

The wavelength of radiation being used determines the smallest object we can detect with it. This is known as the resolving power. The smaller the wavelength, the better the resolution. The resolution in visible light is limited by its wavelength of about $5 \times 10^{-7}\,\mathrm{m}$. In electron microscopes, electrons accelerated through $30\,000\,\mathrm{V}$ have wavelengths of about $10^{-12}\,\mathrm{m}$ and can produce images of objects as small as a nanometre.

The wavelength is also an important consideration when probing matter in particle physics. To provide useful information the accelerated particle has to have a wavelength that is about the same size as the particle it is colliding with.

For example, there is more chance of an electron probing the proton if its de Broglie wavelength is comparable with the proton diameter $(2.4 \times 10^{-15}\,\mathrm{m})$.

The electron momentum must be greater than $2.8 \times 10^{-19}\,\mathrm{N\,s}$.

$$\text{Kinetic energy} = \frac{(mv)^2}{2m} = \frac{(2.8 \times 10^{-19})^2}{2 \times 9.1 \times 10^{-31}} = 4.6 \times 10^{-8}\,\mathrm{J}$$

This is an energy of $3 \times 10^{11}\,\mathrm{eV}$. The electrons in the accelerator at CERN have energies of about $5 \times 10^{10}\,\mathrm{eV}$ ($50\,\mathrm{GeV}$).

## Problem with the Bohr model

Although providing a neat image of the atom, there are some difficulties with Bohr's model (Topic 3.2) in which electrons orbit a nucleus. One problem is that accelerating electrons radiate energy, as they do in an aerial that is transmitting radio signals. The orbiting electrons in Bohr's atom would be accelerating and so they would radiate energy. As they lose this energy the electrons would spiral into the nucleus, just as a satellite does as it loses energy when it enters the Earth's atmosphere. The wave–particle model of matter was used by Bohr to improve his model. He suggested that the electrons could only have certain 'discrete' or quantised energies such that there was a stationary wave with a whole number of 'loops' in the electron orbit (Figure 4). To change from one

### How science works

The wave–particle duality model uses theories that are established to describe the behaviour of light. As long as the model can explain what is observed and be used to successfully predict new events then it is a good model. When the model fails it has to be changed or a new model found.

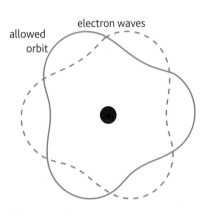

allowed orbit — electron waves

**Figure 4** *de Broglie waves around a nucleus*

energy to another, photons are emitted with energy equal to the difference between the electron energies, so explaining the existence of line spectra.

This approach was the forerunner to the quantum mechanical model of the atom, developed by Erwin Schrödinger.

## Simplified view of the quantum mechanical model

In a simplified view of a hydrogen atom, the electron would be detected somewhere between the nucleus and the outside edge of the atom. It is trapped in a three-dimensional potential 'well' of radius equal to the radius of the atom. The walls correspond to the nucleus and the edge of the atom. To escape from the atom, the electron has to get out of the well.

Within the well, the electron energy must be such that the de Broglie wave is a stationary wave with nodes at the sides.

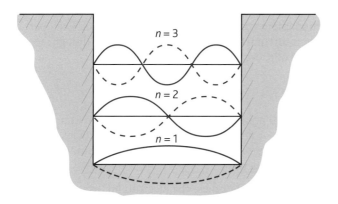

**Figure 5** *Electron stationary waves in a potential well*

In the electron wave model the probabilities of finding an electron in the nucleus and outside the atom are both zero, so the wave amplitude is zero at these points. The electron is most likely to be found (highest probability) where the amplitude is a maximum – midway between the nodes.

### Calculating electron energies

For the electron the momentum $mv = \dfrac{h}{\lambda}$ and the kinetic energy,

$$E_k = \frac{(mv)^2}{2m} = \frac{h^2}{2m\,\lambda^2}$$

The lowest electron energy is when $\lambda = 2r$, so $E_k = \dfrac{h^2}{8mr^2}$

The next possible energy is when $\lambda = r$, so $E_k = \dfrac{h^2}{2mr^2}$ which is four times the lowest energy.

The next will have nine times the minimum energy, the next 16, so the pattern is that each possible $E_k$ is $n^2$ times the minimum energy $\left(n^2 \dfrac{h^2}{8mr^2}\right)$, where $n$ is the number of loops in the stationary wave.

This approach shows that only certain energies are possible, although the actual pattern of energies in atoms is different from this. The Schrödinger model shows a similar quantised behaviour and accurately predicts the possible energies for a hydrogen atom.

**Link**

The production of electron stationary waves is like the way in which stationary waves are produced on a guitar string (Topic 1.3). There must be nodes at the bridges as they cannot move.

### Summary questions

1. Calculate the wavelength of a ball of mass 160 g travelling at 20 m s$^{-1}$.

2. Calculate the speed and kinetic energy of a neutron that has a wavelength of $4.0 \times 10^{-11}$ m. The neutron mass = $1.7 \times 10^{-27}$ kg

3. Explain how electron diffraction experiments suggest that matter can behave like a wave.

4. How does the Bohr quantum mechanical model of a hydrogen atom differ from a classical model?

# 4.3   Fundamental particles

*Learning objectives:*

- Which particles are thought to be fundamental?

- How were neutrinos discovered?

*Specification reference: 3.1.2C*

### How science works

**Creating theories**

The particle model works in the same way as the atomic model did in the discovery of new elements. These models both suggest a pattern which is used to predict new elements (in the atomic model) or identify new particles (in the standard model). Research then focuses on finding the particle.

**Table 1** *The lepton family*

| the 12 leptons | | | | charge | lepton number |
|---|---|---|---|---|---|
| particle | e | μ | τ | −1 | +1 |
| anti-particles | ē | μ̄ | τ̄ | +1 | −1 |
| neutrinos | $\nu_e$ | $\nu_\mu$ | $\nu_\tau$ | 0 | +1 |
| anti-neutrinos | $\bar{\nu}_e$ | $\bar{\nu}_\mu$ | $\bar{\nu}_\tau$ | 0 | −1 |

*When describing the charge on a particle the 'e' is usually implied. For example, the charge of an electron is given as −1 rather than −1e. The charge on an up-quark is given as $+\frac{2}{3}$ rather than $+\frac{2}{3}e$.*

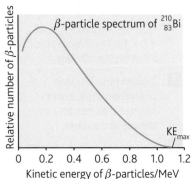

**Figure 1** *Energy spectrum for beta decay*

A comprehensive theory that explains the structure of matter and the forces that hold particles together has become a major goal of scientific research. Cosmologists study the creation of the Universe through a study of distant galaxies. Particle physicists create conditions that would have occurred in the early Universe in their accelerators. The current theory is that the Universe consists of a relatively small number of fundamental particles and four different forces.

## The standard model

The standard model arose from experiments that revealed the decays and interactions between sub-atomic particles. It suggests that there are two types of fundamental particles, **leptons** and **quarks**. Each particle has an equivalent **antiparticle**. All other particles are thought to consist of combinations of these fundamental particles.

## Leptons

Leptons are small point-like particles. Electrons are examples of leptons with a charge of −1 and the corresponding antiparticles, like the positron, have charge +1. Neutrinos and antineutrinos are also leptons and are electrically neutral.

There are three lepton families: the electron (e), muon (μ) and tau (τ). The electron and muon are very light particles but the tau, identified in 2001, is about 1800 times heavier than an electron. For reasons that will be shown later, each lepton is given a lepton number. The particles have lepton number +1 and the antiparticles −1.

The lepton family is shown in Table 1. Only the antiparticle of the electron has its own name, the **positron.**

The neutrinos are intriguing particles; there are three types, one for each charged lepton. They are very difficult to detect and yet come in vast numbers from all directions in space. They pass through the Earth virtually undiminished in intensity and interact so rarely that they would need to pass through lead many light years thick to halve their intensity. So what made scientists look for them in the first place?

## Discovery of neutrinos

The beta particles emitted in beta decay always have a range of energies, anything from virtually nothing to a maximum value. Also the total energy of the beta particle and the recoil nucleus together was not constant. The energy spectrum is shown in Figure 1. So if there is, as we believe, a set amount of energy available for the decay, the question arose where did the rest of the energy go?

When a gun is fired, the gun recoils in the opposite direction to the bullet to conserve momentum. A similar situation would occur in beta decay if the only particle emitted is the beta particle but Figure 2 shows that in practice this does not happen.

These facts led Wolfgang Pauli (1930) to predict a 'particle' that would carry away the energy and momentum. Evidence for the existence of the neutrino (meaning 'little neutral one') was found by Reines and Cowan in 1959. The particle emitted in beta decay is actually an antineutrino for reasons that are explained in Topic 4.4. Although firmly established in the standard model, neutrinos remain mysterious particles and their properties are still under intensive investigation. Originally thought to be massless, recent evidence seems to suggest that a neutrino has a very small mass.

## Quark family

This family also consists of six particles and six corresponding antiparticles. Quarks are never found on their own but exist in **hadrons** formed from various quark combinations.

There are six types (or flavours) of quark, each of which is given a label which has no significance other than for identification. They carry a charge of either $+\frac{2}{3}e$ or $-\frac{1}{3}e$ where $e$ is $1.6 \times 10^{-19}$ C.

These quarks are split into three generations of increasing mass. The first generation contains the up and down quarks. The second contains the strange and charm quarks and the third the bottom and top quarks. The top quark was the last to be positively identified (in 1995), as very high energy accelerators were needed to provide evidence for its existence.

The up, down and strange quarks were discovered first. The up (u) and down (d) quarks are the constituents of the protons and neutrons in the atoms of our own material world.

To explain which particles can exist and the outcome of observed interactions between particles, the quarks are assigned properties described by a numerical value. The quark is given a **baryon number** of $\frac{1}{3}$ and an antiquark $-\frac{1}{3}$.

**Strangeness** is a property that was initially defined to explain the behaviour of massive particles such as kaons and hyperons. These strange particles are created in pairs in collisions and have a longer than expected lifetime ($10^{-10}$ s instead of the expected $10^{-23}$ s). This property of strangeness is conserved during their creation, but not when they subsequently decay. A strange antiquark has a strangeness of $+1$, defined as being the strangeness of a $K^0$ ($ = d\bar{s}$) particle. A strange quark then has a strangeness of $-1$.

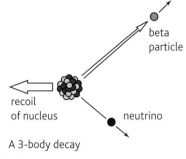

A 3-body decay

**Figure 2** *Particles in beta decay*

**Table 2** *The family of quarks*
*Antiquarks carry the opposite charge*

| quarks with charge $-\frac{1}{3}$ | quarks with charge $+\frac{2}{3}$ | increasing mass |
|---|---|---|
| down | up | |
| strange | charm | ↓ |
| bottom | top | |

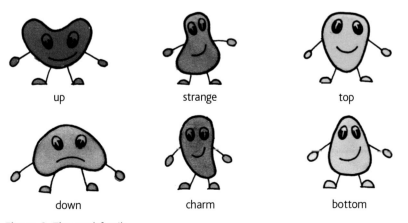

**Figure 3** *The quark family*

## Summary questions

1 How many fundamental particles and antiparticles are there in the standard model?

2 What is the charge on a strange antiquark?

3 What is the baryon number of an anti-up quark?

4 Explain why it was necessary to assume that there was more than one particle emitted in beta decay?

# 4.4 Particles and their interaction

*Learning objectives:*

■ What are the main groups of particles?

■ What is the difference between a baryon and a meson?

■ What are the rules that govern the result of interactions between particles?

*Specification reference 3.1.2C*

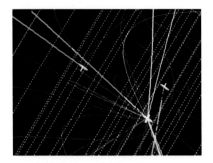

**Figure 1** *Jets of particles produced by electron–positron annihilation*

## 🛈 💡 ⛏ Particles and antiparticles

When new particles are produced in accelerators the production of a particle is accompanied by a corresponding antiparticle. This is called **pair production**.

When a particle meets an antiparticle they disappear. They **annihilate** each other. For example, when an electron meets a positron, a $Z^0$ particle is produced. The $Z^0$ has a short lifetime and at low energies it decays to produce photons of electromagnetic radiation. This is applied in PET scanners used in medical diagnosis. At higher energies the $Z^0$ decays to produce another electron–positron pair or a quark–antiquark pair which results in jets of new particles.

## Baryons and mesons

The particles formed from quarks comprise a class of particles called **hadrons**. These are particles that experience the **strong force** and can be further subdivided into two classes; **baryons** which are made from three quarks and the **mesons** that have only two. The only stable baryon is the proton and all other baryons eventually decay, forming a proton and something else.

The baryons are made from three quarks and have a **baryon number** of 1 or –1. Mesons are made from two quarks and have a baryon number of 0. To find the baryon number of a particle, simply add baryon numbers of the constituent quarks.

## Conservation rules

When particles interact or decay, the event must obey several conservation rules. The fundamental laws of conservation of momentum and energy must always be obeyed. Energy and mass are equivalent so energy may become mass and vice versa.

**In particle physics the total of the charge, baryon and lepton numbers must also be the same after an event occurs as it was before.**

In low energy electron–positron annihilation the sum of the lepton numbers is 0 before the interaction. Lepton number is conserved because the resulting photons are not leptons. At higher energies if a lepton is produced there must be a corresponding anti-lepton.

**Table 1** *Quark structure of protons and neutrons*

| particle | baryon number | charge |
|---|---|---|
| proton uud | $\frac{1}{3}+\frac{1}{3}+\frac{1}{3}=1$ | $\frac{2}{3}+\frac{2}{3}-\frac{1}{3}=1$ |
| antiproton $\overline{u}\overline{u}\overline{d}$ | $-\frac{1}{3}-\frac{1}{3}-\frac{1}{3}=-1$ | $-\frac{2}{3}-\frac{2}{3}+\frac{1}{3}=-1$ |
| neutron udd | $\frac{1}{3}+\frac{1}{3}+\frac{1}{3}=1$ | $\frac{2}{3}-\frac{1}{3}-\frac{1}{3}=0$ |

**Table 2** *Quark structure of some mesons*

| particle | baryon number | charge |
|---|---|---|
| $\pi^+$ u$\overline{d}$ | $\frac{1}{3}-\frac{1}{3}=0$ | $+\frac{2}{3}+\frac{1}{3}=1$ |
| K$^+$ u$\overline{s}$ | $\frac{1}{3}-\frac{1}{3}=0$ | $+\frac{2}{3}+\frac{1}{3}=1$ |

*Examples:*

**1** Showing that when a proton collides with a negative pion it can produce a neutron and an uncharged pion.

The equation for the interaction is $p + \pi^- \longrightarrow n + \pi^0$.

Charge conservation $\qquad +1 -1 \longrightarrow 0 + 0$ ✓

Baryon number $\qquad +1 + 0 \longrightarrow +1 + 0$ ✓

Lepton number $\qquad 0 + 0 \longrightarrow 0 + 0$ ✓

The three rules are obeyed so it is a possible event. The masses on both sides are about the same but further analysis of mass and energy would be needed to confirm whether it can occur.

**2** A neutron decays into a proton by emitting a beta particle so $n \longrightarrow p + e^-$

As it stands this conserves charge as the proton and electron have opposite charges. The neutron and proton both have a baryon number of 1 so that too is conserved. However, before the event there was no lepton but afterwards there is. The electron has a lepton number of +1 so there has to be another lepton emitted which is uncharged but has a lepton number of −1. So an anti-neutrino is emitted as well as the beta⁻ particle.

The full equation for the neutron decay is $_0^1 n \longrightarrow {}_1^1 p + {}_{-1}^0 e + {}_0^0 \overline{v}_e$

- Notice the <u>electron antineutrino</u> accompanies the electron in the decay.

- When the neutron decays into a proton, a down quark decays into an up quark (udd $\longrightarrow$ uud).

- The reaction $d \longrightarrow u + e^- + \overline{v}_e$ occurs in any beta⁻ decay. What happens in beta⁺ decay?

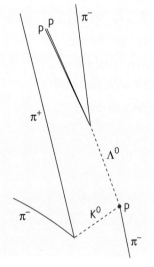

**Figure 2** *Sketch showing the relevant tracks of the pion–proton collision*

## Conservation of strangeness

Particles that contain a strange quark have a strangeness of −1. The $K^0$ meson has a strangeness of +1 so contains a strange antiquark. Particles made from three strange quarks would have a strangeness of −3.

When a strange particle decays through a weak interaction, strangeness is not conserved. For example, strangeness is not conserved when a strange quark decays into an up quark.

**Strangeness is conserved when there is a strong interaction (one in which the strong force is involved).**

This is why strange particles always occur in pairs. If two particles interact to produce a strange particle then a strange antiparticle must also appear.

Figure 2 shows a negative pion interacting with a proton to produce a neutral K-meson ($K^0$) and a neutral particle, a hyperon, called a lambda particle ($\Lambda^0$). These produce no tracks in a bubble chamber.

$$\pi^- + p \longrightarrow K^0 + \Lambda^0$$

There are no strange particles on the left-hand side. The $K^0$ has a strangeness of +1 so the $\Lambda^0$ must have a strangeness of −1. In terms of quarks the equation for the reaction is

$$\overline{u}d + uud \longrightarrow d\overline{s} + sud$$

The $K^0$-meson goes on to decay into positive and negative pions and the lambda particle into a negative pion and a proton. In each of these subsequent decays the strangeness is **not** conserved.

## Summary questions

**1** What is the quark structure of an antiproton?

**2** The quark structure of a particle is duu.

   **a** Is it a meson or a baryon?

   **b** What is its charge?

**3** Identify the unknown particle in the following reaction.

   $$p + \pi^- \longrightarrow n + X$$

**4** A particle Ξ has a structure ssd. What is its charge, baryon number and strangeness?

# 4.5 Forces of nature

## Learning objectives:

■ What holds the particles together?

■ What are the four forces of nature?

■ What is meant by an exchange particle?

*Specification reference: 3.1.2D*

## Forces between particles

The forces and interactions between particles appear to involve four forces. The force between the particles is mediated (or transmitted) by particles called **bosons**. The forces have different ranges and different bosons are responsible for each force. This is summarised in the table below.

| force | occurrence | particle responsible | relative strength | range |
|---|---|---|---|---|
| strong force | in the nucleus between quarks and hadrons | gluons (pions) | 1 | $10^{-15}$ m |
| electromagnetic force | charged particles | photons | $\approx 10^{-2}$ | infinite |
| weak nuclear force | beta decay of nucleus | bosons ($W^+ W^- Z^0$) | $\approx 10^{-6}$ | $10^{-18}$ m |
| gravity | due to mass | gravitons? | $\approx 10^{-40}$ | infinite |

### Exchange forces

The bosons carry the force between particles. For example, an electron can exchange a photon with a neighbouring electron which leads to the electromagnetic force. The exchange particle is said to be a 'virtual' particle because it is not detected during the exchange.

The mass of the exchange particle fixes the range of the force. The exchange particle cannot be detected during its transfer between the particles as this would mean that it would no longer be acting as the mediator of the force between the particles. The larger the rest mass of the exchange particle, the lower the time it can be in flight without it being detected and therefore the lower the range of the force.

### Strong force

This is the strongest of the forces and acts between quarks and therefore between nucleons. This strong force is strong enough to overcome the large repulsive forces acting between the charged protons in the nucleus or between the quarks that make up the protons. The exchange particles responsible are positive and negative pions ($\pi^+$ and $\pi^-$). The strong force is attractive at nuclear distances but if distances are very small, the strong force becomes repulsive.

## Hint

The simplest analogy of how the force can be produced by transfer of a particle is to picture what happens when a heavy ball is thrown backwards and forwards between two boats. The momentum changes as the ball is thrown and caught and this produces a repulsive effect so that they move apart. Whilst this gives the idea of how the exchange of a particle can produce a repulsive force, an explanation of attraction is more tricky, requiring the use of the uncertainty principle, and is beyond what is required in this course.

*The two boats move apart as the ball is exchanged between them.*

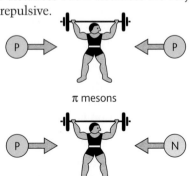

**Figure 1** *The forces of nature – the strong force*

## Electromagnetic force

This is the familiar force that we find exerted between charged particles at rest or in motion. It therefore affects the charged quarks and leptons. The exchange particle that gives rise to the force is the photon. Photons have no mass and this leads to the force having an infinite range.

photons

**Figure 2** *The forces of nature – the electromagnetic force*

## Weak nuclear force

This is responsible for radioactive decay by beta emission. In beta decay a neutron decays to a proton. In this process a W-boson is exchanged as a quark changes from down to up. The W boson then immediately decays into an electron and an electron antineutrino. The W and Z particles responsible for weak interactions are very massive. This leads to the force they give rise to being very short range, only about 0.01 of the diameter of a proton. The weak interaction is the only way in which a quark can change into another quark, or a lepton into another lepton.

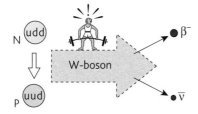

**Figure 3** *The forces of nature – the weak force*

## Gravitational force

This is by far the weakest of the forces. It is long range and is the dominant force that operates within and between galaxies. Theory suggests the existence of a particle called a **graviton** which acts as the exchange particle for gravitational force but such particles have not yet been found.

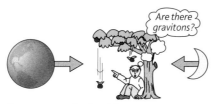

**Figure 4** *The forces of nature – gravitational force*

## Unifying theory

In our Universe the forces are identified as being different. At high energies it has already been found that the electromagnetic force and the weak nuclear force cannot be distinguished. They merge to form a single force, the **electroweak force**. At the time of the Big Bang none of the forces could be seen as separate, but the forces separated out as the Universe cooled. One of the big challenges is to find a theory that would combine the electroweak force with the strong force to produce a Grand Unified Theory for the forces of nature. The next step would then be to find a theory that also includes gravity so that all the forces are unified leading to the so-called Theory of Everything.

### Summary questions

1. State the name of the exchange particle that is responsible for beta decay of a radioactive nucleus.

2. Suggest the property of the exchange particle which determines the range of the force.

3. Which particles feel the strong force?

# 4.6  Big Bang and big questions

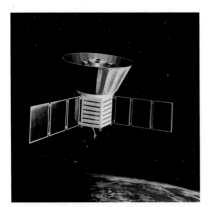

**Figure 1**  *Picture of the COBE satellite*

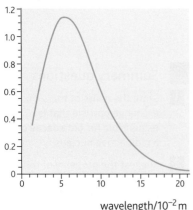

**Figure 2**  *Variation of intensity with wavelength from COBE satellite in agreement with black body at 2.7 K*

From the time they began to think, humans have tried to imagine how the Universe began. The current scientific view is that it began with an explosion referred to as the **Big Bang**.

When you look at a distant star or galaxy you see it as it was in the past. The Sun is seen as it was 8 min before, and the most distant galaxies as they were more than 10 billion ($10^{10}$) years ago. The further away the galaxy, the further back in time you are looking. So cosmology is a way of studying the history of the Universe. Particle physicists study the Universe differently but with the same aims. They try to recreate events that resemble what was happening at different stages of evolution of the universe.

## ■ Summary of the evidence for the Big Bang

Evidence for the Big Bang theory comes from observations that suggest that the Universe is expanding and cooling.

### Red shift

Wavelengths of light from galaxies are longer than expected if they were stationary and suggests that the galaxies are moving further apart.

### Chemical composition of the galaxies

The composition of stars, galaxies and the material between them at different stages of evolution is consistent with a Big Bang theory. The composition and physical processes changed as the temperature fell due to the expansion of the Universe.

### Cosmic microwave background radiation

This theory predicts that the very short wavelength photons produced in the early stages of the formation of the Universe lose energy as the Universe expands. Lower energy photons have a longer wavelength and the theory predicts that the wavelength should now be in the microwave region. The distribution of microwave energy is consistent with radiation from a **black body** at a temperature of 2.7 K as predicted. The cosmic microwave background (CMB) radiation comes from such large distances that it is the oldest detectable signal. The original radiation would have been visible but it has been red shifted so that it is now observed in the microwave region.

### Discovery of CMB radiation

Discoveries in science are often made accidentally but have far reaching implications. The predictions of cosmologists were confirmed by accident when two radio engineers, Arno Penzias and Robert Wilson, were setting up a new microwave receiver. They confirmed that a signal with wavelength 7.4 cm picked up was not a fault with their electronics. It was coming from space and was equally strong in all directions. To confirm the Big Bang theory, it was necessary to look for the energy distribution for other wavelengths, some of which did not penetrate the Earth's atmosphere. The Cosmic Background Explorer (COBE) satellite (Figure 1), launched in 1989, enabled scientists from Berkeley to show that the radiation was black-body radiation at a temperature of about 2.7 K.

## Black-body radiation

A black body radiates all the wavelengths that it can for its temperature. From the distribution of the wavelengths the temperature of the body can be found.

## The 'eras' of the Universe

Scientists have built up a picture of what was happening at different eras (or stages) during the evolution of the Universe (Table 1). It took only about 3 s for protons and neutrons to appear but in those 3 s the Universe went through several stages or 'eras'. In each era the physical processes and the particles that evolved changed as the temperature fell. More information can be found by visiting the European Organization for Nuclear Research (CERN) and Science and Technology Facilities Council (STFC) websites.

### How science works

**Colliders at CERN**

The Large Electron-Positron (LEP) collider was designed to create the conditions a few seconds after the Big Bang. The Large Hadron Collider (LHC), completed in 2008, can accelerate heavy lead ions to energies that will recreate conditions during the heavy particle era just $10^{-7}$ s after the Big Bang. Already scientists are considering how they might investigate times even closer to the Big Bang.

**Table 1**

| age of the Universe | temperature /K | |
|---|---|---|
| **the beginning of time** <br> $10^{-43}$ s | | $10^{-43}$ s is the smallest element of time measurable. The known laws of physics cannot describe what happened before this. All the energy of the Universe was squeezed into a point! |
| $10^{-43}$ to $10^{-34}$ s | $10^{32}$ | Matter and energy squeezed together and continually interchanging. Energy was converted into particle and antiparticle pairs which continually annihilated to produce radiation. A rapid expansion caused the temperature to fall. |
| **Grand Unification era** <br> $10^{-34}$ s | $10^{27}$ | This was a period of 'inflation'. Universe expanded very rapidly. The four forces began to separate. Gravity separated first but the other forces were indistinguishable. Quarks and leptons were also indistinguishable. It is thought that at this time more particles than antiparticles were being created, the surplus particles forming our present Universe. |
| **heavy particle era** <br> $10^{-10}$ s | $10^{15}$ | The strong force separated from the weak force. Heavy particles like W and Z particles existed and decayed. The Universe was still too hot for quarks to combine to form hadrons. Quarks and gluons moved around in a plasma. |
| **light particle era** <br> $10^{-7}$ s to 3 s | $10^{12}$ | Some quarks and antiquarks annihilated but 3 s after the Big Bang the excess quarks and gluons combined to form hadrons. The isotopes of hydrogen and helium formed. After 30 min only protons, neutrons and helium-4 nuclei remained. |
| **radiation era** <br> 10 000 years | 10 000 | Most of the energy is electromagnetic radiation in the form of X-rays, light, ultraviolet or radio waves and eventually this became cosmic background radiation. |
| **matter era** <br> 300 000 years | 3500 | Electrons were captured by the nuclei forming neutral atoms of hydrogen and helium. Early stars began to form. The Universe was 'transparent' meaning that light could now pass unimpeded through the Universe. The expansion continued and the CMB radiation comes from this time. |
| **galaxies formed** <br> about $10^8$ years | 10 | The temperature of the Universe was about 10 K and galaxies started to form. The Sun formed in the Milky Way galaxy and the Earth appeared as a satellite to the Sun about $5 \times 10^9$ years ago. |
| **present** <br> about $1.5 \times 10^{10}$ years | 2.7 | As we see it! |

## Big questions

Although a lot has been discovered about the Universe there are still important questions that physicists are hoping to answer with experiments using the LHC at CERN.

### Are quarks and leptons really fundamental?

Research so far suggests that there are 12 fundamental quarks and 12 leptons but physicists have been here before. Protons and neutrons were once thought to be fundamental. Perhaps the quarks and leptons can be broken down into yet smaller particles? The high energies of the LHC accelerator may produce surprises.

## What is mass?

Why do some quarks have a much higher mass than others? The theory is that mass is caused by particles interacting with another particle called the **Higgs boson**. Massive particles interact more strongly with the Higgs particle than lighter ones. Mass is a measure of a body's inertia, that is, how difficult it is to accelerate it. According to this theory a massive object finds it harder to move because it is interacting more strongly with the particles in the Higgs field that fills space.

One way to picture this is to imagine lifting a smooth sphere and a rough sphere of similar mass out of a viscous fluid. The smooth sphere will be easier to lift. Because there is less friction the sphere interacts less with the fluid than the rougher sphere so it will feel lighter. In a similar way when particles move through the Higgs field some 'pick up' less mass than others.

Until the Higgs particle has been observed however, the origin of mass remains only a theory.

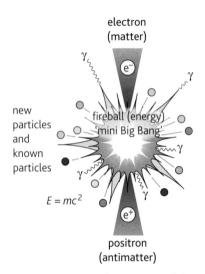

**Figure 3** *Matter and antimatter collide producing conditions soon after the Big Bang*

## What is dark matter?

So far only about 4% of the matter in the Universe has been accounted for. The motion of the stars and galaxies suggests that there is much more mass but what form this takes is still a mystery; 20–25% is thought to be non-baryonic dark matter, weakly interacting massive particles. The rest is dark energy which is only known to exist because it is continually increasing the rate at which the universe is expanding.

## Why is there only matter in the Universe?

During the Big Bang, matter and antimatter should have been created equally and they should have annihilated each other. So how did our matter Universe come about? There must have been an imbalance during the early stages of the Big Bang, with more matter than antimatter being created, but why did this happen?

## Will the Universe expand for ever?

There are three possibilities for the fate of the Universe depending on the density of the Universe. The density can be defined in terms of the density parameter $\Omega$, where:

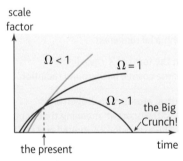

**Figure 4** *The Future of the Universe?*

$$\Omega = \frac{\text{actual density of the Universe}}{\text{critical density}}$$

The critical density is the density for a flat Universe in which there is just enough matter for the Universe to continue to expand to a maximum limit but the rate of expansion would decrease with time. This is thought to be the least likely scenario.

If $\Omega < 1$ the Universe would be open and continue to expand forever.

If $\Omega > 1$ then the Universe would be closed. It would eventually stop expanding and then collapse and end with a 'Big Crunch'.

The dark energy factor however, raises further questions, so there is a lot still to be discovered.

## Summary questions

1. Explain the origin of cosmic microwave background radiation.

2. How long after the Big Bang did the protons and neutrons form?

3. When did the first atoms appear?

4. What particle do scientists think is responsible for mass?

1   (a) State what is meant by the *photoelectric effect* and explain how **two** observations
        made in photoelectric experiments suggest that electromagnetic radiation
        behaves like a stream of particles rather than a wave.                    *(7 marks)*

    (b) Photons with energy $1.1 \times 10^{-18}$ J are incident on a metal surface. The maximum
        energy of electrons emitted from the surface is $4.8 \times 10^{-19}$ J.

        (i)  Calculate the work function of the metal.

        (ii) Calculate the wavelength of the de Broglie wave associated with the emitted
             electrons.                                                           *(2 marks)*

2   (a) A photocell contains a metal that emits electrons when visible light is incident on
        it. The electrons are emitted with almost zero kinetic energy when yellow light of
        wavelength 570 nm is incident on the photocell.

        (i)  Show that the photoelectric threshold frequency of the metal in the photocell
             is about $5 \times 10^{14}$ Hz.

        (ii) Calculate the work function, in J, of the metal in the photocell.    *(4 marks)*

    (b) Ultraviolet radiation of photon energy $4.7 \times 10^{-19}$ J that has the same intensity as
        the visible light in part (a) is now incident on the cathode.

        (i)  Calculate the maximum velocity of the emitted electrons.

        (ii) State and explain the effect on the number of electrons emitted per second
             resulting from this change in the photon energy of the incident radiation.  *(6 marks)*

3   (a) Explain what is meant by the *work function* of a metal.                  *(2 marks)*

        A metal emits photoelectrons when light is incident on it. The graph shows
        the results obtained when the maximum kinetic energy of these emitted
        photoelectrons was measured over a range of incident light frequencies.

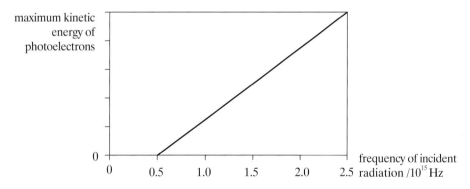

    (b) Use the graph to determine the work function of the metal.               *(3 marks)*

    (c) The experiment is repeated but with the light incident on a different metal that
        has a lower work function.

        Copy the graph shown in part (a) and draw a new line to show how the results will
        change. Label the original line **A** and your new line **B**.            *(2 marks)*

**4** The equation represents the collision of a neutral kaon with a proton, resulting in the production of a neutron and a positive pion.

$$K^0 + p \longrightarrow n + \pi^+$$

(a) Show that in addition to energy and momentum conservation, this collision obeys the **three** conservation laws relating to baryon number, lepton number and charge. *(3 marks)*

(b) The neutral kaon has a strangeness of +1.

Write down the quark structure of the following particles:

(i) $K^0$

(ii) $\pi^+$

(iii) p *(4 marks)*


**5** Light of frequency $5.0 \times 10^{14}$ Hz is shone onto a specimen of potassium and a photoelectron is emitted from the metal.

work function of potassium $= 2.9 \times 10^{-19}$ J

(a) Calculate the maximum speed of emission that this photoelectron can have. *(2 marks)*

(b) Calculate the corresponding de Broglie wavelength for this electron. *(2 marks)*

AQA, 2005


**6** Data for this question:

a negative muon $\mu^-$ is 207 times more massive than an electron

rest mass of an electron $= 9.1 \times 10^{-31}$ kg

rest mass of neutral pion $= 2.4 \times 10^{-28}$ kg

(a) Calculate the de Broglie wavelength of a negative muon travelling at $3.0 \times 10^6 \, \text{m s}^{-1}$. *(2 marks)*

(b) Calculate the ratio $\dfrac{\text{rest mass of } \pi^0}{\text{rest mass of } \mu^-}$ where $\pi^0$ is a neutral pion. *(2 marks)*

(c) Calculate the speed necessary for a neutral pion to have the same de Broglie wavelength as that of the negative muon in part (a). *(2 marks)*


**7** (a) (i) Give an example of an exchange particle other than a $W^+$ or $W^-$ particle and state the fundamental force involved when it is produced.

(ii) State the roles that exchange particles can play in an interaction. *(4 marks)*

(b) From the following list of particles

$$p \quad \bar{n} \quad \nu_e \quad e^+ \quad \mu^- \quad \pi^0$$

identify all the examples of:

(i) hadrons

(ii) leptons

(iii) antiparticles

(iv) charged particles *(4 marks)*

**8**   Describe the main features of the Big Bang theory and the evidence that supports it.   *(6 marks)*

**9**   (a)   Complete the following equations:

$p + e^- \longrightarrow$ ___ $+$ ___

$n + v_\mu \longrightarrow p +$ ___

$p + p \longrightarrow p + p + K^- +$ ___   *(4 marks)*

(b)   Give an equation that represents $\beta^-$ decay, using quarks in the equation rather than nucleons.   *(2 marks)*

(c)   (i)   Which fundamental force is responsible for electron capture?

(ii)   What type of particle is an electron?

(iii)   State the other fundamental forces that electrons may experience.   *(3 marks)*

AQA, 2006

**10**   (a)   (i)   In relation to the photoelectric effect, explain the meaning of the term *threshold frequency*.

(ii)   Sketch a graph of the maximum kinetic energy of photoelectrons against the frequency of the incident electromagnetic radiation. Label the position of the threshold frequency, *f*.

Values are not required on the axes.   *(5 marks)*

(b)   The table gives the work function of some metals.

| metal | work function/$10^{-19}$ J |
|---|---|
| caesium | 3.0 |
| lithium | 3.7 |
| beryllium | 6.2 |
| mercury | 7.2 |
| tungsten | 7.4 |

(i)   Calculate the threshold frequency for caesium.

(ii)   A caesium surface is illuminated with electromagnetic radiation of wavelength $3.0 \times 10^{-7}$ m. Determine the maximum kinetic energy of the ejected photoelectrons.

(iii)   State which metals listed in the table will not emit photoelectrons when illuminated with electromagnetic radiation of wavelength $3.0 \times 10^{-7}$ m.   *(7 marks)*

AQA, 2007

## 5.1 Light from the stars/stellar spectra

Specification reference: 3.1.2E

### Learning objectives:

- What can be learned from a study of spectra from stars?
- How do astronomers classify stars?

By studying the radiation from galaxies scientists learn about the past. So that stars can be compared they are classified into different types. The spectra they emit are one way of classifying them.

The particle reactions inside a star release energy that raises the temperature of the star. A study of the brightness and the wavelengths that are present in the radiation can tell us about its temperature, its chemical composition and the nature of the processes that are taking place to produce the energy.

### Classifying stars by brightness

**Luminosity**

The **luminosity** of a star is the total power (energy per second) it radiates. The power radiated by each square metre of the surface of a star depends on its surface temperature. The luminosity depends on both the power per square metre *and* the surface area of the star. So a cool star that emits half the power per square metre of a hotter star but has twice the surface area has the same luminosity.

### Magnitude of a star

When you look at the stars the first thing that you notice is that they have different **brightnesses**. A star may be less bright than another because it emits less power (energy per second) or it may be just further away. Astronomers refer to the brightness of a star as its magnitude.

The **apparent magnitude** is simply how bright it looks to an observer. Brightness is a comparison of the energy per second that falls on the pupil of the eye. The brightest stars that are visible with the naked eye are referred to as stars of the first magnitude and the dimmest are sixth magnitude stars. This scale is defined so that the intensity of light from the brightest star is 100 times that from the dimmest. A decrease of 1 in magnitude is an increase of $2.51$ ($100^{1/5}$) in the intensity of the light received by the observer.

The Sun is so bright that it has a negative magnitude of $-26.7$ which makes its intensity about $1.2 \times 10^{11}$ ($2.51^{27.7}$) times higher than a first magnitude ($+1$) star.

### How science works

**Using the inverse square law**

As intensity $= \dfrac{\text{power}}{4\pi r^2}$, a star that emits four times the power of another star but is twice as far away from an observer will appear equally bright. Table 1 shows that although the apparent magnitudes show Sirius or Vega to be much dimmer than the Sun they have a much higher luminosity.

**Table 1**

| star | apparent magnitude | distance from Earth/ly | absolute magnitude | relative luminosity |
|------|--------------------|------------------------|--------------------|--------------------|
| Sun | −26.7 | $1.5 \times 10^{-5}$ | 4.8 | 1 |
| Sirius | −1.44 | 8.6 | 1.45 | 22.5 |
| Vega | 0.03 | 25.3 | 0.58 | 50.1 |

What is more important however is a comparison of the real luminosity of a star. That is, how the power emitted by a star compares with other stars. This is the called the **absolute magnitude**. A dim star close to the Earth may seem to be emitting more power than a brighter star that is further away. To make a fair comparison the brightness of each a star is calculated as it would be if it were 10 parsecs (pc) (32.6 light-years) from the Earth.

## Classifying stars by temperature

Although stars look white to us, closer inspection shows that stars have many different colours that are related to surface temperature. Most energy emitted by a cool star is in the infra-red region with some red light. Shorter wavelengths appear in hotter stars so these look yellow or white. Very hot stars look blue as the intensity of the short wavelengths increase. The star types are labelled O, B, A, F, G, K, M , the O type being the hottest. Our Sun is a G type star.

The **emission spectra** from stars fall into one of three types: continuous spectra, band spectra and line spectra.

A **continuous spectrum** comes from hot (incandescent) bodies such as hot or molten iron. In the laboratory this can be investigated using glowing metal in the form of a filament lamp. A determination of where the peak of the energy is in this spectrum gives the temperature of the star.

A **line spectrum** is the result of excitation of atoms. These spectra only contain certain well-defined wavelengths. The wavelengths present are characteristic of the element that produces the light so comparison of the starlight with a laboratory source reveals the elements in the star.

A **band spectrum** is produced in the same way as a line spectrum but is produced by molecules. It consists of bands of light produced by a range of wavelengths separated by gaps.

In a laboratory line spectra are produced when light from electrical discharge tubes, containing gas or vapour, is diffracted through diffraction gratings.

When the continuous spectrum of the light from a star is analysed the spectrum contains dark lines. This is an **absorption spectrum**. Like the emission spectrum, these lines enable analysis of the chemical composition of the star. They are caused by the light passing through atoms and ions in the outer regions of the star. This will be explained in more detail later (see Topic 5.4).

### Table 2

| star type | temperature/K | colour | cause of absorption lines |
|---|---|---|---|
| O | more than 30 000 | blue | ionised helium |
| B | 11 000–30 000 | blue-white | helium atoms and hydrogen |
| A | 7500–11 000 | white | hydrogen and some ionised calcium |
| F | 6000–7500 | yellowish white | ionised calcium and metal atoms |
| G | 5000–6000 | yellow | calcium atoms and metal ions such as iron |
| K | 3500–6000 | orange | metal atoms |
| M | less than 3500 | red | molecules of titanium oxide producing band spectra |

### How science works

**Effect of the atmosphere**

The atmosphere, and particularly atmospheric pollution, absorbs radiation so the appearance of a star depends on where an observatory is placed. This is why scientists place their observatories in remote places and often on high mountains. The best observations are from satellites in orbit outside the Earth's atmosphere.

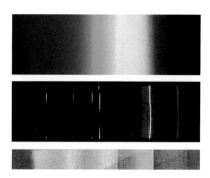

**Figure 1** *Continuous, line and band spectra*

**Figure 2** *Sun's absorption spectrum*

### Summary questions

1. Star A has a luminosity of 20 relative to the Sun and Star B a luminosity of 30. A is 10 light-years and B is 13 light-years away from Earth. Which one appears brightest?

2. Explain why star B could have a lower surface temperature than star A although it has a greater luminosity.

3. Explain the difference between the apparent and absolute magnitudes of a star.

# 5.2 Hertzsprung–Russell diagram

## Learning objectives:

- What are red giants and white dwarfs?
- How did the Sun form?
- What is likely to happen to the Sun in the future?

*Specification reference: 3.1.2E*

In the early 1900s Hertzsprung and Russell independently developed a diagram showing stars placed according to their luminosity and temperature.

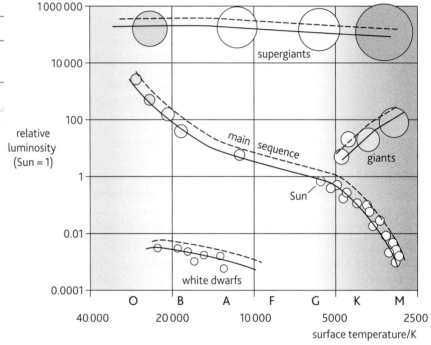

**Figure 1** *Hertzsprung–Russell diagram*

There are some important things to note about the Hertzsprung–Russell diagram.

- By convention the temperature scale runs from high to low so the hottest blue and blue–white stars are on the left hand side and the cooler red stars are to the right.
- The luminosity scale uses the Sun as a reference. So a star with a luminosity of 100 emits 100 times the power of the Sun, etc.
- Because of the large range of temperatures and luminosities, neither of the scales is linear. In going from one grid line to the next, the luminosity increases by a factor of 100. On the temperature scale, the temperature halves from one grid line to the next.

There are a number of observations that can be made when stars are plotted on the diagram. The stars are not randomly spread throughout the plot but are found to occur in groups of particular types. This suggests that there is a particular sequence of events in the evolution of a star and its subsequent 'death'.

## Types of stars

**Main sequence** stars are ordinary dwarf stars like our Sun that produce energy from the fusion of hydrogen and other light nuclei such as helium and carbon. The vast proportion of the stars (over 80%) fit into this category.

**AQA** Examiner's tip

Remember that the luminosity is related to the star's absolute magnitude and its colour depends on its temperature.

**Red giants** are cooler than the Sun and so emit less energy per square metre of surface. However, they have a higher luminosity, emitting up to 100 times more energy per second than the Sun. This means that they must have a much larger surface area to emit the energy. They therefore have a much larger diameter than the Sun, hence the term giant stars.

**White dwarfs** are what remains of old stars. Although they were very hot when they finally stopped producing energy, they have a relatively low luminosity showing them to have a small surface area. These very small hot stars take billions of years to cool down.

**Supergiants** are enormous and very bright. A super giant emitting 90 000 times the energy of the Sun at the same temperature as the Sun must have a surface area 90 000 times larger. This leads to a diameter that is 300 times the diameter of the Sun. A supergiant can therefore have a greater radius than the distance between the Earth and the Sun!

## Formation of a star

The initial process in the formation of a star is the gravitational attraction of interstellar hydrogen nuclei. The loss of potential energy leads to an increase in the gas temperature. The gas becomes denser and when the temperature is high enough the nuclear fusion process begins. This creates helium nuclei and, as the temperature rises, these can also fuse, liberating even more energy. This is what is happening in the main sequence. The luminous stars in the main sequence last for only a short time (perhaps for a million years) whereas the Sun's life is expected to be about 10 000 million years.

## Lives of Sun-like stars

Eventually stars like the Sun collapse as all the hydrogen nuclei in the core are used up. In such stars the core temperature rises as helium nuclei fuse. The hydrogen in the outer layer now starts to fuse. This raises the temperature of the outer layer, which expands. The temperature falls as the star expands and it becomes a red giant.

The fusion of helium nuclei raises the temperature of the core further and even heavier elements form. The star now collapses to become a small hot white dwarf.

So the probable future for the Sun is shown in the diagram in Figure 2 and by the green line in the Hertzsprung-Russell diagram in Figure 3.

What happens when the white dwarf forms depends on the mass of the star. Stars like the Sun would just fade away but white dwarfs with a mass greater than about 1.4 times the Sun's mass can either explode into smaller white dwarfs or collapse suddenly and become an intensely bright supernova.

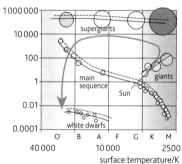

**Figure 3** *Green line shows possible future of the Sun*

### Summary questions

**1** The Sun's luminosity is $L_s$. What type of star has

  **a** a luminosity of $0.005\,L_s$ and a temperature of 1800 K?

  **b** a luminosity of $100\,L_s$ and a temperature of 25 000 K?

**2** State a typical temperature at the surface of a red giant.

**3** What is the likely next stage in the evolution of the Sun?

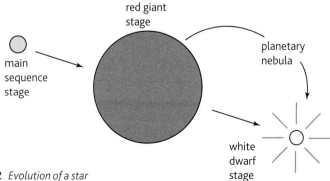

**Figure 2** *Evolution of a star*

# 5.3 Continuous spectra

*Learning objectives:*

- What is black body radiation?

- How does the spectrum of a hot body depend on temperature?

- What is the relation between temperature and power emitted?

*Specification reference: 3.1.2E*

Some bodies are capable of absorbing all the radiation that falls on them. Such an object is called a **black body**. Since it does not reflect energy from any other source, all the energy radiated is thermal energy due to its temperature. When analysed, the resulting radiation forms a continuous spectrum. A hot metal, like the filament of a lamp, is close to being a black body. In the laboratory the radiation from a filament lamp can be investigated as the current is increased, using a spectrometer fitted with a diffraction grating.

## Black body radiation

The radiation from a black body produces a continuous spectrum. As temperature rises, most of the energy at first is in the infrared part of the electromagnetic spectrum. Then the filament glows red as long-wavelength visible radiation is emitted. At yet higher temperatures, the light becomes yellow and then white as the shorter wavelengths appear. In stars which are much hotter than the filament of a lamp, the peak of the curve moves into the blue part of the spectrum so some stars appear bluish-white or blue.

This colour variation as temperature rises can be seen from the series of curves in Figure 1.

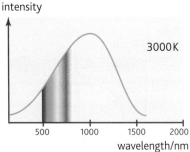

**a** *this star looks red*

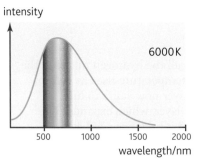

**b** *this star looks yellow-white*

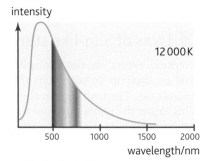

**c** *this star looks blue*

**Figure 1** *Temperature changes the colour of stars*

Whereas the Earth at a temperature of about 300 K emits mostly infra-red radiation, the Sun emits mostly visible light; 43% is visible, 37% is near infra-red and only 7% is ultraviolet.

### Wien's law

As the temperature rises, the peak of the black body radiation graph moves to a shorter wavelength. Wien's law relates the wavelength $\lambda_{max}$ at which most radiation is emitted (the peak of the black body radiation curve) to the absolute temperature $T$ of the body that emits the radiation.

$$\lambda_{max}T = 0.0029 \, \text{m K}$$

You should be able to show that the set of curves shown in Figure 2 agree (approximately) with this equation.

The equation can be used to find the temperature of the surface of a star provided that the peak wavelength is known.

For example, the wavelength of the highest intensity radiation emitted by the Sun is about 500 nm.

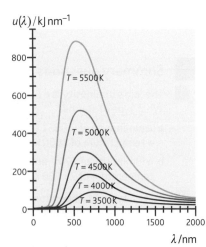

**Figure 2** *Black body radiation curves*

The temperature at the Sun's surface is therefore $\dfrac{0.0029}{500 \times 10^{-9}} = 5800 \, \text{K}$

# Experiments with black bodies

There are a number of experiments that illustrate how black bodies differ from others. Two are described briefly here:

1   If two thermometers, one of which has the bulb painted black, are placed near a heat source, the reading of the thermometer with the black bulb rises more quickly showing that it is absorbing more energy.

2   A metal cube is heated by a light bulb inside it and, by adjusting the voltage, the temperature can be varied. One surface of the cube is smooth and black, one is matt black, one is white matt and the other is a shiny 'silver' surface. The intensity of the radiation from each surface for a particular temperature can be measured using an infrared sensor. The matt black surface produces the highest reading and the silvered surface the least.

It is also possible to adjust the temperature of the surface to investigate the variation of the intensity of the radiation with temperature.

## Effect of temperature on radiated power

The power radiated by a black body increases rapidly with temperature. Double the temperature of a surface (in K) means that the power radiated by each square metre of the surface is 16 ($2^4$) times greater.

The graphs in Figures 3 and 4 show how the power radiated by each square metre of a surface varies with temperature over two different temperature ranges.

Reading from Figure 3, a body at the temperature of boiling water 373 K would radiate about $1000\,\mathrm{W\,m^{-2}}$ and Figure 4 shows that the Sun radiates about $6.5 \times 10^7\,\mathrm{W\,m^{-2}}$ at 5800 K.

The Sun has a radius of $6.96 \times 10^8\,\mathrm{m}$ so its surface area (from $4\pi r^2$) is $6.08 \times 10^{18}\,\mathrm{m^2}$.

The luminosity (power emitted per square metre multiplied by the surface area) $= 4.0 \times 10^{26}\,\mathrm{W}$.

## Calculating the luminosity of stars

The calculation for the Sun can be repeated for any star. The first step is to obtain a record of how the intensity varies with wavelength, such as that shown in Figure 5. The peak is clearly shown, as are the negative going spikes. These spikes show that it is not really continuous due to some wavelengths being absorbed. From the spectrum you can:

- determine the wavelength at which the maximum intensity occurs,
- use Wien's law to determine the temperature,
- determine the power emitted per square metre from the surface.

If the radius is known from astronomical observations, the surface area can be found and hence the luminosity.

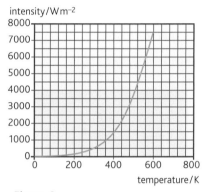

**Examiner's tip**

When using Wien's equation, take care with units. Make sure that the temperature is in kelvin K. Look carefully at the prefixes in any wavelength and convert to m (metres) in standard form.

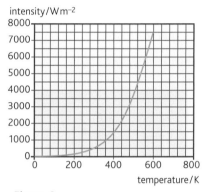

**Figure 3**

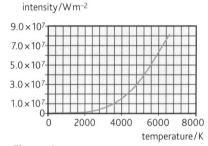

**Figure 4**

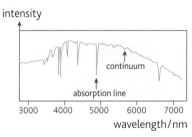

**Figure 5** *Record of spectrum from a star*

## Summary questions

1   Calculate the peak wavelength radiated by a human body at a temperature of 37 °C.

2   A star has a radius that is five times that of the Sun and a surface temperature half that of the Sun. Calculate the ratio of the luminosity of the star to that of the Sun.

3   Calculate the energy emitted by the Sun each second that is in the visible region of the spectrum.

# 5.4 Line spectra

*Learning objectives:*

- Why are only certain frequencies emitted by atoms?

- What is the process that leads to an emission spectrum?

- How does an absorption spectrum occur?

*Specification reference: 3.1.2E*

a *Hydrogen spectrum*

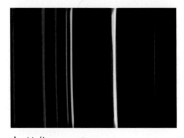

b *Helium spectrum*

**Figure 1** *Spectra for different elements*

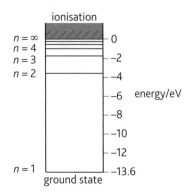

**Figure 2** *Energy levels of a hydrogen atom*

## Emission spectra

Emission line spectra can be seen when light from a gas discharge tube is analysed using a spectrometer. Each line is due to the presence of light of a well-defined wavelength in the emitted light. The set of lines that form the spectrum is unique to the element that is in the gas discharge tube (see Figure 1). The presence of a particular element in a source of light can be shown by identifying some of the wavelengths that are characteristic of the element. This makes the study of line spectra a very useful tool in chemical analysis undertaken in a laboratory and to astronomers in determining the composition of stars and interstellar gases.

In 1868 Joseph Lockyer, an astronomer, identified a spectral line from solar flares that did not belong to any known element. The element was named helium and was not isolated on Earth until 1895. Analysis of the emission line spectrum observed when clouds of interstellar gas are heated by a nearby star can determine which elements are present in the gas.

## Atomic energy levels

Light is emitted when atomic electrons that have moved into **excited states** give up some of their energy. The fact that there are only certain well-defined frequencies present in the spectrum provides evidence for energies of electrons in atoms being quantised. This means that the electrons can only exist in certain well-defined or discrete energies which are referred to as **electron energy levels**.

In a given atom, electrons can only have certain energy levels. They can only move between the energy levels by absorbing or giving up energy in amounts equal to the difference in energies between the levels. Each element has a different set of energy levels which give rise to the unique set of spectral lines.

### Energy of bound electrons

Electrons are bound to atoms. Atoms that are ionized have had one or more electrons removed and energy is needed to do this. An electron that is just free of an atom is defined as having zero energy. For a bound electron, energy has to be added to release it so within the atom the electron has negative energy. Figure 2 shows some of the possible energy levels for a hydrogen atom.

The lowest possible energy that an electron can occupy is called the **ground state**. This is given the level labelled $n = 1$. Notice that the allowed energy levels become closer together as the electron moves to higher energies. These are the **excited states** that the electron can occupy.

Because the energies are small the energies are usually given in electron-volt (eV).

The ground state of the electron in a hydrogen atom is $-13.6\,\text{eV}$, which is $-21.8 \times 10^{-19}\,\text{J}$.

This amount of energy would have to be provided to move the electron from the ground state to the highest level $n = \infty$. The electron would then be free so this is the **ionisation energy** of the atom.

## Definition of an electron-volt

One electron volt (1 eV) is the energy gained by an electron when it is accelerated by a potential difference of 1 V. The energy gained is the potential difference multiplied by the charge ($E = VQ$) so 1 eV is equivalent to $1.6 \times 10^{-19}\,\text{J}$.

## Production of an emission line spectrum

Heating the element in a Bunsen flame or passing a current through a gas in a discharge tube provides energy to cause **excitation** of the atomic electrons. This means that they are raised into one of the higher energy levels. Different atoms will gain different amounts of energy so in a gas atoms will exist in all the possible energy levels. The electrons are said to be in **excited states**.

The excited states are not stable. The electrons remain in these states for only a very short time before releasing energy and returning to lower energy states. This is called **relaxation**.

The electrons lose energy as they move to lower energy states by emitting a photon of electromagnetic radiation. The photon energy $hf$ is equal to the energy difference between the levels.

$$hf = E_1 - E_2 \text{ or } \frac{hc}{\lambda} = E_1 - E_2, \text{ since } c = f\lambda$$

The electron may move to the ground state by emitting a single photon or, if it is in a state higher than $n = 2$, it may do so in stages. Figure 3 shows some transitions for a hydrogen atom in which photons are emitted.

Remember that a more negative energy level has a lower energy. When a photon moves from an energy level of $-3.4$ to $-13.6\,\text{eV}$ the energy lost is: $-3.4-(-13.6) = 10.2\,\text{eV}$ or $16.3 \times 10^{-19}\,\text{J}$

This is equal to the photon energy, so the frequency of the radiation

$$\text{emitted} = \frac{16.3 \times 10^{-19}}{6.63 \times 10^{-34}} = 2.46 \times 10^{15}\,\text{Hz}$$

The corresponding wavelength is $122\,\text{nm}$, which is in the ultraviolet part of the electromagnetic spectrum.

Similar calculations can be done to find the wavelengths for other transitions.

## The hydrogen spectrum

Groups of wavelengths have been identified in the line spectrum of hydrogen. The Lyman, Balmer and Paschen series are named after the scientists who discovered them. The Lyman series is the result of transitions into the $n = 1$ level. This gives rise to high energy photons in the ultraviolet part of the spectrum. The visible Balmer series comes from transitions into the $n = 2$ level. The Paschen series is the result of transitions to the $n = 3$ level and gives infrared radiation.

### How science works

**Developing theories**

Because of the simplicity of the hydrogen atom (one proton and one electron) physicists have been able to produce a theory for the allowed energy levels that fits the observations for hydrogen. The interaction of atomic electrons with each other makes theoretical prediction of the levels for other atoms difficult but the energy level diagrams can be constructed from the frequencies in the line spectrum.

### AQA Examiner's tip

The lines in the line spectrum are not energy levels. Each line in the spectrum is the image of the slit formed by the grating for a particular wavelength. The wavelength itself enables a calculation of a **difference** between energy levels that must exist in the energy level diagram.

### AQA Examiner's tip

When using $hf = E_1 - E_2$, remember that the energies have to be converted to Joules.

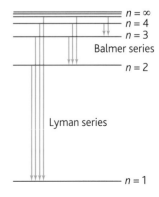

**Figure 3** *Transitions for a hydrogen atom*

## ▨ 💡 Absorption spectra

Although stars behave like black bodies at a very high temperature the spectrum observed from them is not continuous. Dark lines crossing the spectra show that some wavelengths are either missing or have a much reduced intensity. The wavelengths that are missing are characteristic of the elements present in the outer regions of the star through which the light has to pass before reaching Earth. Just as emission spectra tell us what elements are emitting the radiation, absorption spectra tell us which elements are absorbing it, so the chemical composition of the outer regions of the star can be found.

### Formation of an absorption spectrum

Figure 4 shows schematically how light absorbed by interstellar gas may result in an emission or an absorption spectrum. If a star is viewed through the gas then the electrons in the gas atoms are excited into higher energy levels. Only photons that have energy equal to the difference in energy between two levels can be absorbed by the gas. This means that only certain well-defined frequencies are removed from the spectrum.

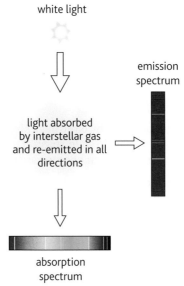

💡 **Figure 4** *Emission and absorption spectrum formed by interstellar gas*

Once the electrons have been excited they are in an unstable state. As they relax into lower states they radiate energy. The intensity of a given wavelength in a particular direction is now reduced for two reasons:

- ■ The light that is re-radiated from the gas cloud travels in all directions so less goes straight on.
- ■ The electrons relax in stages emitting lower energy photons that are in a different part of the electromagnetic spectrum (see Figure 5).

Figure 6 shows that the Sun's spectrum has the same general shape as the black body curve. The dips are those wavelengths that are absorbed by the gas that surrounds the Sun.

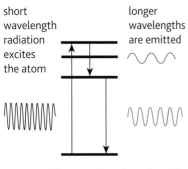

**Figure 5** *Short wavelengths replaced by longer wavelengths*

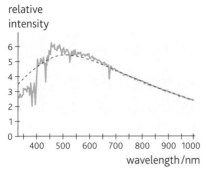

**Figure 6** *Solar spectrum*

## Absorption spectra in the laboratory

An absorption spectrum can be simulated in the laboratory using the arrangement shown in Figure 7. (Details of the spectrometer are not shown.)

Without the bright light source in place, the emission spectrum from the sodium flame consists of a yellow line, corresponding to a wavelength of 590 nm. When a diffraction grating with a very small spacing between the lines is used, the single line can be seen as two yellow lines very close together. If a lamp emitting very bright white light is viewed through the sodium flame, two dark lines cross the lamp's continuous spectrum in exactly the same place as the lines that are seen in the sodium emission spectrum.

An alternative arrangement is to pass white light through iodine vapour produced by gently heating a few iodine crystals in a sealed boiling tube. The continuous spectrum this time consists of equally spaced dark bands. This spectrum is not caused by the energy levels of iodine atoms but by the quantised vibration states that the iodine molecules can exist in. That is, the iodine molecules cannot take in energy in infinitesimally small amounts. They can only take in well-defined 'chunks' of energy.

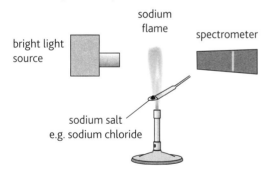

**Figure 7** *Producing an absorption spectrum in the laboratory*

## Summary questions

1 Calculate the photon energy in J resulting from an electron transition from energy level −0.85 eV to −3.4 eV.

2 Calculate the wavelength of the radiation in Question 1 and state the part of the electromagnetic spectrum to which it belongs.

3 How many different wavelengths could be emitted as electrons fall from the $n = 5$ to the $n = 1$ level in a hydrogen atom?

4 What is the highest energy photon that could be emitted by a hydrogen atom?

# 5.5 The expanding Universe

*Learning objectives:*

- What is the Doppler effect?
- How does the red shift suggest an expanding Universe?
- How old is the Universe according to the Hubble law?

*Specification reference: 3.1.2E*

## The red shift

Evidence for the Big Bang comes from observations that show that the Universe is expanding. The main evidence for this is the so-called **red shift**. This is the observation that the wavelength of radiation from some stars has a longer wavelength (lower frequency) than radiation from a similar source in a laboratory on Earth. The Doppler effect predicts such a change when a source of radiation is moving away from an observer. The observation of the red shift leads to the conclusion that stars and galaxies are all tending to move further apart, so the Universe is expanding.

For optical wavelengths the red shift is what it says. The wavelengths are moved **towards** the red end of the spectrum. The faster the motion, the greater the change in wavelength toward the red end of the spectrum. The shift applies to all waves in the spectrum so even the absorption lines in the spectrum are shifted. This is shown in Figure 1.

## The Doppler effect

The Doppler effect is easily observed in the case of sound waves. The sound from the siren on an ambulance changes from a high pitch as it approaches a listener to a lower one as it moves away. The true pitch is heard as the ambulance passes by. The effect is observed whenever there is relative motion between the source and the listener. It does not matter whether one or both are moving as long as they are moving closer together or further apart. In astronomy it is the motion of the source relative to us on Earth that is relevant.

As the source moves, the waves are being bunched into a smaller distance in the direction in which it is moving and stretched in the opposite direction (see Figure 2). This means that wave fronts pass an observer ahead of the source more often so that the sound has a higher frequency.

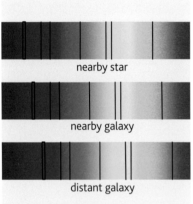

**Figure 1** *Red shift for galaxies moving at different speeds*

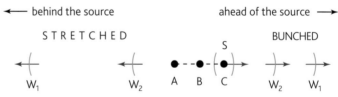

Wave fronts marked $W_1$ emitted when S was at A
Wave fronts marked $W_2$ emitted when S was at B

**Figure 2** *Effect of a moving source*

### Calculating velocity change using the Doppler effect

If a source emitting a frequency $f$ and an observer are stationary then $f$ waves pass the observer every second.

The wavelength is $\frac{v}{f}$

If the source is moving at a speed $v_s$ toward the observer, the wave emitted at the start of a 1 s interval will have travelled a distance $v$. When the last wave in the 1 s interval is emitted the source is a distance $v_s$ closer to the observer.

The $f$ waves now occupy a smaller distance, $(v - v_s)$

The wavelength $$\lambda = \frac{v - v_s}{f}$$

The change in wavelength $$\Delta\lambda = \frac{v}{f} - \left[\frac{v - v_s}{f}\right] = \frac{v_s}{f}$$

$f = \frac{v}{\lambda}$ where $\lambda$ is the 'true' wavelength, so $\Delta\lambda = \frac{v_s}{v}\lambda$ or $\frac{\Delta\lambda}{\lambda} = \frac{v_s}{v}$

If the velocity of the source is small compared with the velocity of the wave $(v_s << v)$ then

$$\frac{\Delta\lambda}{\lambda} = \frac{\Delta f}{f}$$

The approximation can be assumed for the A-level course but make sure you know when it can be used.

*Worked example:*

Radio waves from a distant galaxy are expected to have a wavelength of 210.00 mm but a radio telescope has to be tuned to 210.05 mm in order to detect the signal. Calculate the velocity of the galaxy relative to Earth.

$\frac{v_s}{v} = \frac{\Delta\lambda}{\lambda}$ so $v_s = \frac{\Delta\lambda}{\lambda}v = \frac{0.050}{210.00} \times 3.0 \times 10^8 = 7.1 \times 10^4 \,\text{m s}^{-1}$

The wavelength is longer so the galaxy is moving at 71 km s$^{-1}$ away from Earth.

When the motion is away from the Earth this is called the **recessional speed**.

## Binary stars, rotating stars and galaxies

Some stars consist of two stars rotating about their centre of mass. As they rotate, one star moves away from the Earth so that spectral lines are red-shifted. The other star moves toward the Earth producing a blue-shifted spectrum. The velocities that give rise to the motions can be found from the shifts and the rate of rotation determined. Similarly the spectral lines of light that is emitted from opposite sides of a spinning star (see Figure 3) are blue and red shifted so that its rotational speed can be found.

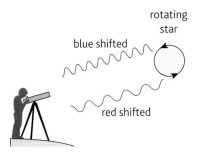

**Figure 3** *Shifted wavelengths for a rotating star*

## Existence of dark matter

The orbital speeds of stars in a galaxy can also be found using the Doppler effect. Such measurements have shown that the orbital periods of stars can be far higher than expected from the estimated mass of the material in a galaxy. This means that some of the mass of the galaxy is unaccounted for. This missing mass is called dark matter and scientists are still unsure what it is. The search for dark matter continues at the present time.

**Developing scientific theories**

In common with many scientific theories, the end result is often the work of several people building on each other's ideas. The red shift was first noticed by Vesto Slipher of Lowell Observatory. Further work by Hubble and Humason determined the law connecting the amount of the shift and the distance of the galaxy.

**Distances in astronomy**

The light-year (ly) and the parsec (pc) are the commonly used distance measurements.

$1\,\text{pc} = 3.26\,\text{ly}$ and $1\,\text{ly} = 9.5 \times 10^{15}\,\text{m}$.

Because of the very large distances, measurements in mega-parsec ($1\,\text{Mpc} = 10^6\,\text{pc}$) are common.

# 🔢 Hubble law

Using observations of red shifts Edwin Hubble suggested that the recessional speeds of galaxies at different distances from the Earth shows they are moving at different speeds. The further away they are the faster they are moving, a factor that is consistent with the Big Bang theory. Working from very poor data he predicted that the velocity $v$ was proportional to the distance $d$ of a galaxy from Earth.

This gives the Hubble law $v = Hd$

where $H$ is the Hubble constant.

The value of the Hubble constant $H$ has changed over the years as measurements of astronomical distances and velocities have been determined more accurately. There were considerable uncertainties in the data Hubble used in 1929. The graph of his data is shown in Figure 4. This gave a value for $H$ of about $500\,\text{km}\,\text{s}^{-1}\,\text{Mpc}^{-1}$. The value today is still uncertain but, using more reliable data, $H$ is thought to about $65\,\text{km}\,\text{s}^{-1}\,\text{Mpc}^{-1}$.

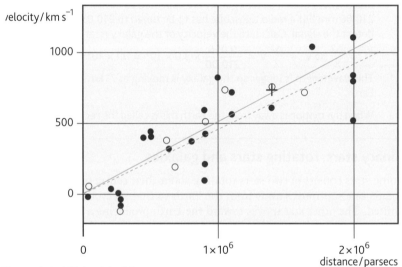

**Figure 4** *Hubble's original data*

## Age of the Universe

The age of the Universe can be estimated from the Hubble constant.

Assuming that it holds for all stars, the maximum speed of a star (one that will be at the edge of the observable Universe) is the speed of light $c$ ($3 \times 10^8\,\text{m}\,\text{s}^{-1}$).

The most distant observable galaxy would be at a distance $\frac{c}{H}$. This is 4600 Mpc away.

This distance is the speed $c$ multiplied by the time $t$ it has taken to get there following the Big Bang ($ct$).

So $ct = \frac{c}{H}$ giving the age of the Universe as $\frac{1}{H}$

This leads to an age of $4.8 \times 10^{17}\,\text{s}$ or $1.5 \times 10^{10}\,\text{years}$.

# Quasars

The red shifts of the radiation from quasars are exceptionally large showing them to be moving at speeds approaching the speed of light. These are the most distant objects that are visible. The nearest quasars show red shifts that correspond to a speed relative to Earth of about $0.15c$ and speeds in excess of $0.93c$ have been measured for the most distant quasars. These are about $1.3 \times 10^{10}$ ly away from Earth. Since light has taken $1.3 \times 10^{10}$ y to reach Earth from these quasars, when studying them scientists are observing some of the earliest events in the creation of the Universe.

Quasars (quasi-stellar radio sources) are the brightest objects that have been observed. The most energetic quasars have a luminosity 1000 times greater than one of the brightest galaxies. The first quasars were discovered from their intense radio emissions (hence their name). However, most quasars discovered since emit visible or X-ray radiation and little or no energy in radio frequencies. Many dramatic images of quasars can be found on the internet.

The energy radiated is thought to be caused by a black hole at the centre of a galaxy. All galaxies are thought to have a black hole at their centres but, in the case of a quasar, the black hole is so massive that it absorbs the gaseous matter in the galaxy at an enormous rate. The gaseous matter reaches speeds close to the speed of light as it approaches the black hole and radiates huge amounts of X-ray, visible and radio radiation as it does so. This leads to the radiation from a relatively small region (about 1 ly across) in the centre of the galaxy being thousands of times greater than that from the rest of the galaxy.

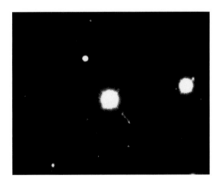

**Figure 5** *Quasar 3C273*

## Summary questions

1  A spectral line has a wavelength of 500 nm when viewed in a laboratory on Earth. Calculate the observed wavelength of this line in light from a galaxy moving at $5.0 \times 10^6$ m s$^{-1}$ away from Earth.

2  Assuming the Hubble constant to be 65 km s$^{-1}$ Mpc$^{-1}$, calculate, in Mpc, the distance between the galaxy in Question 1 and Earth.

3  What is a distance of 45 Mpc in a light years b metres?

4  Explain how quasars have been shown to be distant objects.

5  Why do scientists believe that dark matter exists?

**1** (a) Explain how the intensity of the radiation from a star is related to its luminosity. *(2 marks)*

    (b) **Figure 1** shows the black-body radiation curves for two stars, **X** and **Y**.

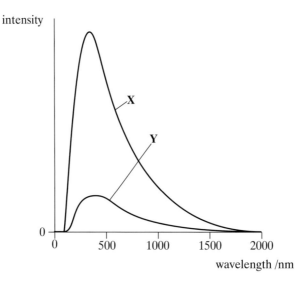

**Figure 1**

       (i) Star **X** is hotter than star **Y**. State **three** other differences between star **X** and star **Y**.

       (ii) Calculate the black-body temperature of star **X**. *(5 marks)*

    (c) The spectrum emitted by star **X** has dark lines across it.

       (i) Describe how these dark lines are produced in the spectrum of a star.

       (ii) Explain the significance of the dark lines to astronomers who are observing the spectra of light from distant galaxies. *(6 marks)*

**2** (a) State in words the Hubble law. *(2 marks)*

    (b) (i) A galaxy at a distance of $2.2 \times 10^{21}$ m is observed to be moving at a speed of $4.6 \times 10^{3}$ m s$^{-1}$ relative to the Earth.

         Calculate the Hubble constant in s$^{-1}$.

      (ii) Calculate the percentage change in the frequency of a spectral line emitted from the galaxy in part (b)(i) when observed on Earth, compared with the same line from a source at rest on the Earth. *(4 marks)*

    (c) State **two** properties of a star (other than its motion) that can be deduced from the study of its spectrum. *(2 marks)*

AQA, 2006

**3** (a) Sketch a Hertzsprung–Russell (H–R) diagram labelling the main sequence stars, dwarf stars and giant stars. Label the *x*-axis with the spectral classes. *(5 marks)*

    (b) On your H–R diagram, mark the present position of the Sun and indicate how it has evolved from its formation and how it will subsequently change to become a white dwarf. *(3 marks)*

**4** A square metre of the Moon's surface that is perpendicular to sunlight receives 1.4 kJ of energy every second from the Sun. Estimate the total energy radiated by the Sun every second assuming that the Sun acts as a point source.

       mean distance of the Moon from the Sun = $1.5 \times 10^{11}$ m *(3 marks)*

AQA, 2004

**5** **Figure 2** shows some of the allowed energy levels in a helium atom.

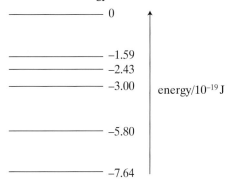

**Figure 2**

(a) (i) Identify the transition that corresponds to the lowest frequency of electromagnetic radiation for these levels.

(ii) Explain what happens in the helium atom when it emits this lowest frequency of electromagnetic radiation. *(4 marks)*

(b) Calculate the wavelength of this lowest frequency of radiation. *(3 marks)*

**6** A binary system is one in which two stars orbit each other bound together by gravitational attraction. One such binary system is 140 parsec from the Earth. Star X in the system belongs to spectral class A and star Y belongs to spectral class G. Each star has an apparent magnitude of 5.1.

(a) A change of 1 in magnitude changes the intensity by a factor of 2.51. Calculate the ratio of the intensity of one of the stars in the binary system to that of a first magnitude star. *(2 marks)*

(b) State and explain which is the hotter star. *(2 marks)*

(c) State and explain which is the smaller star. *(3 marks)*

AQA, 2004

**7** (a) The wavelength of a line in the hydrogen spectrum when measured in the laboratory is 656.28 nm. The same spectral line emitted by a galaxy moving relative to the Earth has a wavelength measured on Earth of 660.86 nm. Show that the galaxy is moving relative to the Earth at a speed of about 2100 km s$^{-1}$. *(3 marks)*

(b) The table gives relative velocities and distances from the Earth for four galaxies. Use these data to plot a suitable graph that will allow you to determine a value for the Hubble constant. *(4 marks)*

| galaxy | velocity/km s$^{-1}$ | distance/Mpc |
|--------|---------------------|--------------|
| A | 1600 | 25 |
| B | 2100 | 33 |
| C | 3500 | 54 |
| D | 4300 | 67 |

AQA, 2005

**8** (a) The Andromeda galaxy is $6.8 \times 10^5$ parsec from Earth.

Calculate the present separation in metres of the Andromeda galaxy from the Earth.

1 parsec $= 3.1 \times 10^{16}$ m *(1 mark)*

(b) A radio signal from atomic hydrogen at a wavelength of 211.121 mm is emitted by sources in the Andromeda galaxy.

Calculate the wavelength at which these will be detected on Earth if the galaxy is moving towards Earth at a speed of 110 km s$^{-1}$. *(2 marks)*

(c) There is a suggestion that Andromeda may collide with the Milky Way galaxy in the future. Estimate the time that will elapse before the collision. *(2 marks)*

## ▇ Unit 1: Harmony and structure in the Universe

### Module 1: The world of music

1    **Figures 1a and 1b** each show a ray of light incident on a water–air boundary. **A, B, C** and **D** show ray directions at the interface.

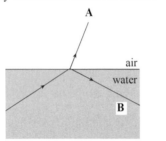

**Figure 1a**                **Figure 1b**

(a)  Which letter below corresponds to a direction in which a ray **cannot** occur?

    **A**       **B**       **C**       **D**

*(1 mark)*

(b)  Which letter below corresponds to the direction of the faintest ray?

    **A**       **B**       **C**       **D**

*(1 mark)*

AQA, 2004

2    **Figure 2** shows a hammer being struck against the end of a horizontal metal rod. A pulse of sound travels along the rod from where the hammer strikes it to the far end and back again. The sound pulse throws the hammer and rod apart when it returns. An electrical timing circuit measures the time for which the hammer and the rod are in contact.

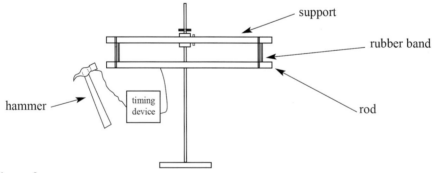

**Figure 2**

(a)  Which word below describes the type of wave that travels along the rod?

    **transverse**      **longitudinal**                *(1 mark)*

(b)  State the name of the effect that causes the sound pulse to return to the hammer.    *(1 mark)*

(c)  The rod is 0.45 m long and the time for which the hammer is in contact with the rod is $1.6 \times 10^{-4}$ s.

Calculate the speed of sound in the rod.                *(3 marks)*

AQA, 2004

3    **Figure 3** shows the Afristar satellite. Afristar orbits the Earth and is used to broadcast high-quality digital signals to parts of Africa. The area over which signals can be received is called the 'footprint' of the satellite.

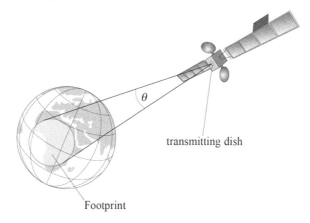

**Figure 3**

(a)  (i)   The satellite broadcasts at a frequency of 1.5 GHz. Calculate the wavelength of the transmitted signal.

speed of electromagnetic radiation, $c = 3.0 \times 10^8 \, \text{m s}^{-1}$

(ii)  The satellite is 36 000 km above the Earth's surface. The footprint of the satellite has an area of radius 3500 km. Calculate the angle, $\theta$, indicated on **Figure 3**, over which signals can be detected.

(iii) Use your answers to part (a) (i) and part (a) (ii) to calculate the maximum diameter of the transmitting dish that is required on the satellite. Assume that the edge of the footprint corresponds to the diffraction minimum.

(iv)  The radio signals are transmitted to the satellite from a ground station that also has a satellite dish. The station is 36 000 km from the satellite. Explain why this dish has a larger diameter than the dish on the satellite.    *(7 marks)*

(b)  The satellite uses *time division multiplexing* to transmit its multi-channel digital audio services. Explain what is meant by *time division multiplexing* and go on to suggest why the satellite uses this technique.    *(7 marks)*

AQA, 2004

4    **Figure 4** shows an arrangement of two loudspeakers used at a concert. The two loudspeakers act as *coherent sources* of sound.

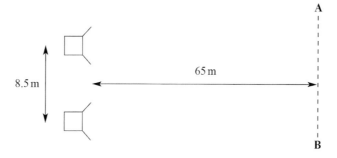

**Figure 4**

(a)  Explain what is meant by the term *coherent sources*.    *(2 marks)*

(b)  In **Figure 4,** the loudspeakers are separated by 8.5 m and are emitting sound of wavelength 0.77 m. A sound engineer is testing the loudspeaker arrangement. When the engineer walks along the line **AB**, 65 m from the loudspeakers, he observes a regular rise and fall in the sound intensity.

(i)   Explain this observation.

(ii)  Calculate the distance moved along **AB** between two consecutive maxima of sound.    *(4 marks)*

AQA, 2004

**5**  (a)  State the conditions necessary for a stationary wave to be produced.  *(3 marks)*

(b)  **Figure 5** shows a stationary wave on a stretched guitar string of length 0.62 m.

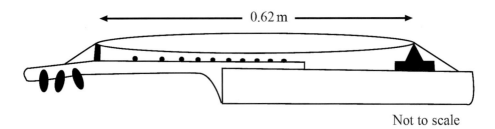

**Figure 5**

The speed of transverse waves along the string is 320 m s⁻¹.
Calculate the frequency of the note being played.  *(3 marks)*

AQA, 2004

**6**  **Figure 6** illustrates one way in which radio signals can be detected beyond the line of sight around the Earth's curvature.

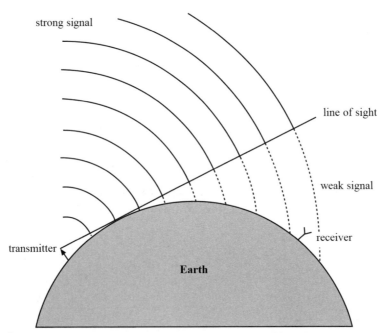

**Figure 6**

(a)  (i)  State the name of the process that allows the weak signal to spread beyond the line of sight.

(ii)  Explain why this effect is more noticeable with long-wave signals than it is with short wave signals.  *(3 marks)*

(b)  State **three** other ways in which telecommunications signals can reach areas beyond the horizon.  *(3 marks)*

AQA, 2005

7    **Figure 7** shows a digital signal input to a long copper cable.

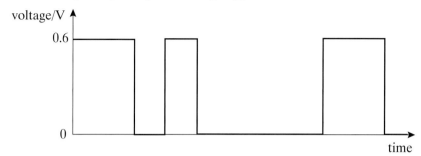

**Figure 7**

(a) (i)   Explain what aspect of **Figure 7** indicates that the signal is digital.

(ii)  State and explain **two** advantages of digital data transmission compared with analogue data transmission.    *(5 marks)*

(b) **Figure 8** shows the output signal at the end of a long copper cable.

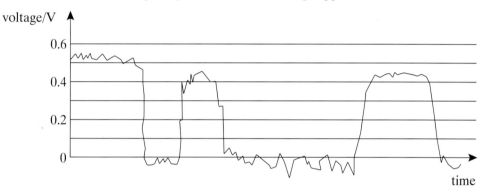

**Figure 8**

(i)   State and explain **two** reasons why the output signal differs from the input signal.

(ii)  Suggest the name of a transmission medium which overcomes these problems.

(iii) Despite the differences between the input and output signals, there may be no error in reading the output signal provided the sensitivity of the coding is appropriate. Choose appropriate voltage ranges to represent 0 and 1 in order to allow the output signal to be correctly read.    *(7 marks)*

AQA, 2001

8    **Figure 9** shows three particles in a medium that is transmitting a sound wave. Particles **A** and **C** are separated by one wavelength and particle **B** is half way between them when no sound is being transmitted.

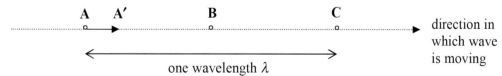

**Figure 9**

(a) Name the type of wave that is involved in the transmission of this sound.    *(1 mark)*

(b) At one instant, particle **A** is displaced to the point **A′** indicated by the tip of the arrow in **Figure 9**. Copy **Figure 9** and show the displacements of particles **B** and **C** at the same instant. Label the position **B′** and **C′** respectively.    *(1 mark)*

(c) Explain briefly how energy is transmitted in this sound wave.    *(2 marks)*

AQA, 2005

## Module 2: From quarks to quasars

**1**     Under certain conditions a γ photon may be converted into an electron and a positron.

    (a)   What is this process called?      *(1 mark)*

    (b)   Explain why there is a minimum energy of the γ photon for this conversion to take place and what happens when a γ photon has slightly more energy than this value.    *(2 marks)*

    (c)   Under suitable conditions, a γ photon may be converted into two other particles rather than an electron and positron.

        Give an example of the two other particles it could create.      *(1 mark)*

AQA, 2006

**2**     (a)   (i)   State the difference between the appearance of a continuous emission spectrum and that of a line emission spectrum.

        (ii)   State **one** laboratory source of a continuous spectrum.      *(2 marks)*

    (b)   The spectrum of the Sun consists of a continuous spectrum crossed by dark lines. State the name for this type of spectrum and explain how the dark lines arise.    *(4 marks)*

AQA, 2004

**3**     (a)   The table summarises the properties of five of the stars in the constellation of Cassiopeia.

| name | absolute magnitude | apparent magnitude | spectral class |
|------|--------------------|--------------------|----------------|
| Achird | 4.6 | 3.5 | G |
| Chaph | 1.9 | 2.3 | F |
| Ruchbah | 0.24 | 2.7 | A |
| Segin | –2.4 | 3.4 | B |
| Shedir | –0.9 | 2.2 | K |

        Explaining your answer in each case, state which star:

        (i)   is the hottest

        (ii)   is likely to appear orange in colour

        (iii) appears the brightest from Earth

        (iv) is less than 10 pc away from the Earth.      *(4 marks)*

    (b)   The constellation Cassiopeia contains another star with an apparent magnitude of 2.2, absolute magnitude of –4.6 and a surface temperature of 12 000 K. Calculate, for this star, the peak wavelength in its black-body radiation curve.    *(3 marks)*

AQA, 2005

**4**     (a)   A particle is made up from an anti-up quark and a down quark.

        (i)   Name the classification of particles that has this type of structure.

        (ii)   Find the charge on the particle.

        (iii) State the baryon number of the particle.      *(3 marks)*

    (b)   A suggested decay for the positive muon ($\mu^+$) is:

$$\mu^+ \longrightarrow e^+ + \nu_e$$

        Showing your reasoning clearly, deduce whether this decay satisfies the conservation rules that relate to baryon number, lepton number and charge.    *(3 marks)*

AQA, 2003

**5** It is believed that the Universe is expanding with the galaxies receding from each other. **Figure 1** shows some of the experimental data which support Hubble's Law. Each point on the scatter diagram represents a galaxy: $v$ is the recession speed of a galaxy and $d$ is its distance from Earth.

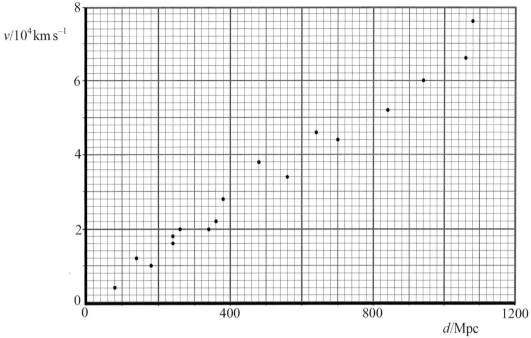

**Figure 1**

(a) Use the data in **Figure 1** to show that the Hubble constant $H$ is about $65\,\text{km s}^{-1}\,\text{Mpc}^{-1}$. *(3 marks)*

(b) A galaxy which can be seen in the constellation of Ursa Major has a recession speed of $17\,000\,\text{km s}^{-1}$. Calculate its distance from Earth in Mpc. *(2 marks)*

(c) An estimate for the age of the Universe can be found by assuming that recession speeds have been constant since the Big Bang. The age, $T$, of the Universe is given by the time it has taken for a given galaxy, travelling at speed $v$, to recede a distance $d$ from ours. Hence

$$T = \frac{d}{v} = \frac{1}{H}$$

Use the above equation to estimate the age of the Universe in years. *(3 marks)*

(d) The recession speed of a galaxy can be measured by comparing its emission spectral lines with those from an equivalent light source on Earth. Explain why this comparison enables the recession speed to be calculated and describe how the measurements are used to find the recession speed. *(6 marks)*

AQA, 2004

This unit consists of two topics which are highly relevant in the twenty-first century. On average, people have increased leisure time and a global economy has meant that long-distance travel is common place; however the feel-good factor is tainted by increasing concerns of diminishing energy resources and global warming. These issues are contextualised in the two topics: 'Moving people, people moving' and 'Energy and the environment.'

## Moving people, people moving

Through the contexts of transportation and sporting excellence, concepts based on statics and dynamics are studied. Much of the topic builds upon **force** and motion studied at GCSE and much of the terminology will be familiar to many students. A wide variety of sports are considered and analysed using the common threads of forces, **impulses**, **momentum**, **energy** changes and kinematics. Efficient, safe transportation provides the other main context in this topic. Ethical considerations in both sport and transportation provide a further important aspect of How science works.

## Energy and the environment

This topic builds upon **energy** considerations studied at GCSE and allows the development of arguments based upon the increased demand for energy internationally offset by the rapidly diminishing resources and the recognition of the harm that unharnessed use of **fossil fuels** is having on the planet. These arguments lead to a detailed study of 'cleaner' methods of generating **electricity** through the use of sources of **renewable energy**. The unit goes on to analyse the use of electrical energy in circuits and how energy can be used efficiently, including the benefits to be gained from the use of **superconductors**.

**What you already know:**

- Speed is distance travelled per unit time and velocity is speed in a given direction.

- The acceleration of an object is its rate of change of velocity.

- An object acted on by two equal and opposite forces is at rest or moves at constant velocity.

- When an object accelerates or decelerates:
  – the greater the resultant force acting on the object, the greater its acceleration
  – the greater the mass of the object, the less its acceleration.

- The gravitational field strength $g$ at any point is the force per unit mass on a small object due to the Earth's gravitational attraction on the object.

- The weight of an object in newtons = its mass in kilograms × $g$

- Work is done by a force when the force moves its point of application in the direction of the force.

- Energy exists in different forms and is measured in joules.

- Energy is transferred by a force when it does work.

- Energy cannot be created or destroyed; it can only be transformed from one form into other forms.

- Energy is eventually transferred to the surroundings, which become warmer.

- Efficiency of a device $= \dfrac{\text{useful energy transferred}}{\text{total energy supplied to the device}}$

- Power is the rate of transfer of energy.

- An electric current is a flow of charge round the circuit due to the movement of electrons.

- Electric current is measured in amperes (A) using an ammeter. Electric potential difference or voltage is measured in volts (V) using a voltmeter.

- For components in series, the current is the same in each component and the sum of the voltages across the components is equal to the total voltage.

- For components in parallel, the voltage is the same across each component and the sum of the currents through the components is equal to the total current.

- For resistors in series, the total resistance is equal to the sum of the individual resistances.

- For resistors in parallel, the current is greatest through the resistor with least resistance.

## 6.1   Record breakers

*Learning objectives:*

- What is the difference between scalar and vector quantities?

- Into which category do speed and velocity fit?

- How are vectors added and subtracted when they are in the same straight line?

*Specification reference: 3.2.1A*

### ■ Scalar and vector quantities

Physical quantities are the calculated or measured quantities that are used in physics. They are written as a number together with a unit. Quantities are subdivided into **scalars** and **vectors**. A scalar quantity is one which has no direction, simply having magnitude (size). A vector has both magnitude and a direction. Table 1 shows examples of scalars and vectors.

Scalars are treated as ordinary numbers when they are used in equations; special algebra is not needed. Vectors, however, do need to be treated differently and require vector algebra when adding or subtracting them.

### Describing a vector

A vector can be fully represented with a line of length proportional to the magnitude of the vector with an arrow that shows its direction. When more than one vector is drawn to add or subtract the same scale must be used for each vector on the diagram. So long as the direction of the vectors is kept the same it does not matter where they are moved to, it will not change the vector. This is very useful when vector quantities are to be added or subtracted.

### Vector quantities in the same straight line

Vectors that are in the same straight line are very easy to deal with; they can simply be added or subtracted depending upon their directions relative to each other (see Figures 1 and 2). They are added so that the tail of the second vector joins the head of the first. Subtraction is simply the addition of the negative vector (a vector of the same length but pointing in the opposite direction).

**Table 1** *Examples of scalar and vector quantities*

| scalars | vectors |
| --- | --- |
| distance | displacement (distance in a given direction) |
| time | velocity |
| mass | acceleration |
| speed | force |
| energy | weight |
| power | momentum |

### ■ Hint

To show vectors into or out of the plane of the page, the convention shown below is used. Here the dot represents the tip of the arrow coming out of the page towards you; the cross represents the tail or flight of the arrow going into the page and away from you.

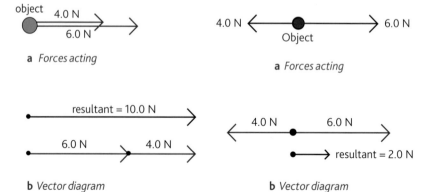

**a** *Forces acting*

**b** *Vector diagram*

**Figure 1** *Two forces acting in the same direction*

**a** *Forces acting*

**b** *Vector diagram*

**Figure 2** *Two forces acting in opposite directions*

## Head-winds and tail-winds

The wind can have a significant effect in athletics. Performances can be improved or worsened when the wind blows; although the order in which athletes finish is unlikely to be changed, the times are affected by the wind. The wind velocity will add to or subtract from the velocity of the athlete alone. This is an example of vector addition. In order for sprinting times and jumping lengths to be ratified as records, the International Athletics Federation rules that the wind speed cannot exceed $2.0\,\mathrm{m\,s^{-1}}$. Long distance events are not stopped by strong winds because runners go around a circular track which means the wind will both help and hinder the athletes meaning that its effect cancels out. Wind that blows in the same direction that the athlete is running is called a tail-wind whilst that blowing in the opposite direction is called a head-wind.

 How science works

### Changing the rules with javelins

Two key physical features of a javelin are its centre of gravity where the weight acts, and the centre of pressure, which is a point nearer the tail of the javelin where the aerodynamic forces of drag and lift can be considered to act. In 1986, the men's javelin world record was increased to beyond 104 m by Uwe Hohn. This length was beyond the capacity of some stadia and so the centre of gravity of the men's 800 g javelin was moved forward by a few centimetres in order to bring it down faster. In 1999, the women's 600 g javelin was modified in the same way. The distance javelins can be thrown is very dependent upon head-winds and tail-winds.

## Airspeed and ground speed

If you have travelled in a large aircraft you may have seen the graphic that shows the aircraft's speed and location relative to its flight path. The speed indicated may have been as much as 700 miles per hour $(313\,\mathrm{m\,s^{-1}})$ at times. At 35 000 ft (10 700 m) the cruise speed of large aircraft is about $250\,\mathrm{m\,s^{-1}}$, so where does the extra speed come from? The answer is a tail-wind. The graphic shows the ground speed of the plane. This is the vector sum of the plane's speed through the air (the airspeed) and the wind speed. So viewed on the Earth's surface the speed is $313\,\mathrm{m\,s^{-1}}$ but relative to the air (which is moving in the same direction as the plane in this case) the speed is $250\,\mathrm{m\,s^{-1}}$. If there is a head-wind this means that the ground speed will be reduced in the same way.

$$v_{\mathrm{ground}} = v_{\mathrm{air}} + v_{\mathrm{wind}}$$

This is vector addition and so the direction of these parallel vectors is crucial.

 Link

Cross-winds act at right angles to the way athletes are moving and have no effect on the forward motion of the athlete; this is because **vectors at right angles do not change one another**. As will be seen in Topic 6.2, vectors at right angles do produce a resultant vector and the athlete will waste energy in overcoming a cross-wind by trying to stay on the track.

How science works

**Have you flown supersonically?**

Speeds greater than the speed of sound are said to be supersonic. The speed of sound at 35 000 ft is just under $300\,\mathrm{m\,s^{-1}}$. So when you are flying at 35 000 ft with a tail-wind, are you flying supersonically? No; it is the speed with which you are flying relative to the airspeed and so this is still only $250\,\mathrm{m\,s^{-1}}$, well below the speed of sound.

### Summary questions

**1** Which of the following quantities are vectors and which are scalars?

  a Mass,

  b momentum,

  c pressure,

  d frequency,

  e gravitational field strength (or acceleration due to gravity),

  f velocity,

  g density.

**2** A javelin is released with a speed of $25\,\mathrm{m\,s^{-1}}$. With winds of $5\,\mathrm{m\,s^{-1}}$ what are the maximum and minimum velocities of the javelin?

**3** Explain the difference between airspeed and ground speed.

# 6.2 Going in the right direction

## Learning objectives:

- How can a scale drawing be used to add perpendicular vectors?

- How is the resultant of two perpendicular vectors calculated?

*Specification reference: 3.2.1A*

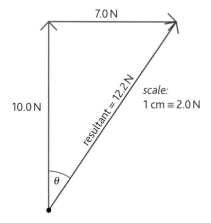

**Figure 1** *Adding two perpendicular vectors*

## Adding vectors using a scale diagram

Vectors can be added by drawing them head to tail; the tail of each vector begins where the head of the last one stopped (as shown in Figure 1). The **resultant** is the vector that joins the tail of the first vector to the head of the last vector. Its length and direction can then be measured using the same scale.

## Calculating the resultant of perpendicular vectors

Looking at Figure 1 again, it would be possible to calculate the value of the resultant vector by using Pythagoras' theorem. The resultant will be $\sqrt{(10.0^2 + 7.0^2)} = 12.2 \, \text{N}$ to 1 decimal place. However, the resultant vector is not complete unless its direction is also specified. The direction can be specified by giving the angle $\theta$ that the resultant makes with the 10.0 N force. This can be found by using the **tan** of the angle; $\tan \theta = $ opposite side of the triangle/adjacent side of the triangle $= \dfrac{7.0}{10}$ This means that $\theta = 35.0°$

### Try or no try?

In rugby it is one of a winger's main jobs to receive the ball close to the touch line and carry it as fast as possible to touch down over the goal line (see Figure 2). Opposing players moving towards the touch line will try to get in a position to tackle and take the winger over the touch line, preventing a try from being scored and gaining control of the lineout. Whether or not this is the case depends upon the two perpendicular forces. Ideally, for the winger, there will be sufficient distance to the touch line to prevent him being carried into touch, being able to cross over the goal line first.

**Figure 2** *Rugby tackle*

## Cross-winds and cross-currents

In many sports including athletics, sailing, rowing, rugby and American football the effect of cross-winds or cross-currents can affect the motion of athlete, boat or ball. Cross-winds are winds that act at right angles to the direction of movement. Similarly cross-currents flow at right angles to the direction of rowing or sailing, etc.

Imagine how a rower would be taken off course when a cross-current is flowing. Say a rower wishes to cross a wide river in a northerly direction but there is a cross-current flowing at $6.0\,\mathrm{m\,s^{-1}}$ from east to west. In what direction must the rower set off in order to reach the opposite bank at the right place? The rower can row at $10.0\,\mathrm{m\,s^{-1}}$ in still water.

To do this problem graphically:

1 Mark a north–south line.
2 Draw the current velocity vector of $6.0\,\mathrm{m\,s^{-1}}$ due west to a chosen scale with its tail on the north–south line.
3 Using a line representing the $10.0\,\mathrm{m\,s^{-1}}$ (drawn to the same scale), join the tail of the rower's velocity vector to the head of the current vector at an angle so that it meets the north–south line.
4 The resultant velocity vector is now in the north–south direction. The angle the rower must make is $\theta$ and his overall velocity relative to the riverbank will be proportional to the length of the resultant.

## Lift, weight, thrust and drag

There are four main forces acting on an aircraft in flight (see Figure 4). The lift acts upwards, the weight of the aircraft downwards, the thrust forwards and the drag backwards.

**Lift** is produced because of the shape of the aircraft's wing. The top surface of the wing is curved more than the bottom surface and so the air that flows over the top of the wing moves faster than that below the wing. The faster moving air produces less pressure above the wing than below it so there is a net upward force which is called lift.

**Thrust** is the driving force produced by the pull of a propeller or the push of a jet engine. A jet engine forces exhaust backwards (see Topic 8.3). These exhaust gases push the aircraft forward.

**Drag** is the resistive force of the air tending to slow an aircraft down. Thrust equals drag for an aircraft that is flying at a constant speed.

When climbing and accelerating forwards the lift must be bigger than the weight and the thrust bigger than the drag. The resultant of each of the pairs of forces therefore gives an overall upward force and an overall forward force. These two perpendicular force vectors can be combined using vector addition in the usual way. Of course when there is a resultant force acting on the plane its direction will change, causing it to climb. Aircraft cannot simply continue to increase the lift and the thrust so there comes a point when the aircraft is said to be at the maximum rate of climb.

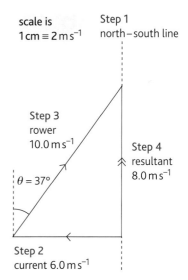

**Figure 3** Rower with cross-current

### AQA Examiner's tip

Be careful when drawing vector diagrams; vectors cannot be mixed up, so displacements or forces should not be included on velocity diagrams.

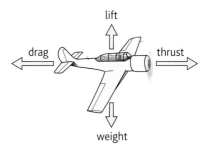

**Figure 4** Forces acting on a aircraft

### Summary questions

1 Explain how to add two vectors which are at right angles and how to calculate the resultant.

2 Draw a scale diagram to find the resultant of a velocity of $7.0\,\mathrm{m\,s^{-1}}$ at an angle of N 60°W added to a velocity of $8.8\,\mathrm{m\,s^{-1}}$ at an angle of N 22°E.

3 A light aircraft of weight $2.8 \times 10^4\,\mathrm{N}$ experiences a vertical lift of $3.6 \times 10^4\,\mathrm{N}$. The horizontal thrust provided by its propellers is $9.0 \times 10^3\,\mathrm{N}$ and the horizontal drag is $3.3 \times 10^3\,\mathrm{N}$. Calculate the angle with the horizontal that the aircraft makes.

# 6.3 Getting the angle

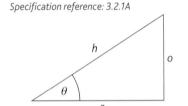

**Figure 1** *Sine and cosine*

## Review of sine and cosine

For a right-angled triangle the sine of an angle is given by the ratio of the opposite side to the hypotenuse of the triangle (*o/h*). Similarly the cosine of the angle is given by the ratio of the adjacent side to the hypotenuse of the triangle (*a/h*) (see Figure 1). This means that since $\sin\theta = o/h$ then $o = h \times \sin\theta$ and since $\cos\theta = a/h$ then $a = h \times \cos\theta$.

## Resolving velocities

In the reverse process of adding vectors, individual vectors can be split up into parts called components. The components are usually chosen to be at right angles to, and therefore independent of, each other. Figure 2 represents the velocity of an aircraft flying horizontally at $50\,\text{m s}^{-1}$ in a direction N 50°E. Using the trigonometric functions cosine and sine, this velocity can be split into an easterly component ($50\cos 40°$) and a northerly component ($50\sin 40°$).

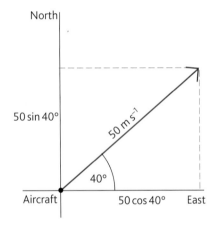

**Figure 2** *Components of flight velocity*

When a rugby player attempts to make a conversion, the ball will be kicked so that it leaves the kicker's boot with a particular speed in a particular direction. As will be seen in a later section, it is helpful to resolve the velocity into horizontal and vertical components. Figure 3 shows that for a ball starting with a velocity *v* at an angle $\theta$ with the horizontal the vertical component of *v* will be $v\sin\theta$ and the horizontal component $v\cos\theta$.

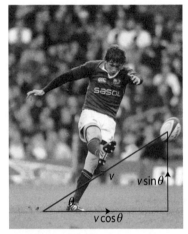

**Figure 3** *Components of initial velocity of rugby ball*

## Components of forces

Like velocities, forces can be resolved to give individual components. The next chapter will demonstrate how useful it is to be able to resolve forces in this way. Figure 4 shows a skier on a drag lift which pulls her up the mountain. The drag rope pulls her forwards and upwards as shown in the figure.

The tension in the tow rope performs two tasks: the horizontal component $T\cos\theta$ overcomes the horizontal friction holding her back; the vertical component $T\sin\theta$ overcomes her weight to make sure that she moves vertically. Of course the two effects are occurring at the same time so she doesn't just fly off into the air.

**Figure 4** *Skier on drag lift showing components of force on the tow rope*

## Free-body diagrams

When dealing with situations involving forces it is necessary to make sure that the analysis is simplified as much as possible. To do this a **free-body** diagram, which is a diagram showing the forces acting on only one object, is often drawn. Although this takes some getting used to, it is an essential skill that must be developed. The following rules are helpful:

- Only draw one body.
- Don't attempt to draw a three-dimensional representation of the body – it just gets confusing, a labelled box is sufficient although sometimes a bit more detail makes the diagram a little clearer.
- Do not mark in forces *and* their resultant.
- Label each force clearly, using the full name of the force not just a symbol (unless the symbols are clearly defined).
- Do not include forces and velocities on the same diagram.
- Be careful with tensions; they pull both objects to which they are attached but only the tension as a pull on the free-body should be marked.

### Forces shown on a free-body diagram

The forces that can be marked on a free-body diagram are limited to the following examples:

- Weight or the pull of gravity acting on the object.
- Tension if the object is being pulled by a string, rope or chain.
- Normal reaction when the object pushes against the ground or a wall etc., the ground or wall pushes back on the object (these are sometimes called perpendicular contact forces or support forces).
- Frictional or drag forces which act to oppose the object moving.
- Lift when the object is caused to move upward by aerodynamic forces.
- Upthrust when the object is displacing a gas or liquid.
- Thrust or driving force.

Figure 5 is a free-body diagram for a weight-lifter holding weights above his head. $P_1$ and $P_2$ are the push of the weights on his hands, $W$ is his own weight and $R_1$ and $R_2$ are the normal reactions of the floor on his feet.

### *Climber in chimney*

Figure 6 is a free-body diagram of a climber in a chimney. Remember it is only necessary to draw a free-body diagram not an artist's impression of the real situation.

Free-body diagrams will be considered again as part of the study of equilibrium in the next chapter.

**Figure 5** *Weight-lifter*

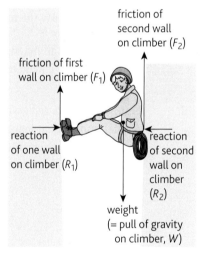

**Figure 6** *Free-body diagram for a climber*

### Summary questions

1  Draw a free-body diagram for a weight suspended by a string when **a** the weight is vertically below its support and **b** when the mid-point of the string is held to the side by a constant force.

2  Explain how to find the horizontal and vertical components of a tennis ball's velocity as it leaves the racket during a serve.

3  A light aircraft takes off at an angle of 8.0° with the horizontal with a thrust of 273 kN. Calculate the vertical thrust on the aircraft.

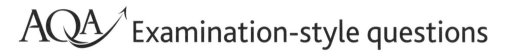

1 **Figure 1** shows the forces acting on a stationary kite. The force $F$ is the force that the air exerts on the kite.

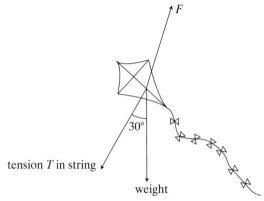

**Figure 1**

(a) Show on a diagram how force $F$ can be resolved into horizontal and vertical components. *(2 marks)*

(b) The magnitude of the tension, $T$, is 25 N.

Calculate:

(i) the horizontal component of the tension

(ii) the vertical component of the tension. *(2 marks)*

(c) (i) Calculate the magnitude of the vertical component of $F$ when the weight of the kite is 2.5 N.

(ii) State the magnitude of the horizontal component of $F$.

(iii) Hence calculate the magnitude of $F$. *(4 marks)*

AQA, 2002

2 **Figure 2** shows a river which flows from West to East at a constant velocity of $0.50\,\mathrm{m\,s^{-1}}$. A small motor boat leaves the south bank heading due North at $1.80\,\mathrm{m\,s^{-1}}$. Find, by scale drawing or otherwise, the resultant velocity of the boat. *(5 marks)*

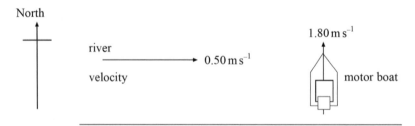

**Figure 2**

AQA, 2006

3 (a) A boat can be rowed at $6.5\,\mathrm{km\,h^{-1}}$ in still water. If it is rowed in a river where the current flows at a speed of $3\,\mathrm{km\,h^{-1}}$, what would be the speed of the boat relative to the river bank if it is rowed:

(i) downstream with the current?

(ii) upstream against the current? *(2 marks)*

(b) (i) The boat in part (a) is now rowed across the river. In what direction must it be steered if it is to travel directly across the river?

(ii) Calculate the resultant velocity of the boat relative to the river bank. *(5 marks)*

4  (a) (i) An aeroplane is at point A which is 80 km northwest of an airport and then later at point B, where it is 80 km northeast of the airport. What is the displacement of the aircraft from A to B?

      (ii) The aeroplane is now displaced 100 km **due north** of point B. What is the magnitude and direction of the displacement from the airport?  *(6 marks)*

5  Passengers A and B at an airport terminal use a moving walkway that is moving at a constant speed of $0.80 \, \text{m s}^{-1}$. Passenger B stands still on the walkway but passenger A walks along it at a speed of $1.2 \, \text{m s}^{-1}$ relative to passenger B. The walkway is 40 m long. Calculate:

      (i) how long passenger B takes to reach the end of the walkway

      (ii) how long it takes passenger A to reach the end of the walkway.  *(4 marks)*

6  **Figure 3** shows an arrow about to be released from a bow.

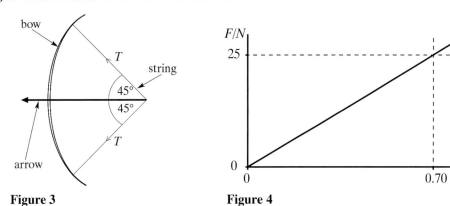

**Figure 3**          **Figure 4**

When the arrow is released the initial forward force on it is 25 N.

   (a) Find, by means of a calculation or scale drawing, the initial tension, $T$, in the string of the bow.  *(2 marks)*

   (b) The graph in **Figure 4** shows the variation of $F$ with $d$, where $F$ is the force on the arrow and $d$ is the distance the string is pulled back. Calculate the initial energy stored in the bow as the arrow is about to be released.  *(2 marks)*

   (c) Calculate the energy stored in the bow when the string is pulled back 0.60 m.  *(2 marks)*

AQA, 2005

7  **Figure 5** shows a ship being pulled along by cables attached to two tugs.

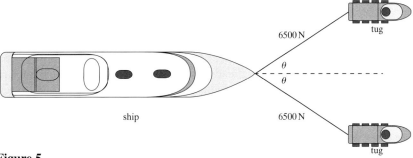

**Figure 5**

   (a) The tension in each cable is 6500 N and the ship is moving at a constant speed of $1.5 \, \text{m s}^{-1}$. When $\theta$ is equal to 35°, calculate:

      (i) the resultant force exerted on the ship by the cables,

      (ii) the work done by the tension in the cables in one minute.  *(4 marks)*

   (b) Explain why work done on the ship doesn't result in a gain in its kinetic energy.  *(2 marks)*

   (c) State and explain the initial effect on the ship if the angle $\theta$ is reduced while the tension in the cables remains constant.  *(3 marks)*

AQA, 2007

## 7.1 Keeping balanced

*Learning objectives:*

- What are the conditions for equilibrium of two or three forces acting through a point?

- How can the force necessary to keep an object in equilibrium be found by a scale drawing or calculation?

- How are the component forces calculated when an object is on a slope?

*Specification reference: 3.2.1B*

### 🛈 💡 ⚠ Forces in equilibrium

Figure 1a is a free-body diagram for an object **O** being pulled by three ropes. The tension in each of the ropes is given by $T_1$, $T_2$ and $T_3$. Adding $T_1$ to $T_2$ would give a resultant which would be equal to $T_3$ but in the opposite direction. This means that the three tensions cancel each other out and O is in **equilibrium**. When three forces are in equilibrium it means that they can be added together in order, making a closed triangle as shown in Figure 1b. In fact any closed polygon made up of a number of forces indicates the equilibrium of forces.

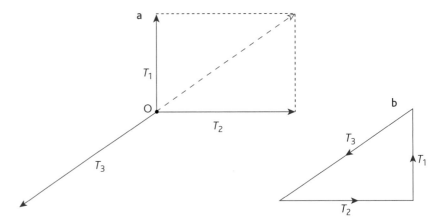

💡 **Figure 1** *(a) Three forces in equilibrium; (b) closed triangle of forces*

### Finding the force needed to ensure equilibrium

As already demonstrated forces can be found by completing a scale drawing or by calculation. In either case it is important to make a sketch of the forces already acting on the object before the force needed for the object to be in equilibrium can be identified. Figure 2 is a demonstration used to illustrate forces in equilibrium. The two weights $W_1$ and $W_2$ are attached to the ends of a string passing over two pulleys. A third weight $W_3$ is added to the middle area of the string and the system comes to rest and is therefore in equilibrium. $W_1$ produces tension $T_1$ in the string and $W_2$ produces tension $T_2$. Assuming the pulleys are friction free $W_1 = T_1$ and $W_2 = T_2$. The resultant of $T_1$ and $T_2$ can be found by drawing a scale diagram. Taking the example where $T_1 = 6.0\,N$ and $T_2 = 4.0\,N$, $\theta_1 = 29°$ and $\theta_2 = 47°$, Figure 3 shows how these tensions are added to give a resultant using a scale diagram.

In order to keep the string in equilibrium a third force must be present which is equal in magnitude and opposite in direction to the resultant. This is the weight $W_3$. It can be seen that the resultant has a magnitude of 8.0 N **upwards**. $W_3$ has magnitude 8.0 N but acts **downwards**.

### ⬛ Hint

Although this will not be examined, the question of whether an object pivoted with two equal forces acting in opposite directions would be in equilibrium may have arisen. The answer is 'no', it would rotate because a couple would be acting on it. In A2, rotational dynamics will be considered when **moments** or **torques** are investigated. For now it is sufficient to state that for an object to be in equilibrium the sum of the clockwise moments must equal the sum of the anticlockwise moments.

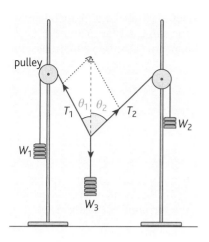

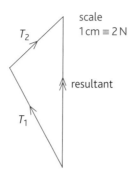

💡 **Figure 2** *Equilibrium demonstration*    💡 **Figure 3** *Addition of tension*

## How is equilibrium identified?

Objects in equilibrium will either be at rest or moving with a constant velocity. It will be shown later that objects obey Newton's law of motion and that an **unbalanced force** means that an object will accelerate.

## ▣ Equilibrium in sport

### Rock climber

Remember the climber in a chimney from Topic 6.3 (Figure 4). The horizontal forces on the rock climber must cancel out and so must the vertical forces. This means that:

$$F_1 + F_2 = W \text{ and } R_1 = R_2$$

### Downhill skier moving at constant velocity

Figure 5a shows the forces acting on a skier moving at constant speed down a slope. To analyse these forces a free-body diagram is drawn as shown in Figure 5b.

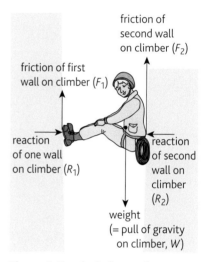

**Figure 4** *Free-body diagram for a climber*

💡 **Figure 5a** *Downhill skier*

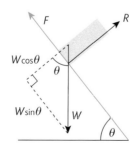

**b** *Free-body diagram for skier*

We can resolve the weight $W$ into components parallel and perpendicular to the slope. The component **parallel** to the slope is $W\sin\theta$ and the component **perpendicular** is $W\cos\theta$. This means that two equations can be written for the forces in the skier:

$$F = W\sin\theta \text{ and } R = W\cos\theta$$

By dividing the force equation by the reaction equation $W$ can be cancelled out and then $\dfrac{F}{R} = \tan\theta$

### Gymnast on rings

The exercise shown in Figure 6 requires immense strength and applies very large forces to the gymnast's muscles. For equilibrium, consider the horizontal and vertical forces. Resolving the tensions vertically gives:

$$T_1\cos\theta_1 + T_2\cos\theta_2 = mg$$

As the angles here are being measured from the vertical, the vertical components in this case are cosine and, furthermore, as the gymnast is not moving horizontally either then the sum of the horizontal components of the tension must cancel, so:

$$T_1\sin\theta_1 = T_2\sin\theta_2$$

**Figure 6** *Free-body diagram for a gymnast*

### Summary questions

1. a Draw a free-body diagram for a parachutist falling at constant speed.
   b Write an equation relating the vertical forces on the parachutist.

2. Two tug boats pull a ship so that it moves with a constant velocity. Each of the tugs produces a tension $T$ at an angle of 28° to the direction the ship is moving. The drag on the ship is 220 kN. Calculate $T$.

3. An object of mass 1.5 kg rests on a slope making an angle of 30° with the horizontal. Calculate:

   a the frictional force and

   b the normal reaction acting on the object. Gravitational field strength = 9.8 N kg⁻¹.

# 7.2 Reaching top speed and slowing down

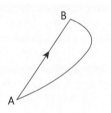

**Figure 1** *Velocity is different from speed*

## Velocity and acceleration

**Velocity** and **acceleration** are **vector** quantities. They can now be considered in more detail. Velocity is defined as the rate of change of **displacement** with time. This is normally written in equation form as

$v = \dfrac{\Delta s}{\Delta t}$ where $\Delta s$ is the change in displacement and $\Delta t$ is the change in time.

Figure 1 illustrates the difference between velocity and speed. Imagine an object moving along the curved path from **A** to **B**. The average speed is calculated by dividing the total distance travelled along the curved path by the time it takes. The average velocity is found by dividing the distance along the straight line **AB** by the time taken and its direction is that of the arrow. The magnitude of the average velocity will be smaller than the average speed. At any instant the speed or velocity might be changing and so this is why average values must be considered. When distances are measured in metres and times in seconds the speed or velocity will be in metres per second $(\mathrm{m\,s^{-1}})$.

Acceleration is defined as being the rate of change of velocity with time. This is normally written in equation form as $a = \dfrac{\Delta v}{\Delta t}$ where $\Delta v$ is the change in velocity and $\Delta t$ is the change in time.

When velocities are measured in metres per second and times in seconds the acceleration will be in metres per second squared $(\mathrm{m\,s^{-2}})$.

## Gradients and areas

Graphs are often effective ways of showing information and helping to analyse situations. The gradients of graphs and the areas below the line are particularly useful in studying motion.

For a distance or displacement–time graph, the area below the line has no physical meaning but the gradient will give the velocity. A negative gradient indicates that the object moves with a velocity in the opposite direction to the one chosen as being positive.

Speed–time graphs provide even more information since the area below the line gives the distance travelled and the gradient gives the acceleration.

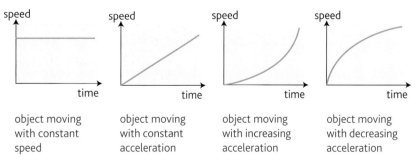

**Figure 2** *Speed–time graphs*

Figure 2 shows four speed–time graphs. When the gradient does not change, as in the first two graphs, it is fairly straightforward to calculate the area under the graph (using base × height for a rectangle or ½ base × height for a triangle – other regular shapes can be broken down into triangles and rectangles). When the graph is not linear the area must be estimated. This is easiest on graph paper where the area of one square can be calculated and then multiplied by the number of squares under the graph; of course this technique works for regular shapes too, if the formula has been forgotten. Negative gradients indicate that the object is decelerating.

## ▦ ◭ 🐥 Equations of motion

These equations apply to objects experiencing a constant acceleration such as that of gravity close to the Earth. Each equation contains four of the five quantities: distance or displacement ($s$), initial speed or velocity ($u$), final speed or velocity ($v$), acceleration ($a$) and time ($t$). Provided three of the four quantities are known the missing one can be calculated by using just one equation. When two of the quantities are unknown two of the equations are required to find the missing quantities. The equations of motion are listed below and are included in the data and formulae booklet supplied in the examinations.

$$v = u + at$$

$$v^2 = u^2 + 2as$$

$$s = \frac{(u + v)t}{2}$$

$$s = ut + \frac{1}{2}at^2$$

### Acceleration of cars

Table 1 shows the 'acceleration' of some pretty impressive cars. In off-road tests the cars were accelerated from a standing start up to 60, 100 and 120 miles per hour (60 mph = 26.8 m s$^{-1}$, 100 mph = 44.7 m s$^{-1}$). The data are given as a series of times, from which the average acceleration can be calculated by dividing the top speed by the time taken to reach it. It is evident from the data that the acceleration is not constant. As the cars go faster the drag increases, reducing the acceleration as the driving force is fixed at a constant value. Giving information in this form helps potential buyers to compare one car with another; such tests need to be completed under the same conditions of road surface, wind speed, incline, etc.

**Table 1** *Acceleration data*

| | Acceleration (seconds) | | | | | |
| | mph | | | | Top gear (mph) | |
| | 0–60 | 0–100 | 0–120 | Rolling 5–50 mph | 30–50 | 50–70 |
|---|---|---|---|---|---|---|
| car A | 6.5 | 16.5 | 25.8 | 7.2 | 3.4 | 4.8 |
| car B | 5.4 | 13.7 | 19.7 | 6.0 | 2.9 | 3.4 |
| car C | 6.1 | 14.0 | 20.7 | 6.3 | 3.2 | 3.8 |

## Stopping distances

Figure 3 is taken from the UK Highway Code and shows thinking and braking distances. The distance travelled between a driver seeing something necessitating braking and starting to brake is the **thinking distance**. The distance travelled while braking is the **braking distance**. These distances added together make the stopping distance.

The braking distance is affected by speed, efficiency of brakes, tyre and road conditions – assuming that the car has been properly serviced with good brakes and tyres, the only thing that can be done to reduce this is to reduce the speed. Thinking distance depends upon the driver; consumption of alcohol or other drugs, tiredness, using a mobile telephone or otherwise being distracted all increase the driver's thinking distance (which of course also depends on speed, since distance travelled = average speed × 'time to think').

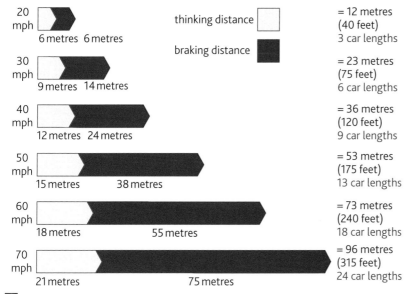

**Figure 3** *Thinking and braking distance Source: UK Highway Code. Crown copyright material is reproduced by permission of the Controller of HMSO.*

### How science works

#### THINK! Road safety

On 27 February 2007 legislation to increase the penalty for using a hand-held phone while driving came into force. The previous fine of £30 was increased to £60 with three penalty points going on the driver's licence. The Department of Transport reported '... Penalty points can mean higher insurance costs. If you get six points within two years of passing your test, your licence will be revoked and you will need to re-sit the test. If the case goes to court, you could risk a maximum fine of £1,000, which rises to £2,500 for the driver of a bus, coach, or heavy goods vehicle ...' These views were informed by the Direct Line Mobile Phone Report 2002 in which the conclusions were that the 'principal hazard of phone use while driving is that it distracts the driver, taking their attention away from the task of driving ... the distraction caused by making or receiving a call can be visual, auditory, mental (cognitive) or physical (biomechanical). The use of mobile phones often involves more than one form of distraction at any one time. A hand-held mobile phone call for instance, could involve all four forms of distractions at the same time.'

### Summary questions

1  Draw a velocity–time graph showing constant acceleration from 0 to 10 m s⁻¹ for 5 s, followed by constant deceleration back to 0 taking a further 10 s. From the graph calculate the total distance travelled.

2  Explain why the stopping distance when travelling at 60 mph is 73 m but only 23 m at half that speed. Calculate the driver's reaction time assumed in the Highway Code.

3  A cyclist travelling at 8.2 m s⁻¹ brakes steadily, coming to rest in 3.5 s. Calculate the cyclist's deceleration and the distance she travels in the time between braking and stopping.

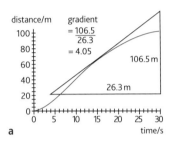

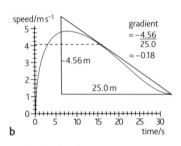

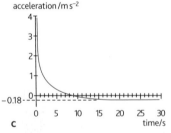

**Figure 1** *Motion of cyclist*

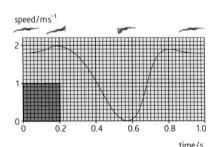

**Figure 2** *Swimming the breast-stroke*

## Using graphs

As has been shown, graphs represent a convenient way to illustrate motion. The motion of athletes or vehicles rarely changes in a regular way and so graphs provide a very useful tool to help with the analysis of motion. Figure 1a is a graph representing the distance travelled by a cyclist over time of 30 s on quite a steep hill. The graph is not a straight line and therefore has a varying gradient. In order to calculate the speed of the cyclist at any instant, the gradient of the tangent to the curve at that moment in time must be found. An example is shown at 15 s. The gradient here shows that the speed is just over $4\,\mathrm{m\,s^{-1}}$. By doing this process for a series of points on the curve (or using a computer package to analyse the curve) the speed–time graph shown as Figure 1b can be generated. The gradient of the tangent to a distance–time curve at a point gives the instantaneous speed at that time.

By calculating the gradients of tangents to the speed–time graph a series of instantaneous accelerations can be found and these can be plotted. Calculating the gradient at 15 s gives a deceleration of just under $-0.2\,\mathrm{m\,s^{-2}}$. By finding the gradients at a series of time points, the acceleration–time graph shown in Figure 1c can be produced. Remember that negative gradients give decelerations; these are shown below the axis.

### The story board

The series of graphs relating to the motion of the cyclist tell the story of the cyclist's motion. As it is known that the cyclist is on a hill and starts from rest it can be seen that the acceleration to start with is very large but gets less, either because the cyclist becomes more tired or the effect of the hill takes its toll. After about 9 s the cyclist starts to decelerate shown by the speed–time graph falling and the gradient (and acceleration) becoming negative. As the cyclist slows the extra distance travelled per second decreases.

### Using areas

The use of the area under a graph is an alternative way of working to that of using gradients. Here it is important to start with the acceleration graph. If an object starts from rest the speed at any time can be found by calculating the area up to that time. A force–time graph can also be used, but here the area under the graph needs to be divided by the value of the accelerated mass to obtain the change in speed. From the speed–time graph, the area under the graph gives the distance travelled.

Figure 2 shows the velocity–time graph for a swimmer making one complete breast-stroke. The area under the graph gives the distance travelled. The shaded squares represent a distance of 0.2 m. Estimating the number of these squares gives a good approximation to the total distance travelled. Check that there are approximately seven of these squares between the line and the time axis and so the distance travelled in one stroke is about 1.4 m.

### The reverse processes

Working from a distance (or displacement) against a time graph the speeds (or velocities) at various times can be found by calculating the gradients of the tangents to the curve at these points. From a reasonable number of speeds a speed–time graph can be plotted and the gradients of the tangents to this graph will give accelerations. If starting with an acceleration–time graph, finding the areas between the curve and the time axis for a range of time intervals would give the velocity change over the whole time interval. A velocity–time graph could be drawn and the areas under this would give values for the distance travelled in each time interval.

## ⁊ When is knowledge of the average value useful?

Looking at the speedometer on a car will give a value of the instantaneous speed of the car or at least the average speed over a very short time. Over the course of a complete journey the details of the time likely to be spent in a traffic queue or the likelihood of meeting every traffic light on red is not taken into account when researching a journey on a 'route-finder' on the internet or by using global positioning satellite (GPS) software. Some speed cameras work by calculating an instantaneous speed using a radar or laser beam; others work by timing vehicles over a fixed distance and calculating an average speed.

### How science works

**Speed or safety cameras?**

There is little question that the presence of the cameras alternatively called 'speed cameras' or 'safety cameras' has an impact on the speed at which drivers travel. A quick internet search will show that there are a considerable number of pressure groups who question the effectiveness of such devices … with emotive statements such as 'Speed on its own does not kill, it's the inappropriate use of speed that kills; something the government seems to have forgotten as the rate of fatalities in road accidents increases, due partly to the decrease in the number of traffic police on duty as the funds are diverted to increase in the number of cameras. Cameras can't catch the careless or dangerous driver, the drugged or drunk driver, the aggressive driver of the poorly maintained vehicle; speed cameras are more revenue generating than you and I are led to believe.' The Government argues that the presence of safety cameras does control the speed on roads where traffic accidents are common place and this is the reason that they are installed.

### How science works

**Scientific models**

In physics, situations are often simplified in order to make them easier to understand; this is called scientific modelling. Calculating the gradients of tangents to curves, estimating areas and using the equations of motion are all examples of scientific models. A good scientific model is one which can help to explain what has already been seen to happen but can also make an accurate prediction of what might happen in a situation before it occurs.

## Summary questions

**1** A displacement against time graph for the motion of a 1500 m runner is provided. Explain how to draw an acceleration–time graph for the runner.

**2** a Find the acceleration after 5 s for the motion in Figure 3a.

   b Calculate the distance travelled in the first 20 s of the motion of Figure 3b.

**3** Suggest why it is very difficult to measure instantaneous speed.

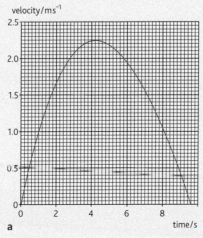

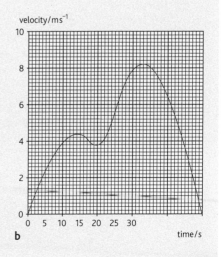

a

b

**Figure 3**

# AQA Examination-style questions

**1** Athlete A, competing in a 100 m race, crosses the finish line in a time of 10.2 s. At the start, the athlete accelerates uniformly to a top speed in 2.0 s and then remains at a constant speed for the remainder of the race.

(a) Calculate:

(i) the average speed of the athlete over the full distance,

(ii) the maximum speed of the athlete if the acceleration were $5.4 \, \text{m s}^{-2}$,

(iii) the distance travelled by the athlete whilst accelerating. *(4 marks)*

(b) **Figure 1** is a speed–time graph for athlete B in the same race. Using the **same** axes, draw a speed–time graph for athlete A. *(3 marks)*

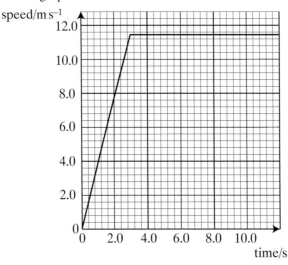

**Figure 1**

(c) Some time after the start of the race the two athletes are running at the same speed. Use your graph to determine:

(i) the time at which this occurs,

(ii) the distance covered by the athletes up to this time,

(iii) how far apart the athletes are at this time. *(4 marks)*

AQA, 2001

**2** (a) A skier of mass 72 kg skis down a slope which makes an angle of 32° to the horizontal. Calculate:

(i) the component of the skier's weight acting parallel to the slope,

(ii) the component of the skier's weight at right angles to the slope. *(3 marks)*

(b) (i) The skier in part (a) moves down the slope at constant velocity. State the total frictional force acting on the skier.

(ii) The angle of the slope increases to 34°. Calculate the initial acceleration of the skier. *(4 marks)*

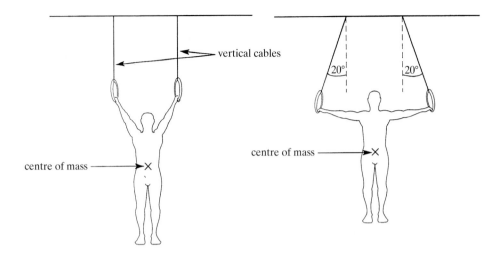

**Figure 2**                                        **Figure 3**

3    **Figure 2** shows a gymnast of weight 720 N hanging centrally from two rings, each
     attached to cables which hang vertically.

     (a)  State the tension in each cable.                                      *(1 mark)*

     (b)  **Figure 3** shows the gymnast after he has raised his body so that his centre of mass
          moves through a vertical distance of 0.60 m.

          Calculate:

          (i)   the increase in gravitational potential energy of the gymnast

          (ii)  the tension in each cable.                                      *(4 marks)*

                                                                          AQA, 2001

4    (a)  A parachutist jumps out of a plane and initially falls freely with negligible air
          resistance. As his speed increases so does air resistance until he reaches a terminal velocity.

          (i)   Sketch a velocity–time graph for the parachutist and explain the main
                features of the graph.

          (ii)  State and explain how the resultant force acting on the parachutist changes
                as he falls.                                                    *(9 marks)*

     (b)  (i)   The parachutist in part (a) has a weight of 720 N. Calculate the resultant
                force on the parachutist when he is travelling at a velocity of 24 m s$^{-1}$ with an
                acceleration of 4.5 m s$^{-2}$.

          (ii)  Calculate the force of air resistance on the parachutist when his acceleration
                is 4.5 m s$^{-2}$.

          (iii) Estimate the terminal velocity of the parachutist if the force of air resistance
                is proportional to the square of his velocity.                  *(6 marks)*

5    (a)  A balloonist is rising at a constant vertical velocity of 6.0 m s$^{-1}$. She drops a coin
          from the balloon when she is at a height of 30 m above the ground. Calculate:

          (i)   the speed of the coin as it hits the ground,

          (ii)  the time it takes for the coin to reach the ground,

          (iii) the maximum height of the coin.                                *(8 marks)*

     (b)  Another balloonist is rising at velocity which has a vertical component of 6.0 m s$^{-1}$
          and a horizontal component of 2.0 m s$^{-1}$. She also drops a coin when the balloon
          is 30 m above the ground. State and explain which of the quantities calculated in
          part (a) would be the same and which would be different.             *(6 marks)*

## 8.1 Diving

**Figure 1** *Diver*

### Diving or jumping?

Diving is the sport of performing acrobatics whilst jumping or falling into water from a platform or springboard (see Figure 1). The mechanics of diving are quite complex and involve putting twists and turns into the motion. However, the simple act of jumping into the water is relatively straightforward to analyse as it is simply an example of a body in **free-fall**. In this section the motion of a diver diving vertically up and down is considered; although in reality without some horizontal motion the diver would hit the diving board on his return. In Topic 8.2 horizontal motion will be taken into account.

### Motion under gravity

Galileo Galilei is often considered to be the first scientist to appreciate that, neglecting the effect of air resistance, all objects in free-fall close to the Earth's surface accelerate vertically downwards with the same acceleration of $9.8\,\mathrm{m\,s^{-2}}$. Neglecting air resistance gives a fairly good approximation to reality for large objects which travel relatively slowly (such as a shot-putt, or a basketball) but it becomes a poor approximation for small objects which travel relatively rapidly (for example, a driven golf-ball or a bullet fired from a rifle).

### How science works

#### Is the acceleration of gravity really constant on the Earth's surface?

The answer to this is 'no'. The average value is around $9.81\,\mathrm{m\,s^{-2}}$ but it does vary from place to place on the Earth. The factors affecting the value of g on Earth include the latitude and height above sea level. In going upwards from the sea level, distance from the centre of the Earth increases and the attraction back to Earth (weight) becomes less. The dependence on latitude is the result of the Earth's rotation. Table 1 shows the acceleration due to gravity for a few places:

**Table 1** *Gravity at different locations*

| location | latitude | height above sea level /m | $g\ /\mathrm{ms^{-2}}$ |
|---|---|---|---|
| North pole | 90°N | 0 | 9.832 |
| Equator | 0°N | 0 | 9.789 |
| Mount Everest | 28°N | 8848 | 9.764 |

### Newton's second law of motion and gravity

Newton's second law of motion is often summarised by the equation $F = ma$ (force = mass × acceleration). This implies that an object of larger mass might be expected to experience a larger force due to gravity

than one of smaller mass. This is the case but the mass of the larger object also means that it has a greater inertia (reluctance to change in motion) and this greater inertia cancels out the effect of the larger force making the ratio $F/m$ (or acceleration) constant. Figure 2 illustrates the *guinea and feather* demonstration in which the guinea (an old British coin) and the feather are placed in a tube from which all the air has been removed (evacuated). Both guinea and feather fall at the same rate when the evacuated tube is inverted. When air is allowed back into the tube the air resistance acts on the feather far more than on the coin and so the feather accelerates far less than the guinea. **For an object in free-fall the only force acting on it is the force of gravity.** The application of Newton's second law of motion to a diver tells us that at the speeds experienced by the diver, whereby air resistance is not significant, the mass of the diver makes no difference to his acceleration.

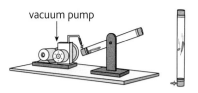

**Figure 2** *Guinea and feather demonstration*

## Equations of motion under gravity

The equations of motion apply to motion under gravity. The acceleration term $a$ is usually replaced by the symbol $g$ but otherwise the equations are identical to those studied in Topic 7.2.

$$v = u + at \quad \text{becomes} \quad v = u + gt$$

$$v^2 = u^2 + 2as \quad \text{becomes} \quad v^2 = u^2 + 2gs$$

$$s = \frac{(v + u)t}{2} \quad \text{stays as it is}$$

$$s = ut + \tfrac{1}{2}at^2 \quad \text{becomes} \quad s = ut + \tfrac{1}{2}gt^2$$

### Motion under gravity graphs for the diver

Figure 3a shows the variation of acceleration with time. Again neglecting air resistance yields a graph in which there is no variation with time. Taking downwards as negative so the diver has a constant negative acceleration which does not vary in upward or downward motion, Figure 3b shows how the velocity changes with time for the same motion. The velocity of the diver is positive as he goes up and negative as he goes down. The gradient of this graph gives the acceleration and so is constantly negative irrespective of upward or downward motion (the direction of the velocity cannot be obtained from the acceleration graph but its magnitude can be). Figure 3c shows how the diver's displacement changes with time. This shape is a parabola and indicates that in equal intervals of time the diver gains height more gradually until he stops and then loses height more rapidly until he reaches the same level as the diving board and then goes below it.

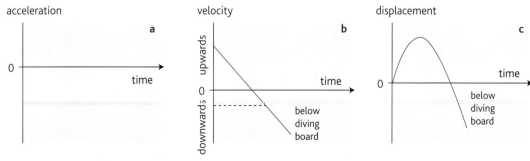

**Figure 3** *Motion under gravity graphs*

Providing air resistance can be neglected, the motion of an object in free-fall is symmetrical. If a diver jumps upwards from a board at a certain velocity, by the time he returns to the level of the board he will be moving with his initial speed but in the opposite direction. In the same way, the time taken to reach his maximum height will be the same as the time taken to fall from that height to the level of the diving board.

### ■ Link

We have seen that close to the surface of the Earth (up to about 20 km from the Earth's surface) the gravitational field strength is approximately constant. Further from the Earth $9.8\,N\,kg^{-1}$ cannot be used because the gravitational field strength falls off rapidly (as an inverse square law relationship, like intensity as described in Topic 1.4). This will be studied during the A2 course.

## ⓘ Acceleration of free-fall or gravitational field strength?

'Gravitational field strength' is a term used to express the magnitude of the force of gravity action on a mass of 1 kg. Since $F = ma$ then $F/m = a$; so $a$ will be the acceleration of free-fall and have units $m\,s^{-2}$ as has already been shown. However, $F/m$ is also the gravitational field strength and has units of $N\,kg^{-1}$. **Gravitational field strength** $(9.8\,N\,kg^{-1})$ is used for forces on an object and **acceleration of free-fall** $(9.8\,m\,s^{-2})$ is used when dealing with the motion of objects. They are equivalent quantities.

### Summary questions

1. A diver jumps from a 3.0 m board (the height of the board above the water) with an initial upward velocity of $4.0\,m\,s^{-1}$. Taking the acceleration of gravity to be $9.8\,m\,s^{-2}$, calculate:

   a  the maximum height of the diver's jump,

   b  the diver's velocity at the water surface,

   c  the time for which the diver is in the air.

2. Taking downwards as being positive, sketch graphs to show the variation of displacement, velocity and acceleration for a ball thrown vertically. What assumptions are made?

3. Weight = $mg$. Explain whether or not an object in free-fall is weightless.

# 8.2  Ski jumping

*Learning objectives:*

- How is the motion on the slope analysed?

- What is the path of an object when projected?

- What is meant by the independence of two motions at right angles?

*Specification reference: 3.2.1D*

## 💡 🔢 The sport of ski jumping

Ski jumping (see Figure 1) is a winter sport performed on snow in which athletes ski down a snow-covered track which eventually curves upwards as a take-off ramp. The aim of the sport is to travel the greatest horizontal distance. The hills can be up to 130 m high and distances well in excess of 200 m are possible. The aerodynamics of the skis (long and wide) helps the jumper to stay in the air rather than falling under gravity. In our analysis of ski jumping, air resistance is ignored.

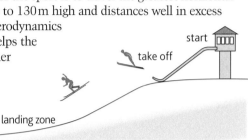

**Figure 1** *Ski jumping – the hill*

## Perpendicular motions

As shown in Topic 2.1, perpendicular vectors have no effect on each other; they are independent of each other. This is the case with velocities. In analysing the motion of a ski jumper, the vertical and horizontal motions can be considered as being independent. This is true for anything moving in this way (known as a **projectile**). The vertical motion is subjected to the acceleration of free-fall as shown in the last section. The horizontal motion is one of constant velocity (if air resistance is neglected). By considering the two motions independently in this way it is possible to cope with quite complex projectile motion.

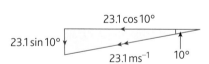

**Figure 2** *Skier's velocity resolved*

*Worked example:*

A ski jumper leaves the ramp at the end of a hill at an angle of 10° below the horizontal with a speed of 23.1 m s$^{-1}$. The skier travels a horizontal distance of 109 m, so how far will the skier have dropped vertically? (Measurements give a distance of 54 m for this). Figure 2 shows how to resolve the skier's velocity into horizontal and vertical components.

The horizontal component of the initial velocity is $23.1 \cos 10°$ and the vertical component is $23.1 \sin 10°$. For the calculation, downwards has been chosen as being the positive vertical direction, and to the left as the positive horizontal direction.

For the **horizontal motion** the velocity is unchanged since gravity only affects the vertical motion, so the initial and final velocity ($u$ and $v$) are each $= 23.1 \cos 10°$ ($= 22.7$ m s$^{-1}$), the distance travelled ($s$) is 109 m.

Using $s = ut + \frac{1}{2}at^2$ and as $a = 0$ gives $s = ut$ so $t = \dfrac{s}{u} = \dfrac{109}{22.7}$ or 4.8 s
This is the time the skier is in the air.

For the **vertical motion** the initial velocity ($u$) $= +23.1 \sin 10°$ ($= 4.01$ m s$^{-1}$), the vertical acceleration $= +9.8$ m s$^{-2}$ and the time taken is 4.8 s.

Using $s = ut + \frac{1}{2}gt^2$ for this component gives

$$s = 4.01 \times 4.8 + \tfrac{1}{2} \times 9.8 \times 4.8^2 = 133 \text{ m}$$

When compared with the measured value of 54 m, this shows that the lift generated by the skis must very significant and that the net downward

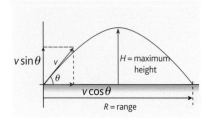

💡 **Figure 3** *Parabolic trajectory*

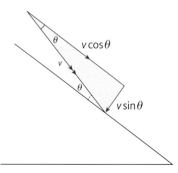

**Figure 4** *Ski jumper landing on slope*

## Summary questions

**1** Draw graphs to show how the height, velocity and acceleration of a projectile vary with time. Ignore air resistance.

**2** Suggest how having a ski jump hill curved as in **Figure 1** both increases the length of jump and protects the ski jumper from injury on landing.

**3** A shot putter releases a shot from a height of 2.1 m with a speed of $13.5\,\text{m s}^{-1}$ at an angle of 40° to the horizontal. Calculate:

  **a** the maximum height above the ground that the shot reaches,

  **b** the time to reach the maximum height,

  **c** the total time that the shot is in the air, and

  **d** the range of the shot. ($g = 9.8\,\text{m s}^{-2}$, ignore air resistance).

acceleration is only about $3.0\,\text{m s}^{-2}$ (calculating a value for $g$ by substituting $s = 54\,\text{m}$ into $s = ut + \frac{1}{2}gt^2$)

## ■ Ramps at different angles

If a ramp that projected the ski jumper steeply upwards were to be used, the jumper could travel further horizontally but this would be unsafe as shown in Topic 8.3. In contrast freestyle aerial skiers use ramps with positive gradients to give them the height that they need to perform tricks.

Assuming that the aerial skier moves at a much slower speed than the ski jumper, let's say $10.0\,\text{m s}^{-1}$, and takes off a ramp at an angle of 45°, what is the range of the skier when landing on a flat surface?

Neglecting the effect of air resistance, the skier will undergo a perfectly parabolic **trajectory** (path of a projectile) as shown in Figure 3.

Consider the **vertical motion** first and take upwards as positive, the initial velocity $u = 10.0 \sin 45°$ and because the motion is symmetrical the final velocity $v = -10.0 \sin 45°$, the acceleration $a = -9.8\,\text{m s}^{-2}$

Using the equation $v = u + at$ gives $-10.0 \sin 45° = 10.0 \sin 45° - 9.8t$

This means that the time $t = \dfrac{-20.0 \sin 45°}{-9.8} = 1.44\,\text{s}$

Now looking at the **horizontal motion,** the velocity is unchanged at $10.0 \cos 45°$ for a time of $1.44\,\text{s}$.

Using the equation $s = ut + \frac{1}{2}at^2$, as $a = 0$,

$s = ut = 10.0 \cos 45° \times 1.44 = 10.2\,\text{m}$

By substituting for different values of $\theta$ it should be possible to convince everyone that $10.2\,\text{m}$ is the maximum range for an aerial skier moving at $10\,\text{m s}^{-1}$.

## ■ Why is the landing hill made to slope?

In Figure 1 it can be seen that the landing hill is curved. This means that the jumper is rarely more than a few metres above the hill; the impact on the jumper is therefore surprisingly small – equivalent to a vertical drop of less than a metre. The reason for this is that in landing on a sloping surface there is little reaction force acting to stop the skier from moving (it is the reaction that is equal and opposite to weight). In Figure 4 the skier is landing with a velocity $v$ at an angle $\theta$ to the landing slope. Resolving the skier's velocity into components parallel and perpendicular to the slope gives $v \cos \theta$ and $v \sin \theta$, respectively. The component parallel to the slope is unchanged by the jumper hitting the slope but the component perpendicular to the slope must be brought to zero by the reaction force acting on the jumper; by making $\theta$ small, $\sin \theta$ and $v \sin \theta$ are small and so the force felt by the skier is very gentle. This is why the ski jumper's trajectory must be nearly matched by that of the slope, a much larger value of $\theta$ and $v \sin \theta$ would mean a much greater reaction force would be needed to bring the perpendicular component to zero.

## ■ Other 'projectile' sports

A significant number of sports involve throwing or kicking a projectile into the air. Examples of such projectiles are rugby drop goals, discus and the golfer's chip shot. In each of these sports the trajectory can always be analysed by considering the horizontal and vertical motions to be independent of each other.

The effects of changing forces

*Learning objectives:*

- What are the effects of frictional forces?
- What is meant by terminal velocity?
- How do objects reach terminal velocity?

*Specification reference: 3.2.1D*

## Frictional forces

Whenever two surfaces rub against each other, frictional forces act to oppose their motion. Friction between rough surfaces can be explained by considering the microscopic bumps and hollows in the surfaces (called **asperities**); these asperities mean that there are only a limited number of points of 'contact' and it is here that the surfaces bind on one another when a force is applied. Experiments show that the frictional force increases as the normal reaction between the surfaces is increased; increasing the normal reaction forces the asperities closer together.

### How science works

#### Another model to explain friction

The 'bumps and hollows' model can explain why a lubricant fills in the hollows and decreases the friction but it cannot explain why very smooth surfaces may stick together or why tyres with no tread at all provide better friction than those with heavy tread. To explain these it is necessary to consider the forces between the molecules in contact with each other; increasing the number of molecules close to one another by increasing the area of overlap can be shown to increase the adhesive force between the surfaces.

## Drag forces

Drag is the force that resists the movement of a solid object through a fluid (a gas or a liquid) as shown in Figure 1. It is a friction force acting in the direction of the external fluid flow and so it acts to oppose the motion of the object. In a moving vehicle the drag acts in the opposite direction to the vehicle's motion. The magnitude of the drag depends on the shape of the object and the **viscosity** of the fluid. In situations where the object is moving through a fluid quickly and stirring the fluid up, the drag force is proportional to the square of the object's speed. At slower speeds the drag is proportional to the speed of the object. In either case, the drag force increases with speed.

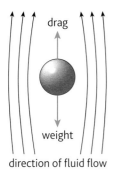

**Figure 1** *Drag forces*

## Skydivers and parachutists

As skydivers fall under the effect of gravity they accelerate and as their speed increases so does the drag (in the form of air resistance). Eventually the drag will be equal and opposite to the weight of each skydiver and the skydiver will travel at a terminal speed (shown graphically in Figure 2). The terminal speed of skydivers is about $50\,\mathrm{m\,s^{-1}}$. Opening a parachute increases the surface area which consequently increases the air resistance reducing the terminal speed to something nearer to $10\,\mathrm{m\,s^{-1}}$.

## Lift forces

We saw in Topic 6.2 that the lift experienced by an aeroplane opposes the weight and is due to the shape of the aircraft's wings. Turning the wing profile upside down produces an aerofoil which is used to increase the downthrust on racing cars. Lift and downthrust will increase with speed.

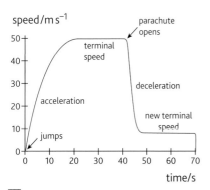

**Figure 2** *Terminal speed*

In Topic 8.2 it was shown that the aerodynamics of ski jumpers and their skis produced a lift that reduced the effective downward acceleration from the usual 9.8 to $3.0\,\mathrm{m\,s^{-2}}$.

## Changing resultant forces

When forces change with speed this means that the acceleration also changes. Newton's second law $F = ma$ still applies but $F$ is not constant and as the resultant force varies so does the acceleration. When an object is falling but the air resistance is significant the equation for its acceleration becomes:

$$mg - F_r = ma \text{ or rearranging } F_r = mg - ma = m(g - a)$$

where $m$ is the mass of the falling object, $g$ the acceleration of gravity, $F_r$ the air resistance force and $a$ the overall acceleration of the body. As $F_r$ increases with speed, this means that $a$ must decrease.

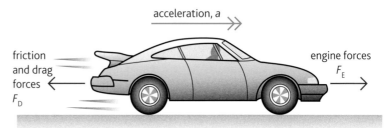

**Figure 3** *Car reaching top speed*

Figure 3 illustrates why a car has a top speed. The resultant force is the difference between the engine drive force $F_E$ and the drag $F_D$ so the acceleration

$$a = \frac{F_E - F_D}{m}$$

As $F_D$ increases with the speed of the car, eventually it will equal $F_E$ and the acceleration will become zero. Under these conditions the car has reached its top speed.

When the car is travelling at its top speed all the chemical energy stored in the fuel is being converted to the **internal energy** of the car and the air around the car (none of it increases the **kinetic energy** of the car).

**Figure 4** *Projectile motion*

## Projectiles when air resistance is not negligible

In Topic 8.2 projectiles were treated as objects having negligible air resistance; this allowed problems to be solved using the symmetry of the motion. As air resistance is not negligible on small, fast-moving objects it is important to consider how this affects projectile motion:

- For the upward vertical motion, the air resistance acts in the same direction as gravity and so the object reaches a lower maximum height than if air resistance is neglected. It comes to rest in a shorter time.

- For the downward vertical motion, the air resistance opposes gravity and so tends to reduce the acceleration of the object. It will therefore take longer to fall through a given height than when air resistance is neglected. It remains in the air for longer.

- For the horizontal motion there is now a deceleration which opposes the horizontal motion and so the object's velocity will reduce and it will not reach the same range as when air resistance is neglected.

- Figure 4 shows a comparison of projectile motion when air resistance is significant or insignificant.

## Summary questions

1 Explain how friction can be both advantageous and disadvantageous; give examples to illustrate your answer.

2 What is a fluid? Explain how different fluids will produce drags on objects moving though them.

3 Draw a graph to illustrate how drag forces restrict the maximum speeds of powered vehicles.

4 A car of mass 800 kg has an engine capable of providing a drive force of 550 N. Calculate the acceleration of the car:

  a when there is negligible air resistance,

  b when the air resistance reaches 330 N.

1   The aeroplane shown in **Figure 1** is travelling horizontally at $95\,\mathrm{m\,s}^{-1}$. It has to drop a crate of emergency supplies.
The air resistance acting on the crate may be neglected.

Q                                                                    R

**Figure 1**

(a) (i)  The crate is released from the aircraft at point **P** and lands at point **Q**. Sketch the path followed by the crate between **P** and **Q** as seen from the ground.

(ii)  Explain why the horizontal component of the crate's velocity remains constant while it is moving through the air.                                       *(3 marks)*

(b) (i)  To avoid damage to the crate, the maximum vertical component if the crate's velocity on landing should be $32\,\mathrm{m\,s}^{-1}$. Show that the maximum height from which the crate can be dropped is approximately $52\,\mathrm{m}$.

(ii)  Calculate the time taken for the crate to reach the ground if the crate is dropped from a height of $52\,\mathrm{m}$.

(iii)  If **R** is a point on the ground directly below **P**, calculate the horizontal distance **QR**.                                                          *(6 marks)*

(c)  In practice air resistance is **not** negligible. State and explain the effect this has on the maximum height from which the crate can be dropped.          *(2 marks)*

AQA, 2004

2   A ball is thrown vertically upwards from a roof of a building and it lands $3.0\,\mathrm{s}$ later on the ground, $7.0\,\mathrm{m}$ below the roof. Calculate:

(a) (i)  the speed with which the ball was thrown upwards,

(ii)  the maximum height of the ball above the ground,

(iii)  the speed with which the ball hits the ground.                       *(8 marks)*

(b)  Another ball is now thrown from the roof at an angle of $70°$ to the horizontal. Calculate:

(i)  the magnitude of the ball's initial velocity if it still takes $3.0\,\mathrm{s}$ to reach the ground,

(ii)  the horizontal displacement of the ball from the point of release to the point of impact with the ground.                                              *(4 marks)*

**3**   **Figure 2** shows how the position of a steel ball which has been projected horizontally from **P** changes with time. The position of the ball is shown at constant time intervals.

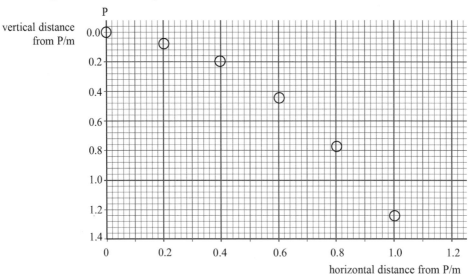

**Figure 2**

(a)  Explain how the horizontal motion of the ball shows that air resistance is negligible.                                                                       *(2 marks)*

(b)  Explain the vertical motion of the ball.                                              *(2 marks)*

(c)  If air resistance were not negligible, describe how this would affect

    (i)   the horizontal motion of the ball,

    (ii)  the vertical motion of the ball.                                         *(3 marks)*

AQA, 2002

**4**   **Figure 3** shows the velocity–time graph for a vertically bouncing ball, which is released above the ground at **A** and strikes the floor at **B**. The effects of air resistance have been neglected.

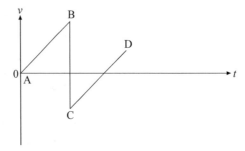

**Figure 3**

(a)  (i)   What does the gradient of a velocity–time graph represent?

    (ii)  Explain why the gradient of the line **CD** is the same as line **AB**.

    (iii) What does the area between the line **AB** and the time axis represent?

    (iv)  State why the velocity at **C** is negative.

    (v)   State why the speed at **C** is less than the speed at **B**.                    *(5 marks)*

(b)  The ball has a mass of $0.15\,kg$ and is dropped from an initial height of $1.2\,m$. After impact the ball rebounds to a height of $0.75\,m$. Calculate:

    (i)   the speed of the ball immediately before impact,

    (ii)  the speed of the ball immediately after impact,

    (iii) the change in momentum of the ball as a result of the impact,

    (iv)  the magnitude of the resultant average force acting on the ball during impact if it is in contact with the floor for $0.10\,s$.                          *(8 marks)*

AQA, 2003

**5**    The table gives data for a skydiver of mass 75 kg during the first phase of a jump.

| time from start of jump/s | 0 | 4.0 | 8.0 | 12.0 |
|---|---|---|---|---|
| velocity/ $m\,s^{-1}$ | 0 | 35 | 55 | 70 |
| acceleration/ $m\,s^{-2}$ | 9.81 | 8.1 | 5.6 | 3.0 |

(a)  For each of the times shown calculate:

(i)   the resultant force on the skydiver,

(ii)  the force of air resistance.    *(8 marks)*

(b)  It is suggested that the force of air resistance is proportional to the square of the skydiver's velocity.

(i)   Use the two sets of data in part (a) to confirm this suggestion.

(ii)  Assuming that the air resistance is proportional to the square of velocity, estimate a value for the skydiver's terminal velocity.    *(5 marks)*

**6**    A ball bearing is released into a tall cylinder of clear oil. The ball bearing initially accelerates but soon reaches terminal velocity.

(a)  By considering the forces acting on the ball bearing, explain its motion.    *(3 marks)*

(b)  How would you demonstrate that the ball bearing reached terminal velocity?    *(2 marks)*

AQA, 2002

**7**    (a)  A trampolinist of mass 68 kg is instantaneously stationary at the bottom of her jump. Her acceleration at this instant is $78\,m\,s^{-2}$. Calculate:

(i)   her weight,

(ii)  the resultant vertical force acting on her at this instant,

(iii) the upward force from the trampoline on her at this instant.    *(5 marks)*

(b)  The net force acting on the trampolinist decreases uniformly to zero in 0.50 s. Calculate her initial velocity as she leaves the trampoline.    *(4 marks)*

**8**    An object is dropped into a column of liquid and the distance it has fallen is measured at regular intervals. The following table contains data from the experiment.

| time/s | 0 | 20 | 40 | 60 | 80 | 100 | 120 |
|---|---|---|---|---|---|---|---|
| depth/mm | 1.67 | 1.89 | 2.19 | 2.54 | 2.91 | 3.28 | 3.65 |

(i)   Plot a graph of depth against time.

(ii)  Explain the shape of your graph.

(iii) Determine the terminal speed of the object from your graph.    *(10 marks)*

**9**    **Figure 4** shows a skier being pulled by rope up a hill of incline 12° at a steady speed. The total mass of the skier is 85 kg. Two of the forces acting on the skier are already shown.

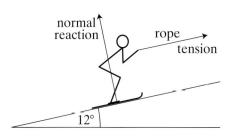

(a)  Copy the diagram and mark with arrows two further forces that are acting on the skier. Label these forces.    *(2 marks)*

(b)  Calculate the magnitude of the normal reaction on the skier.

gravitational field strength, $g = 9.8\,N\,kg^{-1}$    *(3 marks)*

(c)  Explain why the resultant force on the skier must be zero.    *(1 mark)*

**Figure 4**

AQA, 2003

# 9 Looking at energy changes

## 9.1 Energy changes in sport

*Learning objectives:*

- How are the kinetic and potential energy calculated?

- How do kinetic and potential energy change as bodies move?

- What is the difference between work, energy and power?

*Specification reference: 3.2.1E*

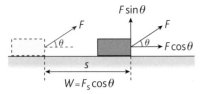

**Figure 1** *Work done by the component of a force*

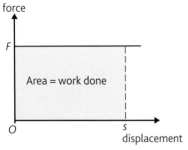

**Figure 2** *Force–displacement graph for a constant force*

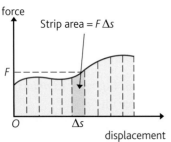

**Figure 3** *Force–displacement graph for a varying force*

## Conservation of energy

One of the most fundamental concepts in physics is the **principle of the conservation of energy**; energy cannot be created or destroyed but it can change from one form to another. It can be transferred from one object to another by **heating** or *by* **doing work**. **Heating** happens if there is a difference in temperature between two objects and takes place by conduction, convection or radiation; **work** is done when a force causes an object to move and is equal to the force multiplied by the displacement of the object in the direction of the force – in equation form

$$W = Fs\cos\theta$$

where $W$ is the work done when the component of a force $F\cos\theta$ moves an object through a distance s (see Figure 1). The component of the force $F\sin\theta$ does no work since it is not lifting the object.

The work done is equal to the area under a force–displacement graph (see Figures 2 and 3). When the force is in newtons and the displacement is in metres the work will be in joules.

## Potential energy

Potential energy is normally considered to be of two types. The potential energy gained by raising the height of something is called **gravitational potential energy** and is calculated using the formula:

$$\Delta E_p = mg\Delta h$$

where $m$ is the mass of the object being raised through a height $\Delta h$ and $g$ is the gravitational field strength.

The potential energy gained when an object is compressed or extended is called **elastic potential energy** and is calculated using the formula:

$$\text{energy stored} = \tfrac{1}{2}F\Delta L$$

where $F$ is the maximum force applied and $\Delta L$ is the extension or compression. This relationship is only applicable when the object extended or compressed obeys Hooke's law (i.e. the extension or compression is directly proportional to the applied force to the object). The energy stored is the area under a force against extension (or compression) graph as shown in Figure 4.

**Potential energy**

In a sense, if energy is considered as being stored, then all types of energy are potential energy until the energy changes to a different form of potential energy. So a car moving at a certain speed has a store of kinetic energy which does not change but the engine is converting chemical energy (stored in the fuel) into the internal energy of the car's body and the air around it by the car doing work on the surroundings.

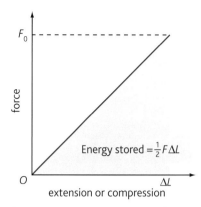

**Figure 4** *Force against extension for object obeying Hooke's law*

## Kinetic energy

The **kinetic energy** of an object is the energy of its motion; the faster it goes the more kinetic energy it has. Kinetic energy is calculated using the formula:

$$E_K = \tfrac{1}{2}mv^2$$

where $m$ is the mass and $v$ the velocity or speed of the object.

## Power

Power is a particularly useful concept. Virtually any quantity of energy can be transferred if enough time is spent transferring it. However, the time span often matters in order to understand the viability of the transfer. Thus **power** is defined as the rate of energy transfer with time or else the rate of work done with time. It can be calculated using one of the formulae:

$$P = \frac{\Delta W}{\Delta t} \quad \text{or} \quad P = Fv$$

where $\Delta W$ is the work done or energy transferred in time interval $\Delta t$, $F$ is the force applied and $v$ is the constant velocity maintained while the force is being applied.

## The sprinter

Let's see how these concepts apply to the sprinter of Figure 5.

As the sprinter pushes back on the starting block, the reaction force at the block pushes the sprinter forwards; in holding the sprint position the sprinter has stored energy in muscle tension and chemical energy is stored in the sprinter's body. The energy changes to kinetic energy as he releases himself from the blocks. As he runs he will reach his top speed which he tries to maintain (with no change in kinetic energy, the energy that he uses will be converted to the internal energy of the air around him as he does work in pushing the air molecules out of the way). As shown in Topic 9.2, the longer the sprinter pushes on the blocks, as he starts his run, the greater will be his impulse and change of momentum; this will mean that he starts with a burst of speed. Of course the overall maximum impulse also depends on the maximum force that the sprinter can apply to the blocks. So there has to be a compromise between the position of the blocks relative to each other and the sprinter's physique.

Initially the useful power of the sprinter will be zero (since any muscle work done will simply raise the internal energy of the sprinter on his blocks). As he accelerates, the work done to increase his kinetic energy will mean that his power increases to a high value but drops as he reaches a steady speed. His power is then constant (to a value $Fv$); the

**The spring stiffness $k$**

It can be useful to discuss the stiffness of objects which stretch or squash. The stiffness (or spring constant) $k$ is defined as the force per unit extension of the object or

$$k = \frac{F}{\Delta L}$$

$k$ has units of $\mathrm{N\,m^{-1}}$.

**Figure 5** *Sprinter*

### AQA Examiner's tip

Provided SI units (kg, m, s, N, etc.) are used throughout, then work and energy will be in J and power will be in W. Be careful to change prefixed units into the correct power of 10 so that kJ need to become J × 10³, ms need to become s × 10⁻³, etc.

dip in speed that normally occurs at the end of the sprint means that his power drops off again. Compared with a long distance runner the work done by the sprinter is much less but it happens at a much greater rate and so the power is much greater.

## ⌛ The pole vaulter or high-jumper

In pole vaulting the principal purpose is to convert the maximum kinetic energy gained during the sprint phase into gravitational potential energy at the point where the vaulter crosses the bar. As the pole vaulter plants her pole at the end of the run-up she should be running at her maximum speed. As she crosses the bar, the vaulter is virtually stationary. Ignoring undesirable energy transformations that occur due to drag forces or imperfections in the pole, whereby the energy stored by the deformed pole is not entirely returned to kinetic energy, then:

$$\tfrac{1}{2}mv^2 = mg\,\Delta h$$

cancelling the mass gives: $\Delta h = \dfrac{\tfrac{1}{2}v^2}{g} = \dfrac{v^2}{2g}$

This means that the weight of the pole vaulter is irrelevant in determining the maximum height of the vault.

The purpose of the pole is to convert the vaulter's horizontal velocity into vertical velocity. At the point where the pole undergoes its maximum deformation $\tfrac{1}{2}mv^2 = \tfrac{1}{2}F\Delta L$, which means that $\Delta L = mv^2/F$; for this to happen the design of the pole needs to be perfect. Good pole vaulters, or high jumpers, will 'curl' around the bar so that their centre of mass will be below the bar giving more height for less speed. High jumpers must use their legs to convert horizontal velocity into vertical velocity; leg muscles are not as efficient as poles at returning all the kinetic energy and so high jumps are much lower than the equivalent pole vault.

**Figure 6** *A pole vaulter*

## ■ The weight lifter

In many weight lifting exercises the bar is moved vertically upwards and downwards transferring the body's chemical energy into gravitational potential energy via kinetic energy. The work done on the weight will be equal to the gravitational potential energy gained by the weight. The power with which the weight lifter must work will depend upon the phase of the lift. Figure 7 shows the velocity of a weight being lifted in the first phases of a **snatch** lift. Up to point **A**, the weight has moved a distance of 0.21 m. By **B** it has moved an extra 0.07 m and by **C** a further 0.125 m, making a total of approximately 0.4 m. Using the equation linking power and work we can see that lifting a 100 kg mass (a weight of approximately 1000 N) means that 400 J of work is done in 0.85 s giving an average power of 470 W. In the three phases of the snatch this amounts to 380 W up to **A**, 470 W between **A** and **B** and 830 W between **B** and **C**. After the snatch the lifter rapidly squats below the bar before lifting it above his head; this requires the momentum of the bar to be carrying the bar upwards while the lifter moves to squat below it.

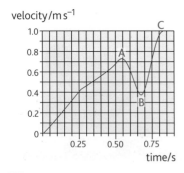

💡 **Figure 7** *Velocity of the bar during the snatch phase of a lift*

## ■ The archer

A bow has many properties in common with a spring. As the archer draws the bowstring he does work on the bow and increases the elastic potential energy by deforming the two limbs of the bow. On releasing the string much of this potential energy is converted into the kinetic energy of the arrow. The tension in the bowstring causes the arrow to accelerate until it leaves the string, when it is subjected to aerodynamic drag. The three feathers on the arrow ensure that the arrow flies in a stable way.

Assuming that all the elastic potential energy is entirely converted into the kinetic energy of the arrow the energy equation is:

$$\tfrac{1}{2}mv^2 = \tfrac{1}{2}FL \qquad \text{or} \qquad v = \sqrt{\frac{FL}{m}}$$

where $m$ represents the mass of the arrow, $F$ the maximum force applied to the bow string and $L$ the displacement of the bowstring.

This is likely to produce an overestimate of the initial speed of the arrow since the bow is likely to stretch unevenly. In addition to this, as the arrow leaves the bowstring, the bow itself moves and takes some of the elastic potential energy.

**Figure 8** *A bungee jumper*

## The bungee jumper

The excitement in **bungee jumping** comes both from the act of free-falling as well as the bouncing up and down. When the jumper jumps, the rope stretches to a maximum before the jumper oscillates up and down. Eventually the rope transfers all the energy to the surroundings.

As a bungee jumper is about to jump she will have an amount of gravitational potential energy due to her height above the ground. As she jumps she is in freefall and her loss of gravitational potential energy becomes entirely kinetic energy (ignoring drag) until the bungee rope is extended to its natural length; at this point she is still not at her maximum speed because she is still accelerating. From this time onwards her acceleration will decrease but she will still be accelerating until the rope stretches sufficiently for the tension in it to equal her weight; she will then have her maximum kinetic energy. As the rope continues to stretch, her rate of loss of gravitational potential energy will decrease but the rope gains elastic potential energy as the result of her loss of both gravitational potential energy and kinetic energy. When she finally comes to rest, the elastic potential energy stored in rope will equal her gravitational potential energy just before jumping.

At the point where the rope just becomes taut $\tfrac{1}{2}mv^2 = mg\Delta h$; when the tension in the rope equals the weight of the jumper $\tfrac{1}{2}mv^2 + \tfrac{1}{2}FL = mg\Delta h$ and when the rope reaches its maximum stretch $\tfrac{1}{2}FL = mg\Delta h$.

### How science works

**Performance-enhancing drugs**

The ethical issues involved in the use of performance-enhancing drugs are wide ranging. Clearly some performance-enhancing drugs are dangerous. Steroids are associated with a range of side effects, including heart attacks and liver cancer.

The International Olympic Committee, which enforces the rules of the Olympic Games, set up the World Anti-Doping Agency (WADA) in 1999 as an independent body charged with coordinating a consistent system for testing Olympic athletes. WADA works with international sports federations and Olympic committees and has begun conducting unannounced, out-of-competition tests on Olympic hopefuls. In doing so the competitors are unlikely to have cleared their bodies of illegal substances prior to in-competition testing.

## Summary questions

1. Explain the difference between the terms force, work, energy and power. Give the unit for each quantity.

2. Calculate the maximum height that a pole-vaulter running at $10.5\,\text{m s}^{-1}$ could vault. Explain why the bar must be lower than this height. $g = 9.8\,\text{N kg}^{-1}$

3. A 75 kg sprinter, starting from rest, reaches a speed of $7.6\,\text{m s}^{-1}$ in 2.0 s with negligible effect due to air resistance. The sprinter then runs the remainder of the race at a steady speed of $7.0\,\text{m s}^{-1}$ under the influence of a 35 N force due to air resistance. Calculate the average power needed to:

   a accelerate the runner, and

   b sustain the steady speed at which most of the race is run.

   (Hint: use the average force in the first calculation.)

4. Suggest why random drug testing in sport can be seen as being unfair to some athletes.

# 9.2 Stopping safely

*Learning objectives:*

■ What is the link between impulse and momentum?

■ What factors affect the force experienced in a collision?

■ How can the force experienced in a collision be reduced?

*Specification reference: 3.2.1E*

## ■ Momentum and impulse

**Momentum** $p$ is a vector quantity with a direction which is the same as the velocity vector. The magnitude of momentum is the product of mass $(m)$ and speed $(v)$.

$$p = mv$$

Momentum can be transferred from one body to another. In an **isolated system** in which momentum is transferred internally, the total initial momentum is the same as the total final momentum. This statement is an example of the conservation of momentum. However, the final momentum is not the same as the initial momentum, i.e. the momentum changes by $\Delta p \, (= F\Delta t)$ when an external force $(F)$ acts on the system for a time $(\Delta t)$. $F\Delta t$ is called the **impulse**. Both impulse and momentum have units $\mathrm{N\,s}$ (this is equivalent to $\mathrm{kg\,m\,s^{-1}}$, which is a unit commonly used for momentum).

## ■ ■ What energy changes occur when a car is ■ ■ brought to rest?

When a car brakes to a stop, its kinetic energy needs to be dissipated as internal energy in the brakes. This causes the temperature of the brake linings and the disc or drum to rise. During the braking process the friction in the brakes does work on the brake disc or drum causing the energy transfer from kinetic energy to internal energy. If the car is brought to rest in a collision then the kinetic energy still must be dissipated but this time it is converted into strain energy of the car and the object that it collided with as well as internal energy.

### Crumple zones

Until the middle of the twentieth century cars were built with an overall structure that was very rigid. Collisions between cars and stationary objects took place over a very short time. For a car travelling at a speed $v$ and having a mass $m$ its momentum is $mv$. When the car is brought to rest its momentum becomes zero so the change in momentum is also $mv$. As shown above the change in momentum is equal to the impulse so here:

$$mv = F\Delta t$$

The mass and velocity of the car are fixed but if the time for which the force acts can be increased, the size of the force will decrease and the force on the passengers will be less. This can be done by designing a car to have crumple zones; these are regions of the car which crumple on impact thus prolonging the time for which the force acts and so reducing the force (see the crumpled bonnets of the cars in Figure 1). Inside the crumple zones is a rigid 'safety cage' which protects the passengers from the impact of the crumpled car body. The crumpling process converts kinetic energy into elastic potential energy and then internal energy as the crumpling parts do work in 'rubbing' against each other. The temperature of the crumpled car parts will rise.

**Figure 1** *Crumpled car bonnets*

## Seat belts

The crumple zones will not prevent the occupants of the car from serious injury if they are not anchored to their seats. Seat belts prevent impacts with the windscreen, steering wheel or (for passengers in the rear) the front seats; such impacts would take place quickly and produce large forces on the passengers. In a similar way to how a crumple zone works the seat belt stretches and reduces the force on the occupant by prolonging the time for which the force acts. The kinetic energy of the car occupant is converted into elastic potential energy of the stretched seatbelt. After a car has been in a collision the seat belts may need to be replaced. They are likely to have passed their *elastic limit* and will not be able to return to their normal length. Figure 2 illustrates how pets should not be considered to be immune from the laws of motion.

**Figure 2** *Pet safety belt*

## Air bags

Sensors at different positions around the car detect any sudden deceleration and impact at places where the impact could harm a car occupant. When a dangerous impact occurs the sensor sends an electrical signal to a transducer in the air bag. The received signal actuates a chemical propellant producing nitrogen gas which inflates the air bag. When the air bag has inflated to its maximum volume, vents at the rear of the bag allow air to leak out as the occupant hits the bag. This leakage prolongs the impact time and cushions the head by reducing the impact force (see Figure 3).

**Figure 3** *Deployed air bag*

## ◪ Other impulsive matters

The concept of reducing forces by prolonging the time of contact has many applications in sport. The mattress used by high-jumpers and pole vaulters is far more user-friendly than the sand pits of bygone days. Athletes' shoes are designed to have a cushion sole with many air spaces which compress when the shoe is put under pressure; again this squashing motion prolongs the time in which it takes the foot to make contact with the track and reduces the forces on the foot and ankle. The reverse of this process can be found when a fixed force maintains contact with something in order to increase the momentum of the object. Athletes in ball games 'follow through' to ensure a prolonged contact between the ball and the hand, foot, bat, club or racquet thereby increasing the momentum and thus the velocity of the ball (see Figure 4). In each of these cases kinetic energy of the club, say, is passed to elastic potential energy of the ball which is then re-converted to kinetic energy, this time of the ball.

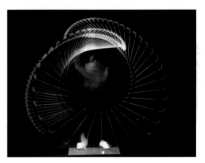

**Figure 4** *Stroboscopic photograph of golf follow through*

### Summary questions

1. Calculate the impulse of the variable force shown in Figure 5.

2. Explain how crumple zones, seat belts and air bags reduce the force on the occupants of a car during a collision.

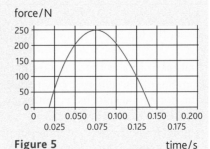

**Figure 5**

3. When a tennis ball is struck with a racquet its momentum changes by 1.2 N s. The tennis ball is in contact with the racquet head for 40 ms. Calculate the average force on the ball.

4. Discuss features that a sensible parent should consider when buying a family car.

### ▪ How science works

**Euro NCAP**

Euro NCAP (the European New Car Assessment Programme) was set up by the Transport Research Laboratory, for the UK Department of Transport. Subsequently other governments have joined the programme (France, Germany, Sweden, The Netherlands and parts of Spain) to provide motoring consumers with an independent assessment of the safety performance of some of the most popular cars sold in Europe. Euro NCAP assess cars for driver, passenger, side and pedestrian safety with five stars being the highest rating available.

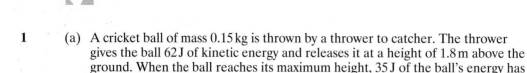

1    (a)  A cricket ball of mass 0.15 kg is thrown by a thrower to catcher. The thrower
          gives the ball 62 J of kinetic energy and releases it at a height of 1.8 m above the
          ground. When the ball reaches its maximum height, 35 J of the ball's energy has
          been converted into gravitational potential energy. Calculate:
          (i)   the speed with which the ball was thrown,
          (ii)  the maximum height of the ball above the ground,
          (iii) the speed of the ball at maximum height.                                *(7 marks)*
     (b)  For the ball in part (a) calculate the angle the initial velocity of the ball makes to
          the horizontal.                                                               *(3 marks)*
     (c)  What is the maximum possible height the ball could reach if it is given 62 J of
          kinetic energy and released from a height of 1.8 m above the ground?          *(3 marks)*

2    (a)  A tennis ball of mass 59 g is moving horizontally at a velocity of 22 m s⁻¹. A tennis
          player hits the ball with a racket so that it returns back along its original path with
          a velocity of 29 m s⁻¹. Calculate:
          (i)   the change in momentum of the ball,
          (ii)  the impulse of the force exerted on the ball,
          (iii) the average force on the ball if it is in contact with the racket for 6.2 ms.  *(5 marks)*
     (b)  What would be the effect on the ball in part (a) if the racket exerts the same
          average force but is in contact with the ball for 3.1 ms?                     *(3 marks)*

3    **Figure 1** shows a skateboarder descending a ramp.

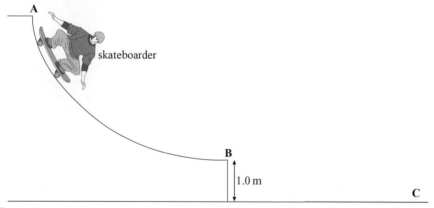

skateboarder

B

1.0 m

C

**Figure 1**

The skateboarder starts from rest at the top of the ramp at **A** and leaves the ramp at **B**
horizontally with a velocity *v*.
     (a)  State the energy changes that take place as the skateboarder moves from **A** to **B**.   *(2 marks)*
     (b)  In going from **A** to **B** the skateboarder's centre of gravity descends a vertical
          height of 1.5 m. Calculate the horizontal velocity, *v*, stating an assumption that
          you make.                                                                     *(3 marks)*
     (c)  Explain why the acceleration decreases as the skateboarder moves from **A** to **B**.   *(2 marks)*
     (d)  After leaving the ramp at **B** the skateboarder lands on the ground at **C** 0.42 s later.
          Calculate for the skateboarder:
          (i) the horizontal distance travelled between **B** and **C**,
          (ii) the vertical component of the velocity immediately before impact at **C**,
          (iii) the magnitude of the resultant velocity immediately before impact at **C**.   *(5 marks)*

AQA, 2006

4    **Figure 2** shows how the momentum of two colliding railway trucks varies with time. Truck **A** has a mass of $2.0 \times 10^4$ kg and truck **B** has a mass of $3.0 \times 10^4$ kg. The trucks are travelling in the same direction.

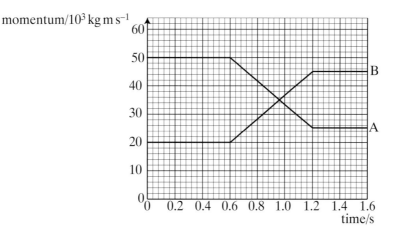

**Figure 2**

(a)   Calculate the change in momentum of:

(i)   truck **A**

(ii)   truck **B**.    *(4 marks)*

(b)   Copy and complete the following table.

|  | initial velocity/ms⁻¹ | final velocity/ ms⁻¹ | initial kinetic energy/J | final kinetic energy/J |
|---|---|---|---|---|
| truck **A** |  |  |  |  |
| truck **B** |  |  |  |  |

*(4 marks)*

AQA, 2005

5    (a)   A trampolinist falls vertically from a height of 2.7 m and lands on a trampoline. She rebounds from the trampoline to a height of 3.4 m. Describe the energy changes that take place as she falls and rebounds from the trampoline.    *(4 marks)*

(b)   (i)   Calculate the speed of the trampolinist in part (a) as she reaches the trampoline mat on the way down.

(ii)   Calculate her speed as she leaves the trampoline mat on the way up.    *(4 marks)*

6    A boy of weight 590 N attempts to determine the power developed by his body by using his arms to do eight pull-ups in 32 s. During a pull-up his centre of gravity rises vertically by 35 cm.

Calculate:

(i)   the gain in gravitational potential energy during each pull-up,

(ii)   the total work done during the eight pull-ups,

(iii)   the power output developed during the exercise.    *(5 marks)*

7    (a)   In a shooting competition a bullet of mass 12 g is fired into a block of wood of mass 3.5 kg. The block is supported by vertical threads and as a result of the impact the block swings and rises through a vertical height of 56 mm. Calculate:

(i)   the gain in gravitational potential energy of the block,

(ii)   the speed of the block immediately after it is struck by the bullet,    *(4 marks)*

(b)   State and explain whether the speed of the bullet is likely to be less or greater than that calculated in (a)(ii)    *(2 marks)*

# 10 Energy in and energy out

## 10.1 Renewable energy

*Learning objectives:*

- What are renewable and non-renewable energy sources?

- Which sources are renewable?

- What is the Sun's role in providing our energy?

*Specification reference: 3.2.2A*

### Link

Later in this chapter there are sections that explain more about the different forms of energy and how they are used.

The use of renewable energy resources is being encouraged internationally to supply the increasing demand for energy. Countries that are less well developed economically tend to advance more slowly in the use of renewable resources because they often have large unexploited reserves of coal, oil and gas. Using these resources can satisfy the relatively huge energy demands of a rapidly growing economy more cheaply and is less demanding technologically.

Most sources of energy, renewable and non-renewable, can be traced back to the Sun, so why is it better to use one rather than the other? Relying on carboniferous non-renewable resources produces serious problems:

- Non-renewable resources will eventually run out
- Their use directly increases the energy input to the Earth and its atmosphere
- They produce by-products that further accelerate global warming.

### Non-renewable resources

The non-renewable resources: oil, gas, and coal, have been formed from decaying organisms. Oil and gas comes from the decay of plankton and bacteria that settled millions of years ago on the sea floor, and coal comes from the decay of plants on land such as trees. The energy for the organisms and plants to grow came from the Sun through the process of photosynthesis in the plants, which in turn provided food for the organisms. As it takes millions of years for these to decay to form coal and oil, they cannot be replaced once used.

When non-renewable resources are used, the energy from the Sun that has been stored in the planet's materials is being released. The stored energy is being added to that arriving naturally from the Sun. Gases such as carbon dioxide, produced when fuels are burned, are released into the atmosphere and give rise to the so-called greenhouse effect which is covered in Chapter 11.

### Nuclear and geothermal energy

Nuclear energy comes from uranium which is a non-renewable source. Fast 'breeder' reactors produce plutonium that can itself be used as a fuel and this increases the energy available from nuclear reactions. However, even this source would eventually be exhausted, so it is non-renewable.

The temperature in the Earth rises approximately 1 K for every 36 m toward the centre of the Earth, so even a few kilometres down, the temperature can be over 250 °C. This geothermal energy can be used directly for heating homes and businesses or used to drive turbines and generators in the production of electricity (see Figure 1). This source of energy is so large that it can be classified as a renewable source.

# Renewable sources

The renewable resources that are being exploited depend on the use of the Sun's energy either directly or indirectly. The Sun's energy is harnessed directly using solar panels or photovoltaic cells and indirectly by generating electricity from wind, rivers and waves. Tidal energy is also a renewable source produced by the gravitational effects of the Sun and Moon. As the Sun is continually fuelling the Earth's climate, the use of these energy sources does not add extra energy to that arriving from the Sun. Our technology transfers the energy into an electrical form that is convenient for transmission and use.

## Wind energy

There are a number of factors that influence the different temperature conditions that exist in the atmosphere and across the surface of the Earth:

- The higher thermal capacity of water compared with rocks, sand and soil result in it generally having a lower temperature than land. The temperature of the land tends to fluctuate more and over a wider range of temperatures and these changes occur more quickly.
- Air close to the Earth is warmer than that higher up.
- Some parts of the Earth such as the equator are closer to the Sun and reach higher temperatures.

These effects result in expansion of the air which lowers density and pressure leading to variations around the Earth. The warm, lower density, air rises forming convection currents and this causes the wind.

Locally, temperature variations result in only gentle breezes from sea to land during the day and in the opposite direction at night (Figure 2). Globally the temperature variations lead to the much more powerful prevailing winds.

The global movement of air is not directly from high to low pressure (like air rushing through an open valve in a bicycle tyre) as might be expected. The rotation of the Earth leads to forces that cause the air movement to spiral inwards into a low-pressure region and spiral outwards for a high-pressure region so that the wind direction is, more or less, along the isobars.

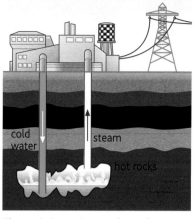

**Figure 1** *Extracting geothermal energy*

## How science works

### Conservation of energy

Remember that energy can only be transferred from one form into another. Burning fuels and producing energy by nuclear fission or fusion reduces mass, in which case an equivalent amount of energy will appear in another form.

The Sun's energy is not strictly renewable – but it can provide energy so far into the future that as far as we are concerned it is a renewable source.

## Hint,

A body with a higher thermal capacity than another needs more energy input to raise its temperature by one degree.

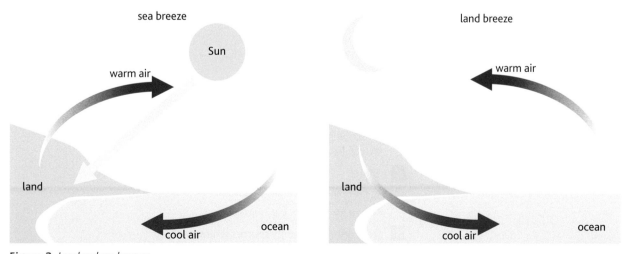

**Figure 2** *Land and sea breezes*

## Wave energy

Waves are caused by a disturbance such as when a stone is thrown into a pond. Tsunami are the destructive waves produced by earthquakes at the bottom of the oceans. The useful sea waves that can be used to provide electrical energy are caused partly by the tidal movement and partly by high winds that drive across the water surface converting the kinetic energy of the wind into kinetic and potential energy in the wave.

## Energy in rivers

The role of the Sun in this case is the production of rain. The sun provides energy to evaporate water, particularly from the large areas of the sea. This rises in the same way as heated air rises in the production of winds. As the vapour rises it gains potential energy. The water vapour condenses as it moves into colder regions in the atmosphere and falls as rain. The rain forms the rivers that gain kinetic energy and lose potential energy as the water returns to the sea from which most of it originated. This kinetic energy can be harnessed in the production of electrical energy.

## Tidal energy

Tides occur due to the gravitational forces exerted on the Earth by the Sun and Moon (Figure 3). The Moon has the greater influence because it is nearer. The highest (spring) tides occur when the Sun and Moon are pulling in the same direction and the lowest (neap) tides when they pull at right angles to each other.

As the Earth and Moon rotate, different parts of the Sea are attracted to the Moon. The combined effect of the Earth's rotation and the gravitational attraction is to create a bulge of water on opposite sides of the Earth. As each point on the Earth's surface is either facing or on the opposite side from the Moon twice in each revolution of the Earth, there are two tides a day.

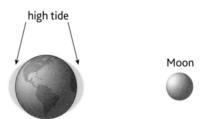

**Figure 3** *Production of tides*

■ Summary questions

1 Describe briefly how the Sun is responsible for the energy that is available from coal.

2 State

  a two renewable energy sources

  b two non-renewable sources.

3 Why are some energy sources renewable?

# 10.2 Energy in

Learning objectives:

- How much energy is available from non-renewable sources in the UK?

- Where are the major non-renewable sources internationally?

- How much energy is produced by renewable sources in the UK?

*Specification reference: 3.2.2A*

## Energy

Energy is 'the capacity to do work'. The energy 'content' of one body can be transferred to another by doing work. The transferred energy then may be in a different form from the original energy. In the case of fuels the energy is originally chemical energy and burning the fuels releases energy that is converted to mechanical energy that drives turbines and generators.

The SI unit of energy is the joule (J).

The rate at which energy is transferred, or the rate at which work is done, is the **power**. The unit is the watt (W). One watt is the same as one joule per second ($1\,W = 1\,J\,s^{-1}$).

When dealing with power production, kW, MW, GW and even TW ($1\,\text{terawatt} = 10^{12}\,W$) are commonly used.

The formula for calculating energy transferred from power is $E = Pt$

Energy transferred (used) = power × time

As the energy produced by power stations and used in the home is large, the unit used is the kilowatt-hour (kWh) or for larger powers the MWh or GWh.

1 kWh is the energy used when using a 1 kW device for 1 h.

So $1\,\text{kWh} = 1000 \times 3600 = 3.6 \times 10^6\,J$

### Energy from the Sun

The power arriving on the Earth's surface from the Sun is about $1.7 \times 10^{17}\,W$. Figure 1 shows what happens to this energy.

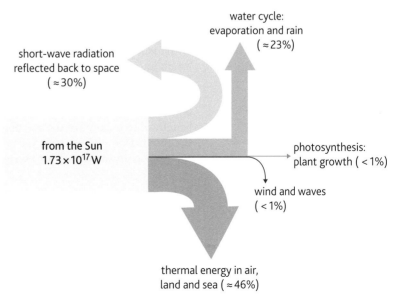

water cycle:
evaporation and rain
($\approx 23\%$)

short-wave radiation
reflected back to space
($\approx 30\%$)

from the Sun
$1.73 \times 10^{17}\,W$

photosynthesis:
plant growth ($< 1\%$)

wind and waves
($< 1\%$)

thermal energy in air,
land and sea ($\approx 46\%$)

**Figure 1** *Energy from the Sun*

## AQA Examiner's tip

Number of kWh used = power rating in kW × the time in hours.

Energy in J = $3.6 \times 10^6$ × energy in kWh.

### How science works

**Sankey diagrams**

In Sankey diagrams (like Figure 1) the arrows are drawn so that their widths represent the relative amount of energy in the different forms. They are an alternative to bar charts and pie charts but have the advantage of indicating 'flow'.

Only about 1% of the power that arrives on Earth is used to generate wind and waves or is absorbed by plants. Of the remainder, about 30% is reflected immediately back into space, about 46% raises the temperature of the Earth and about 23% causes evaporation of water, which eventually returns as rain. A balance is eventually reached in which the energy radiated from the Earth is equal to that arriving from the Sun and the Earth reaches a constant average temperature. Global warming is due to factors that alter this equilibrium condition (see Chapter 11).

## ▓ Energy from non-renewable resources

Internationally there are still abundant supplies of coal, oil and gas. Coal is the most abundant fossil fuel with estimated global reserves of about $9 \times 10^{11}$ tonnes. For gas and oil the current estimated reserves are $170 \times 10^{12} \, m^3$ of gas and $1.1 \times 10^{12}$ barrels of oil. (Oil is sold commercially in 159 litre barrels).

Figures 2, 3 and 4 show how these reserves are distributed in different parts of the world.

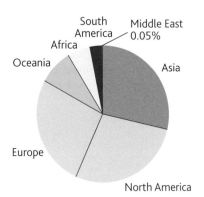

**Figure 2** *Proved coal reserves*

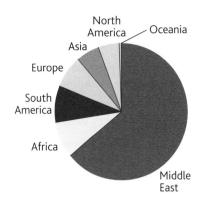

**Figure 3** *Proved oil reserves*

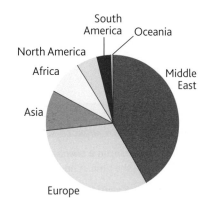

**Figure 4** *Proved gas reserves*

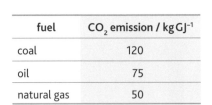

| fuel | $CO_2$ emission / kg GJ$^{-1}$ |
|---|---|
| coal | 120 |
| oil | 75 |
| natural gas | 50 |

The use of these fuels is reliable and safe and capable of supplying much of the world's energy requirements for many years; coal for 250 years, oil for about 40 years and gas for about 30 years. However, the use of fossil fuels, in particular coal and oil, is being challenged for environmental reasons. The table shows that carbon dioxide emissions produced from burning natural gas is much lower than the other fossil fuels so it is beneficial to encourage the use of gas rather than the other fossil fuels in the production of electricity. Geophysicists therefore have an important role to play in the search for new gas deposits.

## 🔋 Available non-renewable energy resources in the UK

The UK production of coal is low and to extract what remains could soon be uneconomic. Projections suggest a decline in the use of coal for energy production from 37% of the total power produced in 2003 to 9% in 2016. In terms of energy produced this represents a fall from 127 TWh to 28 TWh and in terms of coal burned a fall from $5.3 \times 10^{10}$ kg in 2003 to $1.2 \times 10^{10}$ kg in 2016.

In 2006 it was estimated that at the most $3.9 \times 10^{10}$ barrels of oil were available from future UK production. At the same time the upper estimate of available gas was about $2.3 \times 10^{12}\,\mathrm{m}^3$ of gas. Even if these upper ends were possible it still means that almost half the oil and gas in the UK oil and gas fields had already been extracted by 2006.

In general terms this shows that the UK's own supplies of gas, oil and coal are limited and that the UK will become increasingly dependent on imported fuels. This factor and the problem of global warming has led to increased use of renewable resources and a reconsideration of the role of nuclear power in supplying our energy needs.

## 🖊 Energy production in the UK

The mean power demand in the UK is about 32 GW. The conversion of fuels into electricity is not efficient and the mean efficiency of power stations in the UK is only about 38%, so 62% of the energy in fuel is wasted (Figure 5).

Figure 6 shows how energy produced from different sources changed over the period from 1980 to 2005. Even in 2005 the amount produced by renewable sources is barely visible in the chart compared with the total energy production. In 2005 about 4% of the total energy production came from renewable resources and most of this was from waste and landfill gas. However, the target for renewable energy set for the power production industry is 10% of the total by 2010, 15% by 2015, and 20% by 2020 and the use of wind power is likely to increase.

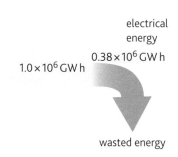

**Figure 5** *Efficiency of power stations*

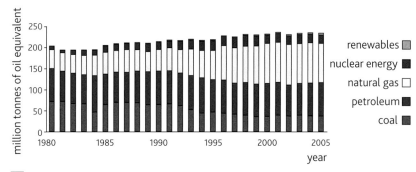

🖊 **Figure 6** *Energy production from different sources*

### Summary questions

1 Assuming the use data in this section, determine:

  a the percentage of the world's potential oil reserves is in the UK oilfields,

  b the percentage of the world's potential gas reserves is in the UK gas fields.

2 How much of the Sun's energy is converted into the energy carried by wind and waves each day?

3 Calculate the mass of $CO_2$ emitted into the atmosphere when producing 1 MJ of energy from coal.

4 How much energy is produced from 1 kg of coal? Give your answer in kW h and J.

5 Referring to Figure 5, calculate the amount of energy wasted in the production of electricity in GW h.

# 10.3 Energy out

*Learning objectives:*

- What factors lead to increasing demand for energy?
- How is energy used in the UK?
- How does energy use affect carbon emissions?

*Specification reference: 3.2.2A*

## How science works

**Positive feedback**

This is a common feature of many scientific phenomena. In medicine an infectious disease like AIDS spreads by such a process. The more people that have the disease the more come into contact with it, so more catch it and so on. Examples in physics include the process of the chain reaction in a nuclear explosion and thermal runaway in transistors.

Access to energy is fundamental to our civilisation, and economic and social development is fuelling a growing demand for reliable, affordable and clean energy. Moreover, nearly 1.6 billion people, or roughly a quarter of the world's population, today lack access to modern energy services.

*World Energy Council (2004)*

Apart from the need for energy to provide the basic necessities and luxury goods, many societies use energy to commute to work, to conduct international business and for leisure travel. This demand has accelerated the rate at which energy is used.

Countries become more prosperous by international trade in natural resources and/or manufactured goods. The latter need energy so this leads to a correlation between living standards as measured by the gross national product and energy consumption. As an economy improves, individuals have more money to spend on necessary and luxury goods, which leads to increased energy consumption. This is an example of **positive feedback** in which an increase in output leads to even further increase. If the current consumption trends continue it is estimated that energy demand will rise by a staggering 50% over the next 25 years. This is not surprising, as roughly a quarter of the world's population cannot access modern energy services and have yet to reach the living standards that are enjoyed by the majority.

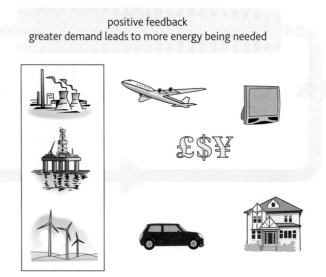

positive feedback
greater demand leads to more energy being needed

**Figure 1** *Increasing energy demands*

## Electrical energy production in the UK

In 2005, power stations in the UK had a power producing capacity of about 65 GW, well in excess of the peak demand of 50 GW. The mean demand was about 43 GW so that the annual energy consumption for domestic and industrial use was 379 000 GW h of which about 50 000 GW h (around 13%) was for domestic use. The remainder was used for transport, commercial and industrial purposes.

The population of the UK is about 60 million, so averaged over the whole population we use about 6300 kWh of electricity per person per year. This compares with an annual world average of around 2600 kWh per person and only 1100 kWh per person in the poorest countries. The 50 000 GWh of the UK's electricity used in homes equates to 830 kWh per person. Our mean total energy consumption is increased by the use of oil for transport and fossil fuels for space and water heating.

Over the period from 1990 to 2005 energy used from **all** fuel sources increased by about 8%. The charts in Figure 2 show how the use by the different sectors has changed in that time. Notice in particular the increase in the proportion used for transport which is primarily due to increased use of cars and other forms of transport, notably air travel for commuting and leisure.

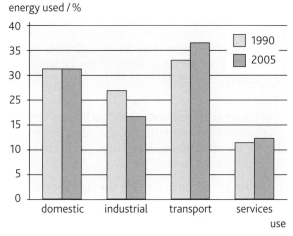

**Figure 2** *Energy use in 1990 and 2005. Source: The Department for Business Enterprise and Regulatory Reform. Crown copyright material is reproduced with the permission of the Controller Office of Public Sector Information (OPSI)*

## Energy use and carbon emissions

Figure 3 shows how carbon dioxide emissions are changing as the world's use of energy increases. While there is a steady increase in emissions in developed countries, the emissions in developing countries such as China are increasing dramatically. The effects of carbon emissions will be discussed in the next chapter.

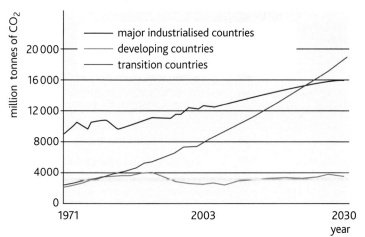

**Figure 3** *Increasing carbon dioxide emissions. Source: IEA, 2004*

**How science works**

**Government decision making**

The Department for Business, Enterprise and Regulatory Reform (BERR; formerly the Department of Trade and Industry (DTI)) produce data on production and use of energy. The Department of the Environment, Food and Rural Affairs (Defra) monitors changes affected by energy use such as pollution, sea levels and average temperature. These inform government decisions on how electricity should be produced in the future. This information can be viewed on the BERR and Defra websites.

**How science works**

**Energy and ethics**

The location and distribution of energy around the Earth is a major influence on international economics and politics. The issues are complex. Developed countries are demanding more energy to sustain living standards and developing countries consume energy to improve their quality of life. The effect is a continual increase in energy demand which is unsustainable and dangerous to the planet in the longer term. The Kyoto agreement is an international agreement (not endorsed by all countries) which sets out goals for trying to resolve the problem.

## Carbon dioxide emissions

Burning coal produces a number of different gases but let us suppose that all the carbon burned produces carbon dioxide.

$1\,kWh$ of electrical energy is used by a $1\,kW$ heater in $1\,h$ and is $3.6 \times 10^6\,J$.

$1\,kg$ of coal produces about $36 \times 10^6\,J$ of thermal energy.

Power stations have an efficiency of about 30% so to produce $3.6 \times 10^6\,J$ of electricity about $330\,g$ of coal (carbon) has to be burned.

$1\,kg$ of carbon completely converted to carbon dioxide produces $3.7\,kg$ of $CO_2$.

So the mass of carbon dioxide produced per $kWh$ is about $1.2\,kg$.

## Carbon footprints

An informative activity is to work out the carbon emissions that result from your own energy use and assess how your contribution to the global production of carbon dioxide might be reduced. Estimates of the average annual carbon emissions per person in the UK vary between $10\,000$ and $11\,000\,kg$. This compares with about $19\,000\,kg$ for the average citizen of the USA.

In calculating the energy used remember that each of us benefits to a greater or lesser extent from transport, industrial, commercial and services provided for us, all of which use energy. So this has to be added to what we use directly in our homes.

Each of us contributes to carbon emissions through the use of:

- electricity and other fuels in the home
- transport for work and leisure
- the manufacture and delivery of food and material goods that we purchase
- use of facilities and materials during our everyday lives (such as a proportion of energy for school heating, lighting and materials)
- services such as roads, hospitals, council and national services, etc.

Remember that any activity that is shared, for example by sharing transport, reduces our individual contribution.

Table 1 shows how one survey arrived at an 'average' carbon footprint of $10.62 \times 10^3\,kg$ per year.

### How science works

**Carbon footprints**

You will find many calculators on the internet that will claim to estimate your carbon footprint based on your home life and activities. These may be calculators that are biased to reflect the interests of the organisation that provides the calculator. Try different ones and think critically about why estimates using different calculators might be different.

### Summary questions

**1** Calculate the percentage of carbon emissions that is produced by air travel.

**2** Use Figure 2 to determine the proportion of the energy used for transport in the UK in 2005.

**3** Describe the ways in which energy is used in road building.

**Table 1**

| energy use | nature of activities | $CO_2$ emissions / $10^3$ kg per year | comments |
|---|---|---|---|
| recreation | trips, leisure activities and goods(tv, video, etc.) | 1.95 | digital tv will increase emissions |
| heating | gas, electricity and oil | 1.49 | lowering by 1K saves 25 kg per year |
| food | cooking, transport, travel to shops | 1.39 | |
| household use | manufacture of furnishings and house | 1.37 | |
| hygiene | in hospitals and homes | 1.34 | showering uses less energy |
| clothing | manufacture, transport and cleaning of clothes | 1.00 | importing adds to the carbon emissions |
| commuting | travelling to and from work | 0.81 | |
| air travel | holidays and business | 0.68 | flight to Malaga (Spain) 400 kg per passenger |
| education | operating schools, travel, books, 'school run' | 0.49 | |
| phones | communications | 0.1 | mobile phone use increasing battery charging |

AQA Examination-style questions

1  (a) **Figure 1** shows the how the use of energy by various modes of transport in the UK has varied since 1970.

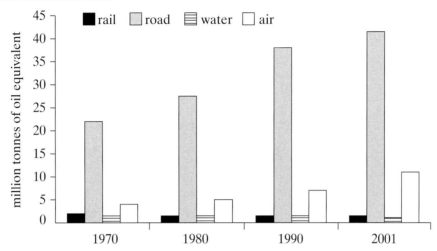

**Figure 1**

*Source: Department for Business Enterprise & Regulatory Reform. Crown copyright material is reproduced with the permission of the Controller Office of Public Sector Information (OPSI)*

State **three** conclusions that you can draw from this chart.          *(3 marks)*

(b) **Figure 2** shows the variation in various modes of transport in the UK over the 30 years ending in 2000.

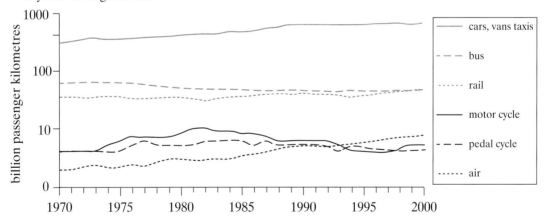

**Figure 2**

*Source: Department for Business Enterprise & Regulatory Reform. Crown copyright material is reproduced with the permission of the Controller Office of Public Sector Information (OPSI)*

(i)   Explain the scale on the *y*-axis of the chart.

(ii)  Identify and calculate the greatest percentage change in mode of transport that occurred between 1970 and 2000.

(iii) One passenger kilometre of air travel results in the emission of about $2 \times 10^{-4}$ tonnes of $CO_2$ into the atmosphere. Use the chart to estimate the total amount of $CO_2$ released as a result of UK travel in 2000.          *(6 marks)*

**2** **Figure 3** below shows the electrical energy generated in the UK from large-scale hydroelectric resources.

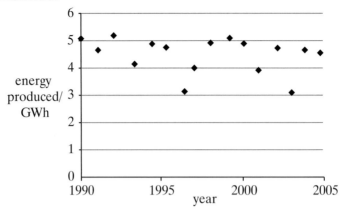

**Figure 3**

(a) Calculate the maximum energy that can be provided by 1.0 kg of water falling through 100 m. *(2 marks)*

(b) Use the graph to estimate the mean energy in joules produced every year in the UK by large-scale hydroelectric resources. *(1 mark)*

(c) Estimate the minimum mass of water that must fall through 100 m in order to generate this energy. *(3 marks)*

**3** **Figures 4 and 5** show data relating to the generation of electricity in the UK for periods up to 2006.

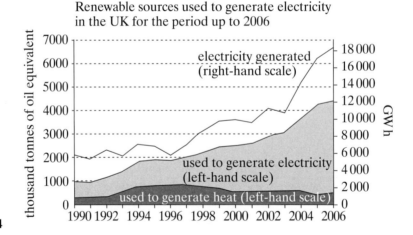

**Figure 4**

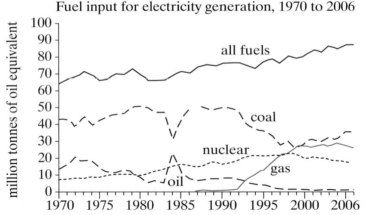

**Figure 5**

*Source: Department for Business Enterprise & Regulatory Reform Crown copyright material is reproduced with the permission of the Controller Office of Public Sector Information (OPSI)*

(a) Explain why the graphs are difficult to compare. *(1 mark)*

(b) One tonne of oil equivalent is equal to $4.2 \times 10^{16}$ J. The mean efficiency of power stations in the UK is about 35%.

Estimate the amount of electrical energy in kW h that was generated from:

(i) coal in 1990,

(ii) renewable sources in 2005. *(4 marks)*

(c) Explain what is meant by a *renewable* fuel. *(1 mark)*

(d) (i) Give an example of a renewable energy source that is not based on the movement of water.

(ii) For your example in part (d)(i), using a diagram, explain how the energy is converted from its original form and give an account of the advantages and disadvantages of the conversion process. *(5 marks)*

**4** **Figure 6** shows how the electrical energy generated in the UK from wind and wave resources has varied over a fifteen-year period. (For the years 1990–1993, 9 GWh of energy were generated.)

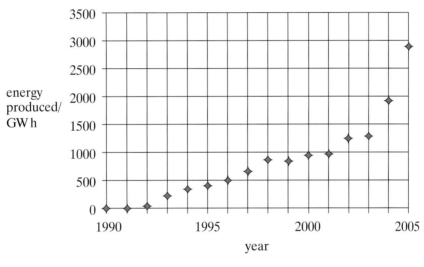

**Figure 6**

(a) Use the graph to give a description of the way in which the amount of electrical energy produced from waves and wind changed during the period shown on the graph. *(3 marks)*

(b) Calculate the energy in joules generated in the year 2004. *(2 marks)*

(c) The area of the UK is roughly 240 000 km² and the Sun delivers roughly 1.4 kW of energy per second to each square metre at the distance of the Earth from the Sun.

Estimate the length of time required for the Sun to deliver the amount of energy you calculated in part (b) to the UK. *(3 marks)*

(d) State and explain whether your estimate in part (c) is a maximum or a minimum. *(3 marks)*

**5** Calculate the energy in joules that is converted in the following:

(i) a 1.2 kW heater running for 5.0 h,

(ii) burning 10 000 cm³ of petrol, if 1 kg of petrol releases $4.8 \times 10^7$ J and the density of petrol is 740 kg m⁻³. *(5 marks)*

**6** Read the following and then construct a Sankey diagram to illustrate the energy usage in the motor car described below.

A car uses 7 dm³ of petrol when it drives 100 km in 1 h. 1 dm³ of petrol releases $4.8 \times 10^7$ J of energy. The engine of the car is 20% efficient. The energy from the engine travels to the transmission losing 3 kW on the way due to resistance and other losses; the transmission system is 75% efficient. The energy reaching the wheels is transferred to air friction and road (rolling) friction in equal amounts. *(7 marks)*

## 11.1    Energy from the Sun

**Learning objectives:**

- How does energy from the Sun reach the Earth?

- How is energy distributed in the Sun's spectrum?

*Specification reference: 3.2.2B*

### Hint

Take care when using $c = f\lambda$. The unit for length in the velocity must be the same as that used for wavelength.

Wavelengths are usually quoted with a prefix, so learn these. For ultraviolet, visible and infrared radiations the prefix 'nano' ($n = 10^{-9}$) is very common. When given in standard form a wavelength of 500 nm is $5.0 \times 10^{-7}$ m.

The temperature of a planet in the Solar system depends on relative rates at which energy arrives from the Sun and the rate at which the planet radiates energy into space. On Earth the correct balance of these factors has produced a climate that has enabled plants and animals to evolve. Maintaining an appropriate balance is important to sustaining a suitable environment to enable life on Earth to continue.

### Solar energy

The Sun's energy is created by nuclear fusion in its core. This produces a temperature of about $1.5 \times 10^7$ K in the core. The temperature falls as the energy is transmitted to the outer surface. At first the energy is in the form of gamma radiation and X-rays which raises the temperature of the outer core. Convection currents in the gaseous outer region of the Sun then transfer the energy to the surface where the temperature is 5760 K. Energy is radiated into space in the form of electromagnetic radiation at a rate of about $6.5 \times 10^7$ W for each square metre of the surface.

The radius of the Sun is $6.96 \times 10^8$ m and using the formula for the surface area of a sphere $(4\pi r^2)$ gives the surface area of the Sun as $6.08 \times 10^{18}$ m$^2$.

Therefore the total power emitted by the Sun =
$(6.5 \times 10^7) \times (6.08 \times 10^{18}) \approx 4.0 \times 10^{26}$ W

Figure 1 shows how much of this energy is radiated at different frequencies in the electromagnetic spectrum. It shows that most of the energy is in the form of visible light and infrared radiation. A smaller proportion is in the more damaging ultraviolet part of the spectrum. About 1% is in the form of microwave and other long wave radiation.

### The electromagnetic spectrum

Some energy from the Sun arrives as ions in the solar wind which gives rise to the northern lights and the tails of comets that enter the solar system. However, most of the energy is in the form of electromagnetic waves. These travel through space at a speed, $c$, of $3.0 \times 10^8$ m s$^{-1}$ taking about 8 min to reach the Earth from the Sun. Figure 2 shows the main regions of the electromagnetic spectrum, their wavelengths and frequencies.

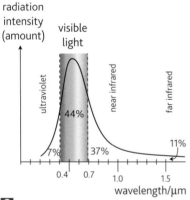

**Figure 1** *Solar radiation*

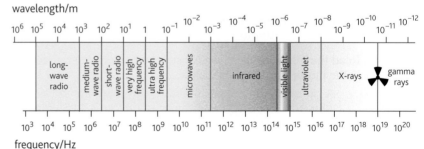

**Figure 2** *The electromagnetic spectrum*

As can be seen from Figure 1 the infrared, visible and ultraviolet are the important regions in solar radiation.

## Relation between frequency and wavelength

When analysing spectra, the wavelength is measured using diffraction gratings. The technique is explained in Topic 2.2.

The wavelength $\lambda$ and frequency $f$ of electromagnetic waves are related by the formula $c = f\lambda$.

The wavelength that emits most energy in the Sun's radiation is about 500 nm which is in the green part of the spectrum. The frequency of green light is therefore:

$$\frac{3.0 \times 10^8}{500 \times 10^{-9}} = 6.0 \times 10^{14}\,\text{Hz}$$

## Effects of electromagnetic radiation

The radiation delivers its energy in the form of photons. The higher the frequency, the higher the photon energy and the more damaging the radiation can be to our health. A single photon of green light has energy of $4.0 \times 10^{-19}$ J whereas a photon of ultraviolet radiation with wavelength 250 nm has twice as much energy, and is sufficient to cause damage to cells in the body.

The shorter wavelength X-rays and gamma radiation are penetrating radiations and are used for medical treatment and diagnosis but they also damage healthy tissue.

Infrared wavelengths cause heating and the longer wavelength microwaves are used for cooking and in mobile phone communication networks.

## Black body radiation and Wien's law

Black bodies emit all the wavelengths that are possible given the temperature of the body.

As temperature rises:

- the total energy emitted increases (doubling the kelvin temperature produces 16 times more radiated energy)
- the wavelength at which the maximum energy is emitted becomes shorter.

The wavelength at which the intensity of the radiation is greatest $(\lambda_{max})$ is related to the temperature by Wien's law.

$$\lambda_{max} T = 0.0029\,\text{m K}$$

For the Sun $\lambda_{max} = \dfrac{0.0029}{5760} = 503 \times 10^{-9}\,\text{m}$

Assuming a temperature of 290 K for the temperature of the Earth

$$\lambda_{max} = \frac{0.0029}{290} = 10\,000 \times 10^{-9}\,\text{m}$$

This is in the infrared part of the electromagnetic spectrum.

See also Topic 5.3.

**How science works**

**Mobile phones**

There is some concern about the possible damaging effects of microwave radiation from the use of mobile phones. As yet there has been no conclusive evidence as to whether they do or do not have damaging effects.

**Hint**

Temperature in Kelvin (K) = temperature in degrees Celsius (°C) + 273

Take care: note that a *temperature difference* in K is the same as the *temperature difference* in °C

Do not add 273 for temperature changes. This is a common error made in examinations.

**Summary questions**

1  Make a table showing the main parts of the electromagnetic spectrum. For each part state a use or an effect that it may have on humans.

2  Calculate the frequency of radiation that has a wavelength of 200 nm.

3  As the Sun becomes older it will cool down. At what wavelength will the peak energy occur when its surface temperature is 4500 K? What colour does this correspond to?

*Learning objectives:*

- What is the inverse square law?

- How much energy reaches the Earth from the Sun?

- What happens to the Sun's energy when it arrives at the Earth?

*Specification reference: 3.2.2D; 3.2.2B*

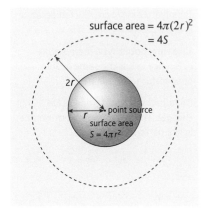

**Figure 1** *Doubling radius spreads energy over 4× the area*

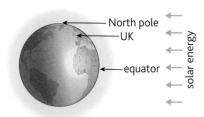

**Figure 2** *Passage of radiation through the Earth's atmosphere*

## Inverse square law

Provided that no energy is lost on the way, the **intensity** of radiation from a point source which radiates energy equally in all directions, obeys an inverse square law.

If the distance from the Sun is large enough (i.e. distance from the Sun >> radius of the Sun), the Sun can be treated as a point source. As distance $r$ from the Sun increases, the energy is spread over a larger surface area, given by the surface area of a sphere, $4\pi r^2$.

So if the power of the source (the Sun) is $P$, the intensity of radiation at a distance $r$ is given by:

$$I = \frac{P}{4\pi r^2}$$

This means that if the distance is doubled, the intensity falls by a factor of four.

The Earth is $1.5 \times 10^{11}$ m from the Sun which radiates a total power of $4.0 \times 10^{26}$ W so, using the law, the intensity of the radiation arriving at the Earth's outer atmosphere:

$$= \frac{4.0 \times 10^{26}}{4\pi(1.5 \times 10^{11})^2} = 1400\,\mathrm{W\,m^{-2}}$$

## Energy at the Earth's surface

Not all the energy arriving at the outer atmosphere reaches the surface. Energy is lost due to:

- **reflection** of radiation back into space

- **absorption** of radiation by the atmosphere.

By the time it reaches the Earth, the intensity (power per m²) is about $1000\,\mathrm{W\,m^{-2}}$ at the equator. Because the radiation has to pass through more of the Earth's atmosphere (shown diagrammatically in Figure 2), this falls to a **maximum** of about $750\,\mathrm{W\,m^{-2}}$ in the UK. However, due to the position of the UK and the variation in intensity between summer and winter, the mean annual power available from the Sun in the UK is only about $150\,\mathrm{W\,m^{-2}}$.

The proportion of energy reflected and absorbed is increased by the presence of cloud, dust and other pollutants which varies during the year. The degree of reflection and absorption depends on the wavelength of the radiation.

### Ultraviolet radiation

Ultraviolet radiation with wavelengths between 1 and 280 nm (UVC) is completely absorbed in the upper atmosphere by the ozone layer. UVB has wavelengths between 280 and 315 nm and is partially absorbed in the upper atmosphere producing ozone. However, the ozone layer has no effect on UVA which has wavelengths 315 to 400 nm, closer to the visible range.

The short wavelength ultraviolet radiation splits up oxygen ($O_2$) molecules to produce atoms of oxygen which then recombine to form ozone ($O_3$) molecules. Although ozone would be a health hazard at ground level, the molecules are useful in the upper atmosphere because they absorb some of the longer wavelength ultraviolet radiation which causes cancers in humans and damages plant life.

There is concern about the release into the atmosphere of pollutants such as chlorofluorocarbons (CFCs). These are used in refrigeration, air conditioners and aerosol sprays and seem to be responsible for a reduction in the amount of ozone in the ozone layer. The result is that a greater amount of short wavelength ultraviolet radiation can reach the Earth's surface. Such wavelengths make some contribution to global warming but, perhaps more importantly, can cause malignant skin cancer so protection is needed particularly during sunny spells.

## Infrared radiation

The temperature of the Earth and its atmosphere is the result of all the energy transfer processes that occur when sunlight reaches the Earth. The processes increase the temperature of the solids, liquids and gases that make up the Earth and therefore the amount of infrared radiation.

The absorption of ultraviolet radiation raises the temperature of the atmospheric gases. These then radiate energy in the longer infrared part of the spectrum. Although some is able to escape back into space, some is trapped by the atmosphere and so the temperature of the atmosphere rises. The infrared radiation in the Sun's radiation is also readily absorbed by atoms of oxygen, methane and carbon dioxide in the atmosphere. Light photons are absorbed by plants in the process of photosynthesis and these plants radiate energy in the infrared region of the spectrum.

The raising of the temperature caused by the trapping of the radiation is the 'greenhouse effect'.

Remember that all bodies above absolute zero emit radiation and, at the Earth's temperature, the energy radiated is infrared.

The Sun–Earth system has established an equilibrium in which the energy received and radiated are balanced and provide a mean temperature for the Earth of about 15°C. In Topic 11.3 you will see that the greenhouse effect has been important in creating suitable conditions for life on Earth as without the effect, the temperature of the Earth would be too low. The problem of global warming is that human activity is upsetting the delicate balance by *enhancing* the greenhouse effect.

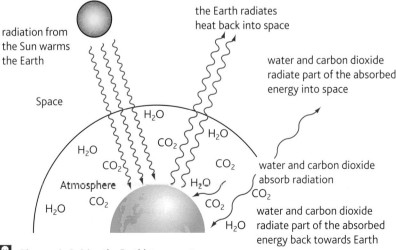

💡 **Figure 4** *Raising the Earth's temperature*

**Figure 3** *'False colour' infrared image of part of UK (red ≈ 1.6 μm, green ≈ 0.87 μm)*

### Summary questions

1. Explain why reduction of ozone in the ozone layer is a health hazard.

2. Mars is $2.28 \times 10^8$ km from the Sun. Calculate the intensity of the Sun's energy on the surface assuming that none is absorbed by its thin atmosphere.

3. Explain how the greenhouse effect affects the temperature of the Earth.

## Learning objectives:

- Why doesn't the energy arriving on the Earth radiate away?

- What is meant by thermal equilibrium?

- What is the greenhouse effect and how is it affecting the environment?

*Specification reference: 3.2.2B*

energy radiated from the Earth's surface

energy in this cone reaches the Earth

**Figure 1** *Energy absorbed and emitted*

What's happened to the greenhouse effect is a common question when extreme cold is recorded? What is generally forgotten is that the rise in mean temperature will be superimposed on the underlying variability of the climate system on the day-to-day, month-to-month and year-to-year timescales. Each year will not be warmer than the last and it may be several decades yet before we can unequivocally state that the rise is due to the build-up of greenhouse gases in the atmosphere, although this is the most likely cause.

*Dr Philip Jones Climate Research Unit, University of East Anglia*

## Equilibrium temperature

Making a few assumptions, it is possible to estimate the temperature that the Earth would reach if there were no energy trapped by the heating of the atmosphere. When equilibrium is reached, the power that is being taken in from the Sun's radiation is equal to that radiated from the Earth.

Assumptions:

- The intensity of the Sun's radiation that raises the temperature of the Earth is about $1000\,W\,m^{-2}$

- The Earth reaches a uniform temperature (of course it is hotter at the equator and cooler at the poles)

- The Earth behaves as a black body:

Assuming that $1000\,W$ is absorbed by each $m^2$ of the Earth,
power $= 1000\,\pi R^2$

Energy radiated = power radiated per $m^2$ $(p) \times$ surface area of the Earth $(4\pi R^2)$

For equilibrium $1000\pi R^2 = 4\pi R^2 p$

$p$, the power radiated $= 250\,W\,m^{-2}$

The graph in Figure 2 shows how the power radiated by a black body varies with temperature of the body. To emit $250\,W\,m^{-2}$ the equilibrium temperature of the Earth would be about $260\,K$ or $-13°C$.

This mean temperature would be too low to sustain life on Earth. The 'greenhouse effect' has enabled the Earth to achieve the higher mean temperature (about $15°C$) necessary for life to evolve.

power radiated / $W\,m^{-2}$

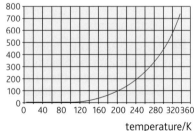

temperature/K

**Figure 2** *Intensity of radiation from a black body*

## Global warming and the effect of carbon dioxide

Venus is similar to Earth and might have once been able to support some form of life in the form of microbes. The intensity of the Sun's radiation arriving at the atmosphere of Venus is $2730\,W\,m^{-2}$. Assuming that all this were used to raise the temperature of Venus, the power radiated would have to be $680\,W\,m^{-2}$ and the temperature would be about $335\,K$. Venus has an atmosphere which is largely carbon dioxide and sulphurous fumes. This has led to 'runaway' global warming so its surface temperature is actually $743\,K$ $(470°C)$ which is hot enough to melt lead. So could the same thing happen on Earth?

The main contributory factors to global warming are the concentrations of water vapour and gases such as carbon dioxide and methane in the atmosphere. The molecules absorb the incoming radiation and re-radiate energy at longer wavelengths which find it more difficult to escape back into space. Water vapour actually absorbs a greater proportion of the Sun's energy than carbon dioxide in the atmosphere. Although it absorbs energy less well, the concentration of carbon dioxide in the atmosphere is increasing because it remains in the atmosphere longer than water vapour. This leads to an increase in the amount of solar energy being absorbed and a rise in the mean global temperature.

The rising temperature causes more water to evaporate and, as water vapour absorbs incoming radiation, more water vapour in the atmosphere could lead to further rises in temperature, enhancing the greenhouse effect. Some measurements suggest that the amount of water vapour in the upper atmosphere could double by the end of the century as the temperature rises.

Figure 3 shows how the temperature has changed over the years. The graphs use the mean temperature between 1960 and 1990 as the reference temperature. They show that the temperature was about 0.5 K below this mean in the nineteenth century. Evidence suggests this had changed little since the twelfth century. Since 1980, however, the temperature has been consistently above this mean and continues to rise.

As temperature rises it is possible that eventually a new equilibrium temperature will be established. However, this new equilibrium temperature could be too high to support life and the effect of the higher temperatures on other conditions on Earth could be disastrous

The climate change that is produced by the effects of global warming brings about many undesirable and destabilising effects. The following are some events that may occur due to global warming.

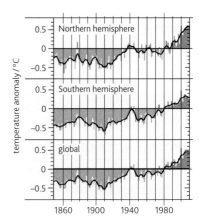

**Figure 3** *Rising global temperatures*

### How science works

**Planning for the future**

The trends in temperature and the apparent link with the carbon content of the atmosphere have led to the international agreements and legislation by governments to plan a low carbon economy. This legislation encourages a reduction in energy consumption in transport, homes and offices and the production of electricity by methods with no, or low, carbon emissions.

### How science works

**Cause and effect**

Climatic changes have taken place naturally and when assessing the effects of global warming on the climate, scientists have to distinguish between natural trends and variations and those which appear to be caused by the influence of human activity.

- The changing weather conditions in different regions of the planet upsets the ecosystems.
- Animals lose their natural habitats.
- Human populations are unable to provide the essential food on which to live.
- Extreme weather conditions bring about hurricanes, floods, heat waves and droughts.
- Melting of icecaps.
- Rising sea levels.

These factors are all interlinked and the Earth's climate is one of interacting dynamic changes.

### Summary questions

**1** Suggest why although Mercury is nearer the Sun than Venus, it has a lower surface temperature.

**2** Use Figure 3 to find the rise in temperature risen in the northern hemisphere during the period from 1910 to 2000.

**3** Explain why the reduction of carbon emissions into the atmosphere reduces the effect of global warming and suggest three means of reducing these emissions.

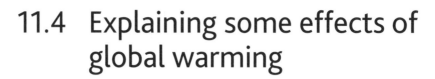

# 11.4 Explaining some effects of global warming

*Learning objectives:*

■ Why are sea levels rising?

■ What is Archimedes Principle?

■ How can Archimedes Principle help us explain environmental changes?

*Specification reference: 3.2.2B*

The consequences of global warming listed in Topic 11.3 are produced by changing climatic conditions. These in turn depend on local changes that are occurring in the temperatures of land, sea and air in different regions of the planet. The effects differ across the planet. Some regions suffer more frequent stormy conditions whilst others have little or no rainfall. One factor influencing the climate is the reduction of the polar icecaps whilst temperatures at the equator are increasing. These changes affect the global convection currents in the water and air across the Earth's surface and therefore the patterns and strengths of the winds.

## ■ Rising sea levels

One obvious effect of rising global temperature is the addition of water to the oceans caused by the melting of the polar icecaps and the glaciers that exist in the Alps, Himalayas, Andes and Rocky mountains.

The rise in the water temperature caused by global warming also causes the water to expand which further increases the water level. The mass of water involved means that this takes place slowly but the effect cannot be ignored.

Observations show that the sea level is rising. Since 1870 the average rate of rise has been 1.44 mm per year. The rate is increasing and since 1950 the rate has increased to 1.75 mm per year. Estimates of the trend vary as to the rise expected over the next 100 years but scientists are anticipating an increase in the range 100 to 900 mm.

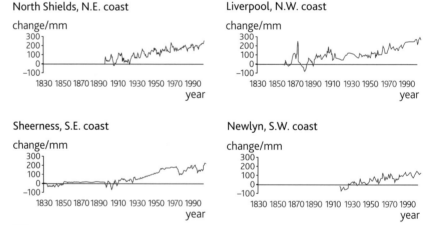

**Figure 1** *Changes in sea levels for the UK*

The rate of rise is not uniform even around Britain's coastline. Local variations in tidal levels can be caused by extra water flow into the sea from rivers and the strength and direction of winds. Furthermore, following the melting of the ice sheet which covered Britain 20 000 years ago, the North and West of Britain is rising but the South-East of England is sinking. The combination of the general rise in sea level and the sinking suggests a rise of 5.4 mm each year in the South-East of Britain.

**Possible disasters**

Internationally more than three hundred million people live within one metre of average sea-level and one-third of the world's population live near the coast. There are major scientific and political issues relating to the protection of the threatened areas by building flood defences and dealing with disasters as and when they arise. The main concern is that large populations will have to be resettled.

The following comment from the Environment Agency summarises the concerns for the UK:

*Around 17 million people live within 10 km of the sea, and much of our manufacturing industry is based at or near the coast. More frequent or serious coastal flooding in low-lying areas will put more of these people and businesses in danger.*

© Environment Agency 2007

# Melting ice

There is a dynamic equilibrium between snowfall that occurs in the colder times of the year and the ice that melts in warmer times. This equilibrium suffers annual variations but, over time, global warming appears to be causing more ice to melt than is being formed. When ice that is resting on a land mass melts it causes the sea level to rise. Ice that is floating, such as an iceberg, may or may not raise the sea level as this depends on the amount of salt in the water in which the iceberg floats. Archimedes Principle can be used to explain why this is so.

## Archimedes Principle

Archimedes Principle states that an object in a fluid (liquid or gas) experiences an upward force (an upthrust) that is equal to the weight of the fluid that the body displaces.

A simple experiment using a newtonmeter demonstrates the presence of the upthrust and how it can be used to to measure the density of an irregular solid.

When readings of the newtonmeter are taken, first when the solid is in suspended air, $W_1$, and then when it is submerged in water, $W_2$, it is found that $W_2 < W_1$.

The difference between the readings $(W_1 - W_2)$ is the upward force exerted by the fluid.

The mass of the fluid displaced $= \dfrac{W_1 - W_2}{g}$

Assuming water to have a density of $1\,\mathrm{g\,cm^{-3}}$, this is equal to the volume of the object in $\mathrm{cm^3}$.

As the mass $\left|\dfrac{W_1}{g}\right|$ is known, the density of the solid can be found:

$$\left(= \dfrac{W_1}{W_1 - W_2}\right)$$

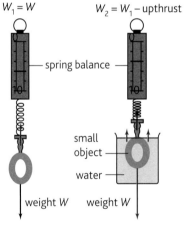

$W_1 = W$  $W_2 = W_1 - \text{upthrust}$

spring balance

small object

water

weight $W$  weight $W$

**Figure 2** *Archimedes Principle*

### Hint

To calculate density, remember that

$$\text{density} = \frac{\text{mass}}{\text{volume}}$$

Density in $\mathrm{kg\,m^{-3}} = 1000 \times$ density in $\mathrm{g\,cm^{-3}}$.

### Principle of Flotation

When an object floats, it is in equilibrium. The upward force, and hence the weight of fluid displaced, is equal to the weight of the object. The fact that a floating object displaces fluid equal to its own weight is the Principle of Flotation.

So what happens when an iceberg made of pure frozen water melts? If it is floating in pure water, the water formed by the melting ice will have a volume exactly equal to the displaced volume of water. (Try it with some ice cubes in a glass of water.) If the iceberg is floating in sea water, which has a greater density than pure water (due to the salt dissolved in it), then the volume of water from the iceberg will more than fill the volume displaced and the level will rise.

## ■ Convection currents

Convection currents are responsible for redistributing energy from the warm equator to colder regions of the Earth's surface. When a body of air is heated it expands and its density falls. The greater the temperature, the lower the density. When this body of air is surrounded by colder air of higher density it behaves like a table tennis ball pushed to the bottom of a bowl of water and released. The upthrust caused by the displaced colder air is greater than the weight of the body of air and the warm air is forced upwards, its place being taken by the colder air around it. The rate at which the air body moves upwards depends on the relative densities of the warm and cold air as shown below.

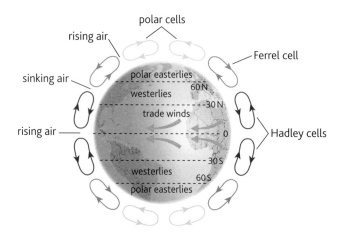

**Figure 3** *Earth's convection currents and winds*

Consider a body of air of volume $V$ and density $d$ surrounded by air of density $\rho$ then:

downward force due to its weight is $W = Vdg$

upthrust on the volume $V = V\rho g$

If $Vdg > V\rho g$ the downward force is greater and the mass of air sinks.

If $Vdg < V\rho g$ the upward force is greater and the mass of air rises.

The greater the difference in densities, the greater the upward force and the faster it accelerates upwards. When the body of air reaches a high temperature this can lead to high winds and hurricanes.

This principle also applies to bodies immersed in liquids and gases.

### ■ How science works

**Simplifying explanations**

In practice, the density of air varies across the Earth's surface and the rotation of the Earth is involved in creating vortices of wind. Convection currents are often explained by simply stating 'hot air rises'. Archimedes Principle goes further and explains why this happens. The Principle can also be shown to be the consequence of the difference in pressure acting on the upper and lower surfaces of an object immersed in a fluid.

# Breezes, thunderstorms and hurricanes

During a hot day at the seaside a sea breeze blows. The land has a relatively low thermal capacity (meaning less energy is needed to raise its temperature by 1 K). Also energy is transferred relatively slowly from the surface to other parts. The surface temperature therefore rises quickly which is very noticeable if you walk barefoot on sand. The air above the ground heats up quickly too.

The intensity of the Sun's energy falling on the sea is the same as that on the land but water needs about 5 times more energy to raise the temperature by 1 K. Also the sea is continually being 'stirred' by winds and waves so the energy is not restricted to the surface. On a particular day the sea temperature remains fairly constant. (It may feel warm in parts of the beach where the water is shallow but this is a local effect.).

As the temperature rises the density of the air above the land falls, so it is forced upwards by the cooler air, over denser air that is over the sea. The warm air is replaced by this cooler air which forms the refreshing breeze. At higher levels, the pressure increases because of the rising air above the land and the wind blows in the other direction. There is therefore a circulating current of air.

In the afternoon, as the intensity of Sun's energy falls, the land quickly cools as energy is lost to the air above it. The air over the sea is now warmer than that over the land and the situation is reversed. This results in a cool land breeze at ground level. Because the land has to cool to below the sea temperature for the land breeze to occur, land breezes only tend to happen in early summer or autumn when the evenings are colder.

Clouds are formed when the convection currents draw warm moist air into the atmosphere. As the moist air rises it cools, forming a cloud of water droplets that eventually falls as rain. When the temperature is very high the dynamics of the event are relatively fast and the water builds up more rapidly. As the air may move to cold regions high up in the atmosphere the water droplets may become frozen and eventually fall as hail stones. The fast turbulent movement of the air masses in the atmosphere can cause some parts to develop a positive charge and some a negative charge. Eventually, when the charge has built up sufficiently, the air masses lose their charge by a discharge from one air mass to another or from the cloud to the Earth, as lightning.

Figure 6 *Thunder cloud developing*

The severity of storms depends on the temperature and particularly that above the oceans. Hurricanes may occur in regions where the sea temperature is about 26 °C or more (clearly not a problem for the waters around the UK). However, the general trend of rising temperatures of the planet, whether or not this is influenced by human activity, is placing more regions at risk, many of which have not experienced such severe storms in the past.

warm air    sea breeze    cool air
28°C                        15°C

Figure 4 *Sea breeze*

cool air    land breeze   warm air
10°C                        15°C

Figure 5 *Land breeze*

## Summary questions

1 State three reasons why there is an increased risk of flooding around Britain's coastline.

2 An iceberg of volume $1.60 \times 10^4 \, m^3$ and density $920 \, kg \, m^{-3}$ floats in sea water of density $1025 \, kg \, m^{-3}$. Calculate:

 a the volume of sea water that it displaces,

 b the volume of water produced when the iceberg melts given that the density of water is $1000 \, kg \, m^{-3}$.

3 Assuming that the water rises uniformly around the Earth's surface and the seas and oceans cover four-fifths of the Earth's surface (Earth's radius 6400 km), calculate the mass of ice that has to melt to raise the sea level by 1.75 mm.

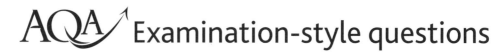

1  (a) State Wien's Law. *(2 marks)*

   (b) The Sun radiates a total power of $4.0 \times 10^{26}$ W.
   Show that about 1.4 kJ of energy falls on one square metre of the Moon each second.
   Sun–Moon distance = $1.5 \times 10^{11}$ m *(2 marks)*

   (c) One-eighth of the radiation that falls on the Moon's surface is reflected back into space.
   Calculate the power absorbed by one square metre of the Moon from the Sun. *(1 mark)*

   (d) **Figure 1** shows how the power radiated by a black body varies with temperature.
   Use the graph to determine the equilibrium surface temperature of the Moon on
   the side facing the Sun. *(1 mark)*

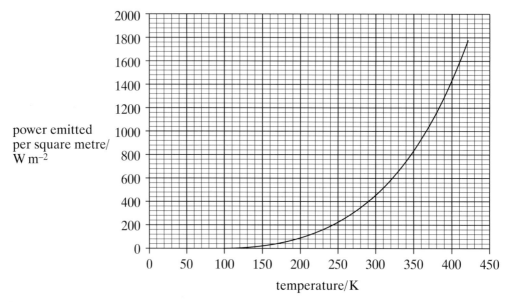

**Figure 1**

   (e) Locations on the Moon spend 14 days in the dark and 14 days in sunlight. Suggest
   the factors that are likely to influence the temperature on the dark side of the Moon. *(2 marks)*

2  Arrange the following list of regions of the electromagnetic spectrum in order of
   increasing *wavelength*.

   Radio    X-ray    Microwave    Visible    Infrared    Ultraviolet

   For **two** of these regions give approximate wavelengths for the radiation and
   indicate two uses of the radiation. *(6 marks)*

**3**   (a)   The planet Mercury has daytime temperatures of 720 K and night-time temperatures of 100 K.

     (i)   Calculate the frequency at which the intensity of radiation emitted by Mercury is at its greatest.

     (ii)   State the region of the electromagnetic spectrum in which this frequency is situated.   *(4 marks)*

   (b)   Venus has a higher average temperature than Mercury even though it is twice the distance from the Sun. State **two** ways in which the emitted energy of Venus differs from that of Mercury.   *(2 marks)*

**4**   The Sun has a surface temperature of 5700 K.

   (a)   (i)   Calculate the wavelength at which the intensity of the Sun is greatest.

     (ii)   State the region of the electromagnetic spectrum in which this wavelength is found.   *(4 marks)*

   (b)   A photograph of the Sun is taken using a photographic plate sensitive only to infrared radiation.

State and explain how the image of the Sun on the infrared plate will differ from that of a photograph taken with visible light.   *(4 marks)*

**5**   (a)   State Archimedes principle.   *(1 mark)*

   (b)   Use your answer to part (a) to explain why a freshwater iceberg melting in a salt water sea leads to a change in sea level.   *(4 marks)*

   (c)   State and explain how your answer to part (b) changes if pure glacier ice melts in a freshwater lake.   *(3 marks)*

**6**   It is suggested that changing levels of carbon dioxide ($CO_2$) in the atmosphere are leading to changes in the mean temperature of the Earth.

   (a)   Explain the role played by $CO_2$ in this change.   *(2 marks)*

   (b)   Explain how water molecules can help to produce 'positive feedback' in this system.   *(3 marks)*

**7**   (a)   Explain what is meant by the 'greenhouse effect'.   *(2 marks)*

   (b)   Explain how the greenhouse effect arises.   *(3 marks)*

**8**   The Antarctic land mass has an area of $14 \times 10^6$ km² and is mostly covered in ice to an average depth of 1.6 km.

   (a)   Calculate the mass of the Antarctic ice.

     density of ice = 920 kg m⁻³   *(3 marks)*

   (b)   Calculate the change in sea level if all this ice were to melt.

     area of ocean on Earth = $3.6 \times 10^8$ km²

     density of water = 1000 kg m⁻³   *(3 marks)*

# 12 Using electrical energy

## 12.1 Making charge flow

**Figure 1** *Solar powered road sign*

Modern lifestyle has become increasingly dependent on the use of electricity. It is used for heating, lighting, producing motion using motors and for the operation of electronic devices such as television sets and computers. This chapter is concerned with the physics behind the conversion of electrical energy into other useful forms.

### Mains supplies, cells and batteries

The mains supply is the means by which we obtain energy using a national grid that transmits power from the renewable and non-renewable power sources. Cells and batteries are the portable devices in which the electrical energy is produced from stored chemical energy. Although commonly referred to as a 'battery', a 1.5 V supply is a single cell. A battery is the correct term for a supply that consists of more than one cell such as a 12 V car battery that consists of six lead–acid cells.

A cell may have a limited lifetime, determined by the type and quantity of the chemicals in the cell, or it may be capable of being recharged from the mains supply using a mains adaptor. Many lights in road signs and bus-stops now work using solar cells that produce electricity directly from the Sun's energy (Figure 1).

Important features of a supply:

- It is the **electromotive force** (emf) of the supply which produces a **potential difference** (pd) across the components in the circuit.
- The **current** that it produces in a circuit is governed by its own **internal resistance** and the **resistance** of other components in the circuit.
- The total energy the supply can provide, i.e. the 'life' of the supply.

A supply may provide a direct or an alternating voltage and current. Heating and lighting use the alternating mains supply directly whilst the electronic circuits found in mobile phones, computers and television sets need a direct supply. Motors may operate from direct or alternating supplies depending on their design.

A supply such as a dry cell produces a direct current (dc) which means that the current is always in the same direction in the circuit. Computers and other similar equipment use electronic devices to produce a direct supply from the alternating mains supply to operate the rest of the electronic circuitry.

### Alternating power supplies

When a supply produces an alternating current (ac) the current changes direction. In the UK the mains supply operates at a frequency of 50 Hz. The emf quoted for the supply, 230 V in the UK, is the equivalent direct voltage. When making calculations of current and power for such circuits, assume that it behaves like a direct supply with this emf.

## What is electric current?

An electric current is produced by the movement of charged particles called charge carriers. In metallic conductors the charge carriers are electrons. Electrical charge is measured in coulomb (C) and each electron carries a charge of $-1.6 \times 10^{-19}$ C.

Before electrons were discovered, the direction of current was defined as the direction of flow of positive charge so it is still assumed to be in the direction from $+$ to $-$. The negatively charged electrons however move towards the positive terminal of the supply. This can be a source of confusion, so take care.

Charge is a conserved quantity so when a circuit is operating, the same quantity of charge leaves a point as enters it in a set time. This is useful when making circuit calculations because, when the current has two or more possible paths from a point,

$$\frac{\text{the sum of the currents}}{\text{entering a junction}} = \frac{\text{the sum of the currents}}{\text{leaving a junction}}$$

It follows that the current going into a supply is equal to that which leaves it.

The electric current at a point in a circuit is a measure of the rate of flow of charge through the point. It is measured using an ammeter. Just as a turnstile counts people into a sporting event (each one carrying their ticket), an ammeter effectively records the number of electrons passing through it (each one carrying its charge).

The **ammeter** therefore must be connected **in series** with the component whose current measurement is needed.

The SI unit of current is the ampère A so 1 coulomb = 1 ampère-second ($1\,C = 1\,As$ or $1\,A = 1\,Cs^{-1}$)

If a current $I$ flows for a time interval of $\Delta t$ the charge $\Delta Q$ that passes each point in the circuit is given by:

$$\Delta Q = I\Delta t \quad \text{so} \quad I = \frac{\Delta Q}{\Delta t}$$

In terms of electrons, if the current is $I$ then the number of electrons that must pass a point in the circuit in $1\,s = \dfrac{I}{1.6 \times 10^{-19}}$

If the current at a point in a circuit is $1\,A$ then $6.25 \times 10^{18}$ electrons pass the point each second.

## Rechargeable cells and batteries

The usefulness of rechargeable cells and car batteries is given in terms of the total charge they can cause to flow. This total charge is equal to the average current the supply delivers multiplied by the time for which it operates before running down. The time is usually measured in hours. Thus the charge is given in amp-hours (Ah) for high capacity batteries such as those used in cars or in mAh for smaller cells used in devices such as digital cameras and mobile phones.

For example a 1300 mAh rechargeable cell for a digital camera can supply a current of 1300 mA for 1 h or 100 mA for 13 h, etc.

One hour is 3600 s so the total charge it supplies $= 1300 \times 10^{-3} \times 3600 = (4680\,C)$.

Recharging such batteries requires this amount of charge to be stored in the cell. This can be supplied by a charger at a rate of 100 mA for 13 h or 200 mA for 6.5 h, etc.

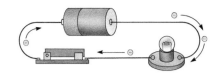

**Figure 2** *Electron flow in a circuit*

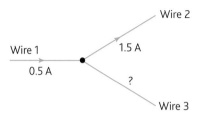

**Figure 3** *Currents at a junction*

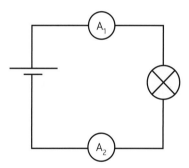

**Figure 4** *Both ammeters record current in the lamp*

### Summary questions

1 A car battery is stated to have a capacity of 30 Ah. For how long could it provide a current of a 1.5 A b 80 A?

2 How many electrons pass a point in a circuit each minute when the current is 2.5 A?

3 Explain why a non-rechargeable cell has a limited life.

# 12.2 Currents in circuits

Learning objectives:

■ What factors affect the current in a component?

■ How are the conductive properties of materials compared?

■ How is the effective resistance of resistors in series and parallel calculated?

*Specification reference: 3.2.2C*

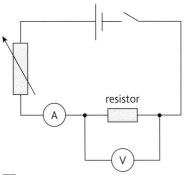

**Figure 1** *Measuring resistance*

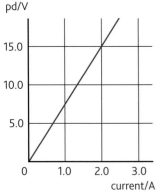

**Figure 2** *V–I graph for an ohmic component*

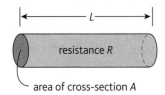

**Figure 3** *Finding resistivity*

The current in a circuit component is determined by the potential difference across it and its resistance to the flow of charge. The **resistance** $R$ is defined as the potential difference $V$ across the component divided by the current $I$ through it.

$$R = \frac{V}{I}$$

When the $V$ is in volts (V) and $I$ is in amperes (A) the $R$ is in ohm ($\Omega$).

When a 750 W heater element is connected to a 230 V mains supply, the current is 3.26 A. So the resistance of the heater element when working normally is 70.6 $\Omega$

$$\left| R = \frac{230}{3.26}\Omega \right|.$$

## ■ Ohm's law

The variation of current with potential difference across a component is called its 'characteristic'. This behaviour is an important factor in determining its applications. The circuit in Figure 1 may be used to investigate the characteristic of an electrical component (in this case a resistor). For some components the resistance is constant when the current and voltage change. The component is then said to obey **Ohm's law** and is referred to as an **ohmic conductor**. The graph of $V$ against $I$ for such a conductor is a straight line through the origin and the gradient of the graph gives the value of the resistance. In Figure 2 the resistance of the component is 7.5 $\Omega$.

An example of an ohmic component is a metallic resistor held at constant temperature.

When the $V$–$I$ graph is a curve (such as that for a filament lamp) the component does not obey Ohm's law and is a non-ohmic conductor (see Topic 12.4).

### Finding resistance from graphs

The gradient only gives the resistance for ohmic conductors. When the graph is curved the resistance for a given voltage is found by dividing that voltage by the corresponding value of current which is read from the graph. This is **not** equal to the gradient of the $V$–$I$ graph at that voltage.

## 💡 ⚗ Electrical resistivity

The resistivity of the material is the property used to compare the ability of different materials to conduct. A perfect conductor would have a resistivity of zero and a perfect insulator an infinite resistivity.

The resistivity $\rho$ is calculated from the formula:

$$\rho = \frac{RA}{L}$$

$R$ is the resistance, $A$ is the cross-sectional area of the conductor and $L$ is the length of the conductor (see Figure 3).

When $R$ is in $\Omega$, $A$ is in $m^2$ and $L$ is in m, the resistivity $\rho$ is in $\Omega\,m$.

Table 1 shows the resistivity for some solid conductors and insulators.

Good conductors such as copper are used for making electrical connections between components. Aluminium is often used in power transmission cables as it has a lower density than copper and gold is used in the manufacture of integrated electronic circuits. These can usually be assumed to have negligible resistance compared with the resistance of the components in the circuit.

Insulators like rubber and polythene are used for both practical and safety reasons. Wires are coated with high resistance insulation to prevent short circuits occurring between conducting wires and to protect the user when high voltages are used.

In terms of resistivity, between the good conductors and insulators there are:

- alloys with resistivities of about $10^{-6}\,\Omega\,m$ which provide resistance to the flow of charge so that electrical energy is transferred to thermal energy
- semiconductors with resistivities of between 0.1 and $60\,\Omega\,m$ that are used in temperature sensors and are essential to the operation of modern electronic devices.

### Heater elements and lamp filaments

The element in an electric heater is made of nichrome wire (approximately 80% nickel and 20% chromium with small amounts of other elements) wound on a grooved rod made of ceramic which is an insulator. The design of the element is a compromise that takes into account the length and diameter of the rod, the power output required and the operating temperature. The operating temperature (about 700 °C) must be well below the melting temperature of the element.

For example, a 750 W element could be made of 0.42 mm diameter nichrome wire. From the formula

$$L = \frac{RA}{\rho}$$

the length $L$ of the filament is 8.9 m $\left(= \dfrac{70.6 \times \pi(0.21 \times 10^{-3})^2}{110 \times 10^{-8}}\right)$.

The wire could be wound on a rod of diameter 15 mm. The circumference of the rod would be 0.047 m so that there would be about 190 turns. (There would actually be fewer turns because the coil is in the form of a spiral so each turn would need a little more than 0.047 m of wire.)

Lamp filaments have to operate at high temperatures so that they emit light. They also need a large surface area to increase the light output. To achieve this each filament consists of a long length of very thin tungsten wire (melting point 3700 K) which is arranged in the form of a coiled coil (Figure 4).

### Lamps in parallel

The headlights and sidelights and all the electrical equipment in a car are all designed to operate from a 12 V supply. They are therefore connected to the supply **in parallel**. As well as ensuring that they operate correctly, connecting them in parallel ensures that if one of the lamps fails the others will continue to operate.

**Table 1**

| material | resistivity / $\Omega\,m$ |
| --- | --- |
| copper | $1.7 \times 10^{-8}$ |
| gold | $2.8 \times 10^{-8}$ |
| nichrome | $110 \times 10^{-8}$ |
| tungsten | $5.4 \times 10^{-8}$ |
| silicon | 0.1–60 |
| glass | $\approx 1 \times 10^{-11}$ |
| polythene | $10^{15}$–$10^{18}$ |
| rubber | $\approx 10^{15}$ |

### Hint

Look carefully at the prefix for units of voltage, current and resistance. A resistance is often given in k$\Omega$ ($10^3\,\Omega$) or M$\Omega$.($10^6\,\Omega$). Currents of mA ($10^{-3}$ A) and $\mu$A ($10^{-6}$ A) are commonly used.

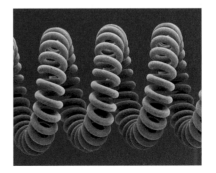

**Figure 4** *Magnified image of coiled coil lamp filament*

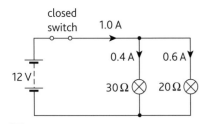

**Figure 5** *Lamps in parallel*

### Summary questions

1. Calculate the current that a 230 V supply would produce in a 1.35 kΩ filament lamp.

2. The 2.5 m long tungsten wire in a filament lamp has a resistance of 880 Ω. Calculate the area of cross-section of the filament.

3. Two 12 V lamps, one with a resistance of 4.0 Ω and the other with a resistance of 6.0 Ω are connected in parallel to a 12 V battery. Calculate the effective resistance of the two lamps and the total current supplied by the battery.

4. a Explain why the headlights in a car are connected in parallel with each other.

   b Two headlamps are designed to operate from a 12 V supply but are incorrectly connected so that they are in series with the 12 V supply. What is the effect of this mistake?

Figure 5 shows the connections to two interior car lamps. The resistance of one of the lamps is 30 Ω and the resistance of the other is 20 Ω.

The current in the 30 Ω lamp $= \dfrac{12}{30} = 0.40\,\text{A}$

The current in the 20 Ω lamp $= \dfrac{12}{20} = 0.60\,\text{A}$

The total current supplied by the battery is therefore 1.0 A

The two lamps behave like a single resistor whose resistance $= \dfrac{12}{1.0} = 12\,\Omega$

### Formula for resistors in parallel

The effective resistance $R$ of two resistors $R_1$ and $R_2$ connected in parallel can be found using the formula:

$$\frac{1}{R} = \frac{1}{R_1} + \frac{1}{R_2}$$

So the two lamps in the above example behave as a single lamp of resistance given by:

$$\frac{1}{R} = \frac{1}{30} + \frac{1}{20}$$

This gives $\dfrac{1}{R} = 0.0333 + 0.05 = 0.0833$ so $R = \dfrac{1}{0.0833} = 12\,\Omega$, as was shown above.

## Lamps in series

Connecting lamps in series is common in strings of lights used for decoration on festive occasions.

In such strings there may be 20 lamps of resistance 72 Ω operating from a 240 V supply. When lamps are connected in series, the current is the same in each lamp. As each lamp has the same resistance, the potential difference across each lamp is also the same. The result is that the supply emf is shared equally between the lamps so that the potential difference across each lamp is $\dfrac{240}{20} = 12\,\text{V}$

This leads to a current of $\dfrac{12}{72} = 0.167\,\text{A}$ in each lamp.

The 240 V supply is producing the current of 0.167 A in the string of 20 lights so their effective resistance is $\dfrac{240}{0.167} = 1440\,\Omega$

### Formula for resistors in series

The effective resistance $R$ of two resistors $R_1$ and $R_2$ connected in series can be found using the formula

$$R = R_1 + R_2$$

In fact, the resistance of any string of resistors connected in series is found by simply adding the individual resistances together.

Notice that in the above example the resistance of the string of lamps (1440 Ω) is the same value as adding all the resistances of the 20 lamps (20 × 72 Ω).

# 12.3　Energy transfer

Learning objectives:

■ How is power in a circuit component calculated?

■ How is energy consumption related to power?

■ What is meant by potential difference?

*Specification reference: 3.2.2C*

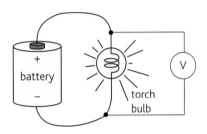

**Figure 1** *Energy from battery to lamp*

## AQA Examiner's tip

The direction of the **conventional current** is defined as the direction of flow of positive charge so is from the positive to the negative terminal of the battery. In metals this is opposite to the direction of movement of the electrons.

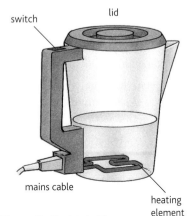

**Figure 2** *Electric kettle*

## ■ Energy transfer in a lamp filament

When a trolley runs down an inclined track it moves from a point where it has high gravitational potential energy to where it has a lower potential energy. As it does so energy is transferred from potential to kinetic energy.

Similarly electrons are made to move through a lamp filament because each electron has a lower potential energy as it moves in the direction of the positive supply terminal and energy is transferred in the process. There is said to be an electrical **potential difference** between the two terminals of the lamp. This is measured by a **voltmeter** connected between the terminals of the lamp.

When a potential difference exists, the free electrons in the filament move toward the positive terminal and energy is dissipated in the filament due to its resistance to the flow of charge.

The potential difference is measured in volts (V). This is the energy in joules transferred to the lamp for each coulomb of charge that passes through it.

One volt is therefore one joule per coulomb ($1\,V = 1\,JC^{-1}$)

For the filament of a lamp the total energy transferred (or dissipated by the filament) $E = VQ$

Since $Q = I\Delta t$ it follows that $E = VI\Delta t$

The **power** (energy per second) used by the lamp $P = \dfrac{E}{\Delta t} = VI$

Using $V = IR$ gives other useful equations for calculating power:

$$P = \frac{V^2}{R} \text{ and } P = I^2R$$

Remember that power is the **rate** at which energy is transferred so it is measured in watts, W ($1\,W = 1\,Js^{-1}$).

An electric kettle using energy at a rate of 1.5 kW from a 230 V supply carries a current of 6.5 A. The resistance of the heating element would be 35 Ω.

The table below shows some device characteristics. You can use the above formulae to show that the data is consistent.

| device | operating pd (*V*) | operating current (*I*) | device resistance (*R*) | power dissipated (*P*) *P = VI* | energy used in 1 h = power in W × 3600 s *E = VIt* |
|---|---|---|---|---|---|
| torch bulb | 1.25 V | 0.30 A | 4.2 Ω | 0.38 W | 1370 J |
| laptop computer | 14 V | 0.60 A | 23 Ω | 8.4 W | 30 240 J |
| car headlamp | 12 V | 8.3 A | 1.45 Ω | 100 W | 360 000 J |

### How science works

#### Mobile phones

A typical mobile phone uses 12 times more power when being used to make a call than in standby. This means that in standby the current is 1/12 of the call current so charge is transferred to the circuit 12 times more slowly.

## ■ Practical energy unit

The joule is a small energy unit. As the table on page 157 shows, while it is suitable for use when analysing small devices, the numbers become very large when considering the operation of high power mains devices. To make numbers more manageable the kilowatt-hour (kW h) is used as the unit of energy consumption. This is the energy used by a 1 kW heater operated for one hour and is equivalent to 3 600 000 J. The quantity 1 kW h is commonly referred to a 'unit' of electricity.

To calculate the number of kW h used, multiply the power of the device by the time in hours for which it is operated:

number of units used (kW h) = power (kW) × time used (h)

The cost of electricity varies according to the time of day it is used. At night electricity is cheaper because the demand is lower. At the time of writing electrical energy costs between 5p and 12p per kW h.

A large office block that has 500 200 W lights left switched on for 8 h overnight would use 100 kW for 8 h which is 800 kW h. The cost at 7p per unit would be £56 per night which is £20, 440 over a year.

## ■ Power use in electric motors

In electric motors, the interaction between a current and a magnetic field produces a force that causes motion and this can be used to drive machinery. In a radio loudspeaker, the signal is in the form of an alternating current from the amplifiers in the radio. This makes a cone inside the loudspeaker vibrate at the same frequency as the signal and transfers energy to the air and hence to the listener. The formula for calculating the power transferred from the supply is still $P = VI$.

### Efficiency of energy transfer

The energy supplied by a power supply is not always useful energy. The energy that appears in the form that the apparatus was designed to generate is the **useful energy**. In an electric kettle, the useful energy is thermal energy, for a filament lamp it is light, for a CD player it is sound and for a motor it is the energy used in lifting or moving something.

The percentage efficiency of the conversion is calculated using:

$$\text{Efficiency (\%)} = \frac{\text{useful energy output}}{\text{corresponding energy input}} \times 100$$

or

$$\text{Efficiency (\%)} = \frac{\text{useful power output}}{\text{power input}} \times 100$$

The conversion of electrical energy to thermal energy in heaters is almost 100% efficient. Some may be emitted as light and some loss may occur in the power leads but even this becomes thermal energy.

Filament lamps are very inefficient. Their purpose is to convert electrical energy to light energy but most is transferred to the surroundings as thermal energy.

In motors, energy is wasted when work is done against frictional forces and due to resistance in the motor wires.

The useful energy supplied by a motor in a crane which is lifting a load of 500 kg through a height of 30 m is 147 000 J (using $mg \Delta h$).

Suppose the motor is driven by a 400 V supply, uses a current of 12 A and takes 40 s to lift the load. The electrical energy supplied to the motor will be 192 000 J (using *VIt*).

The efficiency of the motor is therefore $= \dfrac{147\,000}{192\,000} \times 100 = 76.6\%$

The formula for calculating the percentage efficiency of the motor is
$\dfrac{mgh}{VIt} \times 100$

The percentage of the energy *wasted* is therefore $100 - 76.6 = 23.4\%$

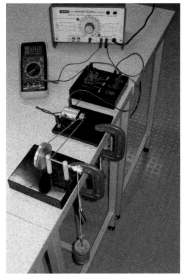

**Figure 3** *Measuring the efficiency of a motor*

## Problems in circuits

Components may be damaged due to mechanical mistreatment or an increase in electrical power dissipation.

When a fault develops in a component such as a lamp in a series circuit one of two things might happen.

- The fault produces an open circuit (i.e. a gap in the circuit) so that none of the other components operate.
- The fault produces a short circuit so that each lamp receives a higher share of the supply e.m.f. The higher potential difference across the other lamps means that they will carry a higher current and are likely to be damaged.

When lamps are connected in parallel

- An open circuit fault in one lamp affects only that lamp.
- A short circuit fault results in a high current through the wires and the supply itself which may cause damage unless there is a fuse in the circuit.

### Summary questions

**1** Calculate the resistance of a filament lamp that operates with a current of 250 mA from a 1.25 V supply.

**2** Calculate the electrical energy in J used by a 1.5 kW electric fire that operates for 3.5 h.

**3** A filament lamp is designed to operate at 12 V, 3 A and an efficiency of 1.5%. Calculate the rate at which light energy is emitted.

### How science works

**Household wiring**

The cable used in wiring for household circuits determines the maximum current that can be safely carried. If a fault occurs in the equipment being used the maximum current could be exceeded. This could cause the wire to overheat and may cause a fire. Protection is provided by incorporating fuses. Some fuses are short lengths of wire connected in series with the appliances. These are designed to melt when the current limit is exceeded, producing an open circuit. Others devices called residual current devices (RCDs) switch off the supply if a fault develops.

# 12.4 Modelling electric current

*Learning objectives:*

- How is electricity conducted through solids, liquids and gases?

- How does electrical energy become thermal energy?

- How does the resistance of metals and thermistors change when temperature changes?

*Specification reference: 3.2.2C*

## How science works

**Models**

The electrical equations are mathematical models that enable us to predict the currents, voltages and power transfers in circuits. This form of circuit analysis is on a **macroscopic scale**. Physicists also create models to explain what is happening at the atomic level, on a **microscopic scale**. The model described in the text is such a model.

**Figure 1** *Insulating supports for conducting cables*

## Conductors and insulators

The ability of a substance (solid, liquid or gas) to conduct electricity depends on the number of free charge carriers per cubic metre. The charge carriers may be **electrons** or **ions**.

When a potential difference is applied, charge carriers experience a force toward the positive or negative terminal depending on the sign of their charge. This causes the free particles to have a net velocity (called the drift velocity) toward one of the terminals. The net movement of charge is the current.

Metals such as copper and gold are very good conductors and transmit electrical energy with little energy loss. Copper has about $10^{28}$ free charge carriers per unit volume which gives it a very low resistivity of about $1.7 \times 10^{-8}\,\Omega\,\text{m}$. Insulators like ceramics and polythene have very few free charge carriers and often only conduct at all due to moisture on their surfaces.

The power dissipated in a conductor depends on its resistance and the current $(I^2R)$. Due to their low resistance, conductors such as copper can carry a high current without wasting power. In the case of insulators the current is very low when used in typical applications so, although the resistance is high, there is little energy dissipated.

### Metallic conductors

Metals are polycrystalline. In solid form, the ions are locked into the lattices of many tiny crystals. Electrons that are not involved in the bonding between the lattice ions are free to move and when there is no applied potential difference, they move randomly.

When there is an emf that causes a current to flow, the free electrons drift through the metal toward the positive terminal of the battery. As they move, the electrons collide with lattice ions. They lose kinetic energy and increase the vibrational energy of the lattice ions. The overall effect is that the electrical energy provided to make the electrons move is transferred to the metal ions so that there is a rise in temperature.

The collisions with the lattice ions affect the rate at which the electrons drift though the metal and therefore limit the rate at which the charge can flow. This limiting effect is the property that we call **resistance**.

The resistivity of a metal is therefore the combined effect of

- the availability of the electrons
- how often the electrons collide with lattice ions (i.e. the frequency of collisions of the electrons)

When the current of electrons passes through suitable metals, as in electrical heaters and filament lamps, the rate at which energy transfer takes place is high enough to provide useful space heating or light.

## Effect of temperature on resistance of metals

When higher voltages (giving higher currents) are connected across a metallic resistor the temperature will rise until it reaches thermal equilibrium with its surroundings. Equilibrium occurs when the electrical energy dissipated in the wire is equal to the energy transferred to the surroundings by conduction and radiation.

When a 750 W 230 V heater element is connected to a 6 V supply the current is 0.091 A. This is higher than the current of 0.085 A that would be expected for the 70.6 Ω heater element.

The 6 V supply produces less power dissipation in the filament wire so its temperature remains constant at room temperature.

Figure 3 shows the shape of the *V–I* graph as the current in the wire of an electric heater is increased from a low value. At 20 °C the wire resistance is 65.9 Ω. This increases as the temperature rises and reaches 70.6 Ω when the wire reaches its working temperature of 700 °C. A filament lamp has a similar characteristic.

As the potential difference increases, the higher current transfers energy to the wire more rapidly than it can be dissipated to the surroundings. The temperature rises until the rate at which the energy can be lost from the wire to the surroundings by conduction and radiation is equal to the rate at which it is being supplied.

As the resistance is lower when a supply is first connected, it follows that when a lamp or heater is switched on there is an initial surge of current which then falls as the temperature rises. This has no real effect on heating elements but the initial surge often causes ageing filament lamps to fail at the instant they are switched on.

### *Explaining the effect*

A higher current leads to an increase in temperature. The amplitude of vibration of the lattice ions in the metal's crystalline structure increases. The ions are now larger targets for the electrons so that the electrons collide more frequently with the ions. The drift velocity of the electrons decreases and if the applied potential difference remains the same then it produces a lower rate of flow of charge, hence a lower current. So as temperature increases the resistance also increases.

## Thermistors

Thermistors are made of semiconductor material. In a pure form the silicon is a good insulator with very few free electrons. When impurity atoms of phosphorus are introduced into the crystal lattice of a silicon crystal (called doping) each one contributes a free electron (see Figure 4).The resistivity of the doped semiconductor therefore largely depends on the number of impurity atoms that have been introduced (i.e. the degree of doping).

As well as the electrons produced by doping, some electrons are liberated from the lattice due to the temperature of the material (see Figure 5). This effect is used in negative temperature coefficient (NTC) thermistors for which resistance falls as temperature rises. .

When the temperature of a thermistor rises, there are two factors that affect its resistance.

▪ As with metals, the frequency of collisions of electrons with the lattice increases. This tends to increases the resistance.

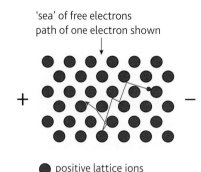

'sea' of free electrons
path of one electron shown

● positive lattice ions

**Figure 2** *Conduction in metals*

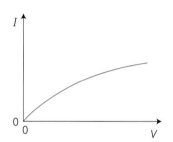

**Figure 3** *V–I graph for heater element*

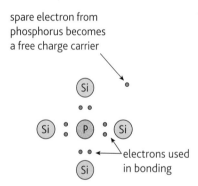

spare electron from
phosphorus becomes
a free charge carrier

electrons used
in bonding

**Figure 4** *Electrons released by doping*

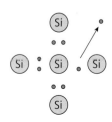

free electron leaves a 'hole' in
the lattice – more are freed at
higher temperatures

**Figure 5** *Electrons released by heating*

■ There is an increase in charge carrier density that tends to decrease the resistance.

The resistance of an NTC thermistor between 0 and 100°C decreases as temperature rises, so the second factor has the greater effect.

## ■ Conduction in liquids and gases

Acids and solutions of salts such as copper sulphate conduct electricity because some salt molecules split up (dissociate) so that the ions are free to move. The more copper sulphate that is dissolved in water the more ions there are in the solution and the lower the resistance.

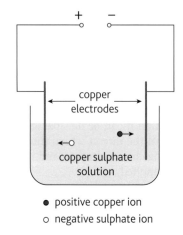

● positive copper ion
○ negative sulphate ion

**Figure 6** *Conduction in liquids*

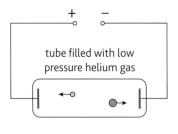

○ negative electron
● positive helium ion

**Figure 7** *Conduction in gases*

**Figure 8** *Lightning strikes*

A high voltage across a gas or sufficiently high temperature can cause ionisation of gas atoms or molecules. The gas then becomes a plasma of positive ions and electrons so the gas becomes conducting. When conduction occurs, the collisions of the ions with gas atoms and molecules produce a rise in temperature of the gas which increases the number of electrons and ions.

The collisions of the accelerated electrons with atoms can also cause the atoms to emit light. The effect is used in gas-filled lamps in home lighting. It also occurs naturally when lightning strikes during thunderstorms. This is caused by a high potential difference between a cloud and the Earth.

### Summary questions

1. Describe the difference between the charge carriers in solids, solutions of salts and gases.

2. State two factors that affect the resistance of a NTC thermistor and explain why the resistance decreases as temperature increases.

3. Describe the mechanism for conduction in copper, sodium chloride solution and a helium-filled gas discharge tube.

# 12.5 Controlling and varying voltages and currents

Learning objectives:

- How can a potential divider be used to produce a low voltage from a high voltage supply?

- How can a temperature-dependent voltage be produced using a thermistor?

- How can current be controlled in an electrical circuit?

*Specification reference: 3.2.2C*

## ⚡ ⚠ Supplies for electronic circuits

There are several types of circuit in a computer and they are often designed to operate using different voltages. These may be derived from the internal mains power supply or in the case of a 'laptop', an internal battery pack. The voltages they need are often much lower than the emf of the battery pack. For example, different circuits in the computer may need a 3 V or 5 V supply whereas the battery pack supplies 14 V. The required voltages can be produced using a potential divider circuit such as that shown in Figure 1.

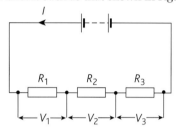

**Figure 1** *Potential divider*

In a potential divider, the current is the same through each component so

$$\frac{V_1}{R_1} = \frac{V_2}{R_2} = \frac{V_3}{R_3}$$

This shows that supply voltage is shared between the resistors in the same ratio as their resistances.

In the computer the 3 V and 5 V could be obtained with resistors $R_1 = 15\,\Omega$, $R_2 = 10\,\Omega$ and $R_3 = 45\,\Omega$ as shown in Figure 2.

Using the ratios above the potential differences across the resistors would be 3 V, 2 V and 9 V. The circuit requiring 5 V supply would be connected across the 15 Ω and 10 Ω resistors.

Any resistors that have the same ratio of values could be used (e.g. 7.5 Ω, 5 Ω and 22.5 Ω). In practice, the values would have to match those that are available commercially. Another problem for designers is that the circuit connected across the output of the potential divider has an effective resistance of its own. This will therefore reduce the overall resistance of that part of the potential divider chain. The output potential difference will therefore be less than the calculated value unless the effective resistance of the circuit is very large.

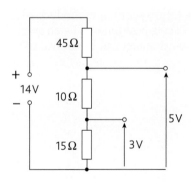

**Figure 2** *Supplies for computer circuits*

### Potential divider formula

The output potential difference $V_0$ across any resistance $R$ in a potential divider chain can be found using the formula:

$$V_0 = \frac{R}{R_t} V_{in}$$

where $R_t$ is the total resistance in the chain and $V_{in}$ is the potential difference across the chain.

For a potential divider consisting of two resistors $R_1$ and $R_2$ the output voltage $V_0$ across $R_1$ is given by:

$$V_0 = \frac{R_1}{R_1 + R_2} V_{in}$$

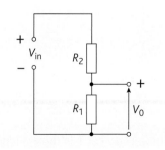

**Figure 3** *Potential divider with two resistors*

**Figure 4** *A potentiometer*

## Volume and balance controls

The volume control for a radio uses a potentiometer such as that shown in Figure 4. The potentiometer resistance is in the form of a coil of resistance wire or a deposit of carbon film on an insulating base. The signal from one part of the amplifying system is connected across the fixed terminals **A** and **B** (shown in Figure 5).

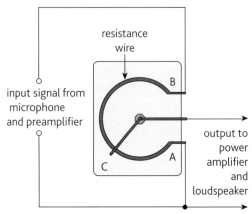

💡 **Figure 5** *Volume control*

The output is taken between one of the fixed terminals **A** and the moving contact **C**. When the control knob of the volume control is turned, the moving contact slides along the resistor. As it moves from end **A** toward **B** the output voltage across **AC** increases. The volume is zero when the moving contact is at end **A** and maximum when at end **B**.

A balance control is often used to compensate for the different characteristics of two loudspeakers in a stereo system or to produce an appropriate balance of sound when the seating position of a listener changes. Figure 6 shows how a linear potentiometer can be connected to control the signals to the speakers.

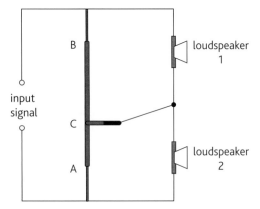

💡 **Figure 6** *Balance control*

The input signal voltage is connected between **A** and **B**. As the contact **C** moves toward **B,** the voltage **AC** that controls speaker 2 increases and the voltage **CB** to speaker 1 decreases by the same amount. When the slider is a quarter of the way along, the voltage controlling speaker 2 is one-quarter of the total and the voltage controlling speaker 1 is three-quarters of the total. When it is half way along, the voltage across each speaker is the same, etc.

## ⚠ Temperature-dependent voltages

Thermostats and temperature sensors require an output that varies with temperature.

A thermistor can be made with a resistance that increases or decreases with temperature. For this course you need to know the behaviour of an NTC thermistor. This has a resistance that decreases as temperature rises, as shown in Figure 7.

Thermistors can be made to operate over a wide range of temperatures and with different characteristics. They can be made small in size so that they need very little energy to change their temperature. This enables them to respond rapidly to changes in temperature which makes them very useful components in temperature sensors that measure or control temperature.

Figure 8 shows how a temperature-dependent potential difference is obtained using a thermistor.

As the temperature rises, the resistance of the thermistor falls so that a greater proportion of the input voltage appears across the terminals of the fixed resistor.

Suppose that in Figure 8 a thermistor is used that has a resistance that changes from $5000\,\Omega$ to $1000\,\Omega$ when the temperature rises from $20\,°C$ to $40\,°C$. If the input voltage is $6\,V$ and the resistor $R$ is $5000\,\Omega$ then the output pd changes from:

$$3\,V\left\{\frac{5000}{5000 + 5000} \times 6\right\} \text{ to } 5\,V\left\{\frac{5000}{5000 + 1000} \times 6\right\} \text{ as the temperature rises.}$$

This pd can be fed to electronic circuits calibrated to give digital readings of the temperature. Alternatively the output can control circuits which switch on a heating or air conditioning system when a predetermined temperature is reached.

### ■ Using a series resistor

Changing the potential difference across a resistor will change the current through it so the output of a potential divider connected across the resistor controls the current.

Alternatively a variable resistor $R_v$ can be connected in series with the resistor $R$ as shown in Figure 9.

As the resistance of the variable resistor $R_v$ increases, the total resistance in the circuit increases so the current through both resistors in the circuit will decrease.

$$\text{The current } I = \frac{\text{emf}}{\text{total resistance}} = \frac{E}{R_v + R}$$

The potential difference $V_R$ across $R$ can be found using the potential divider formula so

$$V_R = \frac{R}{(R_v + R)}E$$

Whichever circuit is used, energy will be dissipated as thermal energy where it is not needed, either in the potentiometer resistance in the first case or in the variable resistor in the second case.

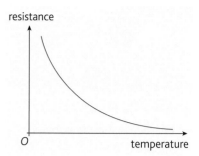

**Figure 7** *Resistance of NTC thermistor*

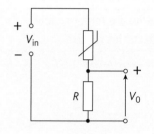

**Figure 8** *Temperature sensor circuit*

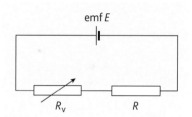

**Figure 9** *Series resistor controlling current*

### ■ Summary questions

**1** A lamp with resistance $6.5\,\Omega$ is connected in series with a $3.5\,\Omega$ resistor and a $12\,V$ supply. Calculate the potential difference across the lamp.

**2** Calculate the percentage of the power supplied that is dissipated by the lamp.

**3** Explain how the voltage would change with temperature if the output is connected across the thermistor instead of across the resistor in Figure 8.

# 12.6 Power supplies

## Learning objectives:

- What are the important characteristics of a power supply?

- What is meant by internal resistance and how does it affect circuit current?

- How are rechargeable batteries rated?

*Specification reference: 3.2.2C*

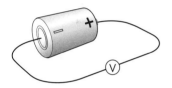

**Figure 1** *Measuring electromotive force*

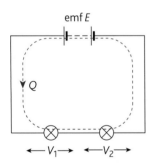

**Figure 2** *Energy dissipated in a circuit*

## ⚠ ⚟ 💡 Power supply characteristics

The important features of a power supply are its

- emf,
- internal resistance,
- capacity, i.e. the total charge or energy it can supply.

### emf

The **electromotive force (emf)**, $\varepsilon$, of a supply causes the free charged particles in a circuit to move. It provides the potential difference across each component in the circuit.

The electromotive force of a supply is measured using a voltmeter connected to the terminals of the supply when there is an open circuit, i.e. when the cell is not delivering any current to a circuit.

The emf, like potential difference, is measured in volts (V). It tells us the energy that the supply delivers to the circuit for every coulomb of charge that the cell moves around the circuit.

A 230 V supply delivers 230 joules of energy for each coulomb.

It follows that the total energy transferred when charge $Q$ flows around a circuit is given by $\varepsilon Q$ and this must equal the sum of the energies that are dissipated in each component in the circuit.

In Figure 2, the same current flows for the same time through the supply and through each component in the circuit. Since $Q = It$

$$\varepsilon Q = V_1 Q + V_2 Q$$

Cancelling the $Q$s shows that the emf is the sum of the potential differences across each component in the series circuit.

$$\varepsilon = V_1 + V_2$$

Since $V = IR$, the emf $\varepsilon = IR_1 + IR_2$

This gives the general formula for the current $I$ in a circuit.

$$I = \frac{\text{emf}}{\text{total resistance}}$$

### Internal resistance

All supplies have an internal resistance. This limits the maximum current that the cell can supply.

In the case of cells that contain chemicals, it is the chemicals themselves that resist the flow of charge through them. In a single fully charged 1.5 V cell this resistance is about an ohm. The internal resistance of the mains and resistance of electronic power packs is due to the resistance of wires and components inside the supply.

The internal resistance has to be added to the load resistance to find the total circuit resistance.

# Summary

## In a series circuit:

- the current in each component is the same,
- the sum of the voltages is equal to the total voltage across the circuit,
- the voltage splits in the same ratio as the ratio of the resistances.

## In a parallel circuit:

- the potential difference across each component is the same,
- the sum of the currents into a junction is equal to the sum of the current out of the junction,
- the larger resistor carries the smaller current.

## emf and total resistance

When cells are connected in series the total emf is the sum of the emf values of the cells.

A car battery consisting of six cells each with emf 2 V and internal resistance $0.02\,\Omega$ has a total emf of 12 V and total internal resistance $0.12\,\Omega$.

From $I = \dfrac{\text{emf}}{\text{total resistance}}$, for the circuit in Figure 3

$I = \dfrac{\varepsilon}{r + R}$ or $\varepsilon = IR + Ir$

$IR$ is the potential difference that is measured across the load resistor $R$. This is the same as the potential difference that would be measured by a voltmeter connected across the terminals of the supply and is referred to as the **terminal potential difference**.

The equation shows that when the cell provides more current, the terminal pd $(= \varepsilon - Ir)$ decreases. The graph in Figure 4 shows the variation of terminal pd with current.

If a wire of negligible resistance connects the terminals of a supply (i.e. if there is a short circuit across the terminals) the current $I$ is $\varepsilon/r$. This is the maximum current that the cell can possibly supply. In this situation all the energy is dissipated inside the supply as thermal energy. This situation can quickly cause damage to an electrical supply and possibly cause a fire – hence the need for fuses.

Take care when carrying spare batteries. It is possible to short circuit the cell if it is carried in a pocket with a set of keys or coins.

## Cells in series

For cells connected in series the total emf is the sum of the emf values of the individual cells. Connecting the cells in series however does not increase the maximum current that can be supplied as the total internal resistance is also the sum of the internal resistances of the cells.

Figure 5 shows the result of connecting cells in series. In the first case they are all the same way round and in the second one of the cells has been reversed. This shows why it is important to ensure that you observe the polarities carefully when replacing batteries in electronic equipment.

**AQA** Examiner's tip

Don't forget to include the internal resistance of the supply when calculating the total resistance of a circuit.

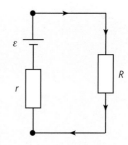

**Figure 3** *emf and internal resistance*

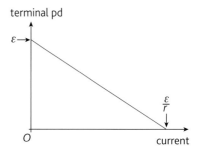

**Figure 4** *Graph of terminal pd against current*

for each cell $\varepsilon = 1.4\,\text{V}$, $r = 0.5\,\Omega$

total emf = 4.2 V
total internal resistance = $1.5\,\Omega$

total emf = 1.4 V
total internal resistance = $1.5\,\Omega$

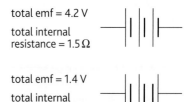

**Figure 5** *Cells in series*

## ■ Car batteries

Car batteries need to supply sufficiently large currents to turn the starter motors of the car. The emf of a car battery is nominally 12 V but is about 12.6 V when fully charged. It contains six lead–acid cells each of emf 2.1 V. The battery has to supply an initial surge current which can be as high as 400 A so the internal resistance has to be less than 0.03 Ω.

During the surge, the power generated is therefore about 4800 W ($VI$) which explains why it is not wise to operate a starter motor for too long when starting a vehicle. If operated for too long the thermal energy generated can cause irreversible damage to the battery.

Car batteries are rated according to their capacity, i.e. the charge or energy that they can supply. A 30 A h battery can (theoretically) supply 30 A for 1 h or 1 A for 30 h. The total energy stored in the battery is 1.3 MJ (given by $\varepsilon It$). When a cell supplies current, the energy comes from chemical processes inside the battery. Energy ceases to be available when all the reacting chemicals have been used. In the case of non-reusable cells the chemical process is not reversible but in rechargeable cells, such as those used in mobile phones and cars, the cell can be restored to a fully charged condition by passing a current through the cell in the reverse direction.

The difference in internal resistance between car batteries and dry cells explains why the dry cells cannot be used as replacements for car batteries. Eight dry cells each of emf 1.5 V and internal resistance 1 Ω would have the same 12 V emf as the car battery but they would have a total internal resistance of 8 Ω. The maximum current that could be supplied is therefore only 1.5 A (12/8 A).

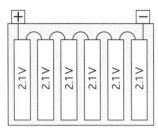

the six cells are linked in series
6 × 2.1 V = 12.6 V

**Figure 6** *Car battery*

## ■ Electrical safety

The human body can sense electric currents through it as small as 1 mA. Currents of only a few mA can be dangerous especially if the current passes through the heart region.

The 230 V mains supply has a low internal resistance. Since with ac even very low currents of a few mA can be painful and 30 mA lethal, contact with bare mains wires must be avoided. The potentially lethal current is achieved with a body resistance of only 7700 Ω. Although when the skin is dry the 'hand to hand' resistance is high, most of the resistance is contact resistance between the wires and the skin. This is reduced considerably if the skin is wet or damp due to perspiration for example.

Although the dangerous current levels when using dc are a little higher, precautions still need to be taken to avoid shocks. In physics laboratories many devices and experiments use high voltages. Mains leads used for connecting circuits have more insulation and the power supplies are designed to have high internal resistances to limit the maximum current. For example a 5000 V supply might have an internal resistance of 10 MΩ. The maximum current when short-circuited is then only 0.5 mA. Although making contact with a wire would cause a slight shock, encouraging immediate release, this current is below a dangerous level.

### Summary questions

1 A 6.0 V motorcycle battery has an internal resistance of 0.025 Ω. It operates a starter motor with resistance of 0.05 Ω. Calculate the initial surge current through the motor.

2 When the motor turns, the current drops to 40 A. Calculate the power dissipated in the battery.

3 A 2500 V supply has an internal resistance 3000 kΩ. In an experiment, a current of 2 mA has to be passed through gas in a discharge tube. Explain why this supply is unsuitable for providing a current of 2 mA.

# 12.7 Transmitting energy

## Learning objectives:

- Why is energy transmitted at high voltages?

- What causes energy loss during transmission of electrical energy?

- How can superconductors improve the efficiency of energy transfer?

*Specification reference: 3.2.2C*

## The National Grid

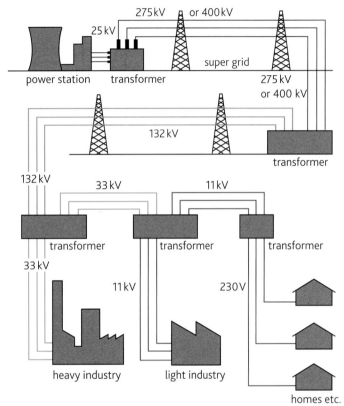

**Figure 1** *The National Grid*

The National Grid (Figure 1) is the network of transformers and cables between the power stations, where the electricity is produced, and our homes and businesses. The electricity is carried either by underground cables or overhead cables on pylons or poles whose size depends on the voltage at which they are working. In the national network there are over 82 000 km of conducting cables and 88 000 transformers. The supply used in our homes is 230 V but it is transmitted over long distances at higher voltages to reduce power losses. Although still dangerous, the 230 V supply can be used safely with less insulation than would be needed for higher voltages.

Alternating supplies are used because alternating voltages can be easily stepped-up (increased) and stepped-down (decreased) using transformers. The transformers vary in size. Some are sited in large substations and can supply a town whereas small transformers on poles can supply an isolated farm.

At the power stations the voltage is increased to either 275 000 V or 400 000 V. It is then reduced to 132 000 V at Grid Supply Points and then in stages to 33 000 V and 11 000 V. Distribution substations finally transform the voltage to 230 V. Without this process of transforming voltages, the losses would be unacceptably large (see below).

To reduce losses an alternative would be to generate the electricity for each area locally. This is possible in some areas by using alternative means of generating electricity especially from renewable resources such as wind, wave or solar energy. In the many cases where the alternative supply is inadequate then the grid system is a necessity even with its environmental drawback.

In the grid system the two factors that affect the **efficiency** of the transmission process are:

▨ the power losses in the transformers,

▨ the power losses due to energy dissipated by the cable.

## ▦ Power losses in cables

The power loss in a cable depends on its resistance and the current in it $(P = I^2R)$.

A cable delivering 1.0 MW of power at 230 V would carry a current of

$$4350\,\text{A} = \left| \frac{1 \times 10^6}{230} \right| \text{A}$$

If the power were transmitted using 20 km of copper cable with a cross-sectional area of 50 mm² (about 8 mm diameter) the cable resistance would be about 6.8 Ω. The power lost in the cable would be 129 MW $(4350^2 \times 6.8\,\text{W})$ and the voltage drop across the cable would be 29 580 V $(4350 \times 6.8\,\text{W})$.

So to deliver 1 MW at 230 V to the user, the power station would need to produce an emf of 29 810 V $((29\,580 + 230)\,\text{V})$ and generate 130 MW $((129 + 1)\,\text{MW})$ of power. This is clearly not practicable.

If the 1 MW of power is transmitted using a voltage of 11 000 V, the current in the cable is reduced to only 91 A.

The efficiency of this transmission line $\left| \dfrac{\text{power supplied to the user}}{\text{power generated}} \right|$ is about 95%.

In practice, higher voltages can be used giving even higher efficiencies.

### Effect of transformers

When a transformer increases or decreases the voltage, some of the energy that is supplied to the input of the transformer is 'lost'. There are a number of reasons for the power loss, one of which is the $I^2R$ heating due to current through the resistance of the wire coils in the transformer. As the current increases, these losses become greater.

A large transformer may have an efficiency of 95% whereas small pole-mounted transformers can achieve 98% efficiency or better. In practice, overall efficiencies of about 93% are achievable. This still means that 7% of the energy generated does not reach the consumer.

The simple arrangement in Figure 2 shows a step-up transformer at the generator, the transmission cables and a step-down transformer near to the user with some typical efficiencies.

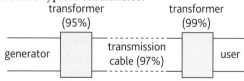

**Figure 2** *Power transmission system*

The overall fractional efficiency of this system is found by *multiplying* the **fractional** efficiencies together.

i.e. $\dfrac{95}{100} \times \dfrac{97}{100} \times \dfrac{99}{100} = 0.95 \times 0.97 \times 0.99 = 0.91$

which gives a percentage efficiency of 91%.

The Sankey diagram in Figure 3 shows the energy flow when a generator supplies 200 kW to the system.

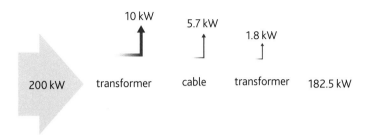

**Figure 3** *Energy changes in a transmission system*

In practice the transformers have to be cooled by their surroundings. To improve energy transfer, oil circulates through an arrangement of pipes with cooling fins. This is a potential fire hazard.

## Use of superconductors

When the temperature of a superconducting material is at or below its **critical temperature,** it has no resistance. Figure 4 shows the variation of the resistance with temperature for a material that becomes superconducting. Because it has no resistance, a superconductor dissipates no energy when a current passes though it.

There is clearly an energy saving benefit of transmitting energy using a superconductor. However, using existing superconductors, the cost of maintaining the cable below the critical temperature ($\approx$130 K) over many kilometres of cable is prohibitive.

Until superconductors are found that operate at or nearer ordinary temperatures, the main use of superconductors in the generation and transmission of electrical power is in increasing the efficiency of generators and transformers. Superconducting transformers do have a significant advantage in that they only require liquid nitrogen to enable the material to become superconducting. As no oil is needed, the fire-risks are eliminated.

### How science works

**Trials with superconductors**

In 2001 a high-temperature superconducting cable, just 30 m long, was successfully used as part of the system supplying 150 000 residents of Copenhagen in Denmark.

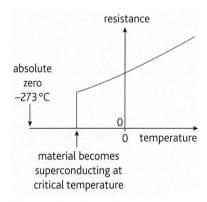

**Figure 4** *Resistance–temperature graph for a superconductor*

## Summary questions

**1** Describe how energy is wasted in the transmission of electrical power.

**2** How much power could be saved each second when 500 kW of power is transmitted at 33 000 V instead of 11 000 V along cable with a resistance of 5.0 Ω.

**3** A transmission system operates with two transformers that are 97% efficient. 2% of the power that reaches the cable is lost during transmission. What percentage of the generated power reaches the users?

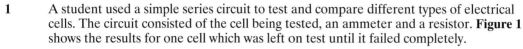

1   A student used a simple series circuit to test and compare different types of electrical cells. The circuit consisted of the cell being tested, an ammeter and a resistor. **Figure 1** shows the results for one cell which was left on test until it failed completely.

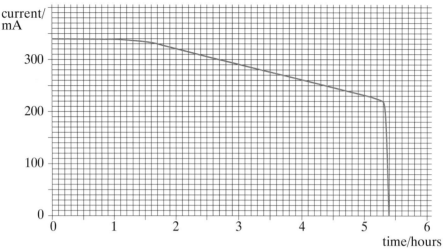

**Figure 1**

(a)   The emf of the cell at the start of the test was 1.6 V.

Calculate the total resistance in the circuit.                                *(1 mark)*

(b)   Use **Figure 1** to estimate the total charge that flowed in the circuit during the test.                                                          *(4 marks)*

(c)   The average emf provided by the cell during the test was 1.4 V.

Calculate the total work done by the cell.                                *(2 marks)*

2   The table shows the potential differences $V$ and the corresponding currents $I$ for three conductors.

|  | $V/V$ | $I/A$ |
|---|---|---|
| **Copper wire** | 0.2 | 4.0 |
| **Copper sulphate solution** | 3.0 | 0.3 |
| **Hydrogen gas** | 2000 | $1.0 \times 10^{-3}$ |

(a)   For each conductor state the charge carriers involved.                  *(3 marks)*

(b)   The data suggest that the resistances of the conductors in each experiment are very different.

(i)   Calculate the resistances for each conductor.

(ii)  Explain in terms of charge carriers why this is the case.              *(6 marks)*

3   The heating circuit of a hairdryer consists of two heating elements $R_1$ and $R_2$ connected in parallel. Each element is controlled by its own switch (**Figure 2**).

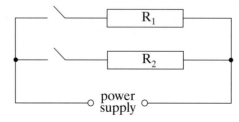

**Figure 2**

The elements are made from the same resistance wire. This wire has a resistivity of $1.1 \times 10^{-6}\,\Omega\,m$ at its working temperature. The cross-sectional area of the wire is $1.7 \times 10^{-8}\,m^2$ and the length of the wire used to make $R_1$ is $3.0\,m$.

(a) Show that the resistance of $R_1$ is about $200\,\Omega$. *(3 marks)*

(b) Calculate the power output from the heating circuit with only $R_1$ switched on when it is connected to a $240\,V$ supply. *(2 marks)*

(c) With both elements switched on, the total power output is three times that of $R_1$ on its own.

    (i) Calculate the length of wire used to make the coil $R_2$.

    (ii) Calculate the total current with both elements switched on. *(4 marks)*

**4**    (a) Define the term *electromotive force* (emf). *(2 marks)*

    (b) **Figure 3** shows a very high resistance voltmeter placed across an $8.00\,\Omega$ resistor connected to a cell of emf $1.56\,V$. The voltmeter registers $1.40\,V$. Show that the internal resistance of the cell must be about $1\,\Omega$.

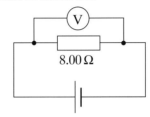

**Figure 3** *(3 marks)*

    (c) A voltmeter with a resistance of $24.0\,\Omega$ replaces the high resistance voltmeter.

       (i) Calculate the combined resistance of this voltmeter and the $8.00\,\Omega$ resistor connected in parallel.

       (ii) Calculate the reading on this voltmeter. *(5 marks)*

    (d) Each lead connecting the resistor to the cell is made from a single strand of copper wire. Each lead is $0.30\,m$ long and has a radius of $1.0\,mm$.

    Show that the potential difference across the two leads is negligible when the cell delivers a current of $0.20\,A$.

    resistivity of copper $= 1.7 \times 10^{-8}\,\Omega\,m$ *(4 marks)*

**5**    **Figure 4** shows components that are to be connected in a circuit to investigate how the current $I$ in a filament lamp varies with the potential difference $V$ across it.

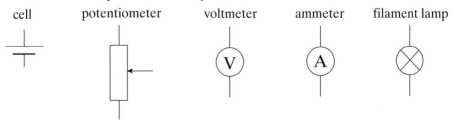

    **Figure 4**

    (a) Draw a circuit diagram to show how these components should be connected together to obtain voltage and current data over the full range from $0\,V$ to the maximum voltage available from the cell. *(2 marks)*

    (b) The lamp used is rated at $1.25\,V$ $0.3\,W$.

    Calculate the current in the lamp when it is working normally. *(1 mark)*

    (c) Sketch the shape of the graph of $I$ against $V$ that the results of this experiment should produce. *(1 mark)*

# 13 Renewable energy

## 13.1 Solar power

- How do solar cells convert solar energy to electrical energy?

- How is the Sun's energy used to provide heating directly?

*Specification reference: 3.2.2D*

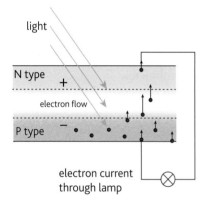

**Figure 1** *Voltage and current in a photovoltaic cell*

### Solar cells

Becquerel discovered the principle of producing an emf from a solar cell in 1839. Selenium-based cells, developed toward the end of the nineteenth century had a low power output and their main use was by photographers to indicate light level. However, the discovery of semiconductor technology and the need to provide electrical energy for satellites led to rapid development of solar cells.

A solar cell (or photovoltaic cell) converts the energy of the electromagnetic radiation from light into electrical energy. A photocell consists of two different types of doped semiconductor material, P-type and N-type, in contact (see Figure 1). An equilibrium situation is reached in which a potential difference (about 0.5 V) is established across the junction. When light photons of the correct energy fall onto the cell charge carriers are liberated. This alters the equilibrium between the P- and N-type materials and, if there is an external circuit, the liberated charge carriers are pushed through the circuit dissipating energy as they go. More light intensity means more photons per second, so more charge carriers are liberated per second. A greater current can be produced and the power available increases.

Photons have energies that depend on their frequency and is given by $E = hf$ where $h$ is the Planck constant. A photon of energy $1.12\,\text{eV}\,(= 1.8 \times 10^{-19}\,\text{J})$ is needed to free an electron from the crystal lattice and make it available for conduction. This means that the energy in the Sun's radiation that is provided by low frequencies cannot be converted into charge carriers, which accounts for the low efficiency of a solar cell. The low frequency radiation simply raises the temperature of the cell. Other losses occur due to radiation being reflected from the surface of the cell (made from glass), the resistance at the connections made to the cell and the internal resistance of the cell itself.

The overall efficiency of the conversion of energy is defined as:

$$\frac{\text{power output}}{\text{solar power incident on cell}} \times 100\%$$

The early cells made of polycrystalline material in the 1950s had efficiencies of only about 6% but modern cells made of single crystals have efficiencies as high as 20%, and 15% is easily achieved.

### Solar panels

A single solar cell produces a maximum emf of about a volt. The low emf limits its usefulness.

Figure 2 shows how the connections are made during the manufacturing process to produce a bank of cells in series.

The use of many cells in series increases the output voltage available. Eight cells in series would produce eight times the output voltage of one cell. However when the cells are connected in series the internal

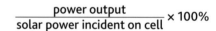

**Figure 2** *A solar module*

resistance also increases. To increase the output current available the banks of series cells have to be connected in parallel.

Figure 3 shows such a circuit using 16 cells.

Assuming each cell to have an output voltage of 0.8 V and an internal resistance of 1.2 Ω, four cells in series have an output of 3.2 V and internal resistance of 4.8 Ω.

The maximum output current of the four cells in series is 0.67 A. By connecting four such sets of cells in parallel, the output voltage remains at 3.2 V but the total internal resistance is reduced to 1.2 Ω. The maximum output current is increased to 2.7 A.

## Characteristics of solar panels

The output voltage and current (and therefore the output power) of a solar panel (or a single cell) depends on the resistance of the load and the intensity of the radiation. The variation of current with voltage for a solar cell or panel can be obtained in the laboratory using the circuit shown in Figure 4. Remember that the light intensity needs to be kept constant. Each set of measurements, taken for a different light intensity, is a characteristic of the solar panel or cell.

Figure 5 shows graphical data for one panel. It shows that the output voltage is at a maximum when zero current is being supplied by the panel. As the load resistance is decreased, the output voltage of the panel decreases and the current drawn from the panel increases. However, for most of the range there is no change in current as the output pd changes due to changing load resistance.

Figure 6 corresponds to the data in Figure 5. The output power is at a maximum a little below the maximum voltage available from the panel. Over the range of where the current remains constant, the power output (*VI*) is directly proportional to the output pd of the solar cell.

For a solar intensity of 1000 W m$^{-2}$ the maximum power available from the panel analysed is ≈ 108 W when the output voltage is ≈ 19 V and the current ≈ 5.7 A. The load resistance used for maximum power was therefore 3.33 Ω. The maximum efficiency for this panel is 10.8%.

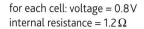

for each cell: voltage = 0.8 V
internal resistance = 1.2 Ω

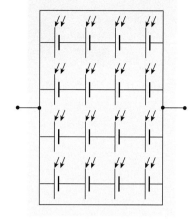

**Figure 3** *Cells connected in series and parallel*

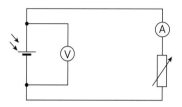

**Figure 4** *Circuit for obtaining cell characteristics*

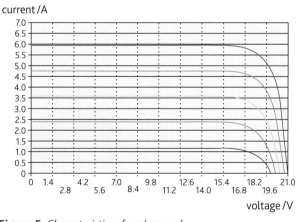

**Figure 5** *Characteristics of a solar panel*

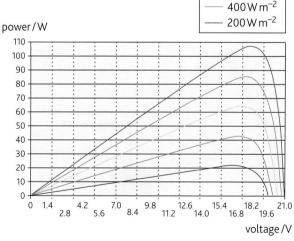

— 1000 W m$^{-2}$
— 800 W m$^{-2}$
— 600 W m$^{-2}$
— 400 W m$^{-2}$
— 200 W m$^{-2}$

**Figure 6** *Power from a solar cell*

## Uses of panels and arrays

The intensity of the solar radiation above the Earth's atmosphere is about 1400 W m$^{-2}$. A satellite solar panel with an efficiency of 15% produces

**Figure 7** *Solar panels on the COBE satellite*

210 W for each square metre of the panel. To ensure maximum output the panel is automatically adjusted to track the Sun, ensuring that the radiation lands normally on the panel. Solar panels deteriorate due to the effects of cosmic radiation but the efficiency falls by only about 1.5% over a 5-year period so they are ideal for powering communication satellites.

Much of the Sun's energy is absorbed in the atmosphere and the maximum intensity at the surface in the UK is about 750 W. This varies throughout the year because the Sun's radiation has to penetrate more atmosphere in the winter when the Sun is low in the sky. Clouds and water vapour also reduce the intensity. This means that to produce a useful output a considerable surface area of solar panels is needed. Assuming an efficiency of 15% and an input power to the panels of 500 W m$^{-2}$, it takes 13 m$^2$ of panel to provide power for a 1 kW electric kettle.

The use of solar panels to produce electrical energy is expensive but the initial cost is gradually falling. However, it still takes a long time to recover the capital costs involved in setting up a solar system using photovoltaic cells. Nevertheless, photovoltaic systems are appearing on houses and factories. In Portugal where the Sun's energy is higher and more reliable than in the UK, a massive array consisting of 52 000 solar panels that generate 11 MW has been built.

## Direct heating using solar radiation

As much as 70% of the annual hot water requirements of a typical home can be provided by direct heating.

Figure 8 shows how a solar panel is connected to provide hot water for the house due to direct heating of the panel. For maximum efficiency the solar collector is sited on a south facing roof and is angled as shown in Figure 9 to receive as much of the Sun's energy as possible.

The Sun's energy falls on a plate designed to absorb the energy efficiently. The absorbed energy heats the fluid (glycol) in the copper pipes. Glycol is used because of its low freezing point. Its use prevents damage in winter. The hot fluid is less dense than cold so unless it is pumped it would simply stay in the collector. The pump forces the hot water down to the heat exchanger in the hot water tank. The water in the tank is heated and the cool fluid returns to the collector.

If the water in the collector is colder than that in the tank then the pump switches off. The hot tank has an alternative means of heating the water when the Sun's energy is too weak to heat the fluid.

### Summary questions

**1** Use data from Figure 6 to plot a graph showing how the output power of a solar panel varies with intensity of illumination when the output voltage remains constant at 14 V.

**2** List the factors that affect the output of a solar panel.

**3** Assuming that the Sun's intensity is 750 W m$^2$ and that the efficiency of the panels is 20%, calculate the total area of the array in the 11 MW Portuguese system.

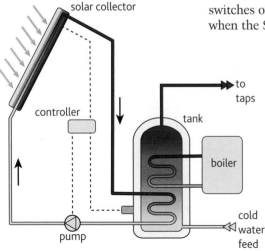

**Figure 8** *Hot water system using solar collector panel*

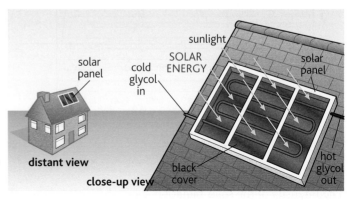

**Figure 9** *Solar heating collector panel*

# 13.2 Wind turbines

*Learning objectives:*

◼ What factors affect a wind turbine when it converts the kinetic energy of the wind into electrical energy?

◼ How much kinetic energy is available from the wind?

*Specification reference: 3.2.2D*

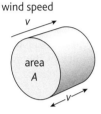

**Figure 1** *Air flow through a turbine*

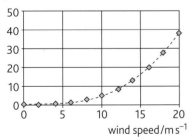

**Figure 2** *Variation of power available with wind speed*

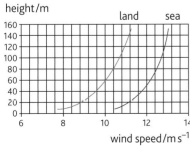

**Figure 3** *Wind speed variations over land and sea*

## ◼ Energy in the wind

Winds are a common feature of the British climate so single turbines providing power for factories and large-scale wind farms that generate energy for the National Grid are becoming increasingly common. One offshore farm near Liverpool consists of 25 turbines. Each turbine provides 3.6 MW so the farm can provide 90 MW of power, sufficient to supply 80 000 homes.

So how much energy is there in the wind that arrives at a turbine? All the energy that arrives in the area $A$ swept out by the blades is available for converting to electrical energy.

If the air in the wind is travelling at velocity $v$, the energy of the air that is available for conversion each second fills a cylinder of length $v$ and area $A$ (see Figure 1).

The volume of air $= Av$

The mass of air in the cylinder $= Av\rho$ ( mass = volume × density )

The kinetic energy of this air $= \frac{1}{2}Av\rho \times v^2 = \frac{1}{2}A\rho v^3$

The energy available is therefore proportional to:

◼ the square of the radius so doubling the blade length quadruples the available power

◼ the cube of the wind speed so when the wind speed doubles the power increases by a factor of eight.

The density of air is $1.23\,\mathrm{kg\,m^{-3}}$. Assuming a blade length of 50 m, the area swept out is $7850\,\mathrm{m^2}$ $(= \pi r^2)$. If the wind speed is $12\,\mathrm{m\,s^{-1}}$, the power available in the wind is 8.34 MW.

The graph in Figure 2 shows how the power available varies with wind speed for the turbine.

### Factors affecting wind speed

The energy available varies from place to place and with the time of the year. The mean annual wind speeds vary from about $6\,\mathrm{m\,s^{-1}}$ in sheltered areas to $9\,\mathrm{m\,s^{-1}}$ at sea and $12\,\mathrm{m\,s^{-1}}$ at the tops of hills.

Due to the resistance between the wind and the Earth and the viscous forces between layers of air, the wind speed is reduced near the ground. Figure 3 shows how the wind speed varies under the same weather conditions over sea, which is relatively smooth, and land which has obstructions such as hedges, agricultural land and housing.

The graph shows that for a turbine with its generator 80 m above ground (or sea) level and with blades 50 m long, the wind speed can vary by as much as $2\,\mathrm{m\,s^{-1}}$ within the region swept out by the blades. The graph also shows the technical advantage of mounting the turbines at sea. The ratio of the wind speeds is $\frac{12.4}{10.4}$ so that the ratio of the power outputs is $\left(\frac{12.4}{10.4}\right)^3$. The power available over the sea is therefore 1.7 times that over typical agricultural land for the same weather conditions.

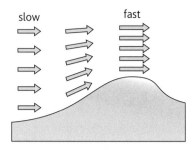

slow　　　　　　fast

**Figure 4** *Funnel effect*

The turbines are often mounted on hilltops to take advantage of the higher wind speeds there. This occurs because of a 'funnel effect' which causes the speed of wind at the top of the hill to increase as air from lower down rises to get past the hill (see Figure 4).

When the wind has passed through a turbine its speed decreases because energy is taken from it by the wind turbine. This causes a wind 'shadow' so a second turbine must be erected well behind the first.

## ■ Harnessing the energy

The most commonly used turbine design has either two or three blades. Maximum efficiency of a turbine is obtained by increasing the number of blades and using long blades with a large surface area However, increasing these factors also increases the mass that has to turn, so low wind speeds may not produce any rotation. Typically there is no, or very little, output for wind speeds below about $5\,\mathrm{m\,s^{-1}}$.

A higher speed of rotation tends to increase the amount of wind energy converted to electrical energy so the turbine will be more efficient. However, the faster the blades turn the more turbulence they produce behind them, which affects the rate of rotation. So there is an optimum speed of rotation that results in maximum efficiency of the system.

The efficiency of a turbine expressed as a percentage

$$= \frac{\text{electrical power output}}{\text{maximum power available from the wind}} \times 100\%$$

Apart from the factors mentioned above and energy losses due to friction, the efficiency is affected by the pitch of the blade (i.e. the angle of the blade relative to the direction of the wind). The optimum angle depends on the wind speed so a computer controls the pitch, changing it by small angles as the wind speed varies to ensure that the maximum power output is obtained.

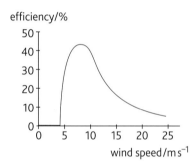

efficiency/%

wind speed/m s$^{-1}$

**Figure 5** *Efficiency versus wind speed*

Figure 5 shows a typical graph of the efficiency of a turbine against wind speed. A turbine can be designed so that it produces the maximum efficiency at any given wind speed. So local conditions, in terms of average wind speed are taken into account when designing a turbine for use in a particular region.

However, the capital cost per kW is more important than the actual efficiency of the machine since the energy source is free.

## ■ Land or sea turbines

The benefit to society of wind turbines is obvious. However, whether on land or sea, various environmental protection groups often object because of the large number of turbines that make up commercial wind farms.

More energy is available when turbines are sited off-shore but there are greater technical problems involved in erection and maintenance. Furthermore, the power has to be transmitted to shore using undersea cables. On the other hand, laying foundations for the huge towers and the subsequent transmission of power is relatively easy for on-shore systems.

Objectors to off-shore development complain of visual 'pollution' and their effect on shipping and marine life. Objectors to on-shore installations also cite the visual impact, the effect on tourism and property prices, the damage to infrastructure during the erection of the plant, damage to animal habitats and the subsequent noise of the swishing blades.

### Summary questions

1 A household uses power at rate of 2.0 kW from a wind generator that has an efficiency of 95%.

　a Calculate the required power of the wind through the turbine.

　b Assuming a wind speed of $7\,\mathrm{m\,s^{-1}}$, calculate the length of the blades of the turbine.

2 For one installation, the wind speed varies between 3 and $8\,\mathrm{m\,s^{-1}}$. Calculate the ratio of the maximum power to the minimum power generated.

3 List the factors that affect the output of a wind turbine.

# 13.3 Hydroelectric power and pumped storage

*Learning objectives:*

- How can electricity be produced using potential energy stored by water?

- How is off-peak electricity 'saved' for use during peak periods?

*Specification reference: 3.2.2D*

**Figure 1** *HEP reservoir fed by glacial melt water*

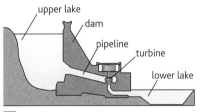

**Figure 2** *A hydroelectric scheme*

**Figure 3** *HEP generators*

## Hydroelectric power

Water power has been used for centuries in water mills where the kinetic energy in water is converted directly into mechanical energy. It is therefore not surprising that it was the first renewable resource to be used commercially for the production of electricity. In 2005 about 3.6% of the electricity generated in the UK came from renewable sources and of this about a third came from hydroelectric power (HEP) stations. A large-scale hydroelectric plant can provide energy within 60 s of switching on so they are usually used during peak periods to supplement the baseload plants that provide electricity continuously. Typically an HEP plant will generate electricity for 1 to 4 h a day.

### Energy conversion

HEP depends on the availability of a high flow rate of water from rivers, natural lakes or man-made reservoirs, high up in mountainous areas, such as that shown in Figure 1.

This water needs to be continually replenished so a suitably high rainfall is required. In one Austrian site, 60% of the water comes from a melting glacier thousands of years old. This is, of course, not renewable.

From the reservoir the water flows through a turbine-generator at the bottom of the dam, as shown in Figure 2. Alternatively, the water may flow through many kilometres of pipes to the generators situated many hundreds of metres below the dam. A typical plant is shown in Figure 3. The gravitational potential energy of the water becomes kinetic energy and this is converted to electrical energy in the turbo-generators.

The second arrangement increases the potential energy available but increases the capital costs and can produce more environmental damage. To avoid unsightly pipes, the water may flow through pipes which are laid in caverns that have been bored through the mountains or just through the actual caverns.

### Energy and power available

For the system shown in Figure 2, the velocity of the water through the turbines decreases as the water level falls. Assuming the sides of a reservoir to be vertical (which is unlikely), and the height through which the water falls between the reservoir and the generators to be $h$, the mean height fallen by the water is $h/2$. The total energy available is then $Mgh/2$, where $M$ is the total mass of water that is above the level of the generators.

For a 150 m high dam with a surface area of $2.5 \times 10^6\,\text{m}^2$, the mass of water in the reservoir basin is $3.75 \times 10^{11}\,\text{kg}$ and the total energy available is $2.76 \times 10^{14}\,\text{J}$.

The maximum possible power $P_{\text{max}}$ output depends on the rate of flow of water through the generators.

This is found from $P_{\text{max}} = \left|\dfrac{m}{t}\right|gh$

where $m$ is the mass of water flowing through the generators in time $t$ and $g$ is the gravitational field strength.

**Table 1**

| advantages | disadvantages |
|---|---|
| generators produce no pollution | limited suitable sites |
| fuel is a natural resource | damage to animal habitats |
| little maintenance needed for the generators | often in isolated areas so long transmission lines needed |
| dams provide side benefits, e.g. flood control | possible need to relocate people |
| the reservoirs can be used for leisure activities | lengthy and costly construction of dams |

**Figure 4** *View of the lower lake at Dinorwig*

## Summary questions

**1** Draw an energy flow diagram that tracks the energy output from a pumped storage system back to energy from the Sun.

**2** The distance between the top of the upper lake and the generators at Dinorwig is 71 m. Assuming an efficiency of 90% for the generation process, calculate the rate of flow of water through the generator house when the system operates at full power.

The power output is actually much lower that that given by the formula because of power losses. The efficiency of the transfer of energy from potential energy to kinetic energy as the water flows from the reservoir to the generators is between 75% and 95% depending on the length and structure of the pipes or caverns.

Losses occur due to frictional drag and turbulence. Also, the turbo-generator system cannot convert all the kinetic energy to electrical energy. The water still has some velocity after passing through the turbine and there will be frictional losses and losses due to electrical resistance. The conversion process has an efficiency of between 95% and 98%.

The most efficient system will therefore have an overall efficiency of about 93% ($0.95 \times 0.98 \times 100\%$) and the most inefficient system an efficiency of only 71%.

### Advantages and disadvantages

Some of the advantages and disadvantages are shown in Table 1. Some scientists have suggested that rotting debris from trees and plants produced by flooding of valleys produces methane. The gas liberated during the generating process adds to the greenhouse gases in the atmosphere so the HEP plants may not be as 'green' as they appear at first sight. This is less of an issue for HEP using natural lakes such as the Scottish lochs.

## ■ Pumped storage system

Power stations such as wind farms and nuclear power stations are **baseload stations** and produce electrical energy continuously. When there is a high demand other stations (**peak power plant**) feed energy to the National Grid to support the baseload stations. Pumped storage systems are one way of satisfying the extra demand.

The arrangement is similar to that in Figure 2 on the previous page. A typical system is operating at Dinorwig in North Wales. During peak times, water flows from a lake to six generators. These can provide up to 288 MW of power to the National Grid for about 5 h. The total energy available is therefore 1440 MWh (about $10^{12}$ J). The generators can go from zero to full power in only 16 s so they can satisfy an increase in demand almost instantaneously.

From the generators the water flows into a lower lake instead of a river (as in HEP schemes). During the night the generators operate in reverse. Energy from the National Grid pumps water back up from the lower lake to the higher one. The lake can be filled to its maximum volume in 7 h using 270 MW of power. The energy input from the National Grid to the pumps is therefore 1890 MWh.

These figures show that the efficiency of the pumped storage system is about 76%. Energy losses occur as water flows through the pipes and in the pump/generator. Some energy may also be lost due to evaporation from water in the upper reservoir.

The photograph in Figure 4 shows that there is little to be seen of the power generating plant. This is because all the pipes and the generators are inside the mountain. The damage to the landscape is the result of earlier slate quarrying.

Photographs and further information about this system, which is the largest in Europe, can be found on the First Hydro Company website.

# 13.4 Tidal and wave power

*Learning objectives:*

- How much energy is available from a tidal barrage?

- What are the alternative methods of capturing energy from the sea?

*Specification reference: 3.2.2D*

There are three methods of using the energy from the sea to produce electricity:

1 Using the potential energy of water trapped behind a tidal barrage when the tide flows in.

2 Using the kinetic energy in a tidal stream as it flows in and out.

3 Using the energy of the waves.

## 💡 Tidal barrage

A tidal barrage is a dam which would normally be built across the mouth of an estuary to a river. As the tide comes in the water is allowed to flow through gaps in the barrage so the estuary fills up. At high tide the gaps are shut and the water is trapped behind the barrage. As the tide goes out there is a difference in levels between the water trapped in the estuary and the sea level on the other side. When there is sufficient difference between the levels, the water is allowed to flow through the turbo-generators producing the electrical energy. Figure 1 shows a cross section through a barrage.

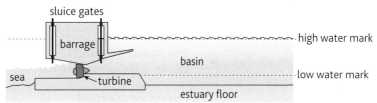

💡 **Figure 1** *A tidal barrage*

The process is similar to the pumped storage system. However, in this case the energy to produce the difference in levels is produced from a renewable source whereas in the pumped storage system the energy has to be provided by another source that feeds the National Grid. This may or may not be a renewable source.

To work effectively and viably there has to be at least a 5 m difference between the water level at low and high tides. In the UK it is estimated that tidal power could produce 10% of our energy needs, of which about 6% could come from a barrage across the Severn estuary which is the second best site in the world for such a project, due to it having the second highest tidal range. The Solway Firth in Scotland is another suitable site.

Figure 2 shows the proposals for the position of the barrier which is undergoing close scrutiny by those for and against its construction.

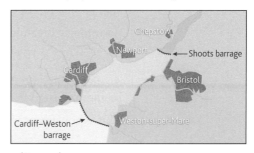

**Figure 2** *Proposed Severn barrage*

A lock on the left-hand side would enable ships to continue to travel up the estuary. Sluices are opened to allow water to flow in. Spin-offs of the barrage would be that it provides defence against flooding and the lagoon created could be used for leisure activities increasing tourism in the area. Those who object are particularly concerned for the irreversible damage that the barrage would do to the ecosystem in the estuary.

### Energy available

The maximum energy available is the potential energy of the water that is trapped.

The potential energy available $= \frac{1}{2}MgH$

where $M$ is the total mass of water that is trapped behind the barrier between the high and low tide levels, $g$ is the gravitational field strength and $H$ is the difference in water levels between the level of high and low tide.

The factor of $\frac{1}{2}$ arises because the average height that the trapped water falls is $\frac{H}{2}$

In the Severn estuary the surface area of the enclosed water is about $480\,\text{km}^2$ ($4.8 \times 10^8\,\text{m}^2$). The tidal range is $11\,\text{m}$ and the mass of water trapped is about $5.4 \times 10^{12}\,\text{kg}$ (using volume of water × density of sea water).

Using the above equation shows that the potential energy available from the trapped water is therefore about $3 \times 10^{14}\,\text{J}$. Assuming that this energy is used over a $10\,\text{h}$ period gives an average power of $8.3\,\text{GW}$.

In practice, losses as the water flows through the pipes, turbines and generators will result in a lower power output than this but extra energy can be gained by making use of the kinetic energy in the incoming tide.

### Power developed

The instantaneous maximum power developed depends on the difference in the water levels at any time.

The velocity $v$ of the water flowing through the generators when the height of water is $h$ given by

$$mgh = \tfrac{1}{2}mv^2 \text{ so } v = \sqrt{2gh}.$$

The mass of water flowing per second through the generators of effective area $A = A\rho v$, where $\rho$ is the density of sea water ($1025\,\text{kg m}^{-3}$).

The kinetic energy of this water $= \frac{1}{2}A\rho v \times v^2 = \frac{1}{2}A\rho v^3$ (compare with the kinetic energy of wind through a wind turbine in Topic 13.2).

The instantaneous power is therefore $\frac{1}{2}A\rho(\sqrt{2gh})^3$.

The generators for the Severn barrage would have a turbine of diameter approximately $9\,\text{m}$ so $A$ is about $64\,\text{m}^2$.

Assuming a mean height of $5.5\,\text{m}$, the power generated by each generator

$$= \tfrac{1}{2} \times 64 \times 1025 \times (\sqrt{2 \times 10 \times 5.5})^3 = 38\,\text{MW}.$$

As there would be about 216 generators, the total power generated would be approximately $8.2\,\text{GW}$.

This is consistent with the $10\,\text{h}$ operating time assumed above.

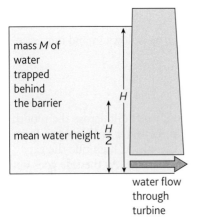

mass $M$ of water trapped behind the barrier

mean water height $\frac{H}{2}$

$H$

water flow through turbine

**Figure 3** *Potential energy from a barrage*

### Power generation time

Figure 4 shows the tide height and how the power output from a turbo-generator varies according to the time of day.

There is no power output as the tide comes in and until the tide has fallen sufficiently there is insufficient head of water to generate power effectively. The result is that the generators produce useful power for about 5 h on each tide (i.e. 10 h per day). This generation time may not coincide with times when there is a demand so some energy production needs to be supplied by other power plant and some energy output from a barrage may need to be stored using pumped storage systems.

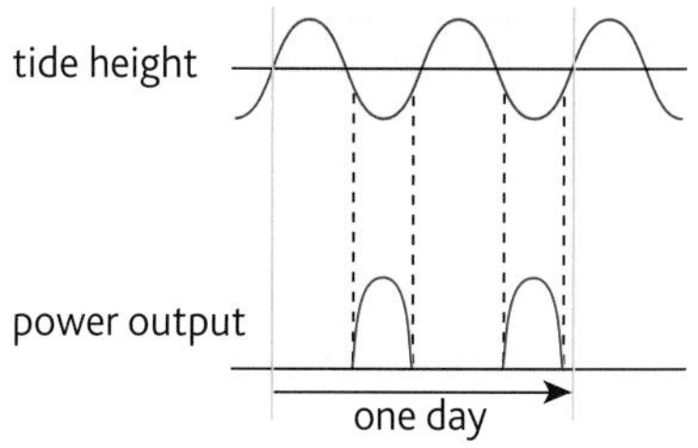

## Tidal lagoons

Another way of using the tide is by creating tidal 'lagoons' in the estuary to capture some of the water at high tide rather than using a full barrage. Figure 5 shows the principle of the lagoon that fills up as the tide comes in and generates power as it goes out. There is a proposal to build a tidal lagoon in Swansea Bay.

This arrangement works in the same way as the full barrage but, although there are some environmental problems, they are not as damaging as a full barrage. As there are no sluices or turbines blocking the estuary, fish can swim unhindered to spawning grounds and the lakes within the lagoons would provide safe havens for wildlife. Many tidal lagoons would be necessary to generate the same power as a barrage but they are cheaper to build and they can be built close to where power is needed, which cuts transmission costs.

## Using the tidal stream

This is the underwater equivalent of a wind farm. The turbines can operate when the tide is coming in and going out but fluctuates according to the rate of flow of the water.

A study has suggested that as much as 8% of the UK's electricity requirements could be generated by tidal streams.

In the Pentland Firth in Scotland the average water speed is about $2\,\mathrm{m\,s^{-1}}$ and this could generate up to 4% of the UK's needs. However, most of the energy available is in deep water and the Pentland Firth has a depth of about 60 m so the technical problems are very demanding. The depth makes fixing turbines to the sea bed too difficult so other solutions have to be found. Furthermore, under-sea turbines can be more easily damaged by sea-weed and debris than is likely with a barrage and they are more difficult to maintain than barrage turbines.

Another problem is that water is 850 times more dense than air (sea water density $1025\,\mathrm{kg\,m^{-3}}$) and although the water has a slower flow rate (the flow rate is not controllable) the turbines have to stand much higher forces.

This leads to turbines with smaller diameters than the turbines used for wind power, so many more turbines are needed. In the design shown in Figure 6 the 4 MW generator is driven by four rotors rather than a single one. This lowers the mechanical stresses on a rotor to an acceptable level.

**Figure 4** *Generation times*

## How science works

**Barrage or no barrage?**

The technical and economic feasibility of the project together with the environmental impact and social issues such as employment creation and spin-offs are used to inform decision making.

Although the capital cost is high (about 14 billion pounds) the economic feasibility of the project is gaining more support as fossil fuels become scarcer and more expensive.

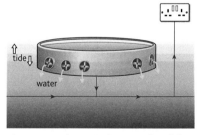

**Figure 5** *Schematic diagram of a tidal lagoon*

**Figure 6** *Under sea tidal electricity generation*

The advantages of tidal stream generation are that there is:

■ a predictable output,
■ little visual impact on the environment,
■ no noise,
■ no use of land sites.

## ■ Wave power

The power available from each metre length of a wave depends on the amplitude of the wave and the wave period $T$, i.e. the time between the arrival of successive waves. The amplitude is half the distance between the peak and the trough. This is the referred to as the wave height $H$.

The power in kW per metre in a pure sinusoidal water wave is given approximately by the formula $P = H^2 T$. Sea waves are more complex and typically the energy available from waves is only $0.5 H^2 T$.

The power of waves that are 3 m high and arrive at 10 s intervals is potentially about 45 kW m$^{-1}$. This shows the immense power that is often available. However, when the wave height halves, the power is reduced to a quarter of the original value. Because the wave height and period are variable, wave power cannot produce a consistent power output and needs backup from other supplies.

### Harnessing the power

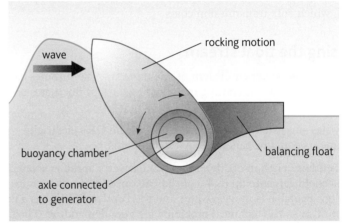

**Figure 7** *A 'duck' for generating wave power*

There are many different arrangements that are used or being developed to capture the wave energy.

Ducks are designed to convert the energy of the wave into rotational energy in the generator and hence to electricity (see Figure 7). Problems include the disruption to shipping and the need to have long underwater transmission lines for connection to the user.

Another arrangement that can be used for large scale power production is shown in Figure 8.

In this case, the air in the chamber is compressed as the wave passes, increasing the pressure. Air is then forced through the turbo-generators at the top. When the water level falls the air flows the other way generating more electrical energy. The generators create a lot of noise but as they are far from shore this is not a major disadvantage.

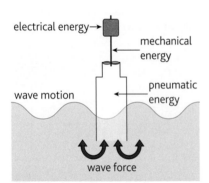

**Figure 8** *Changes in air pressure drive the generator*

### Summary questions

1 Estimate the length of the blades in the 4 MW tidal flow generator assuming a flow rate of 2 m s$^{-1}$.

2 Calculate the number of tidal flow generators that would produce power equivalent to that from the proposed Severn barrage.

3 List one advantage and one disadvantage for each of the following ways of producing power: a barrage, tidal flow and waves.

# 13.5　Making a choice

## Learning objectives:

- What factors govern the choice between different power generation systems?

- What options are available?

- What are the advantages and disadvantages of power generating systems?

*Specification reference: 3.2.2D*

## Comment

Professor David Bellamy, the naturalist, is campaigning against wind farms, warning of 'plans that will make the British coastline ugly and impossible for birdlife'.

*The Times* 2004 (© Jonathan Leake and John Elliot/NI Syndication Limited, 2004)

'when the temperatures rise, the seas roll inland, the trees wither and the moorland retreats, we will not be talking about the survival of the odd sea eagle — we will be lamenting the disappearance of entire species'

*The Times* 2006 (© Magnus Linklater/NI Syndication Limited, 2006)

### 'Planners blown away by storm of objections over wind farm'

#### Objections

'We object to the proposal as it will have an adverse impact on the visual amenity of the local area including the Pentland Hills Regional Park ... This wind farm will not reduce carbon dioxide emissions in any meaningful way'.

#### Response from developers

'We need to weigh up people's perceptions about wind power against the reality of wind power, and the benefits it brings ... Wind power is one of the main ways to fight climate change in the UK'.

*Scotsman* February 2006 (© Scotsman Publications Ltd.)

## 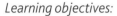 Factors that govern choice

Most people would agree with the need to develop systems that will produce sufficient power to support our standard of living and life style.

Making a choice of how the power is to be provided may be at a home, business, factory, local, national or even international level. That choice inevitably leads to hard decisions and compromise between power output and the environmental impact of the generating plant.

At whatever level the decision is to be made, the following factors need to be considered:

- The suitability of the system(s) to supply sufficient power at the times when power is needed.

- The capital cost: i.e. the cost of setting up the system initially including transmission costs.

- The energy cost in setting up the system:
  - although when using renewable sources the 'fuel' is free, energy is used during manufacture.

- The fuel costs:
  - energy and financial cost of extracting fuel
  - energy and financial cost of transporting fuel.

■ The energy availability i.e.:
  – whether non-renewable fuels are available locally or have to be imported
  – whether renewable sources are available locally and their reliability.

■ Maintenance costs, i.e. cost and availability of labour and parts.

■ Decommissioning costs, i.e. the cost of dismantling and disposing of the equipment when its useful life is over.

■ Environmental issues:
  – air, ground and water pollution
  – damage to habitats
  – visual pollution, i.e. the appearance of the generating plant and the area of land used
  – noise pollution if near to inhabited areas
  – damage caused by creating infrastructure: roads, rail links and transmission lines
  – health and safety of workers and public.

The payback time in terms of energy and money is an issue for consideration. Some methods of production, such as the building of a tidal barrage and nuclear power are expensive compared with those that rely on the burning of fossil fuels. However, these methods become more cost effective as the availability of power from other resources becomes scarcer and therefore more expensive.

### Comment

'… Nuclear facilities including those awaiting 150 years for full decommissioning could be at risk as both sea level and ground waters rise. Salt water corrosion, together with storm surge threat will represent a major worry and cost.'

## ■ What are the options?

Table 1 summarises the options presently available with some of their advantages and disadvantages.

■ **Link**

Refer also to Topic 10.1 and earlier topics in this chapter for further detail about the power generation options.

*Coal-fired power station*

*Nuclear power*

*Wind farm*

**Figure 1** *Power generation options*

**Table 1** *Options for generating power*

| energy source | renewable or non-renewable | advantages | disadvantages |
|---|---|---|---|
| fossil fuels (coal, oil, gas) | non-renewable | well-established technology, power generated where needed, fuel easy to transport, oil and gas are easy to transport through pipelines. | produces greenhouse gases and acid rain, supplies are fairly plentiful but diminishing, pipelines can be easily interrupted. |
| solar | renewable | low maintenance costs, easy to set up to supply individual households, little visual pollution. | costly to set up, energy available from the Sun varies, cells inefficient so large area is needed. |
| wind | renewable | no fuel costs or pollution, economy of scale is reducing capital costs, easy to maintain (easier on land than at sea). | visual impact on environment, variable output, some noise pollution, limited availability of suitable sites. |
| waves | renewable | no fuel cost or pollution. | limited sites around the coastline, unreliable output, energy transfer problems. |
| hydroelectric | renewable | no fuel cost or pollution, easy to maintain, can provide leisure site as a spin-off. | dams destroy local ecology, limited availability of suitable sites, energy transfer over long distances, surface pipes produce visual pollution. |
| tidal | renewable | no fuel cost or pollution, can provide leisure site and flood control as spin-offs, a suitable site can produce a lot of energy, barrage attracts tourists. | barrage damages local environment, visual impact of the barrage on the environment, effect on the local infrastructure during building. |
| geothermal | renewable | no fuel cost or pollution. | not suitable for large scale electricity production in UK. |
| biomass | renewable | uses energy from burning crops so no fuel cost. | burning produces greenhouse gases, large amount of crop needed to produce limited power output. |
| nuclear fission | may be considered renewable or non-renewable | still plenty of raw material available, process can breed fuel for further reaction, no greenhouse gases, large power output per reactor. | large capital cost, large cost of processing fuel, danger to workers and public of accidents in the plant, decommissioning cost are very high, problem of disposal of radioactive waste. |

## Summary questions

1  Imagine that you live in a small village. A local farmer has applied for planning permission to build a wind farm that will supply the farm and also generate a surplus energy that will supply the National Grid. The generators will be on a hill overlooking the village.

a Write a letter to the local paper making objections on scientific and environmental grounds to the proposed plan. Offer alternative suggestions which the farmer could use to produce energy.

b Write a letter to the local paper supporting the farmer's application using scientific and environmental points in your letter.

2  Write a short article that expresses your view on 'Power production in the UK for the 21st century'. Make sure that you include reasons for the points you make in the article.

# AQA Examination-style questions

1. Climate change and increasing global demand for oil and other fossil fuels have led to the development of ways of using renewable sources of energy to generate electricity. In the UK, wind turbines are the most widely used form of renewable energy technology .

    (a) On average, over a 24-h period, a wind turbine is rotated by $3.0 \times 10^9 \, m^3$ of moving air at a wind speed of $8.5 \, m \, s^{-1}$.

        (i) Calculate the total kinetic energy of this moving air.

        density of air = $1.3 \, kg \, m^{-3}$

        (ii) The wind turbine converts 45% of this kinetic energy into electrical energy. Calculate the average power output of the wind turbine. *(6 marks)*

    (b) It has been suggested that tides and waves could also be used to generate electricity for the National Grid. Write about the feasibility of this suggestion, giving both advantages and disadvantages to the power industry and to the environment. *(4 marks)*

2. A small island is situated a long way from the mainland. The islanders require an electricity supply. It is suggested that wind turbine generators could be used together with oil powered generators.

    Explain why such a system of providing islanders with electrical power is seen as being a reasonable proposition. *(4 marks)*

3. Explain the role of the Sun in producing wave energy. *(3 marks)*

4. **Figure 1** shows the relationship between the power generated in a wind turbine generator and the wind speed.

    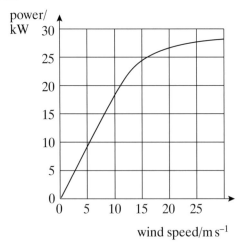

    **Figure 1**

    (a) An island has a mean wind speed of $7.5 \, m \, s^{-1}$. Calculate the maximum energy in MJ that this wind turbine generator could be expected to supply during the course of one year. *(3 marks)*

    (b) Suggest why your answer to part (a) is the maximum amount of energy that could be expected. *(1 mark)*

    (c) Comment on the advantages and disadvantages for the islanders of placing their wind turbine generator well out to sea. *(4 marks)*

5  (a)  Using a clear labelled diagram, explain the principle of a hydroelectric pumped storage plant.  *(5 marks)*

   (b)  For a hydroelectric pumped storage plant, the water falls a mean distance of 370 m between the reservoir and the generator. The mass of water stored in the reservoir when it is full is $1.0 \times 10^9$ kg.

   (i)  Show that the useful gravitational potential energy stored when the reservoir is full is about $4 \times 10^{12}$ J.

   (ii)  Calculate the maximum speed of the water as it reaches the generator.

   (iii)  State the assumption you made in part (b)(ii).

   (iv)  The pumped storage plant has four 100 MW generators.

   Calculate the longest time for which the stored energy alone could provide power at maximum output. Assume that all the stored gravitational potential energy can be converted to electrical energy.  *(8 marks)*

   (c)  In practice, not all the energy that is stored in the system can be retrieved as electrical energy. State and explain how energy is lost in the system.  *(3 marks)*

6  A 250 MW generating station is to supply the energy needs of a large but isolated community. The choice is between a coal-fired station and a nuclear station; the projected lifetimes of both stations are about 25 years. Discuss and compare the relative costs and the environmental impacts of both types of station.  *(5 marks)*

7  The hydroelectric plant at Pitlochry in Scotland has a maximum flow rate of water through the turbines of 12 700 litres s⁻¹. The water head (distance between water source and turbines) is 27 m.

   1 litre = $0.001 \, \text{m}^3$

   density of water = $1000 \, \text{kg m}^{-3}$

   gravitational field strength $g = 9.8 \, \text{N kg}^{-1}$

   (a)  Calculate the maximum power available from the falling water.  *(3 marks)*

   (b)  The quoted output of the station is 3440 bhp (brake horsepower).

   Calculate the overall efficiency of the station.

   1 bhp = 745 W  *(3 marks)*

8  Suggest and explain ways in which renewable energy sources could replace non-renewable sources in the generation of electrical energy in the location where you live.  *(5 marks)*

## 14.1 Energy transfer

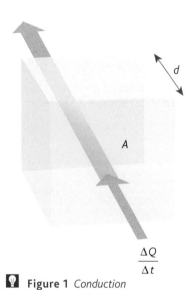

▼ **Figure 1** *Conduction*

An object at a higher temperature has more **internal energy** than an object at a lower temperature. Internal energy is the sum of the kinetic and potential energy of the atoms and molecules in the object. The electrical energy that we consume at work and at home is used to produce motion and also increase internal energy so that we have heat and light. Doing these things as efficiently as possible is an important part of reducing the demand for energy. This means ensuring that as much energy as possible is used to do what we want it to do and as little as possible is wasted. However, remember that all the energy that is used ends up in heating the Earth and atmosphere.

### ■ Transfer processes

The transfer of thermal energy can take place by **conduction**, **radiation** and **convection.**

### Conduction

This is the process by which energy is lost through solids. It is important when considering the choice of building materials such as glass and brick. Conduction can occur in two ways:

■ The atoms that are vibrating in hot parts of the body pass on their energy to neighbouring atoms in cooler parts of the body.

■ Free electrons carry energy from one atom to another in a process that is similar to the transfer of charge by electricity.

The second of these processes is much more effective than the first, so solids, such as aluminium and copper, which are good conductors of electricity, are also good conductors of thermal energy. Metal window frames last longer than wooden ones but are not such a good idea as far as energy loss is concerned.

Some conduction can occur through liquids like water but there is very little conduction in gases as the atoms are so far apart. Even so, the gap between the panes of glass in double glazing is often filled with argon rather than air as it has lower conductivity.

#### *Factors affecting conduction*

The rate of energy transfer by conduction depends on a number of factors.

■ A property of the material called its thermal conductivity $k$. A poor conductor has a low thermal conductivity and transfers energy more slowly.

■ The thickness of the conductor $d$. A thicker conductor transfers energy more slowly.

■ The temperature difference across the conductor, $\Delta\theta$. A lower temperature difference lowers the rate of energy transfer.

■ The area $A$ through which energy is transferred. A smaller area lowers the rate of energy transfer.

These factors are summarised in the equation $\frac{\Delta Q}{\Delta t} = \frac{kA\Delta\theta}{d}$ where $\frac{\Delta Q}{\Delta t}$ is

the energy flowing through the conductor every second.

The thermal conductivity of copper is almost 5000 times greater than that of polystyrene so for the same thickness, area and temperature difference copper transfers energy 5000 times faster. The low conductivity of polystyrene explains its use as an insulator in the lining of freezers and refrigerators.

The thermal conductivity of glass is 40 times that of air. So a layer of air, as used in double glazing, reduces energy loss by conduction considerably. Likewise air trapped between the fine hairs on the bodies of humans and animals provides a very good insulating layer.

## Radiation

This is the process that transfers energy by electromagnetic waves. Radiation is the only process that does not need a material medium and is covered in detail in Chapter 11.

All bodies above absolute zero (0 K) radiate energy. At temperatures around 300 K this radiation is in the infrared region. This is used in infrared thermography to produce images such as that shown in Figure 2.

This shows the relative temperature of the outside walls of a building. The red and yellow parts show the warmer regions, which are where most energy is being transmitted from the inside of the building. Such images help insulation installers to advise householders and owners of business premises how best to reduce their energy needs.

**Figure 2** *Infrared thermography image*

In the home, radiated energy is used to cook when using electrical grills, toasters and electric hobs that use a light source.

## Convection

This occurs in fluids (liquids and gases) where atoms and molecules are free to move. If one part of the fluid is heated it becomes less dense than the fluid around it. This leads to a pressure difference between the top and bottom layer causing it to move upwards (see also the ideas behind Archimedes Principle in Topic 11.4). Cooler air then replaces the warmer air and the process continues (see Figure 3).

A central heating radiator is misnamed. Energy is transferred from hot water or an electric heater element to the metal 'radiator' by conduction. Although some energy is radiated most is transferred to the air in the room by the convection process.

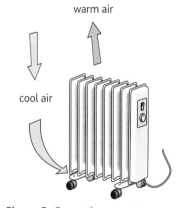

**Figure 3** *Convection currents*

### Forced convection

Allowing the surrounding air to push warmer air upwards is called natural convection. If air is blown across a surface by a fan or by wind then forced convection takes place. The forced flow of air removes the warmer boundary layer at the surface and the rate of loss of energy from the warm surface is increased.

This is similar to the wind chill factor which we experience. For the same air temperature we feel colder in a breeze. The layer of insulating air, trapped by the fine hairs on the body, is swept away by the breeze so our bodies lose energy faster. Table 1 shows some actual and perceived temperatures for different wind speeds. Remember that these are only the effective temperatures for humans. The effect of wind on animals and

**Table 1**

| wind speed / mph | temperature/°C | | | |
|---|---|---|---|---|
| 0 | 5 | 0 | −5 | −10 |
| 10 | −1 | −7 | −13 | −19 |
| 20 | −6 | −13 | −20 | −27 |
| 30 | −9 | −16 | −24 | −31 |
| 40 | −10 | −18 | −26 | −34 |
| 50 | −11 | −19 | −27 | −35 |
| 60 | −11 | −19 | −27 | −35 |

How science works

**Analogies**

This is a mathematical or formal analogy. When the rate of change of quantity at any instant is proportional to the value of the quantity at that time then the change is an *exponential change*. Such changes produce a constant 'half-life' and are studied in more detail in A2.

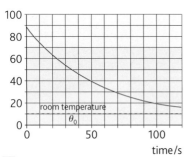

**Figure 4** *Graph showing forced convection cooling*

## Summary questions

**1** Explain why windows with metal frames are likely to transmit heat at a greater rate than wooden or UPVC windows.

**2** What is the difference between natural and forced convection?

**3** Explain why a pair of scissors made of metal seems colder than the wooden desk top when touched although they are at the same temperature.

**4** Air at a steady temperature of 20 °C is blown over the bricks in an electric thermal storage heater. They lose thermal energy at a rate of 400 W when the temperature is 70 °C.

**a** Newton's law of cooling is obeyed. Calculate the rate at which energy is lost to the air when, after 3 h, the temperature of the bricks is 45 °C.

**b** What would be the temperature of the bricks after a further 3 h?

birds with their better insulation is less. Water in a car radiator can only freeze when the *actual* air temperature is 0°C or lower.

Forced convection also affects the rate at which a house loses thermal energy. The outside wall of a house is warmer than the surroundings due to the heat conducted from the inside. The thermal energy in the wall is transferred to the surroundings quicker when a wind is blowing. This lowers the temperature of the outside surface so the temperature difference across the wall is greater leading to a greater rate of loss of energy from inside the house

Some heaters transfer energy to a room by the use of fans which blow air across an electric heater element. The principle is also used in Electric Thermal Storage heaters. These use off-peak electricity at night to store large quantities of thermal energy in ceramic bricks. The ceramic bricks are insulated so that the energy can be retained over long periods and released in the day time when required. A room can then be heated by blowing air over the hot bricks.

## ⚠ Newton's law of cooling

Newton discovered that under forced convection conditions the rate of loss of heat $\Delta Q/\Delta t$ is proportional to the temperature difference between the body and the surroundings,

i.e. $$\frac{\Delta Q}{\Delta t} \propto (\theta - \theta_0)$$

where $\theta$ is the temperature of the body and $\theta_0$ the temperature of the surroundings.

Because the rate of loss of heat is proportional to the rate of fall of temperature,

$$\frac{\Delta \theta}{\Delta t} \propto (\theta - \theta_0)$$

### Comparison with radioactive decay

In radioactivity the count rate always takes the same time to fall to half.

This arises because the **rate at which atoms decay** is proportional to the **number of radioactive atoms**.

In forced convection conditions the rate of fall of temperature is the same as the rate at which the temperature difference changes.

So the **rate of change of temperature difference** is proportional to the **temperature difference**.

Therefore it is logical to expect that it would always take the same time for the **temperature difference** between the hot body and the surroundings to halve.

One way of testing Newton's law of cooling is to blow air over a calorimeter containing hot water and plotting a graph such as that shown in Figure 4.

In Figure 4, Room temperature is 10 °C. The temperature falls from 90 °C to 50 °C in 35 s and from 50 °C to 30 °C in a further 35 s, which is as expected when Newton's law is obeyed.

# 14.2  Energy efficiency in the home

*Learning objectives:*

- How can the energy required from the mains electricity supply be reduced?

- How does a house lose thermal energy?

- How can less energy be used in the home?

- How can energy losses be reduced?

*Specification reference: 3.2.2D*

> If everyone boiled only the water they needed to make a cup of tea instead of 'filling' the kettle every time, we could save enough electricity to run practically all the street lighting in the UK
>
> **Department of Environment, Food and Rural Affairs (DEFRA)**
> *Crown copyright material is reproduced with the permission of OPSI*

## Generation of power locally

Energy losses that occur during transmission through the National Grid can be reduced by generating power locally. Generators may supply a single home or a small group of homes. These may be wind powered generators, solar powered photovoltaic cells (see Chapter 13) or even small hydroelectric schemes. Although there are many such generators appearing, there are often issues relating to planning consent because of the visual impact.

The local supply needs to be supported by power from the grid at times when the renewable sources are not able to provide sufficient (or any) energy. Some people can install generators that supply more than they need so they sell the surplus to the national power providers.

## Reducing energy requirements

Converting electrical energy to thermal energy is almost 100% efficient. Energy efficiency is therefore achieved by reducing the rate at which the energy is lost to the outside and use of thermostats and timers to control the operation of the heating system. For other uses of electricity, savings can also be made by using appliances that are more efficient (i.e. ensuring that a greater proportion of the electrical energy we consume is used to do the task we want done).

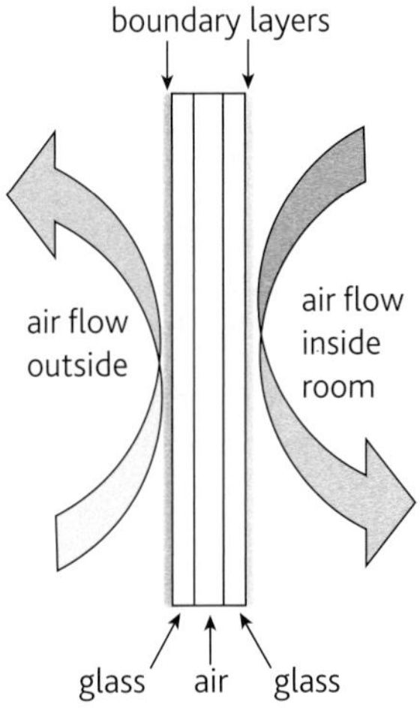

### U-values

Using $U$-values, a comparison can be made of energy losses that occur when using different building materials or structures. When energy is transferred through a window or wall, the rate of transfer is governed by surface conditions at the hot and cold parts of the surface as well as the thermal conductivity of the glass or brick.

As shown in Figure 1, warm air inside the room cools down at the window. It becomes more dense so moves downwards. This produces convection currents at the window surface. Similar convection currents exist on the outside surface where the air is warmed by the transmitted heat so it moves upwards. The air at the window surface is relatively still due to friction as the air flows across the glass surface. This sets up a thin **boundary layer** of air at both surfaces. Because air is a poor conductor, this reduces the rate of energy transfer.

The $U$-value takes account of the boundary layer effects, the thermal conductivity and the thickness of the material. It also takes into account the use of multilayered structures such as cavity walls or double glazing.

The $U$-value is the rate of heat transfer through one square metre of the conducting material for each kelvin temperature difference between the hot and cold surfaces. A building material with a lower $U$-value will result in a lower heat transfer rate.

**Figure 1** *Double glazing and boundary layers*

**Table 1**

| material | U-value / W m⁻² K⁻¹ |
|---|---|
| external door | 2.2 |
| unfilled cavity wall | 1.0 |
| insulated cavity wall | 0.6 |
| single-glazed window | 5.0 |
| double-glazed window | 1.7 |

The rate of heat transfer in $J\,s^{-1} = UA\,\Delta\theta$

$$\text{The } U\text{-value} = \frac{\text{energy per second / W}}{\text{area / m}^2 \quad \times \quad \text{temperature difference / K}}$$

The unit of $U$ is therefore $W\,m^{-2}\,K^{-1}$.

To save energy losses from a building the two controllable factors are the use of materials with lower $U$-values and reduction in the temperature of the interior of the building. Table 1 shows some typical $U$-values for walls and windows.

Insulating a loft space with 100 mm of insulation reduces the $U$-value from 0.6 to $0.3\,W\,m^{-2}\,K^{-1}$.

Suppose the temperature of a room is 20 °C and the outside temperature is 5 °C. An outside wall might consist of an unfilled cavity brick wall of surface area 12 m² and a single-glazed window of area 2 m².

The energy per second transmitted through the wall

$$= 1.0 \times 12 \times (20 - 5) + 5.0 \times 2 \times (20 - 5)$$
$$= 180 + 150 = 330\,J\,s^{-1}.$$

This means that a $\frac{1}{3}$ kW heater would be necessary to replace the heat lost through this wall and maintain the temperature of the room at 20 °C. Similar calculations for the other walls, ceiling and floor can be carried out.

Notice that the rate of loss of heat through the window is about the same as through the rest of that wall.

Reducing the temperature of the room by 1 K reduces the loss to $168 + 140 = 308\,J\,s^{-1}$.

## Double glazing

As air is a poor conductor, the energy loss through a window is reduced by separating two panes of glass by an air-filled cavity. The cavity has to be thin enough to prevent convection currents as this would make the insulation less effective. This means that the $U$-value of a window made using two panes of glass 4 mm thick separated by an air gap has a much lower $U$-value than a single pane of glass 8 mm thick. The data in the table above suggests that the rate of transfer for a double glazed window is about $\frac{1}{3}$ of that through a single glazed window.

Figure 2 shows how the temperature varies through a double glazed window. Notice that most of the temperature drop occurs across the air gap. The rate of flow of energy through each part must be the same.

For the **same rate of flow of energy** the **temperature drop** has to be greater across the section that has **lower conductivity**.

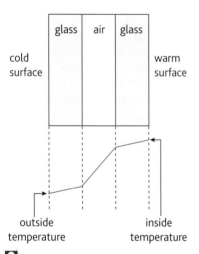

**Figure 2** *Temperature variation across double glazing*

## Cavity walls

Cavity walls provide some insulation for similar reasons to double glazing but the cavities are wide enough for convection currents to exist in the air gap. This reduces the insulating effect. The $U$-value is lowered by filling the cavity with material such as expanded polystyrene. Polystyrene is a poor conductor and the small air cavities in the expanded foam of the material improves its insulating properties.

## Draught exclusion

In older homes, badly sealed windows and doors are a major cause of wasted energy. Warm air leaves a room and cool air enters so energy is

**AQA** Examiner's tip

Remember that the temperature *difference* in K is equal to the temperature *difference* in °C.

Do not add 273 to temperature differences.

continually being used to raise the temperature of this colder air. So, eliminating draughts is a relatively simple and cheap way of energy saving.

## Energy-efficient lighting

A considerable amount of energy is used for lighting. Filament lamps are very inefficient as most of the energy is used simply to keep the filament at the temperature at which it emits white light.

Compact fluorescent lamps (CFLs) are much more efficient and come in many different shapes. They may have two or more gas-filled tubes.

Lamps that use light emitting diodes (LEDs) are also available but these are expensive and at present are more suitable for decorative lighting than for general use.

CFLs consist of a gas-filled tube and a device called a ballast that ensures that the correct current passes through the lamp to optimise the light output. When a current passes through the tube the atoms of the gas (inert gases like argon and mercury vapour) are excited and emit ultraviolet radiation as they relax. The ultraviolet radiation causes the phosphor on the tube to fluoresce and emit visible light.

It is interesting to compare the costs of operating a CFL and a filament lamp over the same time period. Using the data in Table 2, the total cost of operating a 20 W CFL over its 10 000 h lifetime is the sum of the cost of (0.020 × 10 000) kWh of electricity plus the cost of the lamp. At 8p per unit this comes to £21.

The cost of operating standard filament lamps over the same time is (0.1 × 10 000) kWh plus the cost of 10 lamps. The total cost at 8p per unit is £85.

If the lamp is used for 5 h per day this is the cost of operating the lamp over 5.5 years. So the saving per year on just this one lamp is about £11.60.

Using less electrical energy is a clear benefit of energy efficient lamps. The overall environmental benefits must take into account the energy cost in manufacture (more energy is used to make a CFL than a filament lamp) and the possible contamination of the environment with mercury when they are disposed of.

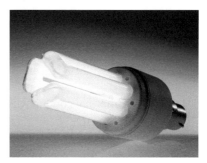

**Figure 3** *Compact fluorescent lamp*

**Figure 4** *LED spotlight*

**Table 2**

| type | filament lamp | CFL |
| --- | --- | --- |
| power consumption (for same light output) | 100 W | 20 W |
| lifetime | 1000 h | 10 000 h |
| approximate prices (2007) | 50p | £5 |

## Summary questions

1. For the example in the text, calculate the energy saved by insulating the 12 m² wall and replacing the single glazed 2 m² window with double glazing when the temperature difference between the inside and outside surfaces is 15 K.

2. Explain why a comparison of *U*-values is more useful when assessing heat loss form a house than a comparison of the relative conductivities of the materials used.

3. A room is to be maintained at a temperature of 17.0 °C. The temperature outside drops from 10.0 °C to 2.0 °C. Calculate the percentage increase in energy consumption necessary to replace the energy transferred through an outside wall.

4. Describe three ways which the owner of an old property could improve the energy efficiency of their home.

# AQA Examination-style questions

**1** The thermal conductivity of a material is given by

$$k = \frac{\Delta Q}{\Delta t} \frac{l}{A\,\Delta\theta}$$

Explain what is meant by

  (i) $\dfrac{\Delta Q}{\Delta t}$

  (ii) $l$

  (iii) $A$

  (iv) $\Delta\theta$ *(4 marks)*

**2** Joists in a house are the horizontal beams used to support floors and ceilings.

**Figure 1** shows one technique used to reduce thermal energy loss in a house, where insulating material is added between the joists as shown.

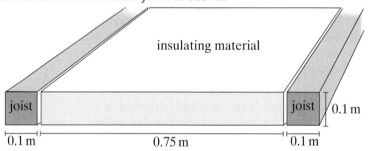

insulating material

joist    joist   0.1 m

0.1 m    0.75 m    0.1 m

**Figure 1**

The air temperature above the joists and insulator is 10°C; the surface temperature below the joists is 22°C.

  (a) The wooden joists are 0.10 m square. Calculate the rate of energy flow through a metre length of a wooden joist.

  $U$-value for the wood = 2.4 W m⁻² K⁻¹ *(4 marks)*

  (b) The wooden joists are 0.75 m apart. Calculate the energy flow through a metre length of the insulating material of $U$-value 0.62 W m⁻² K⁻¹. *(2 marks)*

  (c) Explain why published data of $U$-values for attic floor insulators state that the insulation must be between *and over* ceiling joists for effective reduction in energy loss. *(2 marks)*

**3** Which one of the following gives the correct SI unit for the ratio $\dfrac{k}{U}$, where $k$ is the thermal conductivity of a material and $U$ is its $U$-value?

  A m⁻²    B m⁻¹    C m    D m² *(1 mark)*

**4** In an experiment, the temperature of a hot metal cylinder was measured at 10-s intervals as it cooled under conditions of forced convection.

| time/s | 0 | 20 | 40 | 60 | 80 | 100 | 120 | 140 | 160 | 180 | 200 | 220 | 240 |
|---|---|---|---|---|---|---|---|---|---|---|---|---|---|
| temperature/°C | 95 | 85 | 76 | 68 | 61 | 54 | 49 | 43 | 39 | 35 | 31 | 28 | 25 |

  (a) Explain what is meant by *forced convection*. *(2 marks)*

  (b) (i) Plot a graph of these data.

   (ii) Use the graph to determine whether the data obey Newton's law of cooling.

   *(8 marks)*

5    **Figure 2** shows a saucepan of boiling water heated on an electric hob. The heat source consists of a source of infrared radiation mounted below a transparent glass surface that supports the pan.

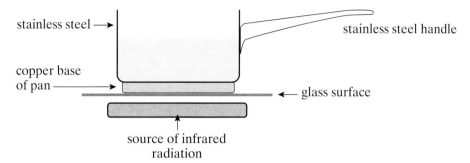

**Figure 2**

The saucepan has a heavy copper base attached to the body of the pan which is made from stainless steel. The thermal conductivity of copper is about twenty times that of stainless steel.

(a)  Outline the processes by which thermal energy heats the base of the pan.    *(3 marks)*

(b)  Outline the way in which thermal energy heats the water in the pan. Describe in detail the processes you mention.    *(6 marks)*

(c)  State and explain how the use of two materials improves the efficiency of the pan.    *(3 marks)*

6    **Figure 3** shows how the wind-chill temperature experienced by a person standing in air of temperature $-1\,°C$ varies with wind speed.

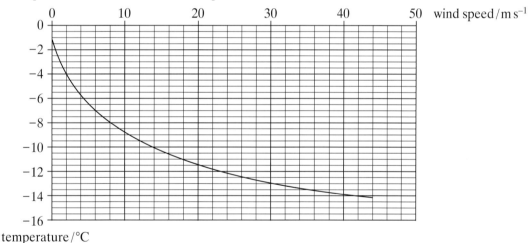

**Figure 3**

(a)  A person is standing outside when the wind speed at 10 m above the ground is $26\,\text{m s}^{-1}$. Use the graph to determine the amount by which the person feels that the temperature is depressed.    *(1 mark)*

(b)  The wind speed used in the equation to determine the chill factor is the wind speed 10 m above ground level, not at ground level itself. Suggest reasons why this is the case.    *(3 marks)*

(c)  State and explain whether the outside surface of a motor vehicle moving at $26\,\text{m s}^{-1}$ through still air reaches the temperature you determined in part (a).    *(3 marks)*

# AQA Examination-style questions

## Unit 2: Physics keeps us going

### Module 1: Moving people, people moving

**1**    In level flight, a pilot of an aircraft sets the course to be $80\,\mathrm{m\,s^{-1}}$ due north. There is a wind blowing from east to west at $20\,\mathrm{m\,s^{-1}}$. Find by scale drawing or otherwise, the resultant velocity of the aircraft.    *(3 marks)*

AQA, 2003

**2**    **Figure 1** shows a speed–time graph for a car that halts at traffic lights and then moves away.

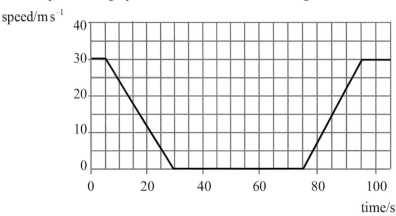

**Figure 1**

(a)  Use the graph to show that the car travels about 380 m whilst decelerating.    *(2 marks)*

(b)  Use the graph to calculate the acceleration of the car for the time interval from 75 s to 95 s.    *(2 marks)*

(c)  Calculate the total distance travelled by the car in the time interval 5 s to 95 s.    *(1 mark)*

(d)  A second car travels the same route without being halted at the traffic lights. The speed of this car is a constant $30\,\mathrm{m\,s^{-1}}$.
Calculate the difference in journey time between the first and second cars.    *(3 marks)*

AQA, 2003

**3**    (a)  A free-fall parachutist falls at a constant vertical speed of $80\,\mathrm{m\,s^{-1}}$ in still air. The wind now begins to blow horizontally at $7.0\,\mathrm{m\,s^{-1}}$.

        (i)  Draw a scale diagram and use it to find the angle the path of the parachutist now makes with the vertical.

        (ii)  Use your scale diagram or a calculation to determine the resultant speed of the parachutist when the wind is blowing.    *(3 marks)*

    (b)  The mass of the parachutist is 75 kg. Calculate the kinetic energy of the parachutist.    *(3 marks)*

    (c)  Calculate the work done by the parachutist as he falls through a vertical distance of 5.0 m in still air.    *(3 marks)*

    (d)  Explain why the parachutist falling vertically through still air eventually reaches a constant speed.    *(4 marks)*

AQA, 2003

**4** **Figure 2** shows a skateboarder of mass 54 kg about to descend a curved ramp in a skate park.

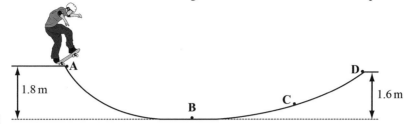

**Figure 2**

The skateboarder can be assumed to be a rigid body during the motion.

acceleration due to gravity $g = 9.8\,\text{m s}^{-2}$

(a) At which of the points **A**, **B**, **C** or **D** is the magnitude of the acceleration greatest along the track? *(1 mark)*

(b) The skateboarder is initially at rest. Assuming that there is no frictional force acting, calculate:

    (i) the kinetic energy the skateboarder would have at **B**,

    (ii) the speed of the skateboarder at **B**. *(4 marks)*

(c) The skateboarder has just enough energy to reach **D** because of friction. The total length of the track between **A** and **D** is 8.0 m. Calculate:

    (i) the energy lost due to friction as the skateboarder moves from **A** to **D**,

    (ii) the magnitude of the overall frictional force assuming it to be constant. *(4 marks)*

(d) State and explain where on the track the skateboarder will have zero acceleration along the track **when there are frictional forces acting**. *(5 marks)*

AQA, 2007

**5** A rugby ball is kicked towards the goal posts shown in **Figure 3** from a position directly in front of the posts. The ball passes over the cross-bar and between the posts.

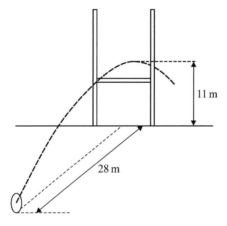

**Figure 3**

(a) The ball takes 1.5 s to reach a point vertically above the cross-bar of the posts.

    (i) Calculate the ball's horizontal component of velocity, $v_h$. Ignore air resistance.

    (ii) The ball reaches its maximum height at the same time as it passes over the cross-bar. State the vertical component of velocity when the ball is at its maximum height.

    (iii) The ball's maximum height is 11 m. Calculate, $v_v$, the vertical component of velocity of the ball immediately after it has been kicked. Ignore the effects of air resistance.

    acceleration due to gravity, $g = 9.8\,\text{m s}^{-2}$ *(6 marks)*

(b) (i) Determine the magnitude of the initial velocity, $v$, of the ball immediately after it is kicked.

    (ii) Determine the angle above the horizontal at which the ball was kicked. *(4 marks)*

(c) State and explain at what instant the ball will have its maximum kinetic energy. *(2 marks)*

AQA, 2002

6   A cycling helmet consists of a hard outer shell which is lined with a plastic foam material which squashes *relatively slowly* when the helmet strikes a hard surface such as the road or a car.

(a) Explain why the process of squashing 'relatively slowly' is helpful in protecting a cyclist wearing the helmet. *(2 marks)*

(b) In one safety test for a cyclist's helmet, the helmet is loaded with a dummy head and dropped so that it reaches a speed of $6.4\,m\,s^{-1}$ before hitting a flat metal block. The helmet 'passes' if the instrumentation connected to the dummy head registers a deceleration of less than $300g$ where $g$ is the gravitational acceleration.

gravitational acceleration = $9.8\,m\,s^{-2}$

(i) The total mass of the dummy head and helmet in one test is 5.0 kg and it rebounds at a speed of $3.1\,m\,s^{-1}$. The time of contact between the helmet and the metal block is approximately 4 ms. Explain whether or not this helmet passes the test.

(ii) The efficiency of the absorbing material is defined as the percentage of the kinetic energy that is absorbed during the test. Calculate the efficiency of the absorbing material. *(6 marks)*

AQA, 2007

7   **Figure 4** shows a cable car being pulled up a 35° slope of length 120 m.

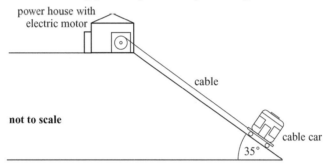

power house with electric motor

cable

not to scale

cable car

35°

**Figure 4**

The cable car has a weight of $1.5 \times 10^4\,N$. The total frictional force resisting motion is $3.0 \times 10^3\,N$.

gravitational field strength, $g = 9.8\,N\,kg^{-1}$

(a) (i) Show that the component of the weight of the cable car parallel to the slope is 8600 N.

(ii) Calculate the tension in the cable when the cable car is moving at a constant speed up the slope. *(2 marks)*

(b) The cable snaps when the cable car is at rest at the top of the slope. The frictional force remains constant at $3.0 \times 10^3\,N$.

Calculate:

(i) the acceleration of the cable car down the slope,

(ii) the speed of the cable car when it reaches the bottom of the slope,

(iii) the time taken for the cable car to reach the bottom of the slope. *(7 marks)*

AQA, 2005

## Module 2: Energy and the environment

1   **Figure 1** shows a circuit that is to be used as a sensor to monitor light intensity. This will allow lamps to be turned on and off as necessary to conserve energy.

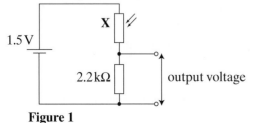

1.5 V

X

2.2 kΩ

output voltage

**Figure 1**

(a) State the full name of the component labelled **X**. *(1 mark)*

(b) Calculate the output voltage when the resistance of **X** is 1.8 kΩ. *(2 marks)*

(c) (i) State and explain how the resistance of component **X** changes when the light intensity falls.

  (ii) State how the output voltage of the sensor will change when the light intensity falls.

*(3 marks)*

AQA, 2007

**2**   **Figure 2** shows a power supply connected to a car battery in order to charge the battery. The terminals of the same polarity are connected together to achieve this.

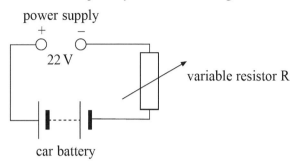

power supply

22 V

variable resistor R

car battery

**Figure 2**

(a) The power supply has an emf of 22 V and internal resistance 0.75 Ω. When charging begins, the car battery has an emf of 10 V and internal resistance of 0.15 Ω. They are connected together via a variable resistor **R**.

  (i) Calculate the total emf of the circuit when charging begins.

  (ii) The resistor **R** is adjusted to give an initial charging current of 0.25 A. Calculate the value of **R**.

*(4 marks)*

(b) The car battery takes 8.0 h to charge. Calculate the charge that flows through it in this time assuming that the current remains at 0.25 A.

*(1 mark)*

AQA, 2003

**3**   **Figure 3** shows how the resistance $R$ of three electrical components varies with temperature $\theta$ in °C.

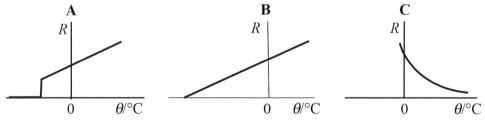

**A**   **B**   **C**

**Figure 3**

(a) Indicate below which one of **A**, **B** or **C** shows the correct graph for:

  (i) a wire-wound resistor,

  (ii) a thermistor,

  (iii) a superconductor.

*(3 marks)*

(b) An experiment is performed at room temperature to find out how the resistance of a wire-wound resistor varies with potential difference over the full range from 0 V to 6 V. The resistance is calculated using readings of potential difference and current.

  (i) Draw a diagram to show the circuit that includes a potential divider to control the potential difference and the correct positions for an ammeter and voltmeter.

(ii) **Figure 4** shows how the current in the wire-wound resistor varies with potential difference. Calculate the resistance of the wire-wound resistor when the potential difference is 3.0 V.

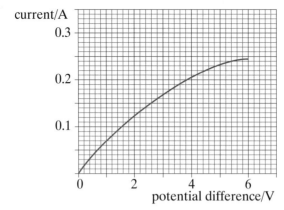

**Figure 4**

(iii) Explain why the graph has the shape shown in **Figure 4.** *(6 marks)*

(c) The metal wire used to manufacture the wire-wound resistor has a resistance per metre of 26 Ω and a diameter of 0.23 mm. Calculate the resistivity of the material from which the wire is made. *(4 marks)*

AQA, 2007

4 (a) Define the *ohm*. *(1 mark)*

(b) An engineer designs a resistor made from a thin layer of graphite mounted on an insulating base. **Figure 5** shows the arrangement.

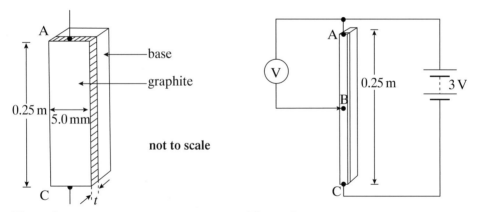

**Figure 5**                    **Figure 6**

The graphite layer has a length of 0.25 m, a width of 5.0 mm, and a resistance of 1.2 kΩ. Calculate the thickness, $t$, of the graphite layer.
resistivity of graphite = $3.0 \times 10^{-5}$ Ω m *(3 marks)*

(c) **Figure 6** shows the circuit in which the resistor will be used. A slider **B** presses onto the graphite to make an electrical connection. The battery has a negligible internal resistance. Calculate the power dissipated in the graphite layer. *(2 marks)*

(d) (i) The slider is placed 0.040 m from end **A**. Calculate the voltmeter reading.

(ii) The slider is now moved to 0.040 m from end **C**. Calculate the **change** in the voltmeter reading. *(4 marks)*

AQA, 2007

5 Geothermal resources are used in some parts of the world for the generation of electrical energy.

Explain what is meant by geothermal energy, describe its origins, and outline briefly the process of conversion from geothermal to electrical energy. State **one** advantage and **one** disadvantage of geothermal energy. *(7 marks)*

AQA, 2003

**6** (a) A wind turbine has blades of total effective area $55\,m^2$ and is used in a head-on wind of speed $10\,m\,s^{-1}$. The density of air is $1.2\,kg\,m^{-3}$.

 (i) Calculate the volume of air striking the blades every second, and hence show that about $650\,kg$ of air strikes the blades every second.

 (ii) Calculate the total kinetic energy of the air arriving at the blades every second.

 (iii) The wind turbine can convert only 40% of this kinetic energy into electrical energy. Calculate the electrical power output of the wind turbine. *(6 marks)*

(b) A town with an electrical power requirement of $100\,MW$ needs a new electricity generating station. The choice is between one oil-fired generating station or a collection of wind turbines. The power output from a small oil-fired generating station is about $100\,MW$; the useful power output of a single turbine is $20\,kW$.

Discuss the advantages and disadvantage of these types of power supply. *(6 marks)*

AQA, 2001

**7** Overhead power supply cables are often constructed from a number of parallel strands of aluminium and steel. Aluminium is used because it is a good electrical conductor and the steel strands provide tensile strength.

(a) Calculate the resistance of a $200\,m$ long strand of aluminium of diameter $3.0\,mm$.

resistivity of aluminium $= 2.8 \times 10^{-8}\,\Omega\,m$ *(3 marks)*

(b) A $10\,km$ length of power cable is used to deliver electricity to a small industrial town. The total resistance of the cable is $0.65\,\Omega$ and the transmission voltage is $400\,000\,V$. At peak times it carries a current of $100\,A$.

 (i) Calculate the power loss due to heating in the cable when the current is $100\,A$.

 (ii) Show that if the same power was supplied at $40\,000\,V$ then the power loss would be greater. Go on to describe how, and explain why, alternating current is used for the distribution of mains electricity. *(9 marks)*

AQA, 2006

**8** **Figure 7** shows several $12\,V$, $21\,W$ lamps connected in parallel. The circuit is protected by a fuse which melts if the current in the circuit exceeds $15\,A$.

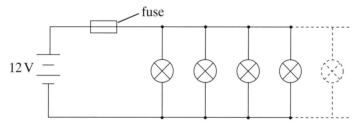

**Figure 7**

(a) Determine the maximum number, $n$, of lamps that can be used without melting the fuse. *(4 marks)*

(b) Show that the working resistance of a single $12\,V$, $21\,W$ lamp is $6.9\,\Omega$. *(2 marks)*

Two of the $12\,V$, $21\,W$ lamps are connected in parallel with a $12\,V$, $4.0\,W$ lamp of resistance $36\,\Omega$ as shown in **Figure 8**.

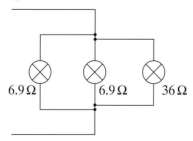

**Figure 8**

(c) Calculate the resistance of the parallel combination of lamps, when they are working normally. *(3 marks)*

AQA, 2002

# Investigative and practical skills

## Moving on from GCSE

Practical work is an integral feature of your AS physics course as it helps you develop your understanding of important concepts and applications. It also teaches you how scientists work in practice. You will find out how important discoveries are made in the subject. You might even make important discoveries yourself. AS level practical skills build on the practical skills you have developed in your GCSE course. For example, you will need to build on your GCSE knowledge of dependent and independent variables, control variables, reliability and precision. In addition, you will be able to learn new skills, such as how to use measuring instruments (e.g. micrometers and oscilloscopes) and how to determine the accuracy of the measurements you make. Always remember that experiments and investigations are at the heart of how science works.

## Assessment overview

During your course, you will carry out practical experiments and investigations to develop your skills and you will be assessed on how well you can:

- **carry out practical work**
- **analyse data from practical experiments and investigations**
- **evaluate the results of practical experiments and investigations.**

Assessment of these skills will take place after you have carried out appropriate practical work as part of your course. There are two separate assessment schemes, T and X. Your teacher will decide which scheme you will be assessed on. The assessment is in two parts.

## Scheme T  The ISA/PSA scheme

1 **The investigative skills assignment (ISA)** consists of a practical task on a topic in the specification followed by a written test on your ability to analyse data and evaluate results. The written test will ask you about the results of your own task and about given results from a related practical investigation. The practical task and the written test are both set by AQA and are taken under supervision after you have studied the relevant topic. The ISA counts for 41 out of the 50 marks for the unit. More details are given about the ISA in Topic 16.1.

2 **The practical skills assessment (PSA)** will assess how well you can follow instructions and on how well you can make measurements. The assessment is made by your teacher towards the end of your course and is based on your practical work during the course, specifically your ability to follow instructions, your skill in using equipment and how well you can organise yourself and work safely in the laboratory. The PSA assessment counts for 9 out of the 50 marks for the unit. More details are given about the PSA in Topic 16.1.

## Scheme X  The AQA-marked scheme

This AQA-marked scheme is in three parts:

1 You are required to carry out 5 short practical exercises in normal class time on measuring tasks set by AQA. Your teacher will check that you have carried out each of these tasks satisfactorily. Some of the measuring skills in these tasks will be assessed in the AQA-set practical experiment in part 2.

**2 and 3** These parts consist of practical experiments and a written test set and marked by AQA. You will need to obtain reliable and accurate results in the experiments (part 2) as you have to analyse and evaluate them in the written test (part 3). More details about scheme X are given in Topic 16.2.

The notes that follow apply equally well to either scheme as the skills you need are the same for both schemes. References in Chapter 15 to PSA or ISA features in scheme T apply equally well to the corresponding features in scheme X unless specifically stated.

# 15 Practical work in physics

## 15.1  Moving on from GCSE

### In the laboratory

The experimental skills you will develop during your course are part of the 'tools of the trade' of every physicist. Data loggers and computers are commonplace in modern physics laboratories, but awareness on the part of the user of precision, reliability, errors and accuracy are just as important as when measurements are made with much simpler equipment. Let's consider in more detail what you need to be aware of when you arc working in the physics laboratory.

#### Safety and organisation

Your teacher will give you a set of safety rules and should explain them to you. You must comply with them at all times. You must also use your common sense and organise yourself so that you work safely. For example, if you set up an experiment with pulleys and weights, you need to ensure they are stable and will not topple over.

#### Working with others

Most scientists work in teams, each person cooperating with other team members to achieve specific objectives. This is effective because, although each team member may have a designated part to play, the exchange of ideas within the team often gives greater insight and awareness as to how to achieve the objectives.

In your AS level practical activities, you will often work in a small group in which you need to cooperate with the others in the group so everyone understands the objectives of the practical activity and everyone participates in planning and carrying out the activity. Part of the PSA assessment is based on how effectively you contribute when you work with others. See the PSA assessment.

#### Planning

At AS level, you may be asked to plan an experiment or investigation. The practical activities you carry out during your course should enable you to prepare a plan. Here are the key steps in drawing up a plan:

1  Decide in detail what you intend to investigate. Note the independent and dependent variables you intend to measure and note the variables that need to be controlled. The other variables need to be controlled to make sure they do not change. A **control variable** that can't be kept constant would cause **the dependent variable to alter.**

2  Select the equipment necessary for the measurements. Specify the range of any electrical meters you need.

3  List the key stages in the method you intend to follow and make some preliminary measurements to check your initial plans. Consider safety issues before you do any preliminary tests. If necessary, modify your plans as a result of your preliminary tests.

4  If the aim of your investigation is to test a hypothesis or theory or use the measurements to determine a physical quantity (e.g. resistivity), you need to know how to use the measurements you make.

### Carrying out instructions and recording your measurements

In some investigations, you will be expected to follow instructions supplied to you either verbally or on a worksheet. You should be able to follow a sequence of instructions without guidance. Part of the PSA assessment is on how well you follow instructions. However, always remember safety first and, if the instructions are not clear, ask your teacher to clarify them.

When you record your measurements, tabulate them with a column for the independent variable and one or more columns for the dependent variable to allow for repeat readings and average values, if appropriate. The table should have a clear heading for each of the measured variables, with the unit shown after the heading, as below.

Single measurements of other variables (e.g. control variables) should be recorded together, immediately before or after the table. In addition, you should record the precision (i.e. the least detectable reading) of each measurement. This information is important when you come to analyse and evaluate your measurements.

**Table 1** *Tabulating the measurements from an investigation of pd against current for a wire*

| potential difference / V | current / A | | | average current / A |
|---|---|---|---|---|
| | 1st set | 2nd set | 3rd set | |
| | | | | |
| | | | | |

length of wire / m = _____
diameter of wire / mm = _____, _____, _____
average diameter of wire / mm = _____

# 15.2 Making careful measurements

## A measurement checklist

At AS level, you should be able to:

- measure length using a ruler, vernier callipers and a micrometer
- weigh an object and determine its mass using a spring balance, a lever balance or a top pan balance
- use a protractor to measure an angle and use a set square
- measure time intervals using clocks, stopwatches and the time base of an oscilloscope
- measure temperature using a thermometer
- use ammeters and voltmeters with appropriate scales
- use an oscilloscope.

In addition you should be able to:

- distinguish between systematic errors (including zero errors) and random errors
- understand what is meant by accuracy, sensitivity, linearity, reliability, precision and validity
- read analogue and digital displays

## Measurements and errors

Measurements play a key role in science, so they must be:

1  **reliable** – which means that a consistent value should be obtained each time the same measurement is repeated. An unreliable weighing machine in a shop would cause the customers to go elsewhere. In science, you can't go elsewhere so the measurements must be reliable. Each time a given measurement is repeated, it should give the same value within acceptable limits.

2  **valid** – which means the measurements are of the required data or can be used to give the required data. For example, a voltmeter connected across a variable resistor in series with a lamp and a battery would not measure the potential difference across the lamp.

Errors of measurement are important in finding out how accurate a measurement is. We need to consider errors in terms of differences from the mean value. Consider the example of measuring the diameter of a uniform wire using a micrometer. Suppose the following diameter readings are taken for different positions along the wire from one end to the other:

$$0.34\,\text{mm}, 0.33\,\text{mm}, 0.36\,\text{mm}, 0.33\,\text{mm}, 0.35\,\text{mm}.$$

- The **range** of the measurements is 0.03 mm. This is the difference between the lowest and the highest reading. We will see later we can use this to estimate the **uncertainty** or probable error of the measurement.

- The **mean value**, $<d>$, is 0.34 mm, calculated by adding the readings together and dividing by the number of readings. If the difference between each reading and $<d>$ changed regularly from one end of the wire to the other, it would be reasonable to conclude that the wire was non-uniform. Such differences are called **systematic errors**. If no such differences can be seen in the set of readings, in other words, there is no obvious pattern or bias or trend in the differences, the differences are said to be **random errors**.

What causes random errors? In the case of the wire, vibrations in the machine used to make the wire might have caused random variations in its diameter along its length. The experimenter might not use or read the micrometer correctly consistently. This shouldn't happen to a skilled experimenter.

The range of the diameter readings above is from 0.33 mm to 0.36 mm. The readings lie within 0.015 mm (i.e. half the range) of the mean value, which we will round up to 0.02 mm. The diameter can therefore be written as $0.34 \pm 0.02$ mm. The diameter is accurate to $\pm\,0.02$ mm. The uncertainty or probable error in the mean value of the diameter is therefore $\pm\,0.02$ mm.

## ⚠ Using instruments

Instruments used in the physics laboratory range from the very basic (e.g. a millimetre scale) to the highly-sophisticated (e.g. a multichannel data recorder). Whatever type of instrument you use, you need to know what the following terms mean.

**Figure 1** *Physics instruments*

### Zero error

Does the instrument read zero when it is supposed to? If not, the zero reading must be taken into account when measuring the gap width otherwise there will be a systematic error in the measurements.

### Uncertainty

The uncertainty in the mean value of a measurement is half the range, expressed as a ± value (e.g. $I = 2.6 ± 0.2\,A$). If the readings are the same, the instrument precision should be used as the uncertainty. At A level, probable error is used as an alternative term for uncertainty.

### Accuracy

An **accurate** measurement is one that has been obtained using accurately-calibrated instruments correctly and where there are no systematic errors. **Accuracy** is a measure of confidence in a measurement and is usually expressed as the uncertainty in the measurement.

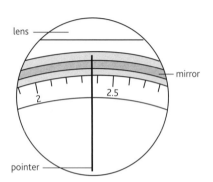

lens
mirror
2
2.5
pointer

**Figure 2** *Magnifying a scale*

### Precision

The **precision** of a measurement is the degree of exactness of the measurement. The precision of an instrument is the smallest non-zero reading that can be measured using the instrument.

- ▨ If the reading of an instrument fluctuates when it is being taken, take several readings and calculate the mean value and range of the measurements. The precision of the measurement is then given by the uncertainty of the readings (i.e. half the range of the readings).

- ▨ If the reading is constant, estimate the precision of a measurement directly from the instrument (or use the stated precision from the instrument specification).

Precise readings are not necessarily accurate readings, because systematic errors could make precise readings all lower or all higher than they ought to be.

### Linearity

This is a design feature of many instruments; it means the reading is directly proportional to the magnitude of the variable that causes the reading to change. For example, if the scale of a moving coil meter is linear, the reading of the pointer against the scale should be proportional to the current.

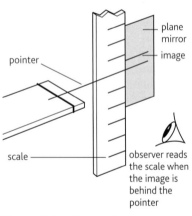

pointer
plane mirror
image
scale
observer reads the scale when the image is behind the pointer

**Figure 3** *Reading a scale*

A lens may be used to read a scale with greater precision. Provided the pointer is thin compared to a scale division, using a lens enables the scale to be read to within 0.2 of a division. In Figure 2, the scale can be read to $±0.02\,A$ (= 0.2 of a scale division × 0.1 A).

Measurement errors are caused in analogue instruments if the pointer on the scale is not observed correctly. The observer must be directly in front of the pointer when the reading is made. Figure 3 shows how a plane mirror is used for this purpose. The image of the pointer must be directly behind the pointer to ensure the observer views the scale directly in front of the pointer.

### Instrument range

Multirange instruments such as multimeters have a 'range' dial that needs to be set according to the maximum reading to be measured. For example, if the dial can be set at 0–0.10 A, 0–1.00 A or 0–10.0 A, you would use the 0–1.00 A range to measure the current through a 0.25 A torchbulb as the 0–0.10 A range is too low and the 0–1.00 A range is more sensitive than the 0–10.0 A range.

**Figure 4** *A multimeter*

# 15.3 Everyday physics instruments

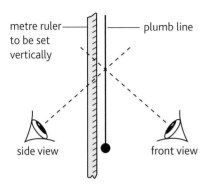

metre ruler to be set vertically — plumb line

side view — front view

If the metre ruler appears parallel to the plumb line from the front and the side, the ruler must be vertical.

**Figure 1** *Finding the vertical*

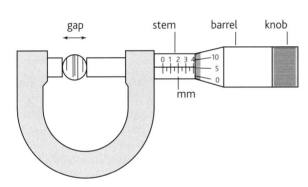

gap — stem — barrel — knob

mm

**Figure 2** *Using a micrometer*

## Rulers and scales

Metre rulers are often used as vertical or horizontal scales in mechanics experiments.

To set a metre ruler in a vertical position:

- use a set square perpendicular to the ruler and the bench, if the bench is known to be horizontal, or
- use a plumb line (a small weight on a string) to see if the ruler is vertical. You need to observe the ruler next to the plumb line from two perpendicular directions. If the ruler appears parallel to the plumb line from both directions, then it must be vertical.

To ensure a metre ruler is horizontal, use a set square to align the metre ruler perpendicular to a vertical metre ruler.

## Micrometers and verniers

Micrometers give readings to within 0.01 mm. A **digital** micrometer gives a read-out equal to the width of the micrometer gap. An **analogue** micrometer has a barrel on a screw thread with a pitch of 0.5 mm. For such a micrometer:

- the edge of the barrel is marked in 50 equal intervals so each interval corresponds to changing the gap of the micrometer by 0.5/50 mm = 0.01 mm
- the stem of the micrometer is marked with a linear scale graduated in 0.5 mm marks
- the reading of a micrometer is where the linear scale intersects the scale on the barrel.

Figure 2 shows a reading of 4.06 mm. Note that the edge of the barrel is between the 4.0 and 4.5 mm marks on the linear scale. The linear scale intersects the 6th mark after the zero mark on the barrel scale. The reading is therefore 4.00 mm from the linear scale + 0.06 mm from the barrel scale.

To use a micrometer correctly:

1 Check its zero reading and note the zero error if there is one.
2 Open the gap (by turning the barrel if analogue) then close the gap on the object to be measured. Turn the knob until it slips. Don't overtighten the barrel.
3 Take the reading and note the measurement after allowing if necessary for the zero error.
4 Note that the precision of the measurement is ±0.010 mm because the precision of the reading and the zero reading are both ±0.005 mm. So the difference between the two readings (i.e. the measurement) has a precision of 0.010 mm.

**Vernier callipers** are used for measurements of distances up to 100 mm or more. Readings can be made to within 0.1 mm. The sliding scale of an analogue vernier has ten equal intervals covering a distance of exactly 9 mm so each interval of this scale is 0.1 mm less than a 1 mm interval. To make a reading:

1 The zero mark on the sliding scale is used to read the main scale to the nearest millimetre. This reading is rounded down to the nearest millimetre.

2 The mark on the sliding scale closest to a mark on the millimetre scale is located and its number noted. Multiplying this number by 0.1 mm gives the distance to be added on to the rounded-down reading.

Figure 3 shows the idea. The zero mark on the sliding scale is between 39 and 40 mm on the mm scale. So the rounded-down reading is 39 mm. The 5th mark after the zero on the sliding scale is nearest to a mark on the millimetre scale. So the extra distance to be added on to 39 mm is 0.5 mm (= 5 × 0.1 mm). Therefore, the reading is 39.5 mm.

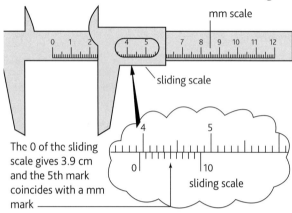

mm scale

sliding scale

The 0 of the sliding scale gives 3.9 cm and the 5th mark coincides with a mm mark

sliding scale

**Figure 3** *Using a vernier*

## Timers

Stopwatches used for interval timings are subject to human error because reaction time, about 0.2 s, is variable for any individual. With practice, the delays when starting and stopping a stopwatch can be reduced. Even so, the precision of a single timing is unlikely to be better than 0.1 s. Digital stopwatches usually have read-out displays with a resolution of 0.01 s but human variability makes such precision unrealistic and the precision of a single timing is the same as an analogue stopwatch.

Timing oscillations requires timing for as many cycles as possible. The timing should be repeated several times to give an average (mean) value. Any timing that is significantly different to the other values is probably due to miscounting the number of oscillations so that timing should be rejected. For accurate timings, a fiducial mark is essential. The mark should be lined up with the centre of the oscillations so it provides a reference position to count the number of cycles as the object swings past it each cycle.

Electronic timers use automatic switches or 'gates' to start and stop the timer. However, just as with a digital stopwatch, a timing should be repeated, if possible several times, to give an average value. Light gates may be connected via an interface unit to a microcomputer. Interrupt signals from the light gates are timed by the microcomputer's internal clock. A software program is used to provide a set of instructions to the microcomputer.

### Balances

A balance is used to measure the weight of an object. Spring balances are usually less precise than lever balances. Both types of balance are usually much less precise than an electronic top-pan balance. The scale or read-out of a balance may be calibrated for convenience in kilograms or grams. The accuracy of an electronic top-pan balance can easily be tested using accurately known masses.

# 15.4 Analysis and evaluation

## Data processing

**For a single reading,** the precision of the measuring instrument determines the precision of the reading. A micrometer with a precision of 0.01 mm gives readings that each have a precision of 0.01 mm.

**For several readings,** the number of significant figures of the mean value should be the same as the precision of each reading. For example, consider the following measurements of the diameter of a wire: 0.34 mm, 0.33 mm, 0.36 mm, 0.33 mm, 0.35 mm. The mean value of the diameter readings works out at 0.342 mm but the third significant figure cannot be justified, as the precision of each reading is 0.01 mm. Therefore the mean value is rounded down to 0.34 mm.

*Note:*

The uncertainty in the mean value is $\pm\ 0.02$ mm (i.e. half the range) as explained in Topic 15.2.

## Using error estimates

How confident can you be in your measurements and any results or conclusions you draw from your measurements? If you work out what each uncertainty is, as a percentage of the measurement (the percentage uncertainty), you can then see which measurement is least accurate. You can then think about how that measurement could be made more accurately.

*Worked example:*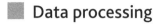

> The mass and diameter of a ball bearing were measured and the uncertainty of each measurement was estimated.
>
> The mass, $m$, of a ball bearing = $4.85 \times 10^{-3} \pm 0.02 \times 10^{-3}$ kg
>
> The diameter, $d$, of the ball bearing = $1.05 \times 10^{-2} \pm 0.01 \times 10^{-2}$ m
>
> Calculate and compare the percentage uncertainty of these two measurements.
>
> *Solution*
>
> The percentage uncertainty of the mass $m = \dfrac{0.02}{4.85} \times 100\% = 0.4\%$
>
> The percentage uncertainty of the diameter $d = \dfrac{0.01}{1.05} \times 100\% = 1.0\%$
>
> The diameter measurement is therefore more than twice as inaccurate as the mass measurement.

*More about errors*

1  When two measurements are added or subtracted, the uncertainty of the result is the sum of the uncertainties of the measurements. For example, the mass of a beaker is measured when it is empty and then when it contains water:

- the mass of an empty beaker = $65.1 \pm 0.1$ g
- the mass of the beaker and water = $125.6 \pm 0.1$ g

## ■ Percentage uncertainty

To work out the percentage uncertainty of $A$, you could:

■ Calculate the area of cross-section for $d = 0.34 - 0.01\,mm$ $= 0.33\,mm$.

This should give an answer of $8.55 \times 10^{-8}\,m^2$.

■ Calculate the area of cross-section for $d = 0.34 + 0.01\,mm$ $= 0.35\,mm$.

This should give an answer of $9.62 \times 10^{-8}\,m^2$.

Therefore, the area lies between $8.55 \times 10\,m^2$ and $9.62 \times 10^{-8}\,m^2$.

In other words, the area is $(9.08 \pm 0.53) \times 10^{-8}\,m^2$

(as $9.08 - 0.53 = 8.55$ and $9.08 + 0.53 = 9.62$).

The percentage uncertainty of $A$ is $\dfrac{0.53}{9.08} \times 100\% = 5.8\%$.
This is twice the percentage uncertainty of $d$.

It can be shown as a general rule that for a measurement $x$, the percentage uncertainty in $x^n$ is $n$ times the percentage uncertainty in $x$.

then the mass of the water could be as much as

$$(125.6 + 0.1) - (65.1 - 0.1)\,g = 60.7\,g, \text{ or as little as}$$
$$(125.6 - 0.1) - (65.1 + 0.1)\,g = 60.3\,g.$$

The mass of water is therefore $60.5 \pm 0.2\,g$.

2 When a measurement in a calculation is raised to a power $n$, the percentage uncertainty is increased $n$ times. For example, suppose you need to calculate the area $A$ of cross-section of a wire that has a diameter of $0.34 + 0.01\,mm$. You will need to use the formula $A = \pi d^2/4$. The calculation should give an answer of $9.08 \times 10^{-8}\,m^2$. The percentage uncertainty of $d$ is $\frac{0.01}{0.34} \times 100\% = 2.9\%$. So the percentage uncertainty of $A$ is $5.8\%$ ($= 2 \times 2.9\%$). The consequence of this rule is that in any calculation where a quantity is raised to a higher power, the uncertainty of that quantity becomes much more significant.

## ■ Graphs and errors

Straight line graphs are important because they are used to establish the relationship between two physical quantities. For example, as explained in Topic 8.4, consider a set of measurements of the distance fallen by an object released from rest and the time it takes. A graph of distance fallen against $(time)^2$ should be a straight line through the origin. If the line is straight, the theoretical equation $s = \frac{1}{2}gt^2$ (where $s$ is the distance fallen, and $t$ is the time taken) is confirmed. The value of $g$ can be calculated as the gradient of the graph is equal to $\frac{1}{2}g$. If the straight line does not pass through the origin, there is a systematic error in the distance measurement. Even so, the gradient is still $\frac{1}{2}g$.

### A best-fit test

Suppose you have obtained your own measurements for an experiment and you use them to plot a graph that is predicted to be a straight line. The plotted points are unlikely to be exactly straight in line with each other. The next stage is to draw a straight line of best fit so that the points are on average as close as possible to the line. Some problems may occur at this stage:

1 There might be a point much further than any other point from the line of best fit. The point is referred to as an **anomaly**. Methods for dealing with an anomalous point are as follows:

■ If possible, the measurements for that point should be repeated and used to replace the anomalous point, if the repeated measurement is much nearer the line.

■ If the repeated measurement confirms the anomaly, there could be a fault in the equipment or the way it is used. For example, in an electrical experiment, it could be caused by a change of the range of a meter to make that measurement. If no fault is found, make more measurements near the anomaly to see if these measurements lead towards the anomaly. If they do, it is no longer an anomaly and the measurements are valid.

■ If a repeat measurement is not possible, the anomalous point should be ignored and a comment made in your report (or on the graph) about it.

2 The points might seem to curve away from the straight line of best fit. The uncertainty of each measurement can be used to give a small range or error bar for each measurement. Figure 1 shows the idea. The straight line of best fit should pass through all the error bars. If it doesn't, the following notes might be helpful. You could use the error

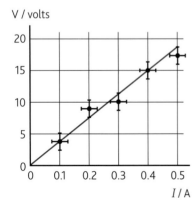

**Figure 1** *Error bars*

bars to draw a straight line of maximum gradient and a straight line of minimum gradient.

- The points lie along a straight line over most of the range but curve away more further along the line. This would indicate that a straight line relationship between the plotted quantities is valid only over the range of measurements which produced the straight part of the line.

- Only two or three points might seem to lie on a straight line. In this case, it cannot be concluded that there is a linear relationship between the plotted quantities. You might need to plot further graphs to find out if a different type of graph would give a straight line relationship. A data analysis software package on a computer could be used to test different possible relationships (or at A2 a log graph could be plotted).

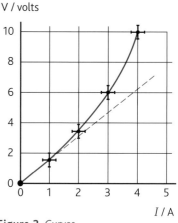

**Figure 2** *Curves*

## Evaluating your results

You should be able to form a conclusion from the results of an investigation. This might be a final calculation of a physical quantity or property (e.g. resistivity) or a statement of the relationship established between two variables. As explained earlier, the degree of accuracy of the measurements could be used as a guide to the number of significant figures in a 'final result' conclusion. Mathematical links established or verified between quantities should be stated in a 'relationship' conclusion.

You always need to evaluate the conclusion(s) of an experiment or investigation to establish its validity. This evaluation could start with a discussion of the strength of the experimental evidence used to draw the conclusions:

- Discuss the reliability of the data and suggest improvements, where appropriate, that would improve the reliability. You may need to consider the effect of the control variables, if the experimental evidence is not as reliable as it should be.

- Discuss the methods taken (or proposed) to eliminate or reduce any random or systematic errors. Describe the steps taken to deal with anomalous results.

- Evaluate the accuracy of the results by considering the percentage uncertainties in the measurements. These can be compared to identify the most significant sources of error in the measurements, which can then lead to a discussion of how to reduce the most significant sources of error.

- Propose improvements to the strategy or experimental procedures, referring to the above discussion on validity as justification for the proposals.

- Suggest further experimental work, based on the strength of the conclusions. Strong conclusions could lead to a prediction and how to test it.

## 16.1 The ISA/PSA scheme (scheme T)

### ■ Investigative skills assignments

Two AS level physics ISAs are set by AQA each year. You will be assessed using one of these ISAs if you are being assessed through the ISA/PSA scheme. Previous ISAs must not be used for assessment purposes although they may be used in preparation for one of the two authorised ISAs. The ISA counts for 41 marks out of the 50 mark total for Unit 3.

The ISA is carried out under supervision and is in two stages.

### Stage 1 The practical task

The practical task requires you to carry out practical work using an AQA task sheet, which outlines the investigation. The task sheet may be prescriptive, giving precise instructions, or it may be more open-ended. Your teacher will tell you in advance when you will carry out the ISA. Also, a few weeks before the ISA task, your teacher will tell you the general topic area of the ISA.

The task is carried out in the laboratory in a timetabled lesson (or lessons) under supervision, and should take no more than about an hour. The task will require you to make measurements and present them in a table of your own design. You will be asked to process the measurement data and to use the data to draw a graph. Your teacher is not allowed to instruct candidates on the presentation of the data, or the choice or presentation of the graph. You are not allowed to take work away from the ISA session and all completed work must be handed to your teacher who will assess the work, using AQA marking guidelines. Your teacher is not allowed to write any marks or comments on your work, as it will be returned to you for use in the written test. The practical task counts for 10 of the 41 marks on the ISA. You will not be allowed to redraft or repeat an ISA.

The practical task itself is an individual task which you will carry out in the laboratory under exam conditions. You will be provided with a complete set of practical equipment necessary for the practical task. This equipment should include familiar items that you have used before (e.g. clamps, stands, metre ruler, stopwatch etc.) but it might include an item or materials specific to the task (e.g. a sealed electrical box). The task sheet will tell you how to use the equipment and what measurements to make. Read it carefully to make sure you set up and use the equipment correctly. If you think an item of equipment is not working, ask your teacher to check it.

### Stage 2 The written test

You will take the written test in a timetabled lesson under supervision, as soon as possible after completion of the practical task. The test is a 1 hour written paper set by AQA, and counts for 31 of the 41 ISA marks. Lines to write your answer are provided after each part-question. Your teacher will mark your written test, using AQA marking guidelines. In the exam room, just before the test begins, you will be provided with the test paper and your completed material from the practical task. The test is in two parts:

a Section A will consist of a number of general questions about the practical task. For example, you might be asked about the control variables in the task or about the precision of your measurements. You will probably not be required to plot a graph here as you will have already done this in the practical task.

b Section B will provide a further set of data on the practical task or a closely related task. The questions in this part will ask about methodology, analysis and evaluation of the data. You may be asked in your evaluation to suggest improvements or to discuss further work that could be done, for example to test a prediction.

The allocation of marks to each question will be shown on the written paper. The balance of marks between the two sections will vary according to the ISA and will generally be about one third on section A and two thirds on section B. A sample ISA giving you a clear idea of the style and format of the questions should be available from your teacher.

**Table 1** *ISA marks*

| component | skill area | mark |
| --- | --- | --- |
| Stage 1 Practical task | Make measurements | |
| | Tabulate and process data | |
| | Plot a graph | 10 |
| Stage 2 Written test | | |
| section A | Evaluate own measurements | |
| section B | Analyse given data on a related task | |
| | Evaluate related task | 31 |

## The practical skills assessment

The skills in the PSA are assessed in practical activities that you will do throughout your course. The practical activities will give you opportunities to demonstrate your practical skills. You will be given some instructions when you carry out these activities and you will need to make decisions for yourself about how you organise yourself and how you use the equipment. You will be assessed on your ability to:

- demonstrate safe and skilful practical techniques and processes
- select appropriate methods
- make measurements precisely and accurately
- make and record reliable and valid observations and measurements
- work with others in experimental activities.

The paragraphs below show how your PSA mark is determined. The three strands are each worth up to 3 marks, giving a total of 9 marks. Your teacher will assess the level you reach by the end of the course in each strand.

### Following instructions and group work

- 3 marks are awarded if you are able to follow instructions on complex tasks[2] without guidance and can work with others making some contribution. **If not, see next.**

## How science works

**Measuring**

Standard laboratory apparatus you will use to make measurements might include:

- basic apparatus (metre rule, set square, protractors, stopclock or stopwatch)
- electrical meters (analogue or digital)
- the micrometer, vernier callipers,
- a top-pan electronic balance, measuring cylinders
- thermometers, newtonmeters.

■ 2 marks are awarded if you are able to follow instructions in standard procedures[1] without guidance and can work with others making some contribution. **If not, see below.**

■ 1 mark is awarded if you are able to follow follow instructions in standard procedures[1] but sometimes need guidance. **If not**, no marks are awarded.

### Selection and use of equipment

■ 3 marks are awarded if you can select and use standard laboratory equipment with appropriate precision[4] and recognise when it is appropriate to repeat measurements. **If not, see below.**

■ 2 marks are awarded if you can use standard laboratory equipment selecting the appropriate range[3]. **If not, see below.**

■ 1 mark is awarded if you are able to use standard laboratory equipment with some guidance as to the appropriate instrument / range[3]. **If not**, no marks are awarded.

### Safety and organisation

■ 3 marks are awarded if you can work safely without supervision or guidance (will have effectively carried out own risk assessment[5]). **If not, see below.**

■ 2 marks are awarded if you can work in an organised manner with due regard for safety with only occasional guidance or reminders. **If not, see below.**

■ 1 mark is awarded if you can work in a safe and organised manner following guidance provided but need reminders. **If not**, no marks are awarded.

*Notes:*

1 Standard procedures above refer to setting up and using standard laboratory apparatus. For example, the setting up and use of a circuit to measure the resistance of a component would be a standard procedure.

2 Complex tasks refer to tasks which are not necessarily straightforward and which may involve several stages, where equipment needs to be rearranged at one or more stages. For example, the investigation of the heating effect of an electric current is a complex task, because the same heater would be used with different currents to heat the same amount of substance for the same length of time.

3 Appropriate instrument/range means choosing the most suitable instrument and range for a particular measurement task.
See Topic 15.2.

4 Precision – see Topic 15.2.

5 Risk assessment: Before you carry out a practical task, you should eliminate (if possible) or minimise any health and safety hazards. A risk assessment requires you to think about the possible hazards in an activity and plan to eliminate or minimise them.

# 16.2 The AQA-marked scheme (scheme X)

## Part 1

This part is carried out under supervision in the laboratory during normal class time. You will be required to work individually and carry out 5 short practical exercises. The exercises for each year are set by AQA at the start of the year and each one may be carried out at any stage during the year during or after coverage of the relevant topic . Your teacher will tell you in advance when you are to do them. You will not be expected to spend more than 3 hours of laboratory time in completing these exercises. The exercises will be typical of the normal practical work that would be expected to be covered as part of any AS course.

In carrying out these exercises, you could be asked to use ammeters, voltmeters, vernier callipers, a micrometer, a stopwatch or stopclock, a thermometer, a newtonmeter and an electronic balance as well sophisticated apparatus such as the oscilloscope. In using these instruments, you will be expected to follow instructions and work safely. In addition, you will be asked to make and record accurate measurements and assess the reliability and accuracy of your results.

At the end of each exercise, your results and observations are to be given to the teacher for verification purposes and may be returned to you for use during the remainder of the course. A sample set of Part 1 exercises are listed below

The practical skills developed during Part 1 will be assessed through the AQA-set practical experiments in Part 2.

**Sample set of Part 1 exercises for AS level**

| | Exercise | Measuring equipment used |
|---|---|---|
| 1 | Measurement to produce the $IV$ characteristic curve of a component | ammeter, voltmeter |
| 2 | Measuring the terminal velocity of a ball falling in oil | stopwatch, metre ruler, set square |
| 3 | Measurement of the density of a cylinder | vernier callipers, micrometer screw gauge, electronic balance |
| 4 | Measurement of the refractive index of a liquid | protractor, millimetre ruler |
| 5 | Using a potential divider with a thermistor as a temperature sensor | thermometer , voltmeter |

## ■ Part 2

In this part, you carry out a short practical task and a longer practical task and experiment based on physics from Unit 1 and/or from Unit 2 of specifications. The practical experiment to be carried out will be AQA set and marked. Once completed, you will not be able to attempt Part 2 again. The measurements and results from these experiments will be analysed and evaluated in Part 3, an AQA-set and marked written paper, thus testing relevant skills developed in the Part 1 exercises. However, you can not carry forward written work from Part 1 to the Part 2 experiment.

Examples of some Part 2 practical experiments for AS level are listed below.

1 Investigation of the relationship between the terminal velocity of a sphere falling in oil and its radius (use of stopwatch, metre rule, set square, micrometer, thermometer).

2 Investigation of the variation of the resistance of a thermistor with temperature (use of an ammeter, a voltmeter, a thermometer, an electronic balance).

3 Investigation of the forces acting on an object in equilibrium (use of metre rule, set square, protractor, electronic balance).

Your teacher will tell you in advance when you are to carry out the Part 2 experiments. This will be near the end of the course between March and the end of May. Because the experiment is a skills test like the 'on the road' part of the driving test, the experiment can be used to test other students at other times.

You have to work individually and be supervised throughout. You will be provided with a task sheet with sufficient information and instructions to enable you to obtain reliable measurements which you have to record, process and discuss. In carrying out the experiment, you will be expected to:

■ manipulate apparatus skilfully and safely,

■ make reliable and accurate measurements,

■ identify anomalous measurements,

■ minimise or take account of the effects of random and any systematic error,

■ tabulate the results in a well organised and systematic way, taking account of the expected conventions,

■ process data,

■ graph, or chart, these data as appropriate.

At the end of the experiment, you have to hand in all your written work (i.e. table of results, calculations, graph, and discussion of errors). This will be returned to you for use in Part 3.

# Part 3

This is an AQA-set and marked written paper of duration of 1 hour 15 minutes. Your teacher will arrange when you are to take this test, preferably as soon as possible after Part 2. Before you commence the test, your written work from Part 2 will be returned to you. At the end of the test, all your written work from Parts 2 and 3 will be collected by your teacher who will send it to AQA for marking together with verification forms for Part 1.

Some of the questions in the paper will require you to:

- use your Part 2 results and graph to carry out further analysis in order to arrive at a conclusion,
- assess the overall accuracy of the outcome of the experiment.

In addition, you may be asked to:

- carry out error calculations on the data from Part 2,
- describe procedures used to overcome uncertainties involved in Part 2,
- comment on the reliability of the evidence or procedures used during Part 2,
- discuss all/some of the measurement techniques developed in Part 1,
- make predictions about alternative outcomes
- discuss ways of extending the range or reliability of the evidence produced during Part 2.

The work produced by the candidates in Parts 2 and 3 will sent to AQA for marking together with candidate Part 1 verification forms.

# 17 More on mathematical skills

## 17.1 Data handling

### Scientific units

Scientists use a single system of units to avoid unnecessary effort and time converting between different units of the same quantity. This system, the **Système International** (or **SI system**) is based on a defined unit for certain physical quantities including those listed in Table 1. Units of all other quantities are derived from the SI base units.

The following examples show how the units of all other physical quantities are derived from the base units.

- The unit of area is the square metre ($m^2$).
- The unit of volume is the cubic metre ($m^3$).
- The unit of density is the kilogram per cubic metre ($kg\,m^{-3}$).
- The unit of speed is the metre per second ($m\,s^{-1}$).

**Table 1** *SI base units*

| physical quantity | unit |
| --- | --- |
| mass | kilogram (kg) |
| length | metre (m) |
| time | second (s) |
| electric current | ampere (A) |
| temperature | kelvin (K) |

### More about using a calculator

1. **'Exp'** (or 'EE' on some calculators) is the calculator button you press to key in a **power of ten**. To key in a number in standard form (e.g. $3.0 \times 10^8$), the steps are as follows:
   - Step 1 Key in the number between 1 and 10 (e.g. 3.0).
   - Step 2 Press the calculator button marked 'Exp' (or 'EE' on some calculators).
   - Step 3 Key in the power of ten (e.g. 8).

   If the display reads '3.0 08' this should be read as $3.0 \times 10^8$ (not $3.0^8$ which means 3.0 multiplied by itself 8 times). If the power of ten is a negative number (e.g. $10^{-8}$ not $10^8$), press the calculator button marked '+/−' after step 3 (or before, if you are using a graphic calculator) to change the sign of the power of ten.

2. **'Inv'** is the button you press if you want the calculator to give the value of the inverse of a function. For example, if you want to find out the angle, which has a sine of 0.5, you key in 0.5 on the display then press ' inv' then 'sin' to obtain the answer of 30°. Some calculators have a 'second function' or 'shift' button that you press instead of the 'inv' button.

3. **'log'** (or 'lg') is the button you press to find out what a number is as a power of ten. For example, press 'log' then key in 100 and the display will show 2, because $100 = 10^2$. Logarithmic scales have equal intervals for each power of ten.

4. **To raise any number to any power**, use the ^ button or $y^x$ button (or $x^y$ on some calculators). For example, if you want to work out the value of $2^8$, key in 2 onto the display then $y^x$ (or ^), then 8, and press =. The display should then show 256 as the decimal value of $2^8$.

power of ten

number displayed = $6.62 \times 10^{-34}$

**Figure 1** *Displaying powers of ten*

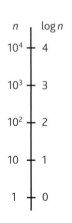

| $n$ | $\log n$ |
| --- | --- |
| $10^4$ | 4 |
| $10^3$ | 3 |
| $10^2$ | 2 |
| 10 | 1 |
| 1 | 0 |

**Figure 2** *A logarithmic scale*

The $y^x$ button can be used to find roots. For example, given the equation $T^4 = 5200$, you can find $T$ by keying in 5200 onto the display, then pressing the $y^x$ button, followed by $(1 \div 4)$ which will give the answer 8.49.

## Significant figures

A calculator display shows a large number of digits. When you use a calculator, you should always round up or round down the final answer of a calculation to the same number of significant figures as the data given. Sometimes, a numerical answer to one part of a question has to be used in a subsequent calculation, in which case, the numerical answer to the first part should be carried forward without rounding it up or down. For example, if you need to calculate the value of $d \sin 65°$, where $d = 1.64$, the calculator will show $9.063077870 \times 10^{-1}$ for the sine of 65°. Multiplying this answer by 1.64 then gives 1.486344771, which should then be rounded off to 1.49 so it has the same number of significant figures as 1.64 (i.e. to 3 significant figures).

*Worked example:*_____

Calculate the cube root of $2.9 \times 10^6$.

*Solution*

Step 1   Key in $2.9 \times 10^6$ as explained earlier

Step 2   Press the $y^x$ button

Step 3   Key in $(1 \div 3)$

Step 4   Press =

The display should show '1.426 02' so the answer is 142.6

---

### Summary questions

Write your answers to each of the following questions in standard form, where appropriate, and to the same number of significant figures as the data.

**1**  Copy and complete the following conversions.

a i   $500 \, mm = $ _____ m,

ii   $3.2 \, m = $ _____ cm,

iii   $9560 \, cm = $ _____ m,

b i   $0.45 \, kg = $ _____ g,

ii   $1997 \, g = $ _____ kg,

iii   $54\,000 \, kg = $ _____ g,

c i   $20 \, cm^2 = $ _____ $m^2$,

ii   $55 \, mm^2 = $ _____ $m^2$,

iii   $0.050 \, cm^2 = $ _____ $m^2$

**2**  a  Write the following values in standard form.

i  150 million km in metres, ii 365 days in seconds, iii 630 nm in metres, iv 25.7 μg in kilograms, v 150 m in millimetres, vi 1.245 μm in metres,

b  Write the following values with a prefix instead of in standard form.

i   $3.5 \times 10^4 \, m = $ _____ km,

ii   $6.5 \times 10^{-7} \, m = $ _____ nm,

iii   $3.4 \times 10^6 \, g = $ _____ kg,

iv   $8.7 \times 10^8 \, W = $ _____ MW = _____ GW

**3**  a  Use the equation 'average speed = distance/time' to calculate the average speed in $m \, s^{-1}$ of:

i   a vehicle that travels a distance of 9000 m in 450 s,

ii   a vehicle that travels a distance of 144 km in 2 h,

iii   a particle that travels a distance of 0.30 nm in a time of $2.0 \times 10^{-18}$ s,

iv   the Earth on its orbit of radius $1.5 \times 10^{11}$ m, given the time taken per orbit is 365.25 days.

b  Use the equation

$$\text{Resistance} = \frac{\text{potential difference}}{\text{current}}$$

to calculate the resistance of a component for the following values of current $I$ and pd $V$.

i   $V = 15 \, V$, $I = 2.5 \, mA$,

ii   $V = 80 \, mV$, $I = 16 \, mA$,

iii   $V = 5.2 \, kV$, $I = 3.0 \, mA$,

iv   $V = 250 \, V$, $I = 0.51 \, μA$,

v   $V = 160 \, mV$, $I = 53 \, mA$.

**4**  a  Calculate each of the following: i $6.7^3$ ii $(5.3 \times 10^4)^2$ iii $(2.1 \times 10^{-6})^4$ iv $(0.035)^2$ v $(4.2 \times 10^8)^{1/2}$ vi $(3.8 \times 10^{-5})^{1/4}$

b  Calculate each of the following:

i   $\dfrac{2.4^2}{3.5 \times 10^3}$

ii   $\dfrac{3.6 \times 10^{-3}}{6.2 \times 10^2}$

iii   $\dfrac{8.1 \times 10^4 + 6.5 \times 10^3}{5.3 \times 10^4}$

iv   $7.2 \times 10^{-3} + \dfrac{6.2 \times 10^4}{2.6 \times 10^6}$

# 17.2 Trigonometry

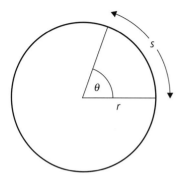

**Figure 1** *Arcs and segments*

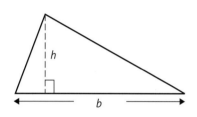

Area $= \frac{1}{2}hb$

**Figure 2** *The area of a triangle*

## Angles and arcs

- Angles are measured in degrees or radians. The scale for conversion is $360° = 2\pi$ radians. The symbol for the radian is rad, so $1\,\text{rad} = 360/2\pi = 57.3°$ (to 3 significant figures).

- The circumference of a circle of radius $r = 2\pi r$. So the circumference can be written as the angle in radians ($2\pi$) round the circle $\times\, r$.

- For a segment of a circle, the length of the arc of the segment is in proportion to the angle $\theta$ which the arc makes to the centre of the circle. This is shown in Figure 1. Because the arc length is $2\pi r$ (the circumference) for an angle of $360°$ ($= 2\pi$ radians), then

$$\frac{\text{arc length, } s}{2\pi r} = \frac{\theta \text{ in degrees}}{360°}$$

## Triangles and trigonometry

### Area rule

As shown in Figure 2,

**the area of any triangle $= \frac{1}{2} \times$ its height $\times$ its base.**

### Trigonometry calculations using a calculator

A scientific calculator has a button you can press to use either degrees or radians. Make sure you know how to switch your calculator from one of these two modes to the other. Many marks have been lost in examinations as a result of forgetting to use the correct mode. For example,

- $\sin 30° = 0.50$, whereas $\sin 30\,\text{rad} = -0.99$

- inv $\sin 0.17$ in degree mode $= 9.79°$, whereas inv $\sin 0.17$ in rad mode $= 0.171$

Also, watch out when you calculate the sine, cosine or tangent of the product of a number and an angle. For example, $\sin(2 \times 30°)$ comes out as 1.05 if you forget the brackets, instead of the correct answer of 0.867. The reason for the error is that, unless you insert the brackets, the calculator is programmed to work out $\sin 2°$ then multiply the answer by 30.

### Trigonometry functions

Consider again the definitions of the sine, cosine and tangent of an angle, as applied to the right-angled triangle in Figure 3.

$$\sin\theta = \frac{o}{h}$$ where $o =$ the length of the side opposite angle $\theta$
$h =$ the length of the hypotenuse
$$\cos\theta = \frac{a}{h}$$ $a =$ the length of the side adjacent to angle $\theta$

$$\tan\theta = \frac{o}{a}$$

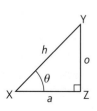

**Figure 3** *A right-angled triangle*

## Pythagoras' theorem and trigonometry

Pythagoras' theorem states that for any right-angled triangle, the square of the hypotenuse = the sum of the squares of the other two sides.

Applying Pythagoras' theorem to the right-angled triangle in Figure 3 gives

$$h^2 = o^2 + a^2$$

Since $o = h\sin\theta$ and $a = h\cos\theta$, then the above equation may be written

$$h^2 = h^2\sin^2\theta + h^2\cos^2\theta$$

Cancelling $h^2$ therefore gives the following useful link between $\sin\theta$ and $\cos\theta$,

$$1 = \sin^2\theta + \cos^2\theta$$

## ■ Vector rules

### Resolving a vector

As explained in Topic 7.1, any vector can be resolved into two perpendicular components in the same plane as the vector, as shown by Figure 4. The force vector $F$ is resolved into a horizontal component $F\cos\theta$ and a vertical component $F\sin\theta$, where $\theta$ is the angle between the line of action of the force and the horizontal line.

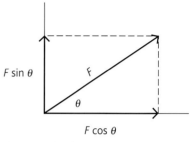

**Figure 4** *Resolving a vector*

### Adding two perpendicular vectors

Figure 5 shows two perpendicular forces $F_1$ and $F_2$ acting on a point object X. The combined effect of these two forces, the resultant force, is given by the vector triangle in Figure 5. This is a right-angled triangle, where the resultant force is represented by the hypotenuse.

■ Applying Pythagoras' theorem to the triangle gives $F^2 = F_1^2 + F_2^2$, where $F$ is the magnitude of the resultant force.
Therefore $F = (F_1^2 + F_2^2)^{1/2}$

■ Applying the trigonometry formula $\tan\theta = o/a$, the angle between the resultant force and force $F_1$ is given by $\tan\theta = F_2/F_1$

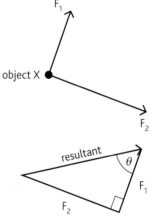

**Figure 5** *Adding two perpendicular vectors*

## Summary questions

**1**  a Calculate the circumference of a circle of radius 0.250 m.
  b Calculate the length of the arc of a circle of radius 0.250 m for the following angles between the arc and the centre of the circle: i 360°, ii 240°, iii 60°

**2**  For the right-angled triangle XYZ in Figure 6, calculate:

  a angle YXZ (= $\theta$) if XY = 80 mm and

  i XZ = 30 mm,

  ii XZ = 60 mm.

  iii YZ = 30 mm

  iv YZ = 70 mm

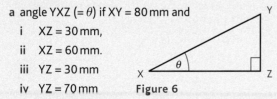

**Figure 6**

  b XZ if i XY = 20 cm and $\theta$ = 30°, ii XY = 22 m and $\theta$ = 45°, iii YZ = 18 mm and $\theta$ = 75°, iv YZ = 47 cm and $\theta$ = 25°

**3**  a A right-angled triangle XYZ has a hypoteneuse XY of length 55 mm and side XZ of length 25 mm. Calculate the length of the other side.
  b An aircraft travels a distance of 30 km due north from an airport P to an airport Q. It then travels due east for a distance of 18 km to an airport R. Calculate i the distance from P to R, ii the angle QPR.

**4**  a Calculate the horizontal component A and the vertical component B of:

  i a 6.0 N force at 40° to the vertical,

  ii a 10.0 N force at 20° to the vertical,

  iii a 7.5 N force at 50° to the horizontal.

  b Calculate the magnitude and direction of the resultant of a 2.0 N force acting due north and a 3.5 N force acting due east

# 17.3 More about algebra

## Signs and symbols

If you used symbols in your GCSE course, you might have met the use of $s$ for distance and $I$ for current. Maybe you wondered why we don't use $d$ for distance instead of $s$ or $C$ for current instead of $I$. The answer is that physics discoveries have taken place in many countries. The first person to discover the key ideas about speed was Galileo, the great Italian scientist, so he used the words 'scale' from his own language for distance and therefore assigned the symbol $s$ to distance. Important discoveries about electricity were made by Ampère, the great French scientist, and he wrote about the intensity of an electric current, so he used the symbol $I$ for electric current. The symbols we now use are used in all countries in association with the **SI system of units**.

**Table 1** *Symbols for some physical quantities*

| physical quantity | symbol | unit | unit symbol |
|---|---|---|---|
| distance | $s$ | metre | m |
| speed or velocity | $v$ | metre per second | $m\,s^{-1}$ |
| acceleration | $a$ | metre per second per second | $m\,s^{-2}$ |
| mass | $m$ | kilogram | kg |
| force | $F$ | newton | N |
| energy or work | $E$ | joule | J |
| power | $P$ | watt | W |
| density | $\rho$ | kilogram per cubic metre | $kg\,m^{-3}$ |
| current | $I$ | ampere | A |
| potential difference or voltage | $V$ | volt | V |
| resistance | $R$ | ohm | $\Omega$ |

## Signs you need to recognise

- Inequality signs are often used in physics. You need to be able to recognise the meaning of the signs in Table 2. For example, the inequality $I \geq 3\,A$ means that the current is greater or equal to $3\,A$. This is the same as saying that the current is not less than $3\,A$.

- The approximation sign is used where an estimate or an order-of-magnitude calculation is made, rather than a precise calculation. For an order-of-magnitude calculation, the final value is written with one significant figure only, or even rounded up or down to the nearest power of ten. Order-of-magnitude calculations are useful as a quick check after using a calculator. For example, if you are asked to calculate the density of a $1.0\,kg$ metal cylinder of height $0.100\,m$ and diameter $0.071\,m$, you ought to obtain a value of $2530\,kg\,m^{-3}$ using a calculator. Now let's check the value quickly:

Volume $= \pi(\text{radius})^2 \times \text{height}$
$= 3 \times (0.04)^2 \times 0.1 = 48 \times 10^{-5}\,m^3$

Density $= \text{mass}/\text{volume}$
$= 1.0/50 \times 10^{-5} = 2000\,kg\,m^{-3}$

This confirms our 'precise' calculation.

- Proportionality is represented by the $\propto$ sign. A simple example of its use in physics is for Hooke's law; the tension in a spring is proportional to its extension.

$$\text{Tension } T \propto \text{extension } \Delta L$$

By introducing a constant of proportionality $k$, the link above can be made into an equation:

$$T = k\Delta L$$

where $k$ is defined as the spring constant. See Topic 9.1. With any proportionality relationship, if one of the variables is increased by a given factor (e.g. $\times 3$), the other variable is increased by the same factor. So in the above example, if $T$ is trebled, then extension $\Delta L$ is also trebled. A graph of tension $T$ on the $y$-axis against extension $\Delta L$ on the $x$-axis would give a straight line through the origin.

**Table 2** *Signs*

| sign | meaning | sign | meaning | sign | meaning |
|---|---|---|---|---|---|
| $>$ | greater than | $>>$ | much greater than | $<x^2>$ | mean square value |
| $<$ | less than | $<<$ | much less than | $\propto$ | is proportional to |
| $\geq$ | greater than or equal to | $\approx$ | approximately equals | $\Delta$ | change of |
| $\leq$ | less than or equal to | $<x>$ | mean value | $\sqrt{}$ | square root |

# More about equations and formulae

## Rearranging an equation with several terms

The equation $v = u + at$ is an example of an equation with two terms on the right-hand side. These terms are $u$ and $at$. To make $t$ the subject of the equation,

1 Isolate the term containing $t$ on one side by subtracting $u$ from both sides to give $v - u = at$

2 Isolate $t$ by dividing both sides of the equation $v - u = at$ by $a$ to give

$$\frac{(v - u)}{a} = \frac{at}{a} = t$$

Note that $a$ cancels out in the expression $\frac{at}{a}$

3 The rearranged equation may now be written

$$t = \frac{(v - u)}{a}$$

## Rearranging an equation containing powers

Suppose a quantity is raised to a power in a term in an equation, and that quantity is to be made the subject of the equation. For example, consider the equation $V = \frac{4}{3}\pi r^3$ where $r$ is to be made the subject of the equation.

1 Isolate $r^3$ from the other factors in the equation, by dividing both sides by $4\pi$, then multiplying both sides by 3 to give $\dfrac{3V}{4\pi} = r^3$

2 Take the cube root of both sides to give $\left(\dfrac{3V}{4\pi}\right)^{1/3} = r$

3 Rewrite the equation with $r$ on the left-hand side if necessary.

### More about powers

1 Powers add for identical quantities when two terms are multiplied together. For example, if $y = ax^n$ and $z = bx^m$, then $yz = ax^m bx^n = ab\,x^{m+n}$

2 An equation of the form $y = \dfrac{k}{z^n}$ may be written in the form $y = kz^{-n}$.

3 The $n^{\text{th}}$ root of an expression is written as the power $1/n$. For example, the square root of $x$ is $x^{1/2}$. Therefore, rearranging $y = x^n$ to make $x$ the subject gives $x = y^{1/n}$.

## Summary questions

1 Complete each of the following statements:

  a If $x > 5$, then $1/x <$

  b If $4 < x < 10$, then _____ $< 1/x <$

  c If $x$ is positive and $x^2 > 100$ then $1/x$ _____.

2 a Make $t$ the subject of each of the following equations:

    i $v = u + at$, ii $s = \frac{1}{2}at^2$, iii $y = k\,(t - t_o)$, iv $F = \dfrac{mv}{t}$

  b Solve each of the following equations:

    i $2z + 6 = 10$, ii $2\,(z + 6) = 10$, iii $\dfrac{2}{z - 4} = 8$,

    iv $\dfrac{4}{z^2} = 36$

3 a Make $x$ the subject of each of the following equations:

    i $y = 2x^{1/2}$, ii $2y = x^{-1/2}$, iii $y\,x^{1/3} = 1$, iv $y = \dfrac{k}{x^2}$

  b Solve each of the following equations:

    i $x^{-1/2} = 2$, ii $3x^2 = 24$, iii $\dfrac{8}{x^2} = 32$, iv $2\,(x^{1/2} + 4) = 12$

4 Use the data given with each equation below to calculate:

  a the volume $V$ of a wire of radius $r = 0.34\,\text{mm}$ and length $L = 0.840\,\text{m}$, using the equation $V = \pi r^2 L$,

  b the radius $r$ of a sphere of volume $V = 1.00 \times 10^{-6}\,\text{m}^3$, using the formula $V = \frac{4}{3}\pi r^3$,

  c the time period $T$ of a simple pendulum of length $L = 1.50\,\text{m}$, using the formula $T = 2\pi(L/g)^{0.5}$, where $g = 9.8\,\text{m s}^{-2}$,

  d the speed $v$ of an object of mass $m = 0.20\,\text{kg}$ and kinetic energy $E_k = 28\,\text{J}$, using the formula $E_k = \frac{1}{2}mv^2$.

# 17.4  Straight line graphs

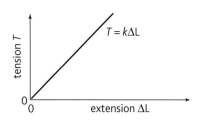

**Figure 1**  *Straight line graph*

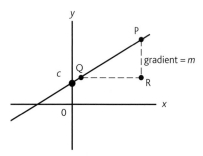

**Figure 2**  $y = mx + c$

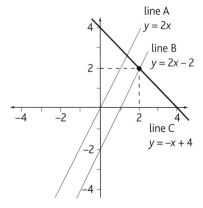

**Figure 3**  *Straight line graphs*

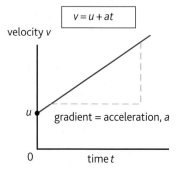

**Figure 4**  *Motion at constant acceleration*

## The general equation for a straight line graph

Links between two physical quantities can be established most easily by plotting a graph. One of the physical quantities is represented by the vertical scale (the 'ordinate', often called the $y$-axis) and the other quantity by the horizontal scale (the 'abscissa', often called the $x$-axis). The coordinates of a point on a graph are the $x$- and $y$-values, usually written $(x, y)$ of the point.

The simplest link between two physical variables is where the plotted points define a straight line. For example, Figure 1 shows the link between the tension in a spring and the extension of the spring; the gradient of the line is constant and the line passes through the origin. Any situation where the $y$-variable is directly proportional to the $x$-variable gives a straight line through the origin. For Figure 1, the gradient of the line is the spring constant $k$. The relationship between the tension $T$ and the extension $\Delta L$ may therefore be written as $T = k\Delta L$.

The general equation for a straight line graph is usually written in the form

**$y = mx + c$,**   where m = the gradient of the line, and c = the y-intercept.

- The gradient $m$ can be measured by marking two points P and Q far apart on the line. The triangle PQR, as shown in Figure 2, is then used to find the gradient. If $(x_p, y_p)$ and $(x_Q, y_Q)$ represent the $x$- and $y$-coordinates of points P and Q respectively, then

$$\text{gradient } m = \frac{y_p - y_Q}{x_p - x_Q}$$

- The $y$-intercept, $c$, is the point at $x = 0$ where the line crosses the $y$-axis. To find the $y$-intercept of a line on a graph that does not show $x = 0$, measure the gradient as above, then use the coordinates of any point on the line with the equation $y = mx + c$ to calculate $c$. For example, rearranging $y = mx + c$ gives $c = y - mx$. Therefore, using the coordinates of point Q in Figure 2, the $y$-intercept $c = y_Q - mx_Q$.

### Examples of straight line graphs

- Line A:   $c = 0$ so the line passes through the origin. Its equation is $y = 2x$

- Line B:   $m > 0$ so the line has a positive gradient; its equation is $y = 2x - 2$

- Line C:   $m < 0$ so the line has a negative gradient; its equation is $y = -x + 4$

## Straight line graphs and physics equations

You need to be able to work out gradients and intercepts for equations you meet in physics that generate straight line graphs. Some further examples in addition to Figure 1 are described below.

1  **The velocity $v$ of an object moving at constant acceleration $a$ at time $t$** is given by the equation $v = u + at$, where $u$ is its velocity at time $t = 0$. Figure 4 shows the corresponding graph of velocity $v$ on the $y$-axis against time $t$ on the $x$-axis.

Rearranging the equation as $v = at + u$ and comparing this with $y = mx + c$ shows that

- the gradient $m$ = acceleration $a$
- the y-intercept, $c$ = the initial velocity $u$.

**2 The pd, $V$, across the terminals of a battery of emf $\varepsilon$ and internal resistance $r$** varies with current in accordance with the equation $V = \varepsilon - Ir$. Figure 5 shows the corresponding graph of pd, $V$, on the $y$-axis against current $I$ on the $x$-axis.

Rearranging the equation as $V = -rI + \varepsilon$ and comparing this with $y = mx + c$ shows that

- the gradient $m = -r$
- the y-intercept, $c = \varepsilon$ so the intercept on the y-axis gives the emf $\varepsilon$ of the battery.

**3 The maximum kinetic energy $E_{Kmax}$ of a photoelectron** emitted from a metal surface of work function $\phi$ varies with frequency $f$ of the incident radiation, in accordance with the equation $E_{Kmax} = hf - \phi$. Figure 6 shows the corresponding graph of $E_{Kmax}$ on the y-axis against $f$ on the x-axis.

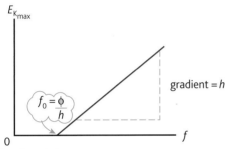

**Figure 6** *Photoelectric emission*

Comparing the equation $E_{Kmax} = hf - \phi$ with $y = mx + c$ shows that

- the gradient $m = h$
- the y-intercept, $c = -\phi$

Note that the x-intercept is where $y = 0$ on the line. Let the coordinates of the x-intercept be $(x_0, 0)$. Therefore $mx_0 + c = 0$ so $x_0 = -c/m$. Applied to Figure 6, the x-intercept is therefore $\phi/h$. Since the x-intercept is the threshold frequency $f_0$, then $f_0 = \phi/h$.

### Simultaneous equations

In physics, simultaneous equations can be solved graphically by plotting the line for each equation. The solution of the equations is given by the coordinates of the points where the lines meet. For example, lines B and C in Figure 3 meet at the point $(2, 2)$ so $x = 2$, $y = 2$ are the only values of $x$ and $y$ that fit both equations.

Solving simultaneous equations doesn't require graph plotting if the equations can be arranged to fit one of the variables. Start by rearranging to make $y$ the subject of each equation, if necessary. Considering the example above:

Line B: $y = 2x - 2$

Line C: $y = -x + 4$

At the point where they meet, their coordinates are the same, so solving $2x - 2 = -x + 4$ gives the x-coordinate. Rearranging this equation gives $3x = 6$ so $x = 2$.

Since $y = 2x - 2$, then $y = (2 \times 2) - 2 = 2$

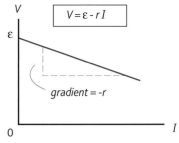

$$V = \varepsilon - rI$$

*gradient = -r*

**Figure 5** *Pd v current for a battery*

### Summary questions

**1** For each of the following equations that represent straight line graphs, write down i the gradient, ii the y-intercept, iii the x-intercept:

a $y = 3x - 3$    b $y = -4x + 8$

c $y + x = 5$    d $2y + 3x = 6$

**2** a A straight line on a graph has a gradient $m = 2$ and passes through the point $(2, -4)$. Work out i the equation for this line, ii its y-intercept.

b The velocity $v$ (in m s$^{-1}$) of an object varies with time $t$ (in s) in accordance with the equation $v = 5 + 3t$. Determine i the acceleration of the object, ii the initial velocity of the object.

**3** a Plot the equations $y = x + 3$ and $y = -2x + 6$ over the range from $x = -3$ to $x = +3$. Write down the coordinates of the point P where the two lines cross.

b Write down the equation for the line OP, where O is the origin of the graph.

**4** Solve the following pairs of simultaneous equations after making $y$ the subject of each equation, if necessary:

a $y = 2x - 4$, $y = -x + 2$

b $y = 3x - 4$, $x + y = 8$

c $2x + 3y = 4$, $x + 2y = 2$

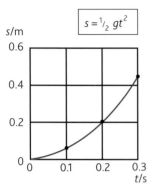

**Figure 1** *s against t*

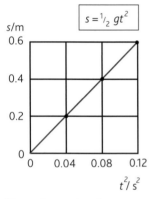

**Figure 2** *s against t²*

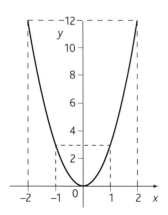

**Figure 3** *y = 3x²*

## ▨ Curves and equations

Graphs with curves occur in physics in two ways.

**1** In practical work, where one physical variable is plotted against another and the plotted points do not lie along a straight line. For example, a graph of p.d. on the $y$-axis against current on the $x$-axis for a filament lamp is a curve that passes through the origin.

**2** In theory work, where an equation containing two physical variables is not in the form of the equation for a straight line $(y = mx + c)$. For example, for an object released from rest, a graph of distance fallen, $s$, on the $y$-axis against time, $t$, on the $x$-axis is a curve, because $s = \frac{1}{2}gt^2$. Figure 1 shows this equation represented on a graph.

Knowledge of the general equations for some common curves is an essential part of physics. When a curve is produced as a result of plotting a set of measurements in a practical experiment, few conclusions can be drawn as the exact shape of a curve is difficult to test. In comparison, if the measurements produce a straight line, it can then be concluded that the two physical variables plotted on the axes are related by an equation of the form $y = mx + c$.

If a set of measurements produces a curve rather than a straight line, knowledge of the theory could enable the measurements to be processed in order to give a straight line graph, which would then be a confirmation of the theory. For example, the distance and time measurements that produced the curve in Figure 1 could be plotted as distance fallen, $s$, on the $y$-axis against $t^2$ on the $x$-axis (where $t$ is the time taken). Figure 2 shows the idea.

If a graph of $s$ against $t^2$ gives a straight line, this would confirm that the relationship between $s$ and $t$ is of the form $s = kt^2$, where $k$ is a constant. Because theory gives $s = \frac{1}{2}gt^2$, it can then be concluded that the theory applies to this set of measurements and that $k = \frac{1}{2}g$.

## ▨ From curves to straight lines

### Parabolic curves

These curves describe the flight paths of projectiles or other objects acted on by a constant force that is not in the same direction as the initial velocity of the object. In addition, parabolic curves occur where the energy of an object depends on some physical variable.

The general equation for a parabola is $y = kx^2$. Figure 3 shows the shape of the parabola $y = 3x^2$. Equations of the form $y = kx^2$ pass through the origin and they are symmetrical about the $y$-axis. This is because equal positive and negative values of $x$ always give the same $y$-value.

**The flight path for a projectile** projected horizontally at speed $u$ has coordinates $x = ut$, $y = \frac{1}{2}gt^2$, where $x$ = horizontal distance travelled, $y$ = vertical distance fallen and $t$ is the time from initial projection. See Topic 8.2.

Combining these equations gives the flight path equation $y = \dfrac{gx^2}{2u^2}$

which is the same as the parabola equation $y = kx^2$ where $\dfrac{g}{2u^2}$ is represented by $k$ in the equation.

A set of measurements plotted as a graph of vertical distance fallen, $y$, against horizontal distance travelled, $x$, would be a parabolic curve as shown in Figure 3. However, a graph of $y$ against $x^2$ should give a straight line (of gradient $k$) through the origin, because $y = kx^2$

### Inverse curves

An inverse relationship between two variables $x$ and $y$ is of the form $y = \dfrac{k}{x}$, where $k$ is a constant. The variable $y$ is said to be inversely proportional to variable $x$. If $x$ is doubled, $y$ is halved. If $x$ is increased tenfold, $y$ decreases to a tenth.

Figure 5 shows the curve for $y = \dfrac{10}{x}$

The curve tends towards either axis but never actually meets the axes. The correct mathematical word for 'tending towards but never meeting' is 'asymptotic'. Consider the following example.

The resistance $R$ of a wire of constant length $L$ varies with the wire's area of cross-section, $A$, in accordance with the equation $R = \dfrac{\rho L}{A}$, where $\rho$ is the resistivity of the wire. See Topic 12.2.

Therefore, $R$ is inversely proportional to $A$. A graph of $R$ (on the vertical axis) against $A$ would therefore be a curve like Figure 5. However, a graph of $R$ (on the vertical axis) against $1/A$ is a straight line through the origin. The gradient of this straight line is $\rho L$.

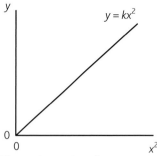

**Figure 4** $y$ against $x^2$

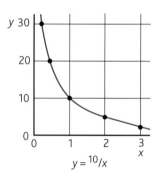

**Figure 5** $y = \dfrac{10}{x}$

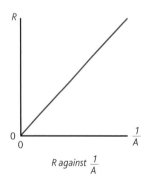

**Figure 6** The resistance of a wire

### Summary questions

**1** The potential energy, $E_p$, stored in a stretched spring varies with the extension $\Delta L$ of the spring, in accordance with the equation $E_p = \frac{1}{2}k\,\Delta L^2$. Sketch a graph of $E_p$ against a $\Delta L$, b $\Delta L^2$.

**2** The energy $E_{ph}$ of a photon varies with its wavelength $\lambda$ in accordance with the equation $E_{ph} = hc/\lambda$, where $h$ is the Planck constant and $c$ is the speed of light. Sketch a graph of $E_{ph}$ against a $\lambda$, b $1/\lambda$

**3** The current $I$ through a wire of resistivity $\rho$ varies with the length $L$, area of cross-section $A$ and pd $V$, in accordance with the equation $I = \dfrac{VA}{\rho L}$

  **a** Sketch a graph of $I$ against i $V$, ii $L$, iii $1/L$.

  **b** Explain how you would determine the resistivity from the graph of $I$ against i $V$, ii $1/L$.

**4** An object released from rest falls at constant acceleration $a$ and passes through a horizontal beam at speed $u$. The distance it falls in time $t$ after passing through the light beam is given by the equation $s = ut + \frac{1}{2}at^2$

  **a** Show that $\dfrac{s}{t} = u + \frac{1}{2}at$

  **b i** Sketch a graph of $s/t$ on the vertical axis against $t$ on the horizontal axis.

    **ii** Explain how $u$ and $a$ can be determined from the graph.

# 17.6 Graphs, gradients and areas

## Gradients

1 The gradient of a straight line = $\Delta y / \Delta x$, where $\Delta y$ is the change of the quantity plotted on the $y$-axis and $\Delta x$ is the change of the quantity plotted on the $x$-axis. As shown in Figure 1, the gradient of a straight line is obtained by drawing as large a gradient triangle as possible, and measuring the height $\Delta y$ and the base $\Delta x$ of this triangle, using the scale on each axis.

Note: As a rule, when you plot a straight line graph, always choose a scale for each axis that covers at least half the length of each axis. This will enable you to draw the line of best fit as accurately as possible, as explained in Topic 5.4. The measurement of the gradient of the line will therefore be more accurate. If the $y$-intercept is required and it cannot be read directly from the graph, it can be calculated by substituting the value of the gradient and the coordinates of a point on the line into the equation $y = mx + c$

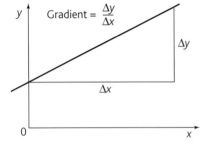

**Figure 1** *Constant gradient*

2 The gradient at a point on a curve = the gradient of the tangent to the curve at that point.

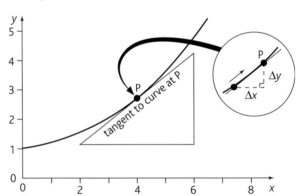

**Figure 2** *Tangents and curve*

The tangent to the curve at a point is a straight line that touches the curve at that point, without cutting across it. To see why, mark any two points on a curve and join them by a straight line. The gradient of the line is $\Delta y / \Delta x$, where $\Delta y$ is the vertical separation of the two points and $\Delta x$ is the horizontal separation. Now repeat with one of the points closer to the other; the straight line is now closer in direction to the curve. If the points are very close, the straight line between them is almost along the curve. The gradient of the line is then virtually the same as the gradient of the curve at that position. See Figure 2. In other words, the gradient of the straight line $\Delta y / \Delta x$ becomes equal to the gradient of the curve as $\Delta x \longrightarrow 0$. The curve gradient is written as $\dfrac{dy}{dx}$ where $\dfrac{d}{dx}$ means 'rate of change'.

The gradient of the tangent is a straight line and is obtained as explained above. Drawing the tangent to a curve requires practice. This skill is often needed in practical work. The **normal** at the point where the tangent touches the curve is the straight line perpendicular to the tangent at that point. An accurate technique for drawing the normal to a curve using a plane mirror is shown in Figure 3. At the point where the normal intersects the curve, the curve and its mirror image should join smoothly without an abrupt change of gradient where they join. After positioning the mirror surface correctly, the normal can then be drawn, and then used to draw the tangent to the curve.

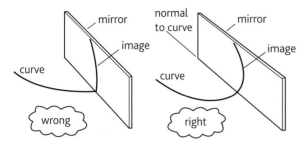

**Figure 3** *Drawing the normal to a curve*

## Turning points

A turning point on a curve is where the gradient of the curve is zero. This happens where a curve reaches a peak with a fall either side (i.e. a maximum) or where it reaches a trough with a rise either side (i.e. a minimum). Where the gradient represents a physical quantity, a turning point is where that physical quantity is zero. Figure 4 shows an example of a curve with a turning point. This is a graph of the vertical height against time for a projectile that reaches a maximum height, then descends as it travels horizontally. The gradient represents the vertical component of velocity. At maximum height, the gradient of the curve is zero, so the vertical component of velocity is zero at that point.

*Note:*

If the equation of a curve is known, the gradient can be determined by the process of **differentiation**. This mathematical process is not needed for AS level physics. The essential feature of the process is that, for a function of the form $y = kx^n$, the gradient (written as $dy/dx$) $= nkx^{n-1}$

For example, if $y = \frac{1}{2}gt^2$, then $\dfrac{dy}{dt} = gt$

## ◼ Areas and graphs

The area under a line on a graph can give useful information if the product of the $y$-variable and the $x$-variable represents another physical variable. For example, consider Figure 5(a), which is a graph of the tension in a spring against its extension. Since 'tension × extension' is 'force × distance' which equals work done, then the area under the line represents the work done to stretch the spring.

Figure 5b shows a tension against extension graph for a rubber band. Unlike (a), the area under the curve is not a triangle, but it still represents work done, in this case the work done to stretch the rubber band. See Topic 9.1.

The product of the $y$-variable and the $x$-variable must represent a physical variable with a physical meaning if the area is to be of use. A graph of mass against volume for different sizes of the same material gives a straight line through the origin. The mass is directly proportional to the volume, and the gradient gives the density. But the area under the line

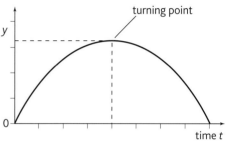

**Figure 4** *Turning points*

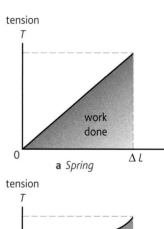

**a** *Spring*

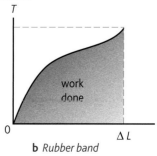

**b** *Rubber band*

**Figure 5** *Tension v extension*

has no physical significance since mass × volume does not represent a physical variable.

Note that even where the area does represent a physical variable, it may not have any physical meaning. For example, for a graph of pd against current, the product of pd and current represents power, but this physical quantity has no meaning in this situation.

More examples of curves where the area is useful include:

- velocity against time where the area between the line and the time axis represents displacement
- acceleration against time where the area between the line and the time axis represents change of velocity
- power against time where the area between the curve and the time axis represents energy
- potential difference against charge where the area between the curve and the charge axis represents energy

## Summary questions

**1**  a Sketch a velocity against time graph (with time on the x-axis) to represent the equation $v = u + at$, where $v$ is the velocity at time $t$.

  b What feature of the graph represents i the acceleration, ii the displacement?

**2**  a Sketch a graph of current (on the y-axis) against pd (on the x-axis) to show how the current through an ohmic conductor varies with pd.

  b How can the resistance of the conductor be determined from the graph?

**3**  An electric motor is supplied with energy at a constant rate.

  a Sketch a graph to show how the energy supplied to the motor increases with time.

  b Explain how the power supplied to the motor can be determined from the graph.

**4**  A steel ball bearing was released in a tube of oil and fell to the bottom of the tube.

  a Sketch graphs to show how i the velocity, ii the acceleration of the ball changed with time from the instant of release to the point of impact at the bottom of the tube.

  b What is represented on graph a i by i the gradient, ii the area under the line?

  c What is represented on graph a ii by the area under the line?

# For reference

## Useful data for AS Physics Specification B

### Fundamental constants and other numerical data

| Quality | Symbol | Value | Units |
|---|---|---|---|
| speed of light in vacuo | $c$ | $3.00 \times 10^8$ | $m\,s^{-1}$ |
| Planck constant | $h$ | $6.63 \times 10^{-34}$ | $J\,s$ |
| gravitational constant | $G$ | $6.67 \times 10^{-11}$ | $N\,m^2\,kg^{-2}$ |
| gravitational field strength | $g$ | $9.81$ | $N\,kg^{-1}$ |
| acceleration due to gravity | $g$ | $9.81$ | $m\,s^{-2}$ |
| electron rest mass | $m_e$ | $9.11 \times 10^{-31}\,kg$ $5.5 \times 10^{-4}\,u$ | $kg$ |
| electron charge | $e$ | $-1.60 \times 10^{-19}$ | $C$ |
| proton rest mass | $m_p$ | $1.67(3) \times 10^{-27}\,kg$ $1.00728\,u$ | $kg$ |
| neutron rest mass | $m_n$ | $1.67(5) \times 10^{-27}\,kg$ $1.00867\,u$ | $kg$ |
| permeability of free space | $\varepsilon_0$ | $8.85 \times 10^{-12}$ | $F\,m^{-1}$ |
| molar gas constant | $R$ | $8.31$ | $J\,K^{-1}\,mol^{-1}$ |
| Boltzmann constant | $k$ | $1.38 \times 10^{-23}$ | $J\,K^{-1}$ |
| Avogadro constant | $N_A$ | $6.02 \times 10^{23}$ | $mol^{-1}$ |
| Wein constant | $\alpha$ | $2.90 \times 10^{-3}$ | $m\,K$ |

### Geometrical equations

| | |
|---|---|
| arc length | $r\theta$ |
| circumference of circle | $2\pi r$ |
| area of circle | $\pi r^2$ |
| surface area of sphere | $4\pi r^2$ |
| volume of sphere | $\frac{4}{3}\pi r^3$ |
| surface area of cylinder | $2\pi rh$ |
| volume of cylinder | $\pi r^2 h$ |

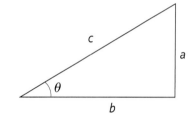

$$\sin \theta = \frac{a}{c}$$
$$\cos \theta = \frac{b}{c}$$
$$\tan \theta = \frac{a}{b}$$
$$c^2 = a^2 + b^2$$

### Unit conversions

| | |
|---|---|
| 1 atomic mass unit (u) | $1.661 \times 10^{-27}\,kg$ |
| 1 year (y) | $3.15 \times 10^7\,s$ |
| 1 parsec (pc) | $3.08 \times 10^{16}\,m$ $3.26\,ly$ |
| 1 light year (ly) | $9.45 \times 10^{15}\,m$ |

### Particle properties

**Properties of quarks**
Antiparticles have opposite signs

| type | charge | baryon number | strangeness |
|---|---|---|---|
| u | $+\frac{2}{3}e$ | $+\frac{1}{3}$ | 0 |
| d | $-\frac{1}{3}e$ | $+\frac{1}{3}$ | 0 |
| s | $-\frac{1}{3}e$ | $+\frac{1}{3}$ | $-1$ |

**Properties of leptons**

| lepton | lepton number |
|---|---|
| particles: $e^-, \nu_e; \bar{\mu}, \nu_\mu; \bar{\tau}, \nu_\tau$ | $+1$ |
| antiparticles: $e^+, \bar{\nu}_e; \mu^+, \bar{\nu}_\mu; \tau^+, \bar{\nu}_\tau$ | $-1$ |

# ■ AS formulae

## Waves

| | |
|---|---|
| wave speed | $c = f\lambda$ |
| period | $T = \dfrac{1}{f}$ |
| intensity | $I = \dfrac{P}{A}$ |
| stretched string frequency | $f = \dfrac{1}{2l}\sqrt{\dfrac{T}{\mu}}$ |
| beat frequency | $f = f_1 - f_2$ |
| fringe spacing | $w = \dfrac{\lambda D}{s}$ |
| diffraction grating | $n\lambda = d\sin\theta$ |
| half beam width | $\sin\theta = \dfrac{\lambda}{a}$ |
| refractive index of a substance $s$, | $n_s = \dfrac{c}{c_s}$ |

For two different substances of refractive indices $n_1$ and $n_2$,

| | |
|---|---|
| law of refraction | $n_1\sin\theta_1 = n_2\sin\theta_2$ |
| critical angle | $\sin\theta_c = \dfrac{n_2}{n_1}$   for $n_1 > n_2$ |

## Mechanics

| | |
|---|---|
| speed or velocity | $v = \dfrac{\Delta s}{\Delta t}$ |
| acceleration | $a = \dfrac{\Delta v}{\Delta t}$ |
| equations of motion | $v = u + at$ |
| | $s = \dfrac{(u+v)}{2}t$ |
| | $v^2 = u^2 + 2as$ |
| | $s = ut + \tfrac{1}{2}at^2$ |
| force | $F = ma$ |
| change in potential energy | $\Delta E_p = mg\,\Delta h$ |
| kinetic energy | $E_k = \tfrac{1}{2}mv^2$ |
| momentum | $p = mv$ |
| impulse | $F\Delta t = \Delta(mv)$ |
| spring stiffness | $k = \dfrac{F}{\Delta L}$ |
| energy stored for $F \propto L$ | $E = \tfrac{1}{2}F\Delta L$ |
| work | $W = Fs$ |

| | |
|---|---|
| power | $P = \dfrac{\Delta W}{\Delta t} = Fv$ |
| density | $\rho = \dfrac{m}{V}$ |

## Quantum physics and astrophysics

| | |
|---|---|
| photon energy | $E = hf$ |
| Einstein equation | $hf = \varphi + E_{Kmax}$ |
| line spectrum equation | $hf = E_1 - E_2$ |
| de Broglie wavelength | $\lambda = \dfrac{h}{p} = \dfrac{h}{mv}$ |
| Doppler shift for $v \ll c$ | $\dfrac{\Delta f}{f} = -\dfrac{\Delta\lambda}{\lambda} = \dfrac{v}{c}$ |
| Wein's law | $\lambda_{max}T = 0.0029\,\text{m K}$ |
| Hubble law | $v = Hd$ |
| intensity for a point source | $I = \dfrac{P}{4\pi r^2}$ |

## Electricity

| | |
|---|---|
| current | $I = \dfrac{\Delta Q}{\Delta t}$ |
| electromotive force (emf) | $\varepsilon = \dfrac{E}{Q}$ |
| | $\varepsilon = IR + Ir$ |
| resistance | $R = \dfrac{V}{I}$ |
| resistors in series | $R = R_1 + R_2 + R_3 + \ldots$ |
| resistors in parallel | $\dfrac{1}{R} = \dfrac{1}{R_1} + \dfrac{1}{R_2} + \dfrac{1}{R_3} + \ldots$ |
| resistivity | $\rho = \dfrac{RA}{L}$ |
| power | $P = VI = I^2R = \dfrac{V^2}{R}$ |
| potential divider formula | $V_0 = \left(\dfrac{R_1}{R_1 + R_2}\right) \times V_i$ |
| energy | $E = VIt$ |
| efficiency | $\dfrac{\text{useful output power}}{\text{input power}}$ |

## Energy production and transmission

rate of heat transfer by conduction $= UA\,\Delta\theta$

maximum energy for a wind turbine $= \tfrac{1}{2}\pi r^2 \rho v^3$

# Glossary

## A

**absolute magnitude:** the magnitude a star would have if it were viewed from a distance of 10 pc.

**absorption:** process of removing sound or light energy.

**absorption spectrum:** continuous spectrum crossed by dark lines or bands due to reduction of energy of particular frequencies when the light passes through a medium.

**acceleration:** change of velocity per unit time.

**accuracy:** a measure of the confidence in an accurate measurement, often expressed as an uncertainty in the measurement.

**accuracy, degree of:** the degree of accuracy of a measurement is usually quoted as the probable error or uncertainty.

**alias:** the false waveform regenerated from data that has been sampled at too low a sampling rate.

**amplitude:** maximum displacement of a vibrating particle.

**amplitude modulation:** process of transferring information by varying the amplitude of a wave.

**analogue:** a continuously varying signal; its value is proportionally a physical quantity.

**annihilate:** when a particle and its antiparticle meet, they destroy each other and become radiation.

**antinode:** fixed point in a stationary wave pattern where the amplitude is a maximum.

**antiparticle:** there is an antiparticle for every particle. A particle and its corresponding antiparticle have equal rest mass and, if charged, equal and opposite charge.

**apparent magnitude:** the magnitude of a star as it is observed from Earth.

**asperity:** roughness of a surface.

**attack:** the beginning of a musical sound when a note is played on an instrument.

## B

**band spectrum:** the coloured bands observed from molecules at high temperature; observed as a range of frequencies.

**bandwidth:** the range of frequencies in a transmitted signal.

**baryon number:** numbers assigned to quarks and hadrons that must be conserved in an interaction.

**baryons:** a hadron consisting of three quarks.

**Big Bang:** theory that all the energy of the Universe was originally at one point and that the Universe began with an expansion at that point.

**bit rate:** number of binary digits transmitted per second.

**black body:** a body that emits all possible wavelengths for the temperature of that body.

**bosons:** particles like photons, kaons and pions; gauge bosons carry the fundamental forces between particles.

**brightness:** the observed intensity of a source.

## C

**channel bandwidth:** the range of frequencies allocated to a user.

**compressions:** regions of high pressure for a longitudinal wave.

**conduction:** process of transferring thermal energy or charge.

**consonant:** two or more notes which when played together produce a pleasing sound.

**constructive interference:** interference in which two waves superpose to produce a wave with amplitude equal to the sum of the amplitudes of the two waves.

**continuous spectrum:** spectrum that contains no gaps; all frequencies are present.

**convection:** process of transferring thermal energy due to movement of warm bodies of fluid.

**critical angle:** the angle of incidence that a light ray must exceed for *total internal reflection* to occur.

**critical temperature:** temperature at which a conductor of electricity becomes superconducting.

**current:** rate of flow of charge.

## D

**decay:** process occurring when radioactive particles emit radiation.

**decibel (dB):** measure of sound intensity; an increase of 3 dB is doubling of intensity.

**deep inelastic scattering:** scattering that occurs when a high energy particle collides with another particle producing new particles.

**demodulating:** process of retrieving the information from a transmitted amplitude modulated or frequency modulated signal.

**destructive interference:** interference in which two waves superpose to produce a wave with amplitude equal to the difference in the amplitudes of the two waves.

**diffraction:** spreading of waves on passing through a gap or near an edge.

**diffraction grating:** a plate with many closely ruled parallel slits on it.

**digital:** information sent in the form of binary digits (0 or 1).

**displacement:** distance from a reference point in a given direction.

**drag force:** the force of fluid resistance on an object moving through the fluid.

**DVD:** Digital Video Disc (or Digital Versatile Disc).

## E

**efficiency:** the ratio of useful energy transferred (or the useful work done) by a machine or device to the energy supplied to it.

**elastic:** a property that enables a solid to regain its shape after it has been deformed or distorted.

**elastic potential energy:** energy stored in a solid when it is extended or compressed by a force.

**electromagnetic wave:** an electric and magnetic wave packet or *photon* that can travel through free space.

**electromotive force:** the amount of electrical energy per unit charge produced by a source of electrical energy.

**electron energy levels:** energies which electrons can have when bound to an atom.

**electron:** fundamental lepton that is a constituent of atoms.

**electroweak force:** term that describes the electromagnetic interaction and the weak interaction between particles.

**emission spectra:** a spectrum that comes from a source without passing through an absorbing medium.

**equilibrium:** situation in which there is no resultant force acting on a body; the body remains at rest or travels at a constant velocity.

**error bar:** line representing the probable error on a graph.

**error of measurement:** uncertainty of a measurement.

**excitation:** process of electrons moving to a higher energy level.

**excited states:** electron states that are higher than the *ground state*.

## F

**Fourier synthesis/analysis:** the process of determining which sinusoidal waves combine to produce a different periodic wave.

**free-body:** diagram which shows the magnitude and direction of all forces acting upon an object.

**free-fall:** situation when the only force acting on a falling body is a gravitational.

**frequency:** the number of cycles of a wave that pass a point per second; the number of complete to and fro oscillations that occur per second.

**frequency modulation:** process of transferring information by varying the frequency of a wave.

**fundamental particles:** particles that are not made from smaller particles.

## G

**geostationary orbit:** orbit of a satellite that remains above the same point on the Earth's surface.

**graded-index core:** glass fibre whose refractive index decreases from the centre to the edge.

**gravitational potential energy:** energy of an object due to its position relative to a particle or body that has mass.

**graviton:** the particle that is thought to mediate the gravitational force.

**ground state:** the lowest energy state that an electron can occupy in an atom.

**ground waves:** transmitted wave that travels along the surface of the Earth.

## H

**hadrons:** particles and antiparticles that can interact through the strong interaction.

**harmonic:** frequencies that are a multiple of the fundamental frequency of an oscillator: $f$, $2f$, $3f$, etc.

**heating:** the process of transferring energy from one body to another due to a difference in temperature.

**Higgs boson:** the particle that has been proposed as being responsible for the mass of particles.

## I

**impulse:** force on a body × time for which the force acts (= change in momentum of a body).

**inelastic:** when a body undergoes an inelastic process some energy that is supplied changes form so it is not recoverable in its initial form.

**infrasound:** sound that has a frequency below the lowest audible sound (about 16 Hz).

**intensity:** the energy per square metre that arrives on a surface each second: measured in $J\,s^{-1}\,m^{-2}$ ($W\,m^{-2}$).

**interference:** formation of points of cancellation and reinforcement where two coherent waves pass through each other.

**internal energy:** the sum of the potential and kinetic energies of all the atoms in a body.

**internal resistance:** resistance inside a source of electrical energy; the loss of pd per unit current in the source when current passes through it.

**ion:** a charged atom.

**ionisation:** process of creating ions.

**ionisation energy:** the energy that has to be supplied to an atom to remove an electron.

**ionising radiation:** radiation that is able to provide energy to ionise atoms.

**isotopes:** atoms of an element with different numbers of neutrons and the same number of protons.

## K

**kinetic energy:** energy due to the motion of a body = ½ $mv^2$.

## L

**leptons:** collective term for fundamental particles such as electrons, muons, taus and neutrinos.

**line spectrum:** spectrum produced by diffraction gratings using radiation produced by excitation and relaxation of electrons in atoms.

**longitudinal wave:** waves with a direction of vibration parallel to the direction of travel of the waves.

**loudness:** a subjective perception of the intensity of a sound.

**luminosity:** the property of a source that gives the perception of brightness of a source.

## M

**mesons:** a hadron consisting of a quark and an antiquark.

**modes:** a possible frequency of vibration.

**modulating:** the process of changing the amplitude or frequency of oscillation of a wave.

**moments:** force × perpendicular distance from the line of action of the force to the point.

**momentum:** mass × velocity.

**multipath dispersion:** the lengthening of a light pulse as it travels along an optical fibre due to rays that repeatedly undergo total internal reflection having to travel a longer distance than rays that undergo less total internal reflection.

**musical interval:** an interval between two notes on a musical scale determined by the ratio of the frequencies of the notes.

## N

**natural frequency:** the oscillation that takes place when an oscillating system is displaced from its original position and allowed to vibrate freely.

**node:** fixed point in a stationary wave pattern where the amplitude is zero.

**nucleon number:** the number of neutrons and protons in a nucleus; also referred to as **mass number**.

**nucleon:** a neutron or proton in the nucleus.

**nuclide:** a nucleus with a particular number of protons and neutrons.

## O

**octave:** musical interval between harmonics that have frequency $f$ and $2f$.

**Ohm's law:** the pd across a metallic conductor is proportional to the current provided the physical conditions do not change.

**oscilloscope:** an instrument that produces an image of the variation with time of a pd.

## P

**pair production:** when a gamma photon changes into a particle and an antiparticle.

**path difference:** the difference in distances from two coherent sources to an interference fringe.

**perfect pitch:** the ability to identify the musical pitch of a note exactly.

**period:** time for one complete cycle of a wave to pass a point; time for one complete oscillation.

**phase difference:** the fraction of a cycle between the vibrations of two vibrating particles, measured either in radians or degrees.

**photoelectric effect:** emission of electrons from a metal surface when the surface is illuminated by light of frequency greater than a minimum value known as the *threshold frequency*.

**photon:** packet or 'quantum' of electromagnetic waves.

**pitch:** a subjective quality relating to the position of a note on a musical scale determined by its frequency.

**polarised:** transverse waves that vibrate in one plane only.

**positron:** *antiparticle* of the electron.

**potential difference:** work done or energy transfer per unit charge between two points when charge moves from one point to the other.

**power:** rate of transfer of energy.

**precision of an instrument:** the smallest non-zero reading that can be measured.

**projectile:** an unpowered object thrown or fired through the air (e.g. a javelin).

**proton number:** number of protons in a nucleus.

**pulse code modulation:** modulation in which a signal is sampled and only certain discrete values of the information are transmitted as a binary coded signal.

## Q

**quality:** the property that enables instruments of the same pitch to be recognised: determined by the frequencies present in the sound.

**quantised:** only certain discrete values of a physical quantity are possible.

**quarks:** fundamental particles that combine to form hadrons (baryons and mesons).

## R

**radiation:** energy transmitted as e-m waves or particles (alpha and beta).

**random error:** error of measurement due to readings that vary randomly with no recognizable pattern.

**range of a set of of a readings:** the range of a set of readings of the same measurement is the difference between the minimum and the maximum reading.

**range of an instrument:** the difference between the minimum and the maximum reading that can be obtained using the instrument.

**rarefactions:** regions of low pressure for a longitudinal wave.

**rays:** paths taken by energy, e.g. light.

**recessional speed:** speed at which galaxies are moving away from the Earth.

**red shift:** the movement of waves to longer wavelengths than those observed from a similar source in a laboratory on Earth.

**reflection:** process in which a wave or particle is directed back into the medium from which it came when it is incident on a surface.

**refraction:** change of direction of a wave when it crosses a boundary where its speed changes.

**relaxation:** the process in which an excited electron returns to a lower energy state by emitting a photon.

**repeaters:** used to boost the energy of a signal during transmission.

**resistance:** pd ÷ current.

**resistivity:** resistance per unit length × area of cross section.

**resonating:** a condition when the body is being driven by a frequency that is equal to its natural frequency leading to a maximum amplitude of vibration.

**resultant:** combined effect of a number of vector quantities (e.g. force or velocity).

## S

**sampling:** a process of taking the value of a physical quantity at regular intervals for transmission or processing.

**scalars:** a physical quantity with magnitude only.

**sky waves:** transmitted radio waves that are received back on Earth after being deflected by the ionosphere.

**space waves:** short wavelength radio waves that penetrate the ionosphere and can only be used for line-of-sight communication on Earth.

**standing wave:** wave pattern with nodes and antinodes formed when two or more progressive waves of the same frequency and amplitude pass through each other.

**stationary waves:** alternative name for standing wave.

**strangeness:** a strangeness number is assigned to every particle and antiparticle on the basis that strangeness is always conserved in the strong interaction but not in a weak interaction or decay involving a strange quark or antiquark.

**strong force:** attractive force between nucleons that holds the nucleons in the nucleus.

**superposition:** the effect of two waves adding together when they meet.

## T

**third:** interval between the first and third note of a major musical scale.

**threshold frequency:** minimum frequency of light that can cause *photoelectric effect*.

**threshold of hearing:** the lowest intensity of sound that is audible $0\,dB = 2 \times 10^{-5}\,Pa$.

**timbre:** see 'quality'.

**torque (see moment):** force $\times$ perpendicular distance from the line of action of the force to the point.

**total internal reflection:** a light ray travelling in a substance is totally internally reflected at a boundary with a substance of lower refractive index if the angle of incidence is greater than a certain value known as the *critical angle*.

**transverse wave:** waves with a direction of vibration perpendicular to the direction of propagation of the wave's energy.

**travelling waves:** waves for which the position of maximum displacement moves so that energy is propagated.

**tremolo:** a note played by continually changing the amplitude of the note or a continuous rapid change between two notes.

## U

**ultrasound:** sound that has a higher frequency than the highest audible sound (20 000 Hz).

**ultraviolet catastrophe:** the failure of classical physics to explain the nature of the radiation from a black body.

**unbalanced force:** a force for which there is not an equal and opposite force acting on a particular object.

## V

**vector:** a physical quantity with magnitude and direction.

**velocity:** change of displacement per unit time.

**vibrato:** a note played with a slight quick continually varying pitch.

**viscosity:** property of a fluid (liquid or gas) to oppose the motion within it.

## W

**wavefronts:** a surface or line along which all oscillations for a given frequency are in phase (wavefronts are perpendicular to rays).

**wavelength:** distance equal to the least distance between two successive crests or compressions.

**wave–particle duality:** matter particles have a wave-like nature as well as a particle-like nature; photons have a particle-like nature as well as a wave-like nature.

**work:** force $\times$ distance moved in the direction of the force.

**work function :** minimum amount of energy needed by an electron to escape from a metal surface.

# Answers to summary questions

## 1.1
1. $0.5\,m\,s^{-1}$
2. 512 Hz and 1024 Hz
3. e.g. 30 000 Hz and 1.1 cm
4. see text

## 1.2
3. 14.7 s

## 1.3
2. 88.0 Hz
3. 425 Hz, 212.5 Hz, 640 Hz, 850 Hz, etc.
5. 10 Hz, 0.10 s

## 1.4
2. $3.1 \times 10^{-6}\,W\,m^{-2}$
3. 40 dB

## 2.2
2. 14.6°

## 2.3
3. 10 kHz

## 2.5
2. 0.24 s
4. a 1.06°  b $13.4 \times 10^{5}\,m$
   (or $14 \times 10^{5}\,m$ to 2 sf)

## 2.6
2. 60.1°

## 3.2
1. $10^{5}$

## 3.3
1. 6 protons, 6 neutrons, 6 electrons;
   95 protons, 146 neutrons,
   95 electrons;
   8 protons, 8 neutrons, 8 electrons
2. 238
3. $x = 86, y = 216°, x = 234, y = 92$
4. If gamma radiation then laws of conservation of momentum and energy would not have been obeyed.

## 4.1
2. a $5.01 \times 10^{14}\,Hz$
   b $3.04 \times 10^{5}\,m\,s^{-1}$

## 4.2
1. $2.1 \times 10^{-34}\,m$
2. $9.7 \times 10^{3}\,m\,s^{-1}; 8.0 \times 10^{-20}\,J$

## 4.3
1. 12 particles and 12 antiparticles
2. $+\frac{1}{3}$
3. $-\frac{1}{3}$

## 4.4
1. $\overline{u}\overline{u}d$
2. (a) baryon (b) 1
3. $\pi^{0}$
4. −1, 1, −2

## 4.5
1. W boson
2. Rest mass
3. Quarks and nucleons (protons and neutrons)

## 4.6
2. about $10^{-7} - 3\,s$
3. after about 300 000 years
4. the Higgs particle (Higgs boson)

## 5.1
1. A

## 5.2
1. a white dwarf
   b Main sequence blue star
2. In range 2500 – 4000 K
3. It could become a red giant

## 5.3
1. $93 \times 10^{-7}\,m$
2. 25/16 or 1.56
3. $1.7 \times 10^{26}\,W$

## 5.4
1. $4.1 \times 10^{-19}\,J$
2. 485 nm – visible green
3. 10
4. 13.6 eV

## 5.5
1. 508 nm
2. 77 Mpc
3. a $1.5 \times 10^{8}\,ly$  b $1.4 \times 10^{24}\,m$

## 6.1
1. s, v, s, s, v, v, s
2. $30\,m\,s^{-1}, 20\,m\,s^{-1}$

## 6.2
2. $12\,m\,s^{-1}$; N 13.3°W
3. 54.5°

## 6.3
3. 38 kN

## 7.1
2. 125 kN
3. a 7.4 N  b 13 N

## 7.2
1. 75 m
2. 0.67 s
3. $-2.3\,m\,s^{-1}$, 14 m

## 7.3
2. a Must lie between 0.14 and $0.16\,m\,s^{-2}$
   b Must lie between 61 and 65 metres

## 7.4
1. a 0.82 m above the board
   b $8.6\,m\,s^{-1}$  c 1.3 s

## 8.1
1. a 0.82 m above the board
   b $8.6\,m\,s^{-1}$
   c 1.3 s

## 8.2
3. a 5.9(4) m
   b 0.89 s
   c 2.0 s
   d 21 m

## 8.3
4. a $0.69\,m\,s^{-2}$
   b $0.275\,m\,s^{-2}$

## 9.1
2. 5.6 m
3. a 1080 W or 1.1 kW (to 2 sf)
   b 245 W or 0.25 kW (to 2 sf)

## 9.2
1. 17–18 N s
3. 30 N

**.2**

**1** a 3.5%

 b 1.4%

**2** Less than 1%

**3** 0.12 kg

**4** 2.4 kWh, $8.6 \times 10^6$ J

**5** $0.62 \times 10^6$ GWh

## 10.3

**1** 6.4

**2** 36%

## 11.1

**2** $1.5 \times 10^{15}$ Hz

**3** 644 nm red

## 11.2

**2** 613 W m$^{-2}$

## 11.3

**2** About 1 °C

## 11.4

**2** a $1.43 \times 10^4$ m$^3$

 b $1.47 \times 10^4$ m$^3$

**3** $7.2 \times 10^{14}$ kg

## 12.1

**1** a 20 h  b 22.5 minutes

**2** $9.4 \times 10^{20}$

## 12.2

**1** 0.17 A

**2** $1.5 \times 10^{-10}$ m$^2$

**3** 2.4 Ω, 5.0 A

## 12.3

**1** 5.0 Ω

**2** $1.9 \times 10^7$ J

**3** 0.54 W

## 12.5

**1** 7.8 V

**2** 65%

## 12.6

**1** 80 A

**2** 40 W

## 12.7

**2** 9.2 kW

**3** 92%

## 13.1

**3** 73 300 (or $7.3 \times 10^4$) m$^2$

## 13.2

**1** a 2.1 kW  b 1.8 m

**2** 19:1

## 13.3

**2** $4.6 \times 10^5$ kg s$^{-1}$ or 460 m$^3$ s$^{-1}$

## 13.4

**1** 9 m (NB there are 4 rotors)

**2** 2050 (assuming 8.2 GW for the barrage)

## 14.1

**4** a 200 W  b 32.5 °C

## 14.2

**1** 171 J s$^{-1}$

**3** 114%

## 17.1

**1** a i 0.500 m  ii 320 cm

  iii 95.6 m

 b i 450 g  ii 1.997 kg

  iii $5.4 \times 10^7$ g

 c i $2.0 \times 10^{-3}$ m$^2$

  ii $5.5 \times 10^{-5}$ m$^2$

  iii $5.0 \times 10^{-6}$ m$^2$

**2** a i $1.50 \times 10^{11}$ m

  ii $3.15 \times 10^7$ s

  iii $6.3 \times 10^{-7}$ m

  iv $2.57 \times 10^{-8}$ kg

  v $1.50 \times 10^5$ mm

  vi $1.245 \times 10^{-6}$ m

 b i 35 km  ii 650 nm

  iii $3.4 \times 10^3$ kg

  iv 870 MW (= 0.87 GW)

**3** a i 20 m s$^{-1}$  ii 20 m s$^{-1}$

  iii $1.5 \times 10^8$ m s$^{-1}$

  iv $3.0 \times 10^4$ m s$^{-1}$

 b i $6.0 \times 10^3$ Ω  ii 5.0 Ω

  iii $1.7 \times 10^6$ Ω

  iv $4.9 \times 10^8$ Ω  v 3.0 Ω

**4** a i 301  ii $2.8 \times 10^9$

  iii $1.9 \times 10^{-23}$  iv $1.2 \times 10^{-3}$

  v $2.0 \times 10^4$  vi $7.9 \times 10^{-2}$

 b i $1.6 \times 10^{-3}$  ii $5.8 \times 10^{-6}$

  iii 1.7  iv $3.1 \times 10^{-2}$

## 17.2

**1** a 1.57 m

 b i 1.57 m  ii 1.05 m

  iii 0.26 m

**2** a i 68°  ii 41°

  iii 22°  iv 61°

 b i 17 cm

  ii 16 m (15.6 m to 3sf)

  iii 4.8 mm  iv 101 cm

**3** a 49 mm

 b i 35 km  ii 31°

**4** a i 3.9 N, 4.6 N

  ii 3.4 N, 9.4 N  iii 4.8 N, 5.7 N

 b 4.0 N, 30° to 3.5 N

## 17.3

**1** a 0.2  b 0.1, 0.25

 c < 0.1

**2** b i 2  ii –1

  iii 4.25  iv ⅓

**3** b i 0.25  ii ± 2.8

  iii ± 0.5  iv 4

**4** a $3.1 \times 10^{-7}$ m$^3$

 b $6.2 \times 10^{-3}$ m

 c 2.5 s

 d 17 m s$^{-1}$

## 17.4

**1** a i 3  ii –3  iii 1

 b i –4  ii 8  iii 2

 c i –1  ii 5  iii 5

 d i –1.5  ii 3  iii 2

**2** a i $y = 2x - 8$  ii –8

 b i 3 m s$^{-2}$  ii 5 m s$^{-1}$

**3** a (1, 4)  b $y = 4x$

**4** a $x = 2, y = 0$  b $x = 3, y = 5$

 c $x = 2, y = 0$

## 17.5

**3** b i use gradient $= \dfrac{A}{\rho L}$

  ii use gradient $= \dfrac{VA}{\rho}$

**4** b ii $u = y$-intercept, ½$a$ = gradient

## 17.6

**1** b i gradient

  ii area under line

**2** b Resistance $= \dfrac{1}{\text{gradient}}$

**3** b The power is constant and is represented by the gradient of the line.

**4** b i acceleration

  ii distance fallen

 c velocity

# Index

# Acknowledgements

## Photograph Acknowledgements

The authors and publisher are grateful to the following for permission to reproduce photographs and other copyright material in this book.

**Alamy/UpperCut Images:** p 124; **Alamy/Mark Boulton:** p 125; **Alamy/Martin Bond:** p 126; **Alamy/ Juniors Bildarchiv:** p 127; **Alamy/Jack Sullivan:** p 127, **Alamy/Caro:** p 98 (top); **Alamy/Associated Sports Photography:** p 98 (bot); **Alamy/CW Images:** p 182; **Alamy/ Rami Aapasuo:** p 197(bottom); **Alfred Pasieka/ Still Pictures:** p.193; **Corbis/Lester V. Bergman:** vii; **Corbis/Lester V. Bergman:** p 40; **Corbis/Arno Balzarini/epa:** p 95; **Corbis/David Madison:** p 105; **Corbis/Randy Faris:** p 112; **Digital Vision 6 (NT):** p 32; **Digital Vision SC (NT):** p 123; **Digital Vision 6 (NT):** p 178; **Fotolia/Alison Bowden:** p 96; **Gilbert Iundt/Jean-Yves Ruszn:** p 127; **Ken Price:** p 154, p 181 (top), p 181 (bottom), p 188 (bottom right); **NASA/ESE, M. Roberto (Space Telescope Science Institute/ESA) and the Hubble Space Telescope Orion Treasury Project Team:** p 3; **Nuffield Curriculum Centre/Mike Vetterlein:** p 161; **Photodisc 24 (NT):** p 9; **Photodisc 83 (NT):** p 55 (top); **Photodisc 31 (NT):** p 93; **Photodisc 51 (NT):** p 103; **Photodisc 31 (NT):** p 164; **Photodisc 4 (NT):** p 188 (top); **Science Photo Library/ Andrew Lambert Photography:** p 5, p 23, p 42, p 166, p 206. p 210; **Science Photo Library/David Parker:** p 36, p 71 (top); **Science Photo Library/Prof. Peter Fowler:** p 44, p 48 (top left); **Science Photo Library/ Maximilien Brice, CERN:** p 48 (top right); **Science Photo Library/CERN:** p 48 (middle), p 48 (bottom); **Science Photo Library/Omikron:** p 55 (bottom); **Science Photo Library/Philippe Plailly:** p 60; **Science Photo Library/NASA:** p 64; **Science Photo Library/Department of Physics, Imperial College:** p 71 (middle), p 71 (bottom); **Science Photo library/ Ted Kinsman:** p 76 (top, bottom); **Science Photo Library/NOAO/AURA/NSF:** p 83; **Science Photo Library/NRSC Ltd:** p 145; **Science Photo Library/Kaj R. Svennson:** p 151; **Science Photo Library/Steve Gschmeissner:** p 157; **Science Photo Library/Martin Bond:** p 162; **Science Photo Library/Skyscan:** p 188 (bottom left); **Science Photo Library/Tek Image:** p 197 (top); **Science Photo Library/Sheila Terry:** p 207, p 209 (top); **Science Photo Library/Cristina Pedrazzini:** p 209 (bottom).

Every effort has been made to trace and contact all copyright holders and we apologise if any have been overlooked. The publisher will be pleased to make the necessary arrangements at the first opportunity.

## Authors' Acknowledgements

In addition to my thanks for the encouragement and consistent advice offered by Ken, I would like to thank my students past and present and my colleagues in both the Bromsgrove School Physics Department and the AQA Physics B teams: Andy Burton, Michael Thompson, Emma Rein and David Wilson and John Avison, David Homer, Gerard Kelly, Barrie Lancaster and Roger Oakley; each of you has influenced my views of physics in subtle and sometimes less subtle ways. Above all I would like to thank my wife, Adele, for always keeping my feet on the ground and putting working on this book into perspective.

*Mike Bowen-Jones*

I, too, would like to thank those colleagues from AQA who Mike has already mentioned and also all those teaching and examining colleagues with whom I have had the pleasure to work over the years. The influence of the many hours of discussion with them in formulating my views on the teaching, learning and examining of physics is immeasurable. My thanks too to all those students whose questions and enthusiasm for the physics have stimulated my own exploration of the subject. Finally, and most of all, I would like to thank my wife, Lynette, for her tireless support and encouragement throughout the project.

*Ken Price*

The authors also wish to thank the publishing team at Nelson Thornes, in particular Carol Usher, Eleanor O'Byrne and Sharon Thorn, for their highly professional support throughout the project. Thanks also to the development editors, Ros and Chris Davies for their invaluable work on the drafts and suggestions for improvements.